CHILDHOOD: CHANGING CONTEXTS

COMPARATIVE SOCIAL RESEARCH

Series Editor: Fredrik Engelstad

Recent Volumes:

COMPARATIVE SOCIAL RESEARCH   VOLUME 25

CHILDHOOD: CHANGING CONTEXTS

EDITED BY

ARNLAUG LEIRA

*Department of Sociology and Human Geography,
University of Oslo, Norway*

CHIARA SARACENO

*Department of Social Sciences, University of Turin,
Italy, and Social Science Research Center Berlin,
Germany*

Emerald

JAI

United Kingdom – North America – Japan
India – Malaysia – China

JAI Press is an imprint of Emerald Group Publishing Limited
Howard House, Wagon Lane, Bingley BD16 1WA, UK

First edition 2008

British Library Cataloguing in Publication Data
A catalogue record for this book is available from the British Library

ISBN: 978-0-7623-1419-5
ISSN: 0195-6310 (Series)

Awarded in recognition of
Emerald's production
department's adherence to
quality systems and processes
when preparing scholarly
journals for print

INVESTOR IN PEOPLE

Books are to be returned on or before
the last date below.

This book was originally accepted by Elsevier for publication as Volume 25 of the Comparative Social Research series. While the present volume was in the last stages of production, Elsevier transferred ownership of the series to Emerald Group Publishing Limited. Volume 25, and subsequent volumes of Comparative Social Research, will therefore appear under the Emerald logo.

CONTENTS

LIST OF CONTRIBUTORS

Maria Carmen Belloni   Department of Social Sciences, University of Turin, Italy

Cecilia Benoit   Department of Sociology, University of Victoria, Canada

Renzo Carriero   Department of Social Sciences, University of Turin, Italy

Nadina Christopoulou   Greek Council for Refugees, Athens, Greece

Sonja de Leeuw   Media and Culture Studies, University of Utrecht, The Netherlands

Jeanne Fagnani   Economic Center of the Sorbonne, University of Paris-1, CNRS, France

Gunhild O. Hagestad   Faculty of Economics and Social Sciences, University of Agder, Kristiansand, and NOVA, Norway

Helga Hallgrimsdotter   Department of Sociology, University of Victoria, Canada

Tina Hyder   Save the Children, United Kingdom

Mikael Jansson   Department of Sociology, University of Victoria, Canada

An-Magritt Jensen   Department of Sociology and Political Science, the Norwegian University of Science and Technology (NTNU), Trondheim, Norway

Jane Jenson   Department of Political Science, University of Montréal, Canada

Wolfgang Keck   Social Science Research Center Berlin,
                         Germany

Trudie Knijn   Department of Interdisciplinary Social
                         Science, Utrecht University,
                         The Netherlands

Arnlaug Leira   Department of Sociology and Human
                         Geography, University of Oslo, Norway

Ruth Lister   Department of Social Sciences,
                         Loughborough University,
                         United Kingdom

Antoine Math   Institute of Economic and Social Research,
                         Paris, France

Claire O'Kane   Save the Children, United Kingdom

Ilona Ostner   Institute of Sociology, Georg August
                         University, Göttingen, Germany

Janneke Plantenga   Utrecht School of Economics, Utrecht
                         University, The Netherlands

Chantal Remery   Utrecht School of Economics, Utrecht
                         University, The Netherlands

Eric Roth   Department of Sociology, University of
                         Victoria, Canada

Chiara Saraceno   Department of Social Sciences, University
                         of Turin, Italy; and Social Science Research
                         Center Berlin, Germany

Loredana Sementini   Applica, Brussels, Belgium

Melissa Siegel   Maastricht Graduate School of
                         Governance, Maastricht University,
                         The Netherlands

Andy West   Save the Children, China

Cecile Wetzels   Department of Economics, University of
                         Amsterdam, The Netherlands

EDITORIAL BOARD

CHILDHOOD: CHANGING CONTEXTS

Arnlaug Leira and Chiara Saraceno

INTRODUCTION

Children – their number, their welfare, their property (whom they belong to), their education – have long been a matter of public concern. What a "proper" childhood should be is always a highly politicized issue never left entirely in private hands. Modern societies in particular have rendered explicit and institutionalized the existence of a public interest in children and in childhood as constituted within, but also outside, families. In this volume, we use the expression "politicizing of childhood" in a broad sense in reference to the ways in which childhood is conceptualized not only as a primary family or parental responsibility, but, in addition, as a matter of public importance and concern, something for (welfare) state intervention. "Politicizing of childhood" encompasses the public motivation and mobilization for childhood change; the political processes in which policies are formulated, legislated and enacted; the response to policy interventions that may in turn feed back into public and political discourse, policy formulation and so on (see Ellingsæter & Leira, 2006, p. 4). The contributions in this volume illustrate one or more of these processes.

First in the Western world, but later also in other parts of the world, the definitions of *school age* and of *non-work age* have been the first explicit forms of the institutionalization of childhood, of its normalcy, timing and

Childhood: Changing Contexts
Comparative Social Research, Volume 25, 1–24
ISSN: 0195-6310/doi:10.1016/S0195-6310(07)00016-6

curriculum. Analogously with the legal definition of "legitimate" and "illegitimate" children, the age grading of children defines parents' powers and the duties and boundaries between "proper" and "deviant" childhood and children. The definitions also show how "childhood" is being constituted in the interplay of different institutional settings. Their content may have changed over time and space, but the issues they framed – to whom the children belong, who should be responsible for them, the proper setting for their growing up, what are they expected to do and where – run through the various turns of discourse and policy practice since then.

The present politicization of childhood, i.e. the fact that children and childhood are increasingly the subject of public debate and enter the political agenda, therefore, is not a wholly new phenomenon, although its aims and content may be relatively new (see, e.g. Jenson, Lister, this volume). In other words, we are presently witnessing an instance in history in which the issue of children, and concern over childhood change, is explicitly entering the public and political discourse, and in which the public discourse over children – as well as the actors constructing it – is being reframed.

The concern with childhood world-wide is most clearly evidenced in how standards of "proper childhood" and children's rights have become increasingly universal, at least in principle, through the work of children's advocates, social science researchers, international organizations and so forth and even inscribed in international agreements – see the UN Convention on the Rights of the Child of 1989 with additional protocols. The European Union (EU) recognizes children's rights in the Charter of Fundamental Rights and the European Commission Communication (2006) "Towards an EU Strategy on the Rights of the Child" highlights some of the serious problems children world-wide and specifically in EU member states are facing in the early 2000s. The great majority of children live in developing countries, as do the great majority who die before the age of five, and the great majority of children who lack access to primary education – most of whom are girls. Children in these countries more often find themselves in forced labour and/or suffer sexual abuse. Many lack food, suffer from malnutrition and inadequate health services (see Commission of the European Communities, 2006, p. 4). In the EU, the Commission's communication states, children are at a higher risk of living in relative poverty than older people. Furthermore, the EU document refers to the racism suffered by children from minority backgrounds and to the need to protect the rights of immigrant, refugee and asylum-seeking children. Violence inflicted on children in various forms is a concern, whether occurring in the family, school or in child trafficking, prostitution or pornography. Finally, the document observes (p. 4) that there is a wide gap between the good intentions of international agreements and the real-life situation of children world-wide.

International agreements and declarations notwithstanding, in many countries not only are universal standards difficult to achieve, they are often systematically denied to large groups of children because of, inter alia, poverty, persecution, war and sheer exploitation. Sometimes they are enforced alongside more traditional expectations. For example, in some countries, children are sent to school, but they are still expected to provide for themselves and to contribute to the needs of the family. Thus, "the right to attend school" and to education is a further, often very strenuous, task that has to be done (see, e.g. Bey, 2003). The right to have a family, whatever "a family" means, is weakened by epidemics, famine and war. In other cases, migration, and the economic difficulties encountered in the process, may worsen the conditions of immigrant children even if they settle in countries where the ideals and norms of children's rights are most upheld. Migrant children might find themselves forced to work illegally, and sometimes even in the criminal economy. Even within richer and more developed countries and among more socially fortunate children, the rights and needs of children occasionally conflict with social organization and with adult's rights and needs. Child poverty is far from eradicated; even in the first world, there are signs that it might actually be increasing (see UNICEF/Innocenti Research Center, 2007). Old risks persist, as new risks are increasing (e.g. Benoit et al., this volume). Moreover, the "right to have a family" is reduced, or at best redefined, by the fragility of partnerships among adults, which disrupts the routine access to both parents. There is an increasing diversification of family forms, norms and values, with the family, in Therborn's words (2004, p. 315), returning to its "modern historical complexity". While this may create new options, it will also create new forms of insecurity for children in so far as rules and responsibilities are no longer clear and widely shared. Furthermore, demands by the labour market on parental time are often highly unfriendly to adults with children, and thus to children themselves (see, e.g. Moen, 2003). Families, and norms and values concerning what families are about, have become increasingly diverse.

No univocal trends can therefore be detected in the present situation of children, even within the developed world. The forms in which a new public interest in children and childhood is framed, the agenda it proposes, the set of actors it involves, may also vary widely across countries. This occurs not only because of different "objective" circumstances, such as different child poverty rates or different marriage instability patterns, but because of specific cultural and political developments, welfare regime traditions, family and gender arrangements and so forth. It is not surprising that researchers, too, may have alternative readings of the processes under way.

In the following, we touch upon some of the changing contexts of childhood influential in shaping the situation of children and the politics of childhood. Although our focus is mainly on the developed world, Europe in particular, we address issues of wider globalization through both immigration and the impact of modernization in the developing world.

FALLING FERTILITY AND POPULATION AGEING: THE FEW CHILDREN OF AGEING SOCIETIES

In a global perspective, low birth-rate is not a problem, while the contrary, a rising birth-rate and widespread poverty among children in high-fertility countries, has long been considered an issue of profound concern. Society-wide fertility control has been and still is considered a precondition for development, although controversy is rife over the social and political means of achieving it. Yet, in recent years "scarcity of children" has become a concern not only in the richest and most developed countries, but also in some of the developing ones. In China and India, for instance, the scarcity of girls appears particularly problematic due to population policies that have greatly reduced the number of children parents may have, thus inducing selective abortions in societies where medical technological progress is super-imposed on persistent traditional gender cultures and arrangements. The Indian journalist Gita Aravamudan (2007) has recently published a book – *Disappearing daughters* – denouncing a practice increasingly adopted by educated, urban, middle class families in India, where it seems that baby girls have less chance of being born into relatively affluent urban middle class families than into "backward" rural families. For similar reasons, selective abortion may occur in low-fertility developed countries, when parents want to have fewer (or only one) children, but of the "right" sex.

At the societal level, however, the low number of children (irrespective of their sex) is experienced as a problem particularly in European countries, where population decline and population ageing are among the reasons why children have become a focus of concern in recent public discourse. The changing age structure of both population and kinship networks brought about in almost all developed societies by the dual phenomenon of increasing life expectancy and low fertility has, in fact, rendered children scarce. This is not an entirely new concern, however. As Gauthier (1996) pointed out in her history of family policies, national concern over falling birth-rates was at the origin of the first wave of family policy measures in Europe in the 1920s and 1930s. They have come to the forefront once again in recent years because of the consequences of the long duration of the fertility decline and of the unprecedented increase in life expectancy. Throughout Europe, the number of people over 65 is already higher than the number under 15. But the ratio in the year 2000 ranged from 1.07 in Northern Europe to 1.40 in Southern Europe (compared to 0.76 in North America). Although trends are similar, projections indicate that cross-country differences will be even greater in 2050, ranging from 1.87 in Northern Europe to 2.76 in Southern Europe (1.56 in North America) (UN, 2005).

In many European countries facing declining birth-rates, a scarcity of children means a scarcity of siblings for many children. How children experience being an only child has not been the focus of much research. At societal level, the "scarcity of children" prompts different concerns: (a) the inability of society to reproduce itself (and to support the costs of ageing); (b) inter-generational conflict; (c) age segregation and age discrimination. In all these concerns, one might detect a common framing of issues based on two assumptions/perspectives: on the one hand, children are looked at mainly in terms of the future prospect of a society; on the other, ageing of the population is perceived as inevitably bringing about inter-age and inter-generational conflicts (see, e.g. Jensen, in this volume).

While there is some evidence of age segregation, however, there is little evidence of inter-generational conflict (see Alber & Kohler, 2005; Keck, Blöme, 2007; Hagestad, in this volume). Furthermore, most discourses focus on redistributive issues at the level of society and population, ignoring what happens at the level of families and kinship networks. Both inter-generational redistribution and the impact of ageing offer a different prospective when looked at from the family perspective. Empirical research, in fact, shows that within families inter-generational exchanges flow both upwards and downwards (see, e.g. Attias-Donfut & Wolff, 2000; Kohli, 1999). In particular, financial redistribution in developed, rich, societies occurs mostly downwards. Only in poorer societies and social groups in which the elderly are not adequately covered by the pension system is there still an important role for upward financial redistribution from the younger to the older adults. This is the case in immigrant groups, where the adult, working age, generation might experience tension between, on the one hand, investing in themselves and in their own children and, on the other, supporting their own elderly parents. However, for most families and individuals in developed countries the reverse is true. Moreover, owing to long life expectancy, downward financial redistribution might even skip one generation, with grandparents supporting their grandchildren directly, and not just through the mediation of support offered to their children. Care flows both downwards and upwards between generations in families, and both the very young and the very frail elderly are the beneficiaries of care provided within families, with the middle generation – fulfilling at one and the same time the positions of parent, grandparent as well as child in three- and sometimes four-generation families – being the main provider. Actually, increasing life expectancy has greatly enhanced the likelihood of holding multiple (at any rate more than two) generational roles simultaneously. Notwithstanding the fertility decline, more parents become grandparents, and for longer, and more grandchildren have several, even most, of their grandparents while growing up, and one or more of their great-grandparents in their early infancy.

This enormous change in the shape and length of the inter-generational framework which marks the context in which children grow up in contemporary developed societies is seldom, if ever, the focus of studies on children. Ageing of population and kinships is examined mainly from the point of view of what happens to societies and to adults, including the elderly. Children's experiences in ageing societies and kinships have attracted much less attention. Even the sociology of childhood rarely, if ever, takes kinship ageing, i.e. the experience of having grandparents and even great-grandparents while growing up, as a constituent part of contemporary childhood in developed societies. Comparative studies indicate that in all developed countries grandparents are an important presence in the lives of their grandchildren at least until the onset of adolescence, if only because to a large degree they help the parents take care of them when little and see them relatively often until they reach adolescence (see, e.g. Leira, Tobio, & Trifiletti, 2005; Hagestad, 2007, Keck & Saraceno, in this volume). Most research, however, focuses on care given from grandparents and received from grandchildren. Little is known about the grandchildren's perceptions and experiences of the relationship between grandparents and grandchildren – including the experience of being the focus of attention and affection of many adults of different generations, but sharing it with few, if any, peers.

MOTHERS' LABOUR FORCE PARTICIPATION AND THE DECLINE OF THE MALE-BREADWINNER FAMILY

Mothers' labour force participation began increasing in the 1950s in the most highly industrialized countries of the world (see Myrdal and Klein, 1956, for an examination of the mobilization of women for labour market participation in the US, the UK, France and Sweden). The employed-mother family has later spread throughout the industrialized world, but the timing, pace, intensity and patterns have varied. While in Italy and Spain the first generation of young mothers was heading for the labour market in the 1990s, in the Nordic countries the second or third generation was on its way. The pattern of women's participation (e.g. part time/full time, continuous/intermittent, well-paid/low-paid) also varies across Europe and the OECD countries. Policy response to this family change has differed greatly between welfare states (Leira, 2002). These differences have affected the understanding of what is a good mother and what is good for children, and particularly the relationship between children's welfare and mothers' employment. They also affect the way fatherhood is understood, especially the degree to which caring is focused upon as a specific feature of fathering and not just of mothering. Within Europe, these differences interact strongly with welfare state policies, in particular with regard to paid maternity and parental leave and to the provision of affordable good quality childcare services. It is unfortunate, in this perspective, that most studies on the impact on children's well-being and cognitive development of having a working mother (and of attending a childcare service at an early age) have been performed in the US, where both types of state intervention are minimal and therefore variation due to family resources greater than in many European countries (e.g. the Scandinavian, but also France and Belgium).

The phenomenon of increasing women's, especially mothers', labour market participation is at the centre of two competing discourses in Europe, with the dual-earner family model increasingly proposed as the "normal" one. By the mid-1990s, more than half of all EU mothers of children aged under 10 were in the labour force, although with cross-country variation in participation rates (Moss & Deven, 2000). What the dual-breadwinner model implies for the caring needs traditionally addressed through the male-breadwinner family, however, is not really assessed. This is explicit in the changing expectations towards lone mothers. In all countries where lone mothers were once exempted from the requirement to be available for paid work when asking for social assistance support, this requirement has been set in place more or less rigidly in recent years (see, e.g. Lewis, 2006; Orloff, 2006). The "good mother" is no longer the one exclusively caring, but the mother who is both caring and breadwinning. The universal breadwinner parent model de facto implies that all children are expected to be in some kind of non-family care as quickly as possible. To some degree, family (women's/mothers') care for children is being undervalued and undermined (see, e.g. Daly, 2004; Lewis, 2006). Conversely, mothers' economic provision for the family is more highly valued. New hierarchies of "proper motherhood" are emerging, sometimes in contrast to strongly entrenched shared values (e.g. Knijn & Ostner, in this volume) or with the actual resources women and families have to fulfil these normative expectations (e.g. Wetzels, in this volume). Well-paid jobs or good quality and affordable childcare places are not always available. The mass entrance of women/ mothers into the labour market indicates that many mothers – from necessity or from choice – opt for the opportunity of some degree of economic independence. But, considering the different political histories of working motherhood, there might well be considerable variation between countries with respect to what "proper motherhood" is about.

The mobilization of mothers into employment has not only partially defamilialized childcare; it has also spurred on the debate on "work–family conciliation", therefore on the means by which caring needs should be incorporated in the overall societal and (paid) work organization. This has forwarded a diversification of options for child care across and in some cases also within countries, including long parental leaves of absence (Plantenga & Remery, 2005; Fagnani & Math, in this volume). It has also included an increasing focus on fathers as potential carers and on their right to have time to care. In this perspective, family care has been broadened with regard to potential care-givers and fathers have been partly re-familialized. These different focuses and agendas are present also within the EU discourse, where they seem to stand side by side rather than coherently integrated (Daly, 2004; Lewis, 2006). The EU public discourse, in fact, has certainly promoted "conciliation" as an important objective. Yet, it has framed it mainly as a women-only issue (Stratigaki, 2004). In addition, it has stressed more the need for women to be in paid work than the caring needs that risk being neglected, short of an overall re-organization of work time at the day/week/year and life-course levels.

Even more than care, pleasure seems to be disappearing from the public discourse concerning children and the relationship of adults with children. Caught between low-fertility concerns and women's labour force participation, having children appears as a social duty and individual (for women) cost, not a self-fulfilling, pleasurable, creative activity. Although the so-called "child penalty" in the lives and careers of women in paid work has drawn attention to the difficulties women face in having both children and a work career, the framing of the discourse almost exclusively in terms of costs omits the dimensions of pleasure, emotional investment, mutual learning and so forth involved in bringing up children. The public discourse on fertility, in fact, seems to be suggesting that children are to be had because they are our – the societal – future. Since there is a cost in time and money, and potential parents (particularly mothers) no longer seem willing to bear this fully, the state somehow has to find ways of carrying the cost. At best, therefore, children are a common good. In this perspective, policies reconciling or balancing work and childcare commitments may be advocated both as equal opportunities and as pro-natalist measures. The fact that children also represent a pleasure, a learning experience for adults (and a private good), is restricted to the private discourse and risks being experienced, or expressed, mainly in the form of narcissistic or consumeristic investment.

Finally, the rise in women's/mothers' employment, together with ageing of the population and of kinship networks, has meant a reduction in family unpaid care labour, thus exposing weaknesses in the family institution as a "care provider pillar". Lack of family hands and domestic servants for care (sometimes referred to as "care shortage") and, in most countries, the lack of good quality childcare services for the very young, available at affordable prices, have all contributed to transnational, even transcontinental, care migration processes in which women play a crucial part. "Global chains" of care, to use Arlie Hochschild's (2000) formulation, can be seen in the mobilization of Philippine women for care and domestic work, e.g. in Hong Kong; of Mexican women for similar work in the US; of Philippine, Equador, Eastern European and North African women for childcare and other forms of care work (particularly for the frail elderly) in Western and Southern Europe (Da Roit & Sabatinelli, 2005; Gori, 2002). A women-dominated care economy provides paid care work for women migrants who serve as the breadwinners of their families and contribute to their home country's economy, while at the same time supplying care labour serving the caring demand of families and labour markets of the West. A globalizing economy interlinks the national economies of the care-work migrant's home country and work country, and changes the contexts of childhood, motherhood and family in both. There is a growing body of research on what happens to women in this process; but little is known of its impact on children: on the children "left behind" when their mother migrates to provide for their future and on children who are looked after by migrant women whose social status, language and culture are often quite different from those of the children's family. Actually, through women's/mothers' migration as care providers, children and the frail elderly are those in both the sending and receiving countries who experience directly, in their everyday lives, what it means to live in a globalized and transnational labour market.

MARITAL/PARTNERSHIP INSTABILITY: DISSOLUTION OF FAMILY SOLIDARITY TOWARDS CHILDREN?

In many parts of the world, children experience the loss of one or both parents through death or desertion, war, persecution, famine, epidemics. Many children in addition have to live with the long-time absence of one or both parents because of patterns of work migration. In Western Europe, most children are protected from these experiences and still live with two married or unmarried parents; but an increasing number are experiencing the breaking up of cohabitation with one parent and some live in a household with a parent and a step-parent. When children live with one parent only, in Europe they do so generally in a mother-headed family and are exposed to the risk of weakening ties with their fathers. This is in contrast to the trend towards a more intensive presence of fathers in the lives of their children, following cultural and normative changes in the father's role – changes that, as pointed out above, are now increasingly being incorporated in social policies, too. This latter trend, however, may reduce the negative impact of marital separation, in so far as studies have shown that the more a father has been involved in caring for his child/children during marriage, the less he is likely to weaken his relationship with them in the event of parental divorce. Also, the shift towards joint custody in most developed countries is an indicator of this new attention to the father–child relationship, as well as of new forms of regulation of parenthood by the state. As a consequence of social differences in which changes in patterns of fatherhood and parenthood develop, a polarization may occur between children having continuous relationships with highly involved fathers, irrespective of what happens to their parents' relationship, and children having more traditional and distant fathers, who lose contact with them when the parental relationship breaks up. The re-partnering of one or both parents may have opposite consequences for children. In some cases, it further weakens the relationship with the non-cohabitant re-partnered parent. In others, it renders complex but enriches the child's family network (see the special issue of *Childhood*, 2003). In either case, parents' cohabitation – in marriage or consensual union – is being weakened as the basis for a child's cohabitation with both parents. Partnership and parenthood no longer stand "obviously" together. This is being acknowledged slowly in legal regulations, through joint custody and sometimes split residence for children of divorced parents.

Notwithstanding ongoing changes in fatherhood as well as increasing mothers' participation in the labour force, parental break-up continues to put children at economic risk. Owing to the gendered division of labour, to women's lower pay on average, to the not always adequate amount of child support by non-cohabitant fathers, lone mother households have lower income on average than dual-parent households and are at a higher risk of experiencing poverty (see Commission of the European Communities, 2007). Thus, children involved in a parental separation have to deal not only with their parents' emotions and develop new forms of relationships with each of them, with their possible new companions, with kin. Sometimes they also have to deal with downward mobility, if not outright poverty.

SOCIAL INEQUALITY: ECONOMIC AND CULTURAL POVERTY

In many, although not all, OECD countries in the past decade, poverty among families with children, therefore among children, has increased. Social policies in many countries seem to contrast inequalities among children less than among adults and the elderly, even though more attention is now paid to including children as the unit of statistical registrations pertaining to childhood (Qvortrup, 1997; Wyness, 2006).

The Supporting Document to the 2007 Joint Report on Social Exclusion (Commission of the European Communities, 2007, p. 11) states: "... in almost all Member States the poverty risk for children is higher than that for the working age population, while the poverty risk for elderly people varies to a greater extent (but in most Member States it is still significantly above average)". Actually, as the most recent UNICEF/Innocenti Research Center (2007) report shows, some of the European countries belong to the group of OECD countries with the highest incidence of child poverty, whether using a simple monetary definition or a more complex one. Moreover, the highest polarization between well-performing and badly performing countries is found within the EU 24. In fact, the two groups of countries at the extreme poles include Sweden, Finland and Denmark (and Norway), on the one hand, the UK, Ireland, Hungary and Poland, on the other. Growing up in poverty presents specific risks. In addition to meagre material resources, it creates a feeling of exclusion precisely in the life phase when one's own sense of self is forming, while at the same time affecting the development of one's capabilities and opportunities, with possible long-term effects. Furthermore, children with more than one sibling are most at risk everywhere – a situation which casts a shadow over public pleas for raising fertility if not accompanied by adequate redistributive measures.

Concerns over child poverty have taken central place in the political and policy agenda in some (e.g. the UK) but not all countries where poverty among children is high. Moreover, there has been a shift, at least at the discursive level, from an emphasis on transfers to an emphasis on parents', particularly mothers', participation in paid work as a means of avoiding the "poverty trap" and the inter-generational transmission of poverty. Research indicates that both instruments are necessary. While public transfers may be important in lifting children out of poverty (e.g. Sørensen, 1999; Esping-Andersen et al., 2002, Bradshaw, 2006), the best protection is having (also) a working mother and living in a dual-parent/dual-earner household (Esping-Andersen et al., 2002). Yet, since many children do not live in a dual-parent household, they do not have access to this kind of protection, or may lose it when their parents separate. Countries such as the UK, while encouraging mothers to work for pay, have strengthened the duties of non-cohabitant fathers toward supporting their children, thus emphasizing that the main responsibility for children's welfare lies with the parents, the state having only a residual and subsidiary role (see also Jensen, this volume). Only in a few countries, such as Norway and Sweden, the state will act as an intermediary by advancing the payment and taking on the job of reclaiming the money from the non-paying parent.

In recent years, a concern for cultural poverty has emerged, spurred on to a large degree by the finding of the OECD Programme for International Student Assessment (PISA) study on the cognitive skills and performance of adolescents. Together with cross-country variations that point to a different performance of national school systems, the data show relevant intra-country differences by social class and ethnicity. Together with an emerging focus on the knowledge society (Jensen, this volume), these findings have given new impulse to those who argue for early childhood education and care as an investment in future human capital. This position in turn has been criticized by those who believe that children should receive resources, and that their situation should be considered seriously, not because they are society's future human capital, but because they are children (see, e.g. Lister, in this volume). Moreover, focusing exclusively on human capital risks, on the one hand, considering the poor and disadvantaged child's family simply as a liability for the children and, on the other, de-coupling cognitive development from relational and emotional life. Finally, one may remember the 1970s and 1980s debates about the fake neutrality of IQ tests, particularly in light of the fact that developed societies have become increasingly multi-cultural and multi-lingual. Yet, in our view, with all its limitations, this debate on human capital and on PISA's findings has two merits. First, it highlights how severe inequality and deprivation experienced during childhood may have a long-term effect on individual capabilities. This problem is further heightened by immigration and by the growing presence of children with limited knowledge of the language of the country where they attend school, or whose families do not command this language properly. Thus policies on child poverty and inequality must address the issue of how to grant equal chances in the development of capabilities. Second, the debate offers a counter-point to discourses and policies that on the contrary give families and parents almost exclusive responsibility and power over their children's life chances.

IMMIGRATION AND MULTI-ETHNICITY

Immigration (re-)introduces with force the issue and visibility of diversity of childhoods across time and space, and highlights diversification of child-hood within local communities. This diversity, moreover, is often presented and experienced within a culturally and socially hierarchical framework: developed/underdeveloped, "us" and "them", and so forth. In Europe, immigrant children of non-European origin may be the most invisible of children and simultaneously the most visible. They are invisible because all discourses on immigration focus mainly on adults (for different approaches see, e.g. Christopoulou & de Leeuw; West et al., in this volume). The experience of children's immigration thus remains unfocused and a-problematic (except for school performance). Children are visible through their colour, their presence in situations and places where they are not expected to be (e.g. in various forms of paid work, including drug dealing and prostitution), the behaviour of their parents (who may not conform to teachers' or social workers' expectations). More recently, and for several different reasons, the use of dress and religious symbols, especially by young girls, has added to visibility and to the discussion of the rights of minorities and problems of multi-culturalism, of the protection of community versus the individual rights, of the children's right (and ability) to choose and so forth – as illustrated in the many discourses surrounding the use of various forms of headscarves, especially in school.

Furthermore, migration is one aspect of globalization of childhood which stands in sharp contrast to another aspect of the same phenomenon: international adoption. "Foreign" children, in fact, increasingly arrive in developed countries through these two pathways granting them quite different acknowledgements and rights, exposing the contradictory ways in which "universal children's rights" are mediated by their form of access to citizenship and, particularly, by their attachment to a family. Adopted "foreign" children become full nationals and acquire full citizenship rights through their becoming children of national parents. Immigrant foreign children, however, even when they have migrated without their families and are, de facto, unattached to a family, are considered first and foremost as migrants, whose citizenship destiny is linked to that of their actual or presumptive family of origin (e.g. Leiter, McDonald, & Jacobson, 2005 on the US case). They have few rights of their own, particularly when they reach adolescence and come near to legal majority age.

THE CHILD "GOES PUBLIC": PUBLIC REGULATION OF CHILDCARE IN THE EARLY CHILDHOOD YEARS

One of the most striking aspects of the "childhood discourses" of recent past decades has been the extent to which childhood is formulated as an interest of international, state and local – public authorities. In addition to the international conventions already mentioned, national legislation in several countries is expanding public regulation of the early childhood years. Increasingly, non-family institutions are setting norms for family arrangements and for "good" or "proper" childhood. In Western Europe, the traditional boundaries between private and public are being renegotiated and, in some cases, redrawn. Some of these processes are monitored/reported in large comparative studies on early childhood education and care (e.g. OECD, 2006), parental leave policy development (e.g. OECD, 2001; Plantenga & Remery, 2005; Plantenga et al., this volume; Moss & Deven, 2006, Fagnani & Math, this volume), and on the reconciliation of work and family (e.g., the OECD series *Babies and Bosses* I–III, 2001, 2002, 2003, 2004).

These policy developments, and their internal tensions, are apparent at the national level and also at the EU level itself, first in the approval of Leave Directives for parents of young children and then in the setting of EU-wide childcare targets.

Following the Maternity Leave Directive of 1992, the Parental Leave Directive was issued in 1996 after years of debate. It states the minimum entitlements of working parents (mothers and fathers) to unpaid leave for infant care. The second direction is presented in policies for early childhood education and care, for which the EU, in 1993, agreed on a Recommendation. More recently, as part of the European Employment Strategy, the European Council meeting in Barcelona in 2002 set ambitious targets for the provision of childcare services: by 2010, such services should be provided for at least one in three children under 3 and 90% of the older pre-schoolers (European Council, 2002; see also Plantenga et al., this volume). As a consequence of these national and EU developments, in several countries there is an increasing emphasis on both parents as earners and carers and a redesign of responsibility for early childhood education and care.

These processes are not homogenous across all countries and not even within the EU. They occur, in fact, within national specific cultural, legislative and institutional frameworks. Family obligations are defined differently across Europe, and the political history of parenthood and childhood has taken different national specific paths (e.g. Anttonen & Sipilä, 1996). However, since the 1990s a shift in political thinking may be detected, particularly within "old EU" countries, with regard to the responsibility of the state for pre-school children. Increasingly, in many countries, the care of small children has been conceptualized not just as a private, family responsibility, but as a matter of public interest, and even as a *social right* of both parents and children (Ellingsæter & Leira, 2006). This development is taking two, apparently opposite, directions at the policy level. On the one hand, mothers' and parental leaves of absence are being extended and fathers, in particular, are increasingly being acknowledged as having a right to care. Consequently, children are acknowledged a right to be cared for by their parents in the early months of life. The duration of this right, as well as its coverage, varies substantially across countries, although the trend is similar. From this point of view, one could say that policies have actively supported the familialization of care in early infancy through a partial re-familialization of fathers. On the other hand, the "mixed bag" of concerns motivating policy reforms – i.e. encouraging women's (mothers') labour market participation, reducing children's social inequality, preventing social exclusion, investing in human capital and so forth – has increasingly promoted a partial de-familialization of child care.

What the different forms and packages on childcare mean for children has been much debated among professionals, parents and politicians. State-sponsoring of childcare services is advocated, among other things, as advantageous to the child in improving everyday experience; as equalizing the opportunities of children from different social and economic backgrounds; and as being a form of investment in a society's human capital. It has also been argued as being a means of facilitating the work/family arrangements of parents, and as assisting the economy's demand for labour (Anttonen, Johansson, & Leira, 2007). As mentioned previously, pronatalism was an argument for public involvement in childcare in the 1920s and 1930 and is currently resurfacing in some European countries. On the other hand, state-sponsoring of childcare is opposed because it crosses the boundaries between the public domain and the private sphere; it challenges the parental mandate in upbringing; it de-values mothers' care; and it levies costs on the public purse.

Whatever the motivations for policy reforms, changes are taking place in the contexts and settings where childhood is being played out; in the norms of "good" childhood, motherhood and fatherhood; and in what families and parents "are for". While it may be true that the family is bereft of some of its functions, the changing contexts of childhood have created new expectations for what constitutes a "proper childhood". Parental responsibilities are not generally relinquished, but are taking on new dimensions and demands.

The issues we have sketched in this introduction form part of a rich literature, often comparative, but prevalently focused on the institutional, economic and demographic framework in which children live. It rarely, if ever, focuses on children as such, or on how their life's experience is shaped within these changing contexts. Particularly within OECD and EU countries, research on children, demographic research and policy research follow different paths and rarely join forces. In this volume, we have tried to connect these three strands of research from the perspective of what it means for children. Our focus is mainly Europe, although, in order to contextualize our arguments, there are also some chapters on developing countries. Some of the studies presented here focus mainly on policies, some take a macro view of trends, others deal with specific groups of children. The picture that emerges is complex and not univocal. We have not tried to offer a homogeneous presentation, not even at the interpretive level. Diversity concerns not just children and childhoods, but also modes of understanding them and of understanding the ongoing changes.

THE VOLUME

The essays in this volume are organized in four parts. Part I deals with policies of childcare; Part II focuses on children in ageing societies; Part III addresses diversity in childhood contexts and Part IV is a discussion of new discourses in childhood policy debates and the issue of whether we might actually be witnessing a paradigm shift.

Part I: Policies of Children and Families

In the essays included in this first part, a specific set of policies are analysed from a comparative perspective: policies dealing with the needs of young children and their families. The way in which each country constructs its "caring package" has to do not only with conceptions of childhood and children's well being, but also with conceptions of the family and of proper gender roles.

Plantenga and co-authors present a broad overview of childcare policy change in Europe, with a focus on the childcare targets of the EU set at the Barcelona summit of 2002. Central to the EU childcare policy statement is confirmation of the goal of full employment and the need to provide childcare to this end. As pointed out by the authors, monitoring the Barcelona targets is complicated. Statistical complexities and institutional differences render any description of the state of affairs with respect to childcare in EU member states a precarious undertaking. The article approaches the field with a threefold agenda. Starting from the statistical complexities, it contributes to the methodology on assessing childcare provisioning. Secondly, it offers an empirical exploration aimed at identifying countries that have already reached the Barcelona targets. Thirdly, it assesses the significance of the Barcelona targets on the availability of childcare. The resulting picture of differential caring packages suggests that across Europe different ways of understanding children needs are in place, therefore shaping not only different options for families and mothers, but also different contexts for young, and particularly very young, children.

Fagnani and Math compare the "family package" (cash benefits, tax breaks, exemptions from charges, subsidies and/or services in kind, including housing benefits) in 11 affluent European democracies: the four Nordic countries, the UK, Ireland, The Netherlands, France, Austria, Belgium and Germany. They present a general overview of expenditure destined for each country's social protection system and, within it, "family/children" benefits in cash and in kind, and follow with an examination of the structure and principal features of the transfer systems to families, namely cash benefits and tax breaks. The analysis shows that a country's "family package" may be generous to varying degree, not just in general, but also with regard to family size, i.e. specifically – to the number of children in the family. It may also have a prevalent focus on horizontal rather than on vertical redistribution. In their conclusion, the authors suggest hypotheses about the relationships between "family packages", poverty rates among families with children and fertility rates in the selected countries.

Knijn and Ostner focus on the way children enter the public agenda; how their needs are conceptualized in the public discourse and how these discourses enter policy discourse. They argue that the role of ideas, what they call the "rhetorical action" of policy-related actors, is as important for understanding policies as the policies themselves, in so far as they construct worlds of meaning that are instrumental in persuading individuals and families about what "values" should be pursued. Rhetorical action is particularly crucial when the goals and values it promotes contrast with those shared by substantial proportions of the population and previously supported by policies themselves. For instance, this is so in the case of the new model of the dual-worker family and of the working mother. Knijn and Ostner compare two countries – The Netherlands and Germany – which, due to a concern about low fertility, have recently radically changed discourses and policies concerning families with children. The new discourses stress the virtues of the dual-earner model and thus of mothers' participation in the labour market, therefore "defamilializing" not only women and children, but also the family itself. In their view, the mix of discourses and policy practices increases, rather than lessens, the ambivalences and the confusion in which the young now make their decisions concerning family and children.

Part II: Children in an Ageing Society

The essays in this section deal with the experience of being a child in an ageing society at both macro and micro levels, i.e. societal arrangements and family inter-generational relations.

Focusing on the social worlds of children, Hagestad first outlines how age structures of society and family lineages have become less "bottom heavy" and increasingly more "top heavy". Kinship structures, too, have become more "verticalized", with more ties across generations and fewer and more age-homogeneous intragenerational ties. Hagestad goes on to discuss modern life course organization and the relationship to age segregation. The consequences of segregation for children's social networks, support and socialization are also highlighted. In conclusion, the author points at the current gaps in our knowledge of children's inter-generational networks and discusses how social policy can address the needs of children who have few vertical ties either inside or outside the family.

Keck and Saraceno address the experience of being grandchildren. While many studies have examined grandparenthood, little research has been done from the perspective of grandchildren. On the basis of the demographic and research literature, this essay first characterizes the specific life circumstance of today's grandchildren and the major changes in the relationship between grandchildren and grandparents in the last part of the 20th century in European societies. Demographic ageing due to low fertility and increasing life expectancy has changed the family structure, with more grandparents present longer for fewer grandchildren. In the second part of the essay, and based on the few data available, the authors explore the relationship between grandchildren and grandparents in two countries – Germany and Italy – characterized by differences not just in family cultures, but also in recent demographic history, as well as in welfare regimes with regard to the allocation of responsibilities between family and collectivity in providing care and other forms of support. The authors argue that the interplay between these various dimensions shapes distinct patterns of grandchild-hood and of grandchildren–grandparent relationships.

Drawing upon a comparative study of children's welfare in 14 countries, Jensen points to the risk – at societal level at least – that the imbalance at the extremes of the age spectrum could result in a corresponding imbalance in the distribution of resources. The increasing incidence of poverty among children is an indicator of the reality of this risk, which in policy practice and discourse is being addressed mostly through a focus on maternal employment as the main solution. In this perspective, according to the author, while the needs of the elderly are addressed as a social responsibility, those of children are addressed as a purely private, family, responsibility, making children particularly vulnerable.

Part III: Diversities of Childhood

The third group of essays deals directly with the lives of children – their similarities but also socially constructed diversities.

Wetzels addresses a specific dimension of these contradictions: namely that between the implicit norms of behaviour concerning mothers' and fathers' combination of paid work and care for their newborn children included in the Dutch parental leave scheme and the actual material and cultural resources available to the different groups of women and men to help meet these norms. Her focus is on differences between spouses/partners from different backgrounds with regard to residence in The Netherlands. She shows that the majority of first-time mothers prefer to return to work early, following termination of the leave period. They also prefer a long part-time job to either full-time or short part-time. It is noticeable that a quota of fathers opts for the long part-time solution. Both these behaviours closely adhere to the implicit norms framed in the leave scheme. It is, however, either not available or not acceptable to many migrant couples, particularly to women. Many mothers not born in The Netherlands perceive the time allowed by the leave scheme, i.e. 3–5 months, as too short. Whatever the reasons, children born at present in The Netherlands may experience early infancy differently, and not just due to family and ethnic membership and traditions, but also to different family and caring arrangements. "Fully Dutch" children experience non-family care early, while "immigrant background" children experience longer family care but also a higher risk of economic constraints.

Christopoulou and de Leeuw draw upon studies of a research group known as Children in Communication about Migration (CHICAM) in six European countries. Their essay sheds light on the processes through which migrant children adapt and interpret their migratory experience while acting as mediators between family and society in the hosting country. The authors argue that migrant children are in fact charged with double roles. On the one hand, they have to remain faithful to their community and family values, including that of respect for the authority and superior knowledge of adults. On the other hand, they are often better positioned than their parents, particularly their mothers, to learn the language of the hosting country and to take part in its everyday life, mainly through attending school and relating to their native peers. Sometimes they are also providers for their own family. In this difficult process, with its many tensions and contradictions, children appear veritable actors, giving proof not only of resilience, but of imagination and of an ability simultaneously to translate and create the multiple social worlds they inhabit.

West and colleagues address the difficult question of the practical tensions that may arise between the discourse on and implementation of children's rights, on the one hand, and local understanding of what childhood is all about, on the other. Within these conflicts, understanding what is "in the best interests" of a child, not in the abstract, but in the concrete context of living, may prove difficult. Using the rich material collected in working with and for children in developing countries, West and co-authors name the multiple actors, including children themselves, who have to be involved if a practice informed by a locally embedded understanding of the children's best interests is to be developed. In so doing, they offer food for thought for the relationship between children and adults, research and practice, researchers and practitioners.

Belloni and Carriero analyse the time-use patterns of school children and adolescents in an industrial city in Italy. In addition to showing how these patterns are strongly shaped by the two main institutions that regulate children's lives – family and school – this essay offers data problematizing the thesis of an increasing age segregation in contemporary society. Although it is true that children spend most of their time in ad hoc institutions, these include adults who monitor and organize children's lives, including their relationships with each other. Apparently, the issue here is less of segregation than the possibility of self-organization by children. Interesting differences emerge in this perspective, not only, of course, between different age groups, but also between female and male children and between native and immigrant children.

Benoit and colleagues take a life-course approach to understanding the risks facing children and youth living on the street in a Canadian town compared to children of the same age living in the same city with their families. In contrast to interpretations that see these risks as deriving from the deviant, or rebellious, behaviour of youth, the authors contend that it is the family and social context in which they grew up that pushed them to life on the street, forcing them to become precociously adult and to take responsibility for themselves in the very basic needs of shelter and food. The "developmental tasks" they face are similar to those of older children and their behaviour may be accordingly interpreted in the perspective of "emergent youth". The risks they face are the outcome of this too precocious entrance to adulthood in a society with a different normative and institutional timetable.

Part IV: Changing Discourses on Childhood

This last group of essays deals with what looks like an actual paradigm shift in policy discourse: namely, the focus on children as a valuable social resource. The fact that the authors use different perspectives and reach partially different conclusions indicates that this is an area in which consensus is still far from achieved, notwithstanding the apparent convergence in public discourses and documents.

In contrast to the thesis of an increasing privatization/familialization of children's needs, Jenson argues that policy development prompted by the so-called "new social risk approach" in the developed countries has rendered children the major focus of public intervention. Among the many measures involved in this new policy approach, Jenson underlines those aimed at preventing social exclusion in the short, but also long term, due to financial and cultural poverty in childhood and at promoting skills that are adequate to the knowledge economy. She defines this preventive and future investment approach the "*LEGO™ paradigm*" from the well-known brand of toys, i.e. based on constant (life-long) learning, knowledge oriented and stressing involvement and engagement and taking of personal responsibilities. According to her reading, the stress on early childhood education and investment in children's human capital, as means to preventing poverty and to investing in the future of society (of which there are important examples in most OECD countries), in fact may well be synthesized by that paradigm.

Lister, too, addresses the human capital investment approach to childhood policies that informs much of OECD and EU discourse. She agrees that it is a veritable paradigm shift in policy. Her reading (which she shares with the European Children's Network), however, is critical, in so far as this approach focuses on children more as future adults (as "becomings") than as children who live here and now (as "beings"). As a consequence, employability concerns (of parents and particularly mothers, as well as of children when adults) inform the policy agenda to the detriment of other dimensions of children's experience, such as play or emotional needs. Lister uses the British example in showing how this approach risks marginalizing "less profitable children", such as the disabled, gypsies, travellers or simply "deviants". She contrasts this with a model focusing on children's present well-being. This model emerges in debates in many countries, in international organizations and in policies prevalent in the Nordic countries. Although education is an important dimension of this model, too, according to Lister it is more clearly informed by the capability approach and by a focus on the need to provide the means needed for children to develop a full life.

REFERENCES

Alber, J. & Kohler, U. (2005). *Health and care in an enlarged Europe*. European Foundation for the Improvement of Living and Working Conditions, Luxembourg, Office for Official Publications of the European Communities.

Anttonen, A., Johansson, S., & Leira, A. (2007). Childcare and the gendering of citizenship. In: R. Lister & F. Williams, et al. (Eds), *Gender and citizenship in western Europe* (pp. 109–136). Bristol: Policy Press.

Anttonen, A., & Sipilä, J. (1996). European social care services: Is it possible to identify models? *Journal of European Social Policy, 6*(2), 87–100.

Aravamudan, G. (2007). *Disappearing daughters*. London: Penguin.

Attias-Donfut, C., & Wolff, F.-C. (2000). The redistributive effects of generational transfers. In: S. Arber & C. Attias-Donfut (Eds), *The myth of generational conflict* (pp. 22–46). London: Routledge.

Bey, M. (2003). The Mexican child. From work with the family to paid work. *Childhood, X*(3), 287–299.

Bradshaw, J. (2006). Child benefit packages in 15 countries in 2004. In: J. Lewis (Ed.), *Children, changing families and welfare states* (pp. 26–50). Cheltenham: Edward Elgar.

Childhood. (2003). Special issue on "New Perspectives on Children and Divorce", Vol. 10, No. 3.

Commission of the European Communities. (2006). Towards an EU Strategy for the Rights of the Child. Communication from the Commission. Brussels 4.7.2006, COM 367 final.

Commission of the European Communities. (2007). Joint Report on Social Protection and Social Inclusion, Supporting Document, Commission Staff Working Document, Brussels, 6.03, 2007, SEC 329.

Da Roit, B., & Sabatinelli, S. (2005). Il modello mediterraneo di welfare tra famiglia e mercato. *Stato e Mercato, 74*(2), 267–290.

Daly, M. (2004). Changing conceptions of family and gender relations in European welfare states and the third way. In: J. Lewis & R. Surender (Eds), *Welfare state change. Towards a third way?* (pp. 135–154). Oxford: OUP.

Ellingsæter, A. L., & Leira, A. (2006). *Politicising parenthood in Scandinavia*. Bristol: The Policy Press.

Esping-Andersen, G., Gallie, D., Vandenbrucke, F., Hemerijck, A., & Myles, J. (2002). *Why we need a new welfare state*. Oxford: Oxford University Press.

European Council. (2002). Presidency conclusions European Council Barcelona 15 and 16 March 2002. Available online at: http://www.consilium.europa.eu/ueDocs/cons_Data/docs/pressData/en/ec/71025.pdf

Gauthier, A. H. (1996). *The state and the family*. New York, NY: Oxford University Press.

Gori, C. (Ed.) (2002). *Il welfare nascosto*. Roma: Carocci.

Hagestad, G. O. (2007). Transfers between grandparents and grandchildren. The importance of taking a three generational perspective. *Zeitschrift für Familienforschung, 3*, 315–332.

Hochschild, A. R. (2000). Global care chains and emotional surplus value. In: W. Hutton & A. Giddens (Eds), *On the edge: Living with global capitalism*. London: Jonathan Cape.

Keck, W., & Blöme, A. (2007). Is there a generational cleavage in Europe? Age-specific perceptions of elderly care and of the pension system. In: J. Alber, T. Fahey & C. Saraceno (Eds), *Handbook of quality of life in the enlarged European Union* (pp. 73–99). London: Routledge.

Kohli, M. (1999). Private and public transfers between generations: Linking the family and the state. *European Societies, 1*, 81–104.

Leira, A. (2002). *Working parents and the welfare state*. Cambridge: Cambridge University Press.

Leira, A., Tobio, C., & Trifiletti, R. (2005). Kinship and informal support: Care resources for the first generation of working mothers. In: U. Gerhardt, T. Knijn & A. Weckwert (Eds),

Working mothers in Europe. A comparison of policies and practices (pp. 74–96). Cheltenham: Edward Elgar.

Leiter, V., McDonald, J. L., & Jacobson, H. T. (2005). Challenges to children's individual citizenship. Immigration, family and the state. *Childhood, XIII*(1), 11–27.

Lewis, J. (2006). Work/family reconciliation, equal opportunities and social policies: The interpretation of policy trajectories at the EU level and the meaning of gender equality. *Journal of European Public Policy, 13*(3, April), 420–437.

Moen, P. (Ed.) (2003). *It's about time. Couples and careers*. Ithaca, NY: Cornell University Press.

Moss, P., & Deven, F. (Eds). (2000). *Parental leave: Progress or pitfall*. Brussels: NIDI/CBGS.

Moss, P., & Deven, F. (2006). Leave policies and research: A cross-national overview. *Marriage and Family Review, 39*(374), 255–285.

Myrdal, A., & Klein, V. (1956). *Women's two role*. London: Routledge and Kegan Paul.

OECD. (2001). *Balancing work and family life: Helping parents into paid employment*. Paris: OECD.

OECD. (2002). Babies and bosses: Reconciling work and family life. Vol. 1. Australia, Denmark, and the Netherlands. Paris: OECD.

OECD. (2003). Babies and bosses: Reconciling work and family life. Vol. 2. Austria, Ireland and Japan. Paris: OECD.

OECD. (2004). Babies and bosses: Reconciling work and family life. Vol. 3. New Zealand, Portugal and Switzerland. Paris: OECD.

OECD. (2006). *Starting strong II. Early childhood education and care* (Summary). Paris: OECD.

Orloff, A. S. (2006). Farewell to maternalism? State policies and mothers' employment. In: J. Levy (Ed.), *The state after statism*. Cambridge, MA: Harvard University Press.

Plantenga, J., & Remery, Ch. (2005). *Reconciliation of work and private life. A comparative review of thirty countries*. Luxembourg: Office of Official Publications.

Qvortrup, J. (1997). A voice for children in statistical and social accounting: A plea for children's right to be heard. In: A. James & A. Prout (Eds), *Constructing and reconstructing childhood* (2nd ed.). London: Falmer.

Stratigaki, M. (2004). The cooptation of gender concepts in EU policies: The case of 'reconciliation of work and family'. *Social Politics, XI*(1), 30–56.

Sørensen, A.-M. (1999). Family declined, poverty, and social exclusion: The mediating effects of family policy. In: A. Leira (Ed.), *Family change: Practices, policies, values. Comparative social research* (Vol. 18, pp. 1–29). Stamford, CT: JAI Press.

Therborn, G. (2004). *Between sex and power*. London: Routledge.

UN. (2005). World population prospects. The 2004 revision, http://esa.un.org/unpp.

UNICEF/Innocenti Research Center. (2007). *Child poverty in perspective. An overview of child well-being in rich countries*, Report Card. N. 7, UNICEF, Florence.

Wyness, M. (2006). *Childhood and society*. Houndsmills: Palgrave Macmillan.

PART I:
POLICIES OF CHILDCARE

CHILDCARE SERVICES IN 25 EUROPEAN UNION MEMBER STATES: THE BARCELONA TARGETS REVISITED

Janneke Plantenga, Chantal Remery, Melissa Siegel and Loredana Sementini

INTRODUCTION

Personal services are extremely important in the lives of working parents. This applies in particular to childcare services, as care responsibilities constitute a major obstacle to (full) employment. The importance of measures in this area has long been recognised by the European Council and Union. In March 1992, the European Council passed a recommendation on childcare to the effect that Member States 'should take and/or progressively encourage initiatives to enable women and men to reconcile their occupational family and upbringing responsibilities arising from the care of children' (92/241/EEC). Ten years later, at the 2002 Barcelona summit, the aims were formulated more explicitly and targets were set with regard to childcare. Confirming the goal of full employment, the European Council agreed that 'Member States should remove disincentives to female labour force participation and strive, taking into account the demand for childcare facilities and in line with national patterns of provision, to provide childcare by 2010 to at least 90% of children between

Childhood: Changing Contexts
Comparative Social Research, Volume 25, 27–53
ISSN: 0195-6310/doi:10.1016/S0195-6310(07)00001-4

3 years old and the mandatory school age and at least 33% of children under 3 years of age' (European Council, 2002).

Given this target, an effective monitoring of the measures taken in the different EU Member States is of utmost importance. Monitoring is difficult, however, for several reasons. First there is an absolute lack of reliable data. Although especially the OECD has provided extremely rich material on childcare services in several European Member States (Cleveland & Krashinsky, 2004; OECD, 2002, 2003, 2004), no harmonised and comparable statistics are yet available. As a result, most research is based on non-comparable, national data. In addition, statistics on the provision of childcare services – though extremely important – do not seem to provide the full answer. The Barcelona targets refer to the care system of small children, and this is likely to be a very particular mixture of care facilities, leave arrangements and pre-school arrangements, each with its own dynamics and each with its own complexities. A relatively low percentage of children enroled in childcare services, for example, should be assessed differently if the same country offers an extensive system of parental leave and/or a low admission age for (pre-primary) education. An informed assessment of childcare services, therefore, necessitates a broad focus on care, taking into account differences in institutional framework.

In this chapter, we try to fill the gap in childcare statistics by estimating the actual provision of childcare services in the 25 EU Member States (situation 2006). Taking into account the European diversity in childcare arrangements and using a broad perspective on childcare, the aim is to gather as much comparable data on childcare services as possible and to assess the progress made towards the Barcelona targets. In addition, we will provide information whether the Barcelona targets have influenced the national policy agenda, and how the effectiveness of European policy in this field should be assessed.

The structure of the chapter is as follows. In "Childcare Statistics and the EU Employment Strategy", we will describe the available data on childcare services as published in the EU Joint Employment Report 2005/2006 and as reported by the Member States themselves (European Commission, 2006). "Taking into Account Leave Facilities" deals with the wider care system, focusing especially on the provision of parental leave. "Availability of Childcare Services" provides harmonised data on the availability of childcare services for the age category 0–2 and 3–compulsory school age, taking into account the structure of leave facilities. "European Policy: National Effects?" tries to assess the effectiveness of the Barcelona targets, whereas "Conclusions" contains the conclusions.

CHILDCARE STATISTICS AND THE EU EMPLOYMENT STRATEGY

Assessing the availability of childcare services is not an easy task. As stated before, comparable data on the provision of childcare services are not available and national statistics are not easily converted to a common standard, given the fact that each country has its own unique constellation of care arrangements, consisting of services and facilities such as day care centres, kindergarten, leave facilities, (pre-school)education system etc. The difficulties can be easily demonstrated by the figures presented in Table 1. These figures are gathered within the context of the European Employment Strategy, based on the National Action Plans of 2004 and National Reform Programmes of 2005 and 2006, and published in the Joint Employment Report 2005/2006.

In line with the Barcelona targets, the figures indicate the percentages of children cared for by formal arrangements as a proportion of all children of the same age group. It appears that the self-reported coverage rate for young children in 2005 differs from over 75% in Sweden to 0.8% in the Czech Republic. Only Sweden, Slovenia and Estonia score above the Barcelona target, Belgium is close. If we include data for 2004, also Denmark, Spain, France and the United Kingdom are above the Barcelona target. Data are missing for quite a number of countries, though. For children above 3 the situation improves, with most countries indicating a coverage rate above 70% – although the coverage rate in the Netherlands drops to a low 24%.

When interpreting the figures it has to be taken into account that the national statistics most of the time follow the national particularities of the care system. In the Swedish case for example, the figure of (approximately) 75% refers to the category of the 1–4 year olds (with rising rates by age). The youngest age group is excluded because these children are taken care of in the leave system. A recalculation of the Swedish figure for the 0–2 category and inserting '0' for the smallest children gives a considerable lower coverage rate. Indeed, for Sweden the harmonised coverage rate for the age category 0–2 can be estimated at a little bit above 40%.

In addition, the relation between childcare and the education sector may cause problems in interpreting the available data for the age category 3–compulsory school age. The Belgium figure of 100% for example, clearly refers to the high coverage rate of the pre-primary educational system of children aged 3–5; it is extremely doubtful whether this figure can be compared with the figure of 70% for Lithuania, let alone the 24% given for

Table 1. Childcare Coverage in 25 EU Member States as
Percentage of Children in the Relevant Age Category as Reported
in the National Action Plans of 2004 and National Reform Programmes
of 2005 and 2006.

	0–2 Years Old			3 Years to Compulsory School Age		
	2003	2004	2005	2003	2004	2005
Belgium	29.4	30.4	30.6	100	100	100
Czech Republic			0.8			76.6
Denmark		68			92	
Germany	7.0			89.0		
Estonia			33.6			85.8
Greece		5			55	
Spain		37			95	
France	29.4	40.8		100	100	
Ireland						
Italy		23			94	
Cyprus	12.0			82.0		
Latvia			16.4			80.5
Lithuania	17.8		21.3	62.1		69.6
Luxembourg	10.9					
Hungary						
Malta						
Netherlands	24.0	26.0	24.0	89.0	91.0	24
Austria	11.0	8	12.6	85.2	64	84.5
Poland	2			60		
Portugal	22.3	24		70.6	70	
Slovenia			37.4			76.9
Slovakia						
Finland	19.5	27.9		73.0	77.3	
Sweden	73.7	74.4	75.3	95.8	95.4	96.4
United Kingdom		35.0			86	

Source: European Commission, 2006 (last update November 2006).

the Netherlands. It is more likely that this figure of 24% refers to the
percentage of children enroled in after-school care, in addition to pre-
primary education (which, by the way, may also explain the large drop in
the Dutch coverage rate between 2004 and 2005). At a more general level, it
seems likely that national differences in the organisation of pre-primary
education have an impact on the organisation of after school care. In some
countries pre-primary school hours may cover all day whereas in other
countries children might well be cared for both within the educational

system during (pre-primary) school hours and within the care system outside these hours. If the figures do not differentiate in a systematic way between childcare facilities and the educational system, they may provide only partial as well as potential misleading information of the effective scope of childcare facilities (for a full assessment of the methodological complexities see Eurostat, 2004; Plantenga & Siegel, 2004).

Both examples indicate that figures on childcare services are difficult to interpret without any knowledge of the (differences in) institutional background. Nevertheless, the conclusions of the EU Joint Employment Report 2005/2006 with regard to the policy efforts of EU Member States are rather straightforward: 'The potential contribution of women to raising employment rates is not strongly emphasised. Measures concentrate on improving the availability and affordability of care for children and other dependents. Seven Member States set targets for extra care places. However, the Barcelona childcare targets are far from being reached' (European Commission, 2006, p. 10).

TAKING INTO ACCOUNT LEAVE FACILITIES

In order to go below the surface picture as presented in Table 1, and taking the birth of a child as a starting point, this section presents the details of the national systems of leave. The details of the entitlements and the substance of these provisions have been widely and variously compiled, analysed and commented upon (OECD, 1995, 2001; Rostgaard, 2003; Drew, 2005; Moss & Deven, 2006). Yet this is an area in which comparisons are still difficult, given differences in institutional details and lack of harmonised data about persons on leave, duration of leave and level of payment. In addition, leave is a very active policy area, which makes it necessary to provide updates on a regular basis.

Since June 1996, national policy in the field of leave arrangements has been underpinned by a directive of the European Council which obliges Member States to introduce legislation on parental leave that will enable parents to care full-time for their child over a period of at least 3 months. In principle this refers to an individual, non-transferable entitlement. This directive ensures that a certain minimum standard is guaranteed within the Member States. Over and above this, however, there is a broad range of national regulations with countries differing as to payments, duration, flexibility and entitlement. Table A1 of the Appendix gives a detailed overview in this respect, based on two recent EU-publications and covering the situation in 2003–2004 (Plantenga & Remery, 2005; Fagan & Hebson, 2006).

It appears that the duration of parental leave differs substantially, ranging from the period until the child's third birthday in the Czech Republic, Germany, Estonia, Spain, France, Latvia, Lithuania, Hungary, Poland and Slovakia to 3 months (per parent) in Belgium, Cyprus, Malta, the Netherlands and the United Kingdom. In some countries parental leave is unpaid (Greece, Spain, Ireland, Cyprus, Malta, the Netherlands, Portugal and the United Kingdom) while in other countries leave takers are compensated more or less for their loss of earnings. Payments vary from fixed flat rate amounts in Belgium, Czech Republic, Germany, Latvia, Luxembourg, Austria and Poland, to wage related payment in Denmark, Estonia, Italy, Lithuania, Hungary, Finland and Sweden. In addition to differences in length and level of payment, parental leave can be organised along family or individual lines. If the former is used as the basis, parents are in a position to decide who will make use of the parental leave allocated to the family. If both parents have an individual, non-transferable entitlement to parental leave, then both can claim a period of leave. If one parent does not take advantage of this entitlement, the right expires. Especially in the 10 new Member States, the parental leave is often framed as a family right. Finally, it has to be taken into account that countries may differ in the length of maternity leave. Moreover, in some countries the distinction between parental, maternity and paternity leave does not apply.

Obviously, all these differences have a negative effect on the possibility of international comparisons. In order to assess the impact and importance of the leave facilities in the national context, it is, for example, not possible to rank the countries simply on the length of the consecutive weeks of parental leave. Country differences may be overestimated, as formal regulations say little about the actual impact. This calls for information on the take-up rate; that is the actual use of leave facilities. In addition, in order to make a proper comparison between countries and/or between men and women information on take up rates should be combined with information on the length of (maternity and parental) leave (Bruning & Plantenga, 1999). Unfortunately, detailed figures in this respect are not available; only the Nordic countries provide regular consistent statistical accounts of the use of leave (viz. Rostgaard, 2005; Moss & Deven, 2006).

We do know, however, that the use of parental leave depends in particular on whether the leave is unpaid or paid and, if paid, at what level (Moss & Deven, 2006). We have therefore computed the 'effective parental leave' by weighting the duration of the parental leave by the level of payment (see also Plantenga & Remery, 2005). In order not to be impeded by too much detail, the computation is not very intricate; weeks of leave paid by more than

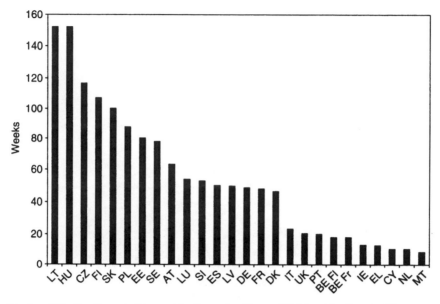

Fig. 1. Effective Parental Leave (the Length of Leave Weighted by Level of Payment and Harmonising Maternity Leave) in 25 EU Member States, 2002–2003. *Source:* Appendix, Table A1.

66% of the national minimum wage are counted fully; weeks paid by 33–66% of the minimum wage are counted for 66%, whereas weeks of leave paid for 0–33% are counted for by 33%. See for more details Table A1 of the Appendix. Despite this crude measure, we believe that this effective parental leave gives a reasonably accurate picture of the importance of the national leave legislation. As Fig. 1 indicates, this effective leave is highest in Lithuania and Hungary (152 weeks) and lowest in Malta (9 weeks), Cyprus and the Netherlands (11 weeks).

As stated before, the leave system influences the need for childcare services. By definition, extended leave facilities, especially in combination with an early admission age for pre-school facilities, lower the need for childcare services. Fig. 2 is rather informative in this respect. It ranks the countries by the number of weeks between the end of the total leave facility available after child birth (estimated as the sum of 8 weeks maternity leave and effective parental leave) and the beginning of the pre-school system (see Table A2 of the Appendix for information on pre-school and compulsory school age). Taking an uninterrupted career of parents as point of departure, it appears that especially Dutch and Greek working parents have to rely

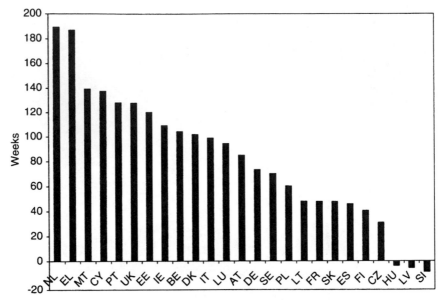

Fig. 2. Difference between Total (Effective Parental + 8 Weeks Maternity) Leave and Pre-Primary School Admission Age in 25 EU Member States, 2002–2003. *Source:* Appendix, Tables A1 and A2.

heavily on the availability of childcare services. In Finland, Czech Republic, Hungary, Latvia and Slovenia the need is considerably less, as a result of extended leave facilities and/or a low admission age of pre-school facilities.

AVAILABILITY OF CHILDCARE SERVICES

Now that we have covered the leave facilities we continue by providing data on childcare services. In the Barcelona targets, the concept of childcare is unspecified, although implicitly the focus seems to be on formal, centre-based arrangements for reasons of stability and reliability. However, narrowing the concept down to formal, centre-based arrangements is inadequate because countries may differ widely in the organisation of services offered, in the division between formal and informal arrangements and/or public and private care. Funding programmes for employers, for example, or tax measures for parents implicate public support for a private market (for a full assessment of the methodological complexities, see Eurostat, 2004).

In order to do justice to the diverse arrangements, the availability of childcare services has been estimated by including – in principle – all childcare facilities, home and centre based and private and public. With this approach, the calculations are in line with the Eurostat publication *'Development of a methodology for the collection of harmonised statistics on childcare'*, which can be seen as a first attempt to provide harmonised statistics on childcare (Eurostat, 2004). The calculation is done as follows: per childcare facility for which data are available, the share of total children cared for was calculated. The indicator of available childcare ('the coverage rate') is calculated by adding the shares per childcare facility. This means that the coverage rate may be underestimated if data for some types of arrangements are not available. At the same time, the coverage rate may be overestimated as a result of double counting. Double counting is, however, avoided as far as possible by excluding arrangements that are clearly overlapping, such as special holiday arrangements. Unfortunately, no consistent data were available on the time during which the care is available. Available childcare could therefore not be calculated in full-time equivalent terms, as a result of which part-time facilities have been given the same weight as full-time facilities. It is likely that this issue is especially important in countries in which the working time regime allows for diverse working time patterns like the Netherlands, the United Kingdom and – to a lesser extent – Denmark and Sweden (see also Plantenga & Remery, 2005).

Childcare Services for the 0–2 Age Group

Fig. 3 summarises the coverage rate of childcare per Member State. On the basis of these more or less comparable figures, it appears that five EU Member States have reached the Barcelona target of 33% childcare for children under 3. Especially, in Belgium-Flanders and Denmark, the coverage by the childcare sector is rather high. France and Sweden also score rather favourably, whereas the Netherlands and Belgium (French part) score just above the target. In several countries, the availability of childcare is below 10%. This is especially the case for Spain, Austria, Czech Republic, Germany, Greece, Italy, Hungary and Poland. Figures of five countries are missing, though.

When interpreting the figures, it should be noted that the data mainly refer to childcare facilities. In a few countries, however, pre-school arrangements are included. In most Member States the admission age to pre-primary education is at least 3. In six Member States, however, children may

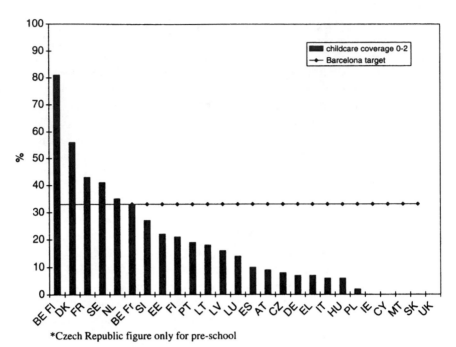

*Czech Republic figure only for pre-school

Fig. 3. Estimated Childcare Coverage Rate (Age Category 0–2) in 25 EU Member States, Recalculated and Harmonised, 2000–2002. *Source:* Appendix, Table A3.

participate from age 2 or 2.5 (Belgium, Germany, Spain, France, Ireland and Italy), whereas in Latvia and Lithuania the admission age to pre-school is set at 1. In fact, especially in the new Member States, the differences between childcare services and pre-school arrangements are not always clear.

As argued before, the availability of childcare facilities does not answer the question whether demand is fully met. The actual demand for childcare is influenced by the participation rate of parents (mothers), levels of unemployment, the length of parental leave, the opening hours of school, the costs of formal arrangements and the availability of alternatives like grandparents and/or other informal arrangements. In Finland, for example, the coverage rate for the youngest age category is, according to Fig. 3, 21%, which is well below the Barcelona target of 33%. Yet, childcare facilities are not in short supply. In fact, since 1990, Finish children under the age of 3 are guaranteed a municipal childcare place, irrespective of the labour market status of the parents. The relatively low coverage rate, therefore, indicates not shortages but alternative ways to look after young children like parental leave facilities. In the Finish case, each family is entitled to 26 weeks of parental leave to be taken after maternity leave. In addition, each family is entitled to a (paid) home care leave until the youngest child is 3 years old or enters public childcare (see Table A1 of the Appendix).

Given the importance of a broader perspective on childcare services, we have combined the information of Figs. 2 and 3 and have calculated an adjusted score that corrects for the extent of available leave facilities. The Finish case can again serve as an example. There are 156 weeks between the birth of a child and the third birthday and we presume that the first 8 weeks are covered by maternity leave. In the Finish case, the effective parental leave is estimated at 107 weeks. Together with the 8 weeks maternity leave, this covers 74% (115/156) of the 0–2 period. If we add this percentage to the childcare coverage rate of 21% (which is calculated over the same 156 weeks), the effective coverage rate is 95%. This effective childcare coverage rate indicates which part of the period between the birth of a child and its third birthday is covered either by services or by parental leave.

Of course, taking into account leave facilities implies that the coverage rate with regard to childcare increases, see Fig. 4. As a result, almost all

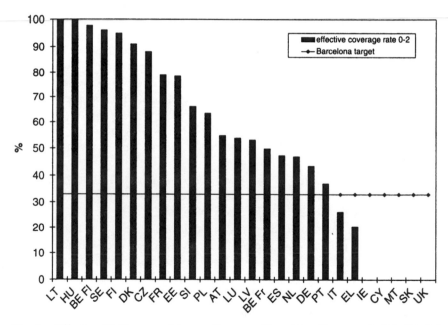

Fig. 4. Effective Childcare and Leave Coverage Rate (Age Category 0–2) in 25 EU Member States, 2000–2002. *Source:* Appendix, Table A3.

Member States seem to have reached the Barcelona target, the only exceptions being Italy and Greece (data for˙ five countries missing). Particularly, the scores of Hungary, Lithuania and the Czech Republic change rather heavily, as these countries have extensive leave provisions, as a result of which the adjusted coverage rate increases rather dramatically. We admit that we may have overestimated the importance of leave facilities in the life of working parents, overstating the effective childcare coverage as indicated by Fig. 4. The point to be taken is, however, that a focus on strictly childcare services may not do justice to the overall care regime and the facilities granted to working parents.

Childcare Services for Children from 3 to Compulsory School Age

The second age group for which the childcare coverage rate is recalculated is children aged 3 to the mandatory school age. The Barcelona target states that the actual coverage should be at least 90%. Again, the national scores have been recalculated, using national sources, and taking into account the different national arrangements. In particular, pre-school arrangements have been included given the impossibility to differentiate between care within and outside of the education system. Fig. 5 shows that eight countries meet the Barcelona target or score rather close: Belgium (French and Flemish part), France, Netherlands, Spain, Denmark, Italy, Sweden and Germany. Greece, Lithuania, Poland and Slovenia score fairly low. When interpreting this graph, it has to be taken into account, that the coverage rate is, to a large extent, influenced by the (high) coverage rate of pre-school arrangements. As in most countries pre-school is only part-time, working parents still need additional childcare facilities, which are much less available.

Summarising the results so far, it seems obvious that effective monitoring of measures taken in the field of childcare depends on the availability of comparable, harmonised data. Reliable data are scarce, however. In addition, the Barcelona targets seem to lack a clear perspective on the interrelation of childcare and leave facilities as a result of which it is not clear whether the data of Fig. 3 or 4 apply when it comes to monitoring childcare developments. As a result, on the basis of the adjusted score, most countries seem to meet the Barcelona target; if the more strict interpretation is followed the national scores are considerably less favourable.

Yet, despite all the difficulties, it can be safely concluded that the European Member States differ widely in the availability of childcare

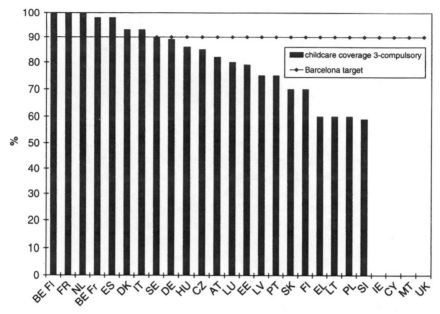

Fig. 5. Estimated Childcare Coverage Rate (3–Compulsory School Age): Recalculated and Harmonised, 2000–2002. *Source:* Appendix, Table A3.

facilities and – more generally – in the care regime towards small children. Given this situation, the question may be asked about the real impact of the Barcelona targets and/or ways to improve the effectiveness of the targets set. Does 'Europe' in any way influence the national policy agenda with regard to childcare services?

EUROPEAN POLICY: NATIONAL EFFECTS?

European policy with regard to equal opportunities used to rely rather heavily on the traditional EU method of regulations and directives. The emphasis, however, changed at the end of the 1990s. The open method of co-ordination (OMC) – a term coined at the summit of Lisbon – implies a movement away from directives towards consultation and joint target setting. O'Connor (2003, p. 1) describes the OMC as 'establishing policy guidelines, setting benchmarks, concrete targets and a monitoring system to evaluate progress via peer group review'. Eberlein and Kerwer (2002, p. 2) add that 'it avoids strict regulatory requirements and allows experiments that are adapted to local circumstances while fostering policy improvement and possible policy convergence, through institutionalised mutual learning processes'. The Barcelona targets are a clear example of this new approach; the targets set should be used as a policy marker; as an important goal to be reached in the near future. Yet they are not obligatory; there is no sanction on non-compliance.

When assessing this new approach, at first sight the results should be rated positively. The European Employment Strategy and the OMC clearly have raised the political relevance of the childcare issue. The targets set keep responsible ministers and civil servants alert and the process of peer review should be seen as an important step in the process of raising awareness. The *Joint Employment Report 2003/2004*, for example, indicates that 'childcare is a policy priority in practically all Member States, even though the approach varies in focus and ambition' (European Commission, 2004, p. 46). An important strength of the OMC is also that there is much more emphasis on gathering relevant information. Childcare figures are now published in the Joint Employment Report and two recent Eurostat publications offer insight into data problems and the complexities of trying to collect harmonised statistics of childcare (Eurostat, 2002, 2004). The targets set also help to legitimise new policy initiatives and to mobilise powers to certain policy decisions that would have been much more difficult to realise without the backing of the Barcelona targets.

There are, of course, also weaknesses. Bureaucracy is one, window dressing is another. European targets might simply add to the administrative burden that national policy makers have to deal with, with no effect on national policy. Indeed, given the fact that care strategies are very closely related to the national identity of a given country and transmit important signals about what is considered the most desirable organisation of society (Alber, 1995), the impact of the European Employment Strategy targets on this particular topic may be rather limited. Increasing investments in childcare facilities may, therefore, be contributed to national policy considerations rather then European targets.

In order to assess whether the Barcelona targets have in fact reached the EU Member States, we scanned the National Action Plans for Employment of 14 'old' Member States (Luxembourg missing) for the period 2002–2004 and the National Reform Programmes for 2005 and 2006 of the 25 Member States (as far as available in English). Table 2 summarises the results.

In 2002, only Ireland refers to the Barcelona childcare targets. In 2003, this has increased to eight countries, whereas in 2004 10 Member States

Table 2.   Number of EU Member States that Make a Reference
in the NAP/NRP towards (the Barcelona Target on) Childcare.

Number of EU Member States that Make a Reference in NAP/ NRP to	2000	2001	2002	2003	2004	2005	2006
Barcelona target	n.a.	n.a.	1	8	10	4	4
Childcare	5	8	9	11	13	16	14

Source: See Appendix, Table A4.

make a reference. The targets seem, however, no longer an issue in the new National Reform Programmes. Both in 2005 and 2006, only four of the 25 Member States make a reference (2005: Portugal, Finland, Sweden and Lithuania; 2006: Ireland, Portugal, Finland and Sweden). In addition, it seems that the countries that make a reference to the targets vary per year. Only three Member States, Portugal, Finland and Sweden, are quite consistent and make a reference to the targets in four (out of five) reports. Ireland refers in three reports to the targets. Greece, Italy and Luxembourg, however, always refrain from any reference. A more global search on the term 'childcare' indicates more interest on this topic, at least until 2005. The number of countries that make a reference increases from 5 in 2000 to 14 in 2006. There is, however, no clear increase after the adoption of the targets in 2002. Moreover, the number of countries that make a reference decreased between 2005 and 2006 from 16 to 14. Again, there is quite some variation between the countries. Ireland, Austria and the United Kingdom mention the term childcare in all seven reports, Denmark and the Netherlands in six reports, and Germany and France in five reports. This suggests that childcare is, at least, a topic of discussion in the country. Of the new Member States, Cyprus, Czech Republic, Estonia and Lithuania make a reference both in the National Reforms Programmes of 2005 and 2006 (see Table A4 of the Appendix for more details).

Summarising the results of this 'administrative scan', it seems that the Barcelona targets have indeed reached the level of nation policy making. This is in line with the conclusion of the Joint Employment Report 2003/2004 cited above. Of course, as stated before, these policy developments are not exclusively related to the Barcelona targets but will also be inspired by the national situation and the need to increase the employment of women. However, the Barcelona targets may have helped to raise the profile of childcare services and the overall level of ambition. At the same time, the figures seem to indicate that the attention for childcare is declining. This may be attributed to the transition of the National Action Plans to the National Reform Programmes and the corresponding change in format (see Rubery, Grimshaw, Smith, & Donnelly, 2006). Another reason might be that the interest in childcare services is indeed declining. Given the current levels of availability, this would underline the necessity to monitor the provision of childcare services also in the near future.

CONCLUSIONS

At the 2002 Barcelona summit, targets were set with regard to childcare. In this article we have estimated the provision of childcare services in the 25 EU Member States, taking into account the differences in institutional frameworks. It appears that a careful monitoring of the Barcelona targets is difficult because of lack of data, and because of the fact that a clear focus behind the targets seems to be missing. Particularly, the position of leave facilities is not clear. If the focus is strictly on childcare services, the available data indicate that services in most countries are still far from sufficient to reach the Barcelona targets. If, however, the full care system is taken into account and the figures for childcare services are recalculated on the basis of the (effective) parental leave, the situation for the youngest age category improves considerably. An analysis of references in national policy documents indicates that the references towards 'Barcelona' and childcare are frequent, though declining. This underlines the importance of a careful monitoring of actual developments.

At a more general level, it is important to note that the Barcelona targets seem to inspire a rather instrumental vision with regard to childcare services: care services are important because they increase the participation rate of women, facilitate economic growth and help to sustain European welfare states. Care services, however, are not only services for working parents; good, high-quality services are services for children. This requires investments not only in the quantity, but also the quality of the care infrastructure. Childcare policy should therefore be pursued as a policy in its own right, rather than as an aspect of policies primary concerned with promoting equal opportunities in the labour market or increasing the female participation rate. As a result, an effective national childcare strategy should address the needs of children, parents, families and communities and not just view childcare from an economic perspective (viz. Eurofound, 2006).

By implication, the debate would shift from childcare services as such, towards the most optimal division between leave facilities, childcare services and the education system. In this search, key factors are equal opportunities, the importance of raising the female participation rate, the healthy and sound development of a child and the importance of parental choice. Given the complexities, it is quite perceivable that the Europe Union will only play a minor role in this debate.

REFERENCES

Alber, J. (1995). A framework for the comparative study of social services. *Journal of European Social Policy*, 5, 131–149.

Bruning, G., & Plantenga, J. (1999). Parental leave and equal opportunities: Experiences in eight European countries. *Journal of European Social Policy*, 9, 195–209.

Cleveland, G., & Krashinsky, M. (2004). *Financing ECEC services in OECD countries*. Paris: OECD. Available online at: http://www.oecd.org/dataoecd/55/59/28123665.pdf

Drew, E. (2005). *Parental leave in council of Europe member states*. Strasbourg: Council of Europe, Equality Division/Directorate General of Human Rights CDEG.

Eberlein, B., & Kerwer, D. (2002). *Theorising the new modes of European Union Governance*. European Integration online Papers (EioP) 6: 5. Available online at: http://eiop.or.at/eiop/texte/2002–005a.htm

Eurofound. (2006). *Childcare for school children: Employment development in the EU*. Available online at: http://www.eurofound.eu.int/areas/labourmarket/childcare.htm

European Commission. (2004). *Joint employment report 2003/2004*. Brussels: European Commission. Available online at: http://ec.europa.eu/employment_social/employment_strategy/report_2003/jer20034_en.pdf

European Commission. (2006). *Joint employment report 2005/2006*. Brussels: European Commission. Available online at: http://ec.europa.eu/employment_social/employment_strategy/jer_en.pdf

European Council. (2002). *Presidency conclusions Barcelona European Council 15 and 16 March 2002*. Available online at: http://www.consilium.europa.eu/ueDocs/cms_Data/docs/pressData/en/ec/71025.pdf

Eurostat. (2002). *Feasibility study on the availability of comparable childcare statistics in the European Union*. Luxembourg: Office for Official Publications of the European Communities. Available online at: http://epp.eurostat.ec.europa.eu/cache/ITY_OFFPUB/KS-CC-02-001/EN/KS-CC-02-001-EN.PDF

Eurostat. (2004). *Development of a methodology for the collection of harmonised statistics on childcare*. Working papers and studies. Luxembourg: Office for Official Publications of the European Communities. Available online at: http://epp.eurostat.ec.europa.eu/cache/ITY_OFFPUB/KS-CC-04-001/EN/KS-CC-04-001-EN.PDF

Fagan, C., & Hebson, G. (2006). *Making work pay' debates from a gender perspective: A comparative review of some recent policy reforms in thirty European countries*. Luxembourg: Office for Official Publications of the European Communities.

Moss, P., & Deven, F. (2006). Leave policies and research: A cross-national overview. *Marriage and Family Review*, 39, 255–285.

O'Connor, J. (2003). Measuring progress in the European social model: Policy co-ordination, social indicators and the social policy agenda in the European Union. Paper prepared for the International Sociological Association Research Committee 19 for workshop at University of Toronto, August 2003, Canada.

OECD. (1995). Long-term leave for parents in OECD countries. In: *OECD, Employment Outlook* (pp. 171–202). Paris: OECD.

OECD. (2001). Balancing work and family life: Helping parents into paid employment. In: *OECD, Employment Outlook* (pp. 129–166). Paris: OECD.

OECD. (2002). *Babies and bosses: Reconciling work and family life. Volume 1. Australia, Denmark and the Netherlands.* Paris: OECD.

OECD. (2003). *Babies and bosses: Reconciling work and family life. Volume 2. Austria, Ireland and Japan.* Paris: OECD.

OECD. (2004). *Babies and bosses: Reconciling work and family life. Volume 3. New Zealand, Portugal and Switzerland.* Paris: OECD.

Plantenga, J., & Remery, C. (2005). *Reconciliation of work and private life. A comparative review of thirty European countries.* Luxembourg: Office for Official Publications of the European Communities.

Plantenga, J., & Siegel, M. (2004). European childcare strategies. Position paper for the conference 'Childcare in a Changing World'. European conference on the socio-economic aspects of childcare, 21–23 October 2004, the Netherlands.

Rostgaard, T. (2003). *Family support policy in Central and Eastern Europe – a decade and a half of transition.* Early Childhood and Family Policy series no. 8. Paris: UNESCO. Available online at: http://unesdoc.unesco.org/images/0013/001337/133733e.pdf

Rostgaard, T. (2005). Diversity and parental leave. In: F. Deven & P. Moss (Eds), *Leave policies and research: A cross-national review.* CBGS Working Papers 2005/3 (pp. 29–39). Brussels: CBGS.

Rubery, J., Grimshaw, D., Smith, M., & Donnelly, R. (2006). *The national reform programme and the gender aspects of the European employment strategy.* The coordinator synthesis report prepared for the Equality Unit, European Commission. Manchester: University of Manchester, EWERC.

APPENDIX

Table A1. Maternity Leave, Parental Leave and Effective Parental Leave in 25 EU Member States.

Country	Leave Regulations					
	Maternity leave	Payment	Parental leave (right)	Total parental leave	Payment	Effective parental leave (weighted by level of payment)[a]
Belgium (BE)	15 weeks	30 days: 82% earnings; remaining: 75% of earnings	3 months (i)	6 months (26 weeks)	Flat rate: ±€550 per month	18 weeks
Czech Republic (CZ)	28 weeks	69% of earnings	156 weeks (f)	156 weeks	€113 per month	117 weeks
Denmark (DK)	18 weeks	100% of wage with max. 3,205 DK per week (±€430)	32 weeks (i)	64 weeks	Payment calculated as for maternity and paternity leave. Limited to 32 weeks	47 weeks
Germany (DE)	14 weeks	100% of earnings	36 months (until the child is 3 years old) (f)	36 months	€300/month for the first 6 months; 7–24 months €300/month but means tested; 25–36 no payment	49 weeks
Estonia (EE)	20 weeks	100% of earnings	36 months (until the child is 3 years old) (f)	36 months	40 weeks are paid at average monthly income; rest unpaid	80 weeks

Table A1. *(Continued)*

Country	Leave Regulations					
	Maternity leave	Payment	Parental leave (right)	Total parental leave	Payment	Effective parental leave (weighted by level of payment)[a]
Greece (EL)	17 weeks (private sector); 5 months (public sector)	100% of earnings	3, 5 months (i)	7 months	Unpaid	13 weeks
Spain (ES)	16 weeks	100% of earnings	36 months (until the child is 3 years old) (f)	36 months	Unpaid	50 weeks
France (FR)	14 weeks	84% of earnings but most collective agreements provide a supplement to full pay	36 months (until the child is 3 years old) (f)	36 months	Unpaid (€460/ month for second or later child)	48 weeks
Ireland (IE)	18 weeks	70% of earnings	14 weeks (i)	28 weeks	Unpaid	13 weeks
Italy (IT)	5 months	Min. 80%, of earnings	10 months (f)	11 months (when father takes 3 months)	30% of earnings	24 weeks
Cyprus (CY)	16 weeks	10 weeks at 100%; 6 weeks at 75% of earnings	13 weeks (i)	26 weeks	Unpaid	11 weeks

Latvia (LV)	16 weeks	100% of earnings	36 months (until the child is 3 years old) (f)	36 months	Flat rate payment, 15 LVL/month	50 weeks
Lithuania (LT)	18 weeks	100% of earnings	36 months (until the child is 3 years old) (f)	36 months	70% of earnings	152 weeks
Luxembourg (LU)	16 weeks	80% of earnings	26 weeks (i)	52 weeks	Minimum wage level (±€1,700 per month)	54 weeks
Hungary (HU)	24 weeks	100% of earnings for insured women	36 months (until the child is 3 years old) (f)	3 years	First two years: 70% of wage with a maximum; third year: minimum wage level	152 weeks
Malta (MT)	14 weeks	13 weeks 100% of earnings and 14th week unpaid	3 months (i)	6 months	Unpaid	9 weeks
Netherlands (NL)	16 weeks	100% of earnings with max of €165 per day	13 weeks (i)	26 weeks	Unpaid	11 weeks
Austria (AT)	16 weeks	100% of earnings	24 months (f) (until the child is two years old)	24 months	€436 per month for 18 months. If the fathers take part of the leave, payment can be extended to 24 months.	63 weeks

Table A1. (*Continued*)

Country	Leave Regulations					
	Maternity leave	Payment	Parental leave (right)	Total parental leave	Payment	Effective parental leave (weighted by level of payment)[a]
Poland (PL)	16 weeks for first birth and 18 for each subsequent birth	100% of earnings	36 months (f)	36 months	400 PLN (±€100)/ month for 24 months	88 weeks
Portugal (PT)	17 weeks	100% of earnings	6 months (i)	12 months	Unpaid	20 weeks
Slovenia (SI)	105 days	100% of earnings	260 days (f)	260 days	100%	53 weeks
Slovakia (SK)	28 weeks	55% of earnings with max. of 472 SKK per day (±€12,50)	36 months (until the child is 3 years old) (f)	36 months	No more than 7,788 SKK per month (±€206)	100 weeks
Finland (FI)	17,5 weeks	43–82% of earnings (66% average)	26 weeks (f)	144 weeks (including childcare leave until the child is 3 years old)	26 weeks: at most 70% of earnings; 118 weeks: about €350 per month	107 weeks
Sweden (SE)	12 weeks	80% of earnings	480 days (f)	480 days	390 days: 80% of earnings 90 days: €6.50 per day	78 weeks

| United Kingdom (UK) | 26 weeks for all women and 26 weeks if employed for 26 weeks with same employer | 6 weeks: 90% of earnings; 20 weeks: flat rate £102.80 per week; 26 weeks unpaid maternity leave who work at least 1 year with the same employer | 13 weeks (i) | 26 weeks | Unpaid | 21 weeks |

[a]Under EU law women must receive 14 weeks of maternity leave and parents are entitled to 3 months unpaid parental leave (Parental Leave Directive 96/34, and Pregnant Workers Directive 92/85).

Effective parental leave = (parental leave in weeks × % payment benefit) + ((maternity leave in weeks–14 weeks) × % payment benefit).

% Payment benefit: If benefit is between 0–33% of minimum wage, then % payment benefit is 33. If benefit is between 34–66% of minimum wage, then % payment benefit is 66. If benefit is between 67–100% of minimum wage, then % payment benefit is 100.

i = individual right, f = family right.

Source: Fagan and Hebson (2006), Plantenga and Remery (2005).

Table A2. Admission Age to Pre-Primary and Compulsory Education in 25 EU Member States.

	Admission Age to Pre-Primary Education	Admission Age to Compulsory Education
Belgium	2.5	6
Czech Republic	3	6
Denmark	3	7
Germany	2.5[c]	6
Estonia	4	7
Greece	4	6
Spain	2	6
France	2	6
Ireland	2.5	6
Italy	2.5	5.5
Cyprus	3	6
Latvia	1	7[a]
Lithuania	4	7[b]
Luxembourg	3	6[a]
Hungary	3	6[a]
Malta	3	5
Netherlands	4	5
Austria	3	6
Poland	3	7[a]
Portugal	3	6
Slovenia	1	6
Slovakia	3	7[a]
Finland	3	7
Sweden	3	7
United Kingdom	3	5

[a]Country has mandatory or obligatory pre-school for certain age groups before compulsory school age.
[b]Compulsory school begins between the ages of 6 and 7 and in some special cases 8.
[c]Most children start at 3.
Source: EU15: Eurostat, 2004, 'Development of a methodology for the collection of harmonised statistics in childcare', 10NMS: National sources.

Table A3. Provision of Childcare in 25 EU Member States, 2003.

Country	Childcare Coverage Rate 0–2 Years (%)	Effective Childcare Coverage Rate 0–2 Years (%)	Childcare Coverage Rate 3–Compulsory School Age (%)
Belgium (Flanders)	81	98	100
Belgium (French)	33	50	98
Czech Republic	8	88	85
Denmark	56	91	93
Germany	7	43	89
Estonia	22	79	79
Greece	7	20	60
Spain	10	47	98
France	43	79	100
Ireland			
Italy	6	26	93
Cyprus			
Latvia	16	53	75
Lithuania	18	121	60
Luxembourg	14	54	80
Hungary	6	109	86
Malta			
Netherlands	35	47	100
Austria	9	55	82
Poland	2	63	60
Portugal	19	37	75
Slovenia	27	66	59
Slovakia			70
Finland	21	95	70
Sweden	41	96	90
United Kingdom			

Source: Own calculations on basis of Eurostat (2004), Plantenga and Remery (2005) and Fagan and Hebson (2006).

Table A4. Reference Made towards (Barcelona Target on) Childcare in Joint Employment Report, National Action Plans (2000–2004) and National Reform Programmes (2005–2006)[a].

Number of times term is mentioned in	2000	2001	2002	2003	2004	2005	2006
JER, no. pages[b]	229	96	123		139	19	17
Childcare	63	16	33		46	4	5
Barcelona target	n.a.	n.a.	5		1	1	1
NAPs							
Belgium, no. pages[b]	*	*	*	*	96	*	84
Childcare					7		1
Barcelona target					1		0
Denmark, no. pages[b]	56	61	125	97	108	152	129
Childcare	0	2	1	14	6	12	1
Barcelona target	n.a.	n.a.	0	1	1	0	0
Germany, no. pages[b]	60	93	151	79	96	*	89
Childcare	0	4	16	4	90		2
Barcelona target	n.a.	n.a.	0	1	1		0
Greece, no. pages[b]	72	56	125	67	62	63	54
Childcare	0	0	6	0	0	0	0
Barcelona target	n.a.	n.a.	0	0	0	0	0
Spain, no. pages[b]	71	86	69	123	151	*	105
Childcare	0	0	0	7	9		0
Barcelona target	n.a.	n.a.	0	0	3		0
France, no. pages[b]	*	48	109	147	176	53	*
Childcare		2	17	16	25	3	
Barcelona target		n.a.	0	1	0	0	
Ireland, no. pages[b]	50	53	106	65	86	74	58
Childcare	53	62	81	42	80	20	55
Barcelona target	n.a.	n.a.	1	0	2	0	1
Italy, no. pages[b]	103	48	*	*	43	*	67
Childcare	1	0			4		2
Barcelona target	n.a.	n.a.			0		0
Luxembourg, no. pages[b]	*	*	*	*	*	*	83
Childcare							0
Barcelona target							0
Netherlands, no. pages[b]	38	46	57	44	50	61	149
Childcare	17	11	25	15	5	22	0
Barcelona target	n.a.	n.a.	0	1	1	0	0
Austria, no. pages[b]	64	73	106	52	75	122	105
Childcare	30	21	59	9	28	13	30
Barcelona target	n.a.	n.a.	0	0	1	0	0
Portugal, no. pages[b]	179	113	103	55	65	208	47
Childcare	0	0	0	3	5	1	0
Barcelona target	n.a.	n.a.	0	1	1	1	1

Table A4. (*Continued*)

Number of times term is mentioned in	2000	2001	2002	2003	2004	2005	2006
Finland, no. pages[b]	53	83	57	57	71	137	111
Childcare	0	0	0	5	3	5	3
Barcelona target	n.a.	n.a.	0	1	1	1	1
Sweden, no. pages[b]	48	60	139	75	75	102	108
Childcare	0	10	19	21	14	11	7
Barcelona target	n.a.	n.a.	0	1	1	1	1
United Kingdom, no. pages[b]	34	33	67	97	92	60	68
Childcare	24	23	38	37	63	26	10
Barcelona target	n.a.	n.a.	0	1	0	0	0
Cyprus, no. pages[b]						145	216
Childcare						1	1
Barcelona target						0	0
Czech Republic, no. pages[b]						36	52
Childcare						3	3
Barcelona target						0	0
Estonia, no. pages[b]						75	122
Childcare						7	6
Barcelona target						0	0
Hungary, no. pages[b]						73	231
Childcare						5	0
Barcelona target						0	0
Latvia, no. pages[b]						52	81
Childcare						9	0
Barcelona target						0	0
Lithuania, no. pages[b]						142	183
Childcare						9	3
Barcelona target						1	0
Malta, no. pages[b]						40	61
Childcare						5	0
Barcelona target						0	0
Poland, no. pages[b]						36	68
Childcare						0	1
Barcelona target						0	0
Slovakia						*	*
Slovenia, no. pages[b]						*	106
Childcare							0
Barcelona target							0

*No English information available.
[a]Search in documents on term childcare/child care and Barcelona.
[b]Includes Annexes.

POLICY PACKAGES FOR FAMILIES WITH CHILDREN IN 11 EUROPEAN COUNTRIES: MULTIPLE APPROACHES

Jeanne Fagnani and Antoine Math

All member countries of the European Union (EU) have developed programmes for providing financial support to families. Complete family packages of cash benefits, tax breaks, exemptions from charges, various subsidies and/or services in kind are all being directed towards assisting parents with the costs of raising children. Moreover, this framework has been developed to favour the long view, guaranteeing the well-being of future generations (Bradshaw, 2006a) and serving to reinforce the shared bond between generations. Clearly, the responsible authorities have recognized, more or less explicitly, the fundamental role families play in upholding the social cohesion (Esping-Andersen, 1999).

It goes without saying, however, that levels of spending in this domain differ considerably between various EU member states (Bradshaw, 2006b). The remarkable generosity of the Nordic countries, for example, contrasts sharply with the modest contributions made by countries in the southern bloc of member states: Greece, Portugal, Italy and Spain. These disparities can no doubt be traced back to cultural differences as to what in fact constitutes family responsibility. Where children are concerned, marked

Childhood: Changing Contexts
Comparative Social Research, Volume 25, 55–78
ISSN: 0195-6310/doi:10.1016/S0195-6310(07)00002-6

differences emerge on how caring responsibility should be divided between State, market and family.

With these considerations in mind and using the model family method, we compared the social and fiscal systems in 11 EU member states for providing financial resources to households with children. We then used these comparisons to answer the following questions: After the impact of various benefits and taxes, what is the difference in the net disposable income of a childless couple compared with a family with children where both families have the same income? To what extent are certain systems of transfers utilized as an instrument of horizontal redistribution and, in particular, how does the level of assistance vary according to the number of children concerned? To what extent are certain transfers used as a means of vertical redistribution, in other words, to what extent do they target the most in need? How do transfers for families with an identical number of children vary according to the families' income levels?

The first part of this paper offers a general overview of expenditures devoted in each country to the social protection system and within this, of the expenditure devoted to families with children, through the provision of both services and cash benefits. The structure and principal features of the transfer systems to families, i.e., cash benefits and tax breaks, is the subject of the second part, along with results of our calculations based on the model family method. Particular attention is paid to France and Germany because both have a long-standing and explicit family policy overseen by public authorities (Fagnani, 2007). The paper concludes with some general reflections on the links that exist between various family packages and poverty rates among families with children, and the effects these have on the fertility rates in the countries we studied.

1. BACKGROUND AND PROBLEMS

Family policies are for the most part inextricably linked to state intervention in other aspects of public policy. Also, support to families is based on numerous historical and social rationales. These include assisting parents with the costs of raising children, fighting against social inequality, tackling market-driven poverty and unemployment, supporting lone parents, helping parents combine family and working life, and encouraging families to have more children. The hierarchical ordering by level of importance of these rationales can vary considerably according to the country concerned.

It is often said that the devil is in the details. This is true of any effort to paint a truly comprehensive picture of the different types of assistance public authorities dispense to families with dependent children. Public policies are further complicated by their place within a broader set of institutional arrangements, which aim to benefit parents active in the workforce, particularly when it comes to public or market-driven childcare provision, childcare subsidies, public programmes for young children (including nursery schools and out-of-school activities) and parental leave. It is well known, for example, that along with the Nordic countries, France leads the EU in public childcare provision and benefits aimed at reducing childcare costs for families (Fagnani & Letablier, 2005; Bradshaw et al., 2005; Leira, 2002). In France, for instance, the range of measures to help working parents has been expanded recently. Public expenditures towards the development of childcare arrangements and parental leaves have dramatically increased over the last two decades. Despite the overall background of cost containment, the system of public crèches has suffered no funding cutbacks. Similarly, in the Nordic countries, there exists a clear political will to further develop the already high-level measures designed to support parents with children. The other countries are also increasing their effort in childcare provision and in supporting dual-earner parent families and working mothers. In the UK, long languishing at the bottom of European league tables in most aspects of family policy, such as provision of parental leave or childcare, the policies pursued by the Blair government have made a significant improvement in the work/family balance, particularly in childcare provision (Lewis & Campbell, 2007). Germany has also made significant strides forward through the recent adoption of new regulations on parental leave, which share many similarities with those found in Sweden, as well as the Day-Care Expansion Act in force since 2005 (Fagnani & Math, 2007).

Because of the constraints imposed by the subject matter of this chapter, we will however limit the analysis of this particular aspect to the overall expenditure devoted to childcare services. In the analysis based on the model families approach, we will consider only the actual cash benefits provided to families.

In order to provide a relatively in-depth comparison, we limited our study to 11 European countries that share an equal level of economic development as well as a willingness to allocate a significant percentage of GDP to social protection programmes. All the countries of the southern bloc – Spain, Italy, Greece and Portugal – show little willingness to commit funds to policies that favour families with children, with only 3–5% of social spending dedicated to families. They have not been included for our comparison.

With the exception of Norway, all countries included in the comparison are EU members. These countries can be divided into three major groups, which we describe using the sometimes criticized typology of social protection systems elaborated by Esping-Andersen in the 1980s and published in 1990.

- The Nordic or 'social democratic' cases include Denmark, Norway, Sweden and Finland (Arts & Gelissen, 2002). The basic characteristics of this welfare-state configuration are well known. They place particular emphasis on public social services, which are by any definition extensive when compared to other countries. The issue of gender equality is high on their policy agenda, and they provide crucial support for women's participation in the labour force. Research has shown, however, that the national schemes developed by Nordic countries to support parents of young children differ from each other in several important aspects (Eydal, 2005; Leira, 2002).
- The United Kingdom (UK) and Ireland are classified as 'liberal welfare' regimes, sometimes also termed 'Anglo-Saxon' (Leibfried, 2001). Taxes and spending have long remained low compared to those of other affluent democracies. Many transfer programmes are still means tested. These welfare-state arrangements operate in the context of liberal market economies.
- France and Germany are part of the cluster of countries whose welfare regimes are qualified 'conservative-corporative', sometimes also termed 'Christian democratic', 'continental', 'corporatist' or 'Bismarckian' (Arts & Gelissen, 2002). Notable features are high levels of spending and pay-roll tax financing, with most benefits dependent on previous contributions and socio-professional status. As far as the main social insurance programmes are concerned, e.g. pension, health care and disability, the French and German welfare states are consistent with this description (Arts & Gelissen, 2002; Pierson, 2001). Their respective family policies also have much in common. Both are linked to employment policy in several ways, and both are explicit, clearly defined and generous in terms of cash benefits. In each country, the appointment of a minister responsible for family issues demonstrates the importance given to this issue. Family policy in the two countries still bears many traces of earlier history. For France, this translates into a system of transfers with their roots in a long-established natalist tradition, which continues to favour large families.

In Germany, legislators have increasingly distanced themselves from the traditional model of the male as 'sole breadwinner' and recently introduced radical changes in the domain parental leave and childcare provision (Fagnani & Math, 2007). As in France, the taxation system still favours married couples where only one of the spouses is in paid work. However, France strongly differs from Germany with regard to childcare policy and public support to working mothers (Fagnani, 2007).

- Austria, the Netherlands and Belgium, also clustered by Esping-Andersen among the 'conservative-corporatist' regime, in some typologies are further specified as 'advanced Christian-democratic' regimes (Arts & Gelissen, 2002; Pierson, 2001).

As far as our countries and types are concerned, consensus has become stronger that hybrid cases are far more numerous than was initially assumed. Indeed, none of the countries, and in particular France and the Netherlands, actually fit the prototype definition of a specific 'ideal-type'. Nevertheless, this typology is somewhat useful for its heuristic and descriptive value.

2. FAMILY-TARGETED PROTECTION SPENDING: DISTINCT DIVERGENCES AND VARIATIONS BETWEEN COUNTRIES

In the affluent democracies we selected, public spending on social security policies varies by country. With Ireland a notable exception, all countries devote more than 26% of GDP to their systems of social protection. Denmark, Sweden and France are particularly distinguished in this area, devoting more than 30% of national spending to these systems. Within the aggregate of social protection expenditures, the portion devoted to family/ children benefits varies from 19.9% in Ireland to only 4.5% in the Netherlands. When it comes to expressing family/children expenditures as a percentage of GDP, Denmark tops the table at 3.9% while the Netherlands and the UK, both allocating less than 2% of GDP, bring up the rear (see Table 1).

The simple label 'family/children benefits' included in Eurostat data on social protection expenditure can be somewhat misleading, and masks the heterogeneous nature of individual measures as well as their underlying logic and final outcomes. We have, therefore, proposed three subcategories

Table 1. Social Protection Expenditure and Share of Family/Children
Benefits as a Percentage of GDP, 2004.

	Total Social Protection Expenditures as % of GDP	Family/Children Benefits	
		As % of GDP	As % of total social protection
Denmark	30.7	3.9	12.7
Ireland	17.0	3.4	19.9
Norway	26.3	3.1	11.6
Sweden	32.9	3.0	9.3
Austria	29.1	3.0	10.4
Germany	29.5	3.0	10.1
Finland	26.7	3.0	11.1
France	31.2	2.5	8.0
Belgium	29.3	2.0	6.7
United Kingdom	26.3	1.7	6.6
Netherlands	28.5	1.3	4.5
UE 25	27.3	2.1	7.8

Source: European System of Integrated Social Protection Statistics (Eurostat).

within the aggregate of family/children benefits for the purposes of trying to
further analyze the different policies:

1. Benefits in kind, which include all social protection expenditures devoted
   to public childcare provision, e.g. crèches and kindergartens, as well as
   public services targeted at families and children coping with hardships in
   their everyday lives (see Fig. 1).
2. Cash benefits related to paternity, maternity and parental leave schemes
   (see Fig. 2).
3. Cash benefits other than leave benefits, particularly child benefits
   including allocations familiales in France and Kindergeld in Germany
   (see Fig. 3).

Groups of countries combine differently, with an internal different
hierarchy, these three kinds of benefits, thus designing specific structures
of opportunities for parents, as well as representing different understanding
of the respective role of the family and the state, of fathers and mothers with
regard to children's well-being. These groups of countries only partially
overlap with Esping-Andersen's typology.

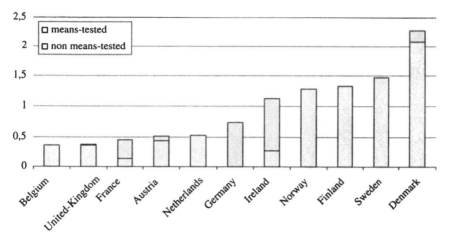

Fig. 1. Family/Children Benefits in Kind – Expenditure as a % of GDP, 2004. *Source:* European System of Integrated Social Protection Statistics (Eurostat).

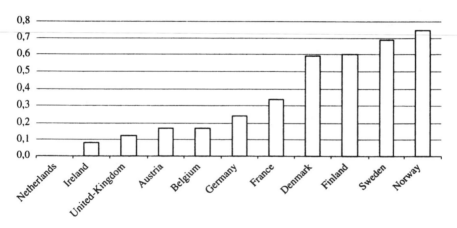

Fig. 2. Cash Benefits for Leaves – Expenditure as a % of GDP, 2004. *Source:* European System of Integrated Social Protection Statistics (Eurostat).

2.1. The Nordic Countries: Priority Given to Public Provision of Services

The Nordic countries have broadened the scope of their welfare services and childcare provision in tandem with Nordic women's increasing participation in the labour force (Eydal, 2005; Leira, 2002). Therefore, they top the table

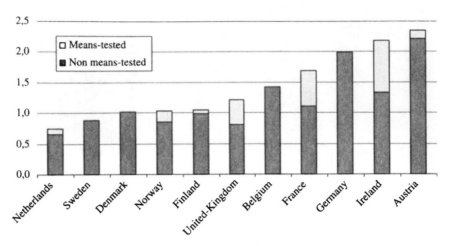

Fig. 3. Cash Benefits Other than Leave Benefits (Child Benefit, Allocations Familiales or Kindergeld) – Expenditure as a % of GDP, 2004. *Source:* European System of Integrated Social Protection Statistics (Eurostat).

in the category of benefits in kind: from 1.3% of GDP in Norway to over 2% in Denmark (see Fig. 1). These benefits in kind are governed by the principle of universality, which provides families with access to services regardless of income.

The Nordic countries also devote a much larger share of their resources towards cash benefits related to funding parental leave, more than any other country in comparison (see Fig. 2). As a matter of fact, thanks to comprehensive public support of parental leave for parents of young children, payment for care leaves is by European standards very generous and functions on a social insurance basis (Math & Meilland, 2004). The logic underlying parental leave in Sweden is different from, for instance, that of France. French parents taking leave receive only a low flat-rate (€530 per month in 2007, if the parent on leave completely stops work) while Swedish parents taking leave receive 80% of their earnings. The Swedish wage-related benefit is explicitly aimed at promoting gender equality at home and at the workplace. It is, however, a counter-redistributive policy from the point of view of cash transfers to families, because well-paid workers receive more than the poorly paid. Nevertheless, this effect is offset by the Swedish fiscal system, which is entirely devoted to vertical redistribution as opposed to the French fiscal system, which fuses both vertical and horizontal redistributions. As a result, well-off Swedish families pay much more income tax than their French counterparts (Bradshaw & Finch, 2004).

On the other hand, the share of GDP devoted by Nordic countries to cash benefits other than leave benefits is comparatively low, only around 1% of GDP compared to 1.7% in France and 2.4% in Austria (see Fig. 3). Only the Netherlands devotes a lower proportion of its GDP in this domain.

2.2. Austria, Germany, France and Belgium: Generous and Universal Child Benefits

A second group comprising Austria, Germany, France and Belgium, is characterized by its generous allocation of funds to universal child benefits (see Fig. 3). France operates rather differently from the other three, however, in that a large proportion of actual cash benefits (about 35%) are means tested, in other words, based on the resources of the individual families concerned.

The levels of family/children benefits in kind as a component of GDP in both Belgium and France lag far behind that of other countries (see Fig. 1). These levels are somewhat misleading, however, and do not take into account the important financial contributions the French and Belgian policies have earmarked for funding public nursery schools.[1] Moreover, generous cash subsidies covering the cost of private childcare arrangements by nannies or registered child minders are not included in our definition of benefits in kind. These programmes, which allow many parents to provide care for their children by qualified individuals meeting the standards laid down by the responsible authorities, are defined as cash rather than benefits in kind.

2.3. UK, Ireland and the Netherlands: The Lowest Share of GDP Devoted to Cash Benefits for Parental Leave

The UK and Ireland have in common the fact that the share of GDP each devotes to remuneration of maternity, paternity or parental leave, despite improvements since the latter end of the 1990s, remains among the lowest in our study (see Fig. 2). In their expenditure on cash benefits other than leave benefits, however, the similarity ends: Ireland is one of the most generous countries, while the UK finds itself in the middle, slightly above the Nordic countries (see Fig. 3). At the same time, cash benefits in the UK and Ireland are more likely to be means tested than in most other countries in our study. Nevertheless, to rely strictly on the data collected by Eurostat is to underestimate the importance of the UK's reliance on the income tax system as a means of distributing resources to families with children. Its Tax Credits system is especially important to low-income families. As for the Netherlands, its overall policies are distinguished by their lack of generosity towards families, whatever the type of benefit, and in this respect they more closely resemble the policies of southern European countries than those of other groups in our analysis.

Financial support for families is multifaceted and family/children benefits systems are by no means the only avenue that must be explored in order to understand the full range of measures in place. The tax system and the housing benefits have a particularly large impact in certain countries. Data which present simply the total levels of spending on family benefits can only give a partial picture and often provide little indication of the redistributive effect of public policies when taken as a whole. How are efforts shared out and adjusted according to different family profiles? By number of dependent children? By income level? Relying solely on Eurostat data imposed limits on our ability to compare countries' benefits systems. Therefore, to ensure that as far as possible like was being compared to like, we utilized the model family method which aspires to overcome these limitations.

3. COMPARISON OF FAMILY PACKAGES USING THE MODEL FAMILY METHOD

The intrinsic value of the model family method is that it allows us to evaluate targeted cash support to family on grounds of dependents. Additionally, this method grants insight into the redistributive effects of these transfers. The goal of our analysis is not to provide an exhaustive inquiry but rather to evaluate how certain transfer systems specifically target families based on the families' configuration and/or income levels.

The method consists of calculating and examining the structure and level of the family benefit package for a range of families constructed taking into account number of children, level of earnings and presence or absence of both parents. The family benefit package is therefore the supplement made to a household's net disposable income and how it compares to a childless couple on the same earnings (see Box 1) after the main transfers and taxes for the family with children have been taken into account. This difference represents the contribution of public policies with respect to children (and being a lone paryent).

Box 1. The Model Family Method.

This method was used to identify a specific range of model families varying in family size and earnings to calculate net income.[a]

A number of model families were selected as follows:

- A childless married couple
- A divorced parent with one child, aged 3, receiving full-time formal childcare
- A lone parent with one child aged 7
- A couple with one child aged 7
- A couple with two children aged 7 and 14
- A couple with three children aged 7, 14 and 17, all at school

This choice enabled us to compare childless couples and families with children, and variations in couples by the number of children.

For each family, a variety of income cases were specified as follows:

- Income case 0: No earners, receiving social assistance
- Income case 1: One earner, wages one-half national average (full-time wage earners only) or, if higher, the minimum wage for a 35-hour week (In France, half-average earnings are slightly higher than full-time employment at minimum wage.)
- Income case 2: One earner, average earnings (In France, about twice the minimum wage.)
- Income case 2 + 1: Two earners, average and half-average earnings (In France, twice and equal to the minimum wage, respectively.)
- Income case 2 + 2: Two earners both average earnings (In France, two salaries each at two times the minimum wage.)

Using these income cases allowed us to compare variations in family packages according to the level of earnings and the number of workers in the household. We included a family with no earners, receiving social assistance (Income case 0). Twenty-six families from each of the 11 EU countries studied were selected for the comparison.

Net income for each family model was calculated by adding or subtracting the following transfers and taxes from earned income:

- Income tax
- Social insurance contributions
- Local taxes
- Family cash benefits (means tested and non-means tested)

- Housing benefits
- Social assistance
- Guaranteed child support

The family package was calculated as the difference between the net income after transfers and taxes for a household with children and the net income of a childless couple where both families received the same earnings. The calculations were made with rules in January 2004.

Figures are calculated per month and are expressed using the purchasing power parity (PPP) system. PPP takes into account some of the variations in cost of living among countries, increasing our ability to make accurate comparisons. PPP figures are based on the purchasing power of €1 in France.[b]

The data relate to 2004, but this is likely to be reasonably representative of the current situation given the slowness with which changes in taxes and transfers, as well as the distribution of earnings tend to occur.

------

[a]We would like to thank Professor Jonathan Bradshaw, University of York, for providing access to the data used in this study. Data specific to France have been calculated through the work of A. Math and C. Meilland of IRES.

[b]Compared to a conversion with real exchange rates, the decision to use PPP as a basis for our calculations actually changes very little when dealing with the majority of countries studied. The impact is most notable in the countries where the cost of living is markedly higher and has the effect of diminishing, in percentage terms, the figures in the following countries to the order of: 20% in Denmark, 17% in Norway and 9% in both Sweden and Ireland.

3.1. Family Income: A Minor or Non-Existent Role in Affecting the Level of Family Benefits

The complete package of family cash benefits (excluding income-related or means-tested benefits and guaranteed child support) almost always increases according to the number of children, but variations exist in the way these benefits are distributed (OECD, 2004).[2] Fig. 4 highlights the significance of earnings when calculating the level of cash benefits for a family of two school-age children.[3] Family policies in the Nordic countries, Germany, the Netherlands and the UK are all guided by a desire to provide equal support to all children regardless of the income levels of their parents; thus, family revenues have no effect on the amount of cash benefits allocated.[4] Belgium would also fall into this

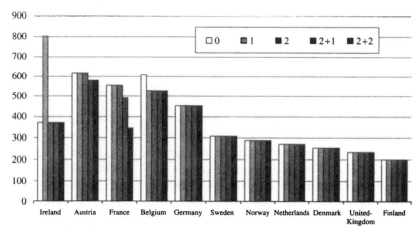

Countries are classed in descending order based on Income case 1. € PPP corresponds to the purchasing power of € 1 in France.

- Income case 0: No earners, receiving social assistance

- Income case 1: One earner, wages one-half national average (full-time wage earners only) or, if higher,

  the minimum wage for a 35-hour week (in France, half-average earnings are slightly higher than full-time

  employment at minimum wage)

- Income case 2: One earner, average earnings (in France, about twice the minimum wage)

- Income case 2 + 1: Two earners, average and half-average earnings (in France, twice and equal to the

minimum wage)

- Income case 2 + 2: Two earners, both average earnings (in France, two salaries at two times the minimum

wage)

Fig. 4. Cash Benefits by Earnings for a Couple Plus Two Children (7 and 14 Years Old) in € PPP per Month. *Source:* International Family Model Database (January 2004).

category were it not for the fact that families on welfare receive more generous assistance than others. Austria provides the highest levels of assistance for families, regardless of family income or makeup, until we consider its reduction in cash benefits for families with three or more children.

France is notable in that families with higher incomes are excluded from access to certain cash benefits that are means tested.[5] In Ireland, all income cases receive equal assistance, except the working poor who receive an extremely generous Family Income Supplement.

Overall, it is clear that when it comes to family cash benefits, the public policies of the countries we studied do not, or little, target or favour one income group over another. Cash benefits seem to be mainly intended as horizontal redistribution between those who do not and those who have children, rather than a vertical redistribution between the rich and the poor.

3.2. Income Taxes: A Means of Support to Families Utilized in Only Certain Countries

When it comes to providing financial support to families, public authorities have a number of measures at their disposal beyond what we classify simply as cash benefits. These include housing benefits, income tax credits, and, for families on social assistance, guaranteed minimum incomes. On the other hand, social contributions and levies are imposed on families across the board with no regard to family makeup. Similarly, in all the 11 countries we studied, the presence of children in a family had little effect on how local tax regimes were organized. The level of housing benefits for low-income families, however, was significantly impacted by the presence of children for families in Denmark, the UK, France, Germany, Sweden and Norway (ranked in descending order by the level of support provided).

3.2.1. The Nordic Countries: The Presence of Children Plays No Role in How Income Tax is Calculated

Income tax systems in all countries studied are progressive, i.e. tax rates increase with the level of income. But it should come as no surprise that in the Nordic countries, where tax regimes were created with the sole objective of vertical redistribution, it makes little difference whether a family has children or not. Norway provides tax deduction up to a certain limit for documented expenses for extra-familial child. All other countries in the study account for the presence of children to varying degrees by employing a number of different measures. Tax credits, tax deductions and the French quotient familial are some examples, and all can vary according to family makeup and size, as well as the age of the children.

For those families that fall into the category sometimes termed 'the working poor' (Income case 1), only the UK offers significant support by means of the Working Family Tax Credit, which is reserved for those in paid employment. For families in higher income brackets, the presence of children provides significant tax advantages in the UK as well as the five continental European countries in our study.

In France and Germany, two countries that practice systems of joint taxation, preference is still given to families with a sole breadwinner, whatever the level of household income.[6] The problem is exacerbated in

Germany, where the splitting system continues to rely on the male-breadwinner model.[7] In France, the quotient familial gives priority to couples (whether married or not) with children, particularly three or more, which satisfies the aim of horizontal redistribution, an objective still supported by numerous politicians at both ends of the political spectrum (Bachel et al., 2005).[8] This contrasts sharply with the policies in Nordic countries, where taxes are assessed on an individual basis, with the result that the partner earning least, usually the woman, is not penalized for this fact.

3.3. The Family Package: Austria in a Class of Its Own

In order to provide a more general picture of the various transfer systems, we have calculated the average whole family package for 15 model couple types with school-age children (one, two and three children for five levels of earnings) and three lone parents with one school-age child (for three levels of earnings) (see Table 2).

Austria clearly leads the pack, providing the most generous family package on average to both couples with children and lone-parent families. The UK also distinguishes itself as one of the most generous countries when

Table 2. Overall Average Family Package – € PPP per Month.

Couples with Children (Average Calculated on the Basis of 15 Model Family Types)		Lone Parent Families (Average Calculated on the Basis of 3 Model Family Types)	
Austria	514	Austria	385
United Kingdom	411	United Kingdom	260
Belgium	388	Denmark	196
Germany	373	Finland	142
France	357	Ireland	139
Ireland	335	Norway	123
Denmark	296	Sweden	111
Sweden	282	Netherlands	101
Finland	266	France	70
Norway	250	Belgium	−34
Netherlands	181	Germany	−55

Note: € PPP corresponds to the purchasing power of €1 in France. For each model family, the family package is calculated as the difference between the net income after transfers and taxes for a household with children and the net income of a childless couple where both families receive the same earnings.

Source: International family model database (January 2004).

it comes to families. This stands in marked contrast to the dearth of
financial support the Netherlands provides to couples with children.
Germany, Belgium and France are all at the top of the table in providing
support to couples with children, but slip to the bottom when it comes to
lone-parent families. Table 2 also confirms that for the Nordic countries
actual cash benefits are of little importance when placed within the overall
context of other measures used to assist families.

3.4. The Family Package by Number of Children: A Means
of Horizontal Redistribution

In all the countries we studied, policy makers clearly took pains to ensure
that policies resulted in horizontal redistribution from families with no
children to those with children. It goes without saying that the family
package is adjusted upwards as the number of children in a family increases.
Nevertheless, the way these packages are calculated can vary significantly
between countries when we take into account the income levels of the
families concerned (see Figs. 5 and 6).

Whatever the size of the family, the UK is by far the most generous
in terms of providing assistance to low-earning families (Income case 1).

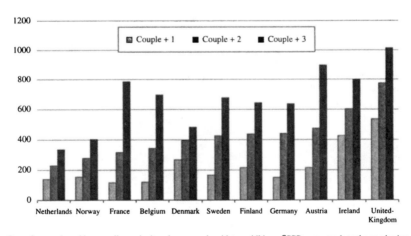

Countries are classed in ascending order based on a couple with two children. €PPP corresponds to the purchasing power of
€1 in France.
* Income case 1: One earner, wages one-half national average (full-time wage earners only) or, if higher, the minimum wage
for a 35-hour week (in France, half-average earnings are slightly higher than full-time employment at minimum wage)

Fig. 5. Family Package by Number of Children – Low-Income Families (in € PPP).

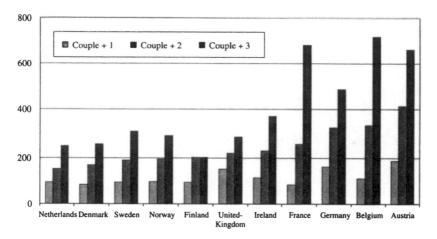

Countries are classed in ascending order based on a couple with two children.
* Income case 2 + 2: Two earners, both average earnings (in France, two salaries at two times the minimum wage).

Fig. 6. Family Package by Number of Children – Higher-Income Dual-Earner Couples (in € PPP).

Once again, we can observe how the policies of France, Belgium and Austria tend to favour larger families. Among all the countries concerned, France and Belgium are particularly modest in providing assistance to families with only one child.

When looking at higher-income dual-earner families (Income case 2 + 2), we can observe a distinct change in the ranking of countries (see Fig. 6). Large families (three or more children) at the top of the income scale in France, Belgium, Austria and, to a somewhat lesser degree, Germany, all receive extremely generous family packages, whereas other countries are rather more modest in assisting this group.

It is clear when observing Figs. 5 and 6 that the UK and, to a somewhat lesser degree, Ireland, have made decisions favouring the working poor and, in particular, have used their system of transfers as a means of redistributing wealth to families of more modest means.

3.5. The Effect of Revenue on Levels of Benefits: A Sharp Emphasis on Vertical Redistribution in the UK

The data in Fig. 7 provides a picture of how family packages vary with earnings for the same family type (in this case a couple with two school-age

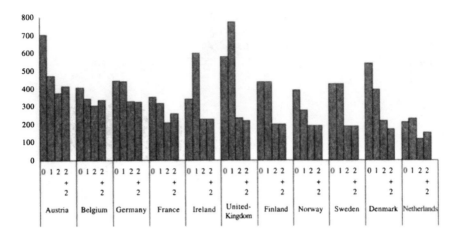

Countries are classed in descending order based on Income case 1. € PPP corresponds to the purchasing power of €1 in France.

- Income case 0: No earners, receiving social assistance
- Income case 1: One earner, wages one-half national average (full-time wage earners only) or, if higher, the minimum wage for a 35-hour week (in France, half-average earnings are slightly higher than full-time employment at minimum wage)
- Income case 2: One earner, average earnings (in France, about twice the minimum wage)
- Income case 2 + 2: Two earners, both average earnings (in France, two salaries at two times the minimum wage)

Fig. 7. Family Package by Earnings – Couples with Two Children (in € PPP). *Source:* International Family Model Database (January 2004).

children). The UK and Ireland are notable in that, while they both provide high levels of benefits to those at the lower end of the economic scale, they place greater emphasis on aiding families classed as the working poor (Income case 1) than those living on social assistance (Income case 0), even though the latter have fewer resources. In the UK, this is accomplished using the Working Families Tax Credit, and in Ireland the Family Income Supplement. Additionally, once the family income surpasses a certain level, and a rather modest one at that, these benefits are no longer available and the total family package is sharply reduced. Still, this does not mean that families are left completely empty-handed.

The UK is also the country where we see the sharpest contrast between family packages for working poor families (Income case 1) and for the well-off families. The Nordic countries, along with Ireland and the Netherlands, also provide low levels of benefits to well-off dual-earner families. In the Netherlands, the family package is comparatively miniscule for all income brackets. Denmark, Finland, Sweden and Norway provide very low income families with social assistance and housing benefits. In contrast, France, Germany and Belgium (and Austria if we leave aside the category of families receiving public assistance) are all distinguished by offering family packages that vary little according to family income.

4. DISCUSSIONS AND CONCLUSIONS

The overlapping nature of the measures contained within different family packages, along with the number of model family types contained in our study, makes drawing any definitive conclusions problematic. Rather, the aim of our comparison and its results is to provide a snapshot from a clearly defined perspective of the current political realities inherent in public policies affecting support for families. The model family method does, however, not allow us to take into account the importance of numerous other measures, such as parental leave or community services for families with children, and the critical role these play in any analysis of cross-country variations.

Despite the previously noted limits of our methodology, distinctive and identifiable trends can be clearly identified in the results of our comparison. Our results also raise important questions about the relationships and interactions between transfer systems, social inequalities, poverty rates and fertility behaviour (see Table 3).

Austria and, to a slightly lesser degree, the UK, are by far the most generous countries when it comes to cash provision to families. Bringing up the rear at the opposite end of the spectrum is the Netherlands. Following their strong traditions of horizontal redistribution, France, Belgium, Austria and, to a lesser degree, Germany, all tend to favour large families, with France and Belgium becoming rather less favourable than the other two when it comes to providing assistance to couples and lone-parent families with only one child. The Nordic countries, the UK and Ireland are all distinguished by a strong emphasis on vertical redistribution, favouring families with modest revenues.

Research has shown that financial support to families plays an undeniable role in reducing the proportion of children growing up in poor households (Bradshaw, 2006a, 2006b). A look at child poverty rates, however, exposes the UK as the worst performer by a considerable margin, in this area which seems to fly in the face of the fact that it is one of the most generous countries when it comes to providing financial support for the working

Table 3. Social Inequalities, Poverty Rates for Children
and Fertility Rates.

Country[a]	Social Inequalities: Gini Index[b]	Poverty Rate for Children[c] (Around 2000)	Total Fertility Rates (TFR) (2004)[d]	Completed Fertility Rates (CFR) for Women Born in 1962[d]
Denmark	24.7	2.4	1.78	1.92
Sweden	25.0	3.6	1.75	2.02
Norway	25.8	3.6	1.81	2.09
Finland	26.9	3.4	1.80	1.94
Germany	28.3	10.9	1.37	1.60
Austria	29.1	13.3	1.42	1.67
Netherlands	30.9	9.0	1.73	1.82
France	32.7	7.3	1.90	2.08
Belgium	33.0	–	1.64	1.82
Ireland	34.3	15.7	1.99	2.30
UK	36.0	16.2	1.74	1.93

Note: Total fertility rate (TFR) is the sum of fertility rates by age for a given year, and completed fertility rate (CFR) is the average number of children born to women of the same generation who have reached the end of their reproductive life. TFR may differ for long periods when fertility timing (or birth calendar) changes: for example, a delay in timing leads to a drop in the TFR even if the completed fertility of the generation is eventually not modified.
[a]Countries are classed by levels of social inequality: from those with the lowest levels to those with the greatest.
[b]World Bank (2006). World Development Indicators 2006. Washington, D.C. The Gini index measures the extent to which the distribution of income diverges from equality, with 1 being the extreme value when a single individual has all the income.
[c]OECD (2007).
[d]EUROSTAT (2006).

poor. Clearly, the goal to increase social justice while decreasing child poverty depends on providing more than simple cash benefits. These need to be complemented by other systems of support. The Nordic countries, where social inequality is less marked and child poverty is virtually non-existent, provide a perfect illustration of this point (see Table 3). Financial support is modest but benefits in kind such as community facilities and services are considerable (see Section 1). Additionally, they offer a coherent, generous and supportive set of provisions to dual-earner families, and this goes hand-in-hand with high employment rates for mothers with children (Eurostat, 2006). Research indicates that in nearly all European countries child poverty rates are significantly higher in single-earner families than those with two earners (Bradshaw, 2006a, 2006b; Whiteford & Adema, 2007). From this perspective, it is not surprising that a recent study carried out by the OECD argues in favour of a more appropriate balance between the so-called 'benefits strategy' and the so-called 'work-strategy', which promotes policies to increase employment among poor families, in particular (Whiteford & Adema, 2007).

While Austria stands head and shoulders above other countries in the level of the family benefit package, levels of fertility remain low, resembling those of Germany and the southern European countries: Total fertility rates (TFR) have fluctuated between 1.50 in 1993 and 1.42 in 2004 (see Table 3). Generous financial support has seemingly failed to motivate Austrian families to increase their fertility rate to a level sufficient to adequately replace previous generations. State policies that favour the work/ family balance remain modest, particularly in the domain of public childcare provision. Despite recent efforts to improve this situation, they pale in comparison to the vast array of measures that make up family policies in France and the Nordic countries. Also, in stark contrast to the Nordic countries, Austria performs rather poorly in terms of social inequalities and its poverty rate for children. These observations, along with those made for the UK, seem to confirm arguments in favour of promoting measures that place greater emphasis on benefits in kind over simple cash benefits.

France finds itself firmly planted in the middle of the ranking when seen through the prism of various model families used throughout our study (discounting the example of families with three or more children). Its system of transfers is less redistributive than those of the Nordic countries and, in terms of reducing social inequality, it remains one of the least efficient. Yet, its fertility rate remains among the highest of the countries studied along with Norway and Ireland (see Table 3). Through the results of other studies, we have attempted to explain this phenomenon by emphasizing the influential role of explicit childcare policies along with the importance of measures supporting the "working mother" model (Fagnani, 2007).

Descriptions of the systems of transfers within various countries sometimes fit rather uneasily into mainstream welfare typologies and social protection systems. The UK and Austria, the two most generous countries, belong to two different social protection systems, while the Netherlands, the country with the most modest contribution, is often categorized alongside France, Germany and Austria. On the other hand, the so-called 'social democratic' welfare states of Scandinavia would seem to justify their inclusion in the same social protection category, as they all exhibit similar characteristics. Their extensive and highly developed systems of social protection, particularly coherent where family policy is concerned, stand in contrast to the hybrid nature of the French system. The logic driving the standard features of welfare regimes (unemployment benefits, pension systems) do not seem fully adequate to explain family policies. At the same time, since family policies can overlap with other policies (e.g. health, education, minimum income), similar policies may result in a certain degree of variation according to the overall social policy package present in each country.

In conclusion, it is clear that in each of the countries contained within our comparative study, public authorities have acknowledged more or less explicitly that the future wealth of any society is its children. States, as well as other social actors, have recognized that children represent a common good and that responsibility for their well-being is far from being a strictly private affair. Indeed, investing in children might be a long-term profitable strategy for society as a whole (Kamerman & Kahn, 2002; Klammer, 2006; Esping-Andersen, 1999; Saraceno, 2000). Guaranteeing the well-being of the children as well as ensuring that each has the opportunity to reach his or her full potential requires a multidimensional and systematic approach, which extends beyond the simple provision of cash benefits, generous as they are. Guaranteeing a living wage and promoting policies that help parents achieve a more balanced work and family life, placing limits on non-standard work schedules[9] and ensuring access to adequate housing – all these are necessary if we are to truly make a difference and work together in the best interest of future generations.

NOTES

1. More than a third (38%) of the children in France aged 2–3 years and 99% of those aged 3–6 now attend free écoles maternelles with on-site cafeterias either on a full-time or part-time basis. Furthermore, local authorities have used financial assistance from the local family allowance funds to considerably develop a recreational infrastructure that keeps schoolchildren occupied after school and on lesson-free Wednesday afternoons.

2. The level of allocations familiales (child benefit) may also vary according to the rank and age of children, like in France.

3. Similar conclusions were reached regardless of the makeup of the family being considered.

4. No benefits in Norway are subject to means testing with the sole exception of those directed at single parents with young children.

5. In France, in addition to universal child benefits (allocations familiales), there is a wide range of means-tested family benefits. The most important ones are for families with three or more children (complément familial), for families with at least one child under three (prestation d'accueil du jeune enfant), for certain lone parents (allocation de parent isolé) and for school charges (allocation de rentrée scolaire).

6. In Germany, however, married couples are offered the choice between joint or individual assessment, which is not the case in France.

7. A married couple's income is added together, then divided by two and taxed separately.

8. The quotient familial (family splitting) operates as follows: every household pays income tax on the basis of its total income divided by a number relating to its size (an 'adult equivalent' for the household). A progressive rate is applied to this income per adult equivalent. For the same income level, a family with three children will pay less than a family with only one child.

9. Strazdins et al. (2006) have demonstrated that non-standard work schedules have detrimental effects on children's well-being and on the quality of interactions within the family.

REFERENCES

Arts, W., & Gelissen, J. (2002). Three worlds of welfare capitalism or more? A state-of-the-art report. *Journal of European Social Policy*, *12*(2), 137–158.

Bachel, A., Dell, F., & Wrohlich, K. (2005). *Income taxation and household size. Would French family splitting make German families better off?* IZA Discussion Paper no. 1894. Institute for the Study of Labour, Bonn.

Bradshaw, J. (2006a). *A review of the comparative evidence on child poverty*. York: Joseph Rowntree Foundation.

Bradshaw, J. (2006b). Child benefit packages in 15 countries in 2004. In: J. Lewis (Ed.), *Children in the context of family and welfare state change*. Cheltenham: Edward Elgar.

Bradshaw, J., & Finch, N. (2002). *A comparison of child benefit packages in 22 countries*. Research Report no. 174. Department for Work and Pensions, London. http://www.dwp.gov.uk/asd/asd5/rrep174.asp

Bradshaw, J., Finch, N., & Mayhew, E. (2005). Financial incentives and mothers' employment: A comparative perspective. In: P. Saunders, (Ed.), *Welfare to work in practice: Social security and participation in economic and social life. International Studies in Social Security* (Vol. 10). Aldershot: Ashgate.

Esping-Andersen, G. (1999). *Social foundations of postindustrial economies*. Oxford: Oxford University Press.

Eydal, G. B. (2005). Childcare policies of the Nordic welfare states: Different paths to enable parents to earn and care? In: B. Pfau-Effinger & B. Geissler (Eds), *Care arrangements and social integration in European societies* (pp. 153–172). Berlin: Policy Press.

Fagnani, J. (2007). Family policies in France and Germany: Sisters or distant cousins? *Community, Work and Family* (10), 39–56

Fagnani, J., & Letablier, M. T. (2005). Caring rights and responsibilities of families in the French welfare state. In: B. Pfau-Effinger & B. Geissler (Eds), *Care arrangements and social integration in European societies* (pp. 153–172). Berlin: Policy Press.

Fagnani, J., & Math, A. (2007). Les récentes réformes de la politique familiale en Allemagne: De nouveaux horizons pour les femmes? *Droit Social* (May), 630–636.

Kamerman, S. B., & Kahn, A. J. (Eds). (2002). *Beyond child poverty: The social exclusion of children*. New York: Institute for Child and Family Policy, Columbia University.

Klammer, U. (2006). Work life balance from the children's perspective. In: J. Lewis (Ed.), *Children in the context of family and welfare state change*. Cheltenham: Edward Elgar.

Leibfried, S. (2001). *Welfare state futures*. Cambridge: Cambridge University Press.

Leira, A. (2002). *Working parents and the welfare state*. Cambridge: Cambridge University Press.

Lewis, J., & Campbell, M. (2007). UK Work/Family Balance Policies and Gender Equality, 1997–2005. *Social Politics, 14*(1), 31–57.

Math, A., & Meilland, C. (2004). Un état des lieux des congés destinés aux parents dans vingt pays Européens. *Revue de l'IRES, 46*(3), 114–136.

OECD (2004). *Income distribution and poverty in OECD countries in the second half of the 1990s.* Mimeo.

Pierson, P. (2001). *The new politics of the welfare state*. Oxford: Oxford University Press.

Saraceno, C. (2000). Gendered policies: Family obligations and social policies in Europe. In: T. P. Boje & A. Leira (Eds), *Gender, welfare state and the market* (pp. 135–156). London: Routledge.

Strazdins, L., Clements, M. S., Korda, R., Broom, D. H., & D'Souza, R. (2006). Unsociable work? Non-standard work schedules, family relationships and children's well-being. *Journal of Marriage and Family* (1), 394–410.

Whiteford, P., & Adema, W. (2007). *What works best in reducing child poverty: A benefit or work strategy?* Working Paper no. 51. OECD, Paris.

THE 'MEANING' OF CHILDREN IN DUTCH AND GERMAN FAMILY POLICY

Trudie Knijn and Ilona Ostner

INTRODUCTION

At the end of the 20th century, birth-rates had fallen below the replacement rate in many Western countries. Changing attitudes towards having children had resulted in very small families, even in childlessness, giving rise to the Vienna Institute of Demography analyzing EUROSTAT data on the most common reasons for Europeans between the ages of 18 and 39 being childless. Almost half of these young adults (48 per cent) said they did not want children because they had general concerns about the future; another 46 per cent lacked a steady partner, while 44 per cent reported enjoying the current childless lifestyle and believed it would be difficult to fit in children; more than a third of these young(er) adults feared the loss of leisure time. 'Harder' facts, such as the expense of having children and job pressures, seemed to matter less for the childless respondents, albeit still more than a third of them gave such reasons (quoted in Theil, 2006, p. 54). Concerns about the future, lifestyle and steady partnership outweigh other worries. The expense of having children, work commitments and related problems in balancing work and family may be further reasons for delaying or foregoing family formation, but are not of prime importance. Societies intent on

Childhood: Changing Contexts
Comparative Social Research, Volume 25, 79–110
Copyright © 2008 by Emerald Group Publishing Limited
All rights of reproduction in any form reserved
ISSN: 0195-6310/doi:10.1016/S0195-6310(07)00003-8

encouraging young people to have children, and at a younger age, must take both concerns into account, i.e. invent a broad discourse on policies for children and families and at the same time design wide-ranging policies. Do they deliver? Can they deliver?

In this chapter, we investigate recent family-related policies, particularly policies intended to tackle declining birth-rates. Discourses matter especially if proposals for policy change target families and expect family members to alter their preferences fundamentally. We therefore study how problems are framed and also the ideas and values used by those arguing for policy change. How does society make a case for children? More analytically, what concepts prevail in the way society thinks about children? How do 'children' enter the public agenda? What does society expect from parents and from children (see Ostner, 2004)? We deal with these questions by comparing current discourses on and policies for children in The Netherlands and Germany. Both countries have initiated changes in family-related policies. We take the German case and compare with the Dutch one, and vice versa. Our 'paired comparison' helps us better understand ways of thinking about children (Skocpol & Somers, 1980, p. 178). By asking similar questions about diverging material on family policy and related discourses we leave room for variations which we hope will provide a fuller account of the meaning of children in society.[1]

The framework for our Dutch–German comparison brings together interpretative approaches in policy analysis and family sociology, emphasizing the importance of ideas in our understanding of children and the family, and for arguing related policies. The next section takes this statement a bit further. In the remainder of our essay, we compare Dutch and German family-related policies and 'messages' that accompany reforms of laws, benefits and advice.

'ARGUING' POLICIES AND THE LIMITS OF DISCOURSE

Importance of Rhetorical Action for Policy Change

Modern society and the welfare state help parents meet the costs of having children. Society invests in children from an early age by providing services and subsidizing education and healthcare costs. Children, on the other hand, are under no obligation to support old or frail and needy parents.

Welfare state benefits and services have largely relieved families from the compulsory solidarity and nurtured affection there has been between children and parents. Having children is a matter of choice. Nowadays, ageing parents are not dependent on their children, so birth-rates have declined to the size desired by the family. Most societies budget for steadily increased spending on families, but so far have refrained from fully compensating parents for the material and immaterial costs of having children. Social policy analysts pinpoint the extent to which welfare states finance generous pensions, early retirement and other forms of employable adults' non-employment, while failing to invest properly in children as future human capital and labor (Esping-Andersen, 2002). Other scholars blame society for snatching the benefits children constitute, while making parents bear most of the costs (Coleman, 1990; Scheiwe, 1999). Scholars differ in their assessment of the family contribution to children's, hence society's, welfare. Prominent proponents of the first group, such as Esping-Andersen (2002, p. 27), emphasize multiple family failures and maintain that 'strong' families who, in our words, monopolize child-raising 'are becoming detrimental for our well-being'. Family conditions, they argue, may undermine children's life chances; hence, policies have to intervene to neutralize the negative impact of families as far as possible. The other group, in contrast, put the accent on the positive contribution of parents, some adherents asking for increased public support. Both groups of scholars perceive children in terms of 'liabilities' for parents and 'assets' for society; and proponents often relate shrinking family sizes or, more generally, young people's reluctance, even unwillingness, to have children to such welfare state failures. Many European welfare states are now facing public debate on a radical re-launch of welfare spending, i.e. towards giving priority to children rather than to those who have already built up personal resources during their working life. Should welfare states turn the tables by recalibrating their social policies to meet the costs of having children? In particular, social policy scholars – and increasingly politicians too – are presently making a plea for investing in children and extending childcare services (Esping-Andersen, 2005, p. 35; Künzler, Schulze, & Van Hekken, 1999; Künzler, 2002; OECD, 2001, 2002). By promoting the continuous employment of mothers and, more generally, the 'dual-earner family', such services are said to be adding to children's resources and, additionally, raising birth-rates.

Once implemented, these recalibrated social policies will affect the nature of the relationship among family members and their idea of solidarity more directly (Daly, 2004), often in ways women and men will not yet have thought of, preferred or desired. In her article, Daly points to the 'anti-familialism' that is needed in speech and practice if society is to invest in children and create new resources for them: from very early on, parents, mothers in particular, would have to share their children with a plurality of providers, hence foregoing the time and space for close bonding with their very special and beloved child. Obviously, measures that promise new resources for tackling children's costs come at a price, especially in the case of parents who stick to norms of female home-based mothering in the decision about care of their smaller children. These norms still matter. ISSP (International Social Survey Programme) data suggest that while 'familialism' and related 'male breadwinner' norms have steadily declined, for instance in the German and Dutch welfare states during the past two decades, only a minority of women and men prefer dual full-time employment when their children are at or below school age. Many (West) German (Huinink, 2001) and Dutch parents still adhere to 'familialist' norms and values of 'mothers' time to care' at home (Knijn & Kremer, 1997; Portegijs, Boelens, & Olsthoorn, 2004; Kremer, 2005). Such parental norms and values strongly conflict with recent proposals for extending mothers' labor market participation, changing welfare policy and the actual norms and values driving that change. Conflicts will further increase once parents have noticed that the reality of dual-earning will often fail to compensate the losses in opportunities, including family time.

The 'rhetorical action' of policy-related actors therefore matters a lot – the strategic use of and appeal to identity-based and value-based arguments rings a bell. Drawing upon Majone (1989), Schmidt (2000, p. 230, 2002) argues that successful political adjustment in the face of interest-based opposition owes much to forms of political communication that are closer to 'arguing' than 'bargaining'. She uses the term 'policy discourse' to describe an 'arguing' rhetorical action which helps demonstrate that policy change is not only necessary, but also appropriate. This discourse would appeal to citizens' moral intuition and convictions by selectively activating ideas and values capable of convincing citizens that, for instance, 'a re-evaluation of the family and a family policy which dares to take new paths' (BMFSFJ, 2006, p. 5) is necessary and that the new paths to be taken are appropriate. Majone (1993, p. 109) distinguishes between the roles of 'ex ante' and 'ex post' ideas in the policy process: ideas that matter before a policy is taken versus after decisions have been taken. Policy-related experts must first formulate or 'frame' the problem to be tackled in ways that create new and extend existing opportunities for immediate and far-reaching intervention. Secondly, they must frame the problem, e.g. lack of children or delayed childbirth, in ways that restrict the options for intervention. The ways selected should be those that lead to new paths. Hence, other lines of argument are needed to persuade the public not just about what is necessary but also about what is impossible (no longer feasible) and why no (better) alternative exists other than doing what is messaged as 'appropriate'. Thirdly, at the stage of implementation, proponents of policy change make strategic use of ideas in order to link hitherto unconnected decisions or make sure that an idea, e.g. 'social investment', will be used by others and become common parlance. Fourthly, 'ex-post' arguing helps facilitate communication among relevant actors: by repeatedly using the same concepts or ideas, one-shot games are transformed into iterated ones. In the end, policy decisions have to be sufficiently communicated and accepted without alternatives.

In the case of family-related policies, proponents of change have linked 'hard' distributional conflicts and questions of efficiency (efficient allocation of taxpayers' money) with 'softer' issues of solidarity and fairness between gender and generations ('framing') and thereby have created moral pressure ('shaming'). It is hard to resist measures intended to increase women's or children's life chances or well-being. Change framed in this way and the corresponding shaming can improve (sometimes even reverse) the weak bargaining power of advocates of a new policy and facilitate policy change in the face of value-based opposition. For instance, welfare states can be steered towards parents' dual earning and an ever earlier institutionalization of children in crèches and pre-schools.

Family Discourses: Powering or Puzzling?

Policy discourses and related reforms will undoubtedly affect the family decisions of young adults, but whether in the ways intended by proponents of change remains an open question. We argue that ongoing discourses on the costs of having children and on family 'failures' largely miss the point about what young adults and parents-to-be believe is in store for them when having children, and so may even further deter already reluctant people from having and bringing up children; they may persuade others to make their decision on whether or not to have children conditional on different types of public support. The 'cost' discourse inevitably triggers more ambivalence, if not anxiety, and initiates a vicious circle: warning young adults – women *and* men – of the costs, burdens or risks that children could bring for them can hardly be met by public policies. It may further devalue parenthood, an important signifier of 'adulthood', ignoring the fact that the latter has already become rather unattractive – as is apparent in the many forms of extended adolescence.

'Costs' literature and related discourses overlook the dynamic they prompt. Why so? The politics of policy change is more about 'powering' and less about 'puzzling' (the problems people face and how they address them). 'Powering' politics and related discourses only strategically engage in problems, e.g. with having children, and only as far as these problems constitute barriers to or windows of opportunities for policy change. Yet, as sociologists, we are more interested in a puzzling 'bottom-up' perspective of young adults who are going to decide for or against having children and their dilemmas and anxieties. Our sociological perspective is broader than positions that perceive children foremost in terms of assets and liabilities. The latter position, we argue, tends to overrate the potential of the welfare state, and by doing so inevitably disappoints citizens' expectations. Welfare states can help mitigate costs by granting benefits and services. Policies are less successful, however, when it comes to dealing with individuals' non-economic ambivalences and feelings of insecurity which stretch far beyond lack of means. As quoted in our introduction, it is dilemmas and uncertainties which shape young adults' ideas about having children. How then, if at all, can welfare states influence young people's attitudes towards children? Welfare states can resort to three means: *legislation*, *money* (redistribution) and *instruction*. They have usually offered a combination of all three. Rhetorical action, *discourse*, constitutes a specific mode of instructing people – a 'second order' instruction which we propose to call *'message'*. Policy changes must be communicated ('messaged') in ways that persuade citizens to change their beliefs. Selectively activating *ideas* ('Deutungsmuster', 'concepts', 'cognitive maps') and *values* that fit planned reforms and resound with citizens' discourses is to provide 'proper' messages and mediate change (Schmidt, 2000).

There is a tradition of family sociology offering politicians 'ideas' and thereby good reasons for engaging in family matters. In the postwar period, following Talcott Parsons' (1951, 1964) structural–functionalist family sociology, it provided arguments for upholding the gendered division of housework and family care and for giving families cash rather than care. During the 1980s, family sociology began to stress the dilemmas, discrepancies and contradictions of modern families (Beck-Gernsheim, 1983; Nave-Herz, 1988; Van Setten, 1986; Weeda, 1989; Kaufmann, 1990; Van Praag & Niphuis-Nell, 1997). Again, it also influenced reform proposals and accompanying policy discourses. Family sociology could regularly do so because, from the outset, family policy has been a weakly institutionalized and highly fragmented field with few resources or legitimacy in either The Netherlands or Germany. It has therefore continuously relied on expertise offered by sociological conceptions of the family that cannot but entail ideas about families' well-functioning or malfunctioning and about what is good or bad for children's development, welfare and well-being. We argue that while family sociology has helped prepare the pending policy change in the two countries under discussion, 'powering' policy-elites and experts have only selectively and instrumentally drawn on sociological arguments, i.e. ignoring their complexity.

At the very same time as Parsons published his structural-functionalist family sociology, Riesman (2001/1961) anticipated a dilemma for contemporary parents (and parents-to-be) in his book *The Lonely Crowd*.[2] He characterized the 20th-century postwar social character as 'other-directed', whereas according to him 'inner-directedness' had prevailed in Western societies during the phase of industrialization and 'tradition-directedness' in peasant societies. He related 'other-directedness' to specific demographic characteristics, such as the incipient population decline due to birth-control and decreasing mortality. Riesman's concept of the 'other-directed social character' helps clarify fundamental dilemmas for young adults and parents-to-be, dilemmas that go well beyond structural or organizational barriers. The 'other-directed' person 'wants to be loved rather than esteemed; he wants not to gull or impress, let alone oppress, others but, in the current phrase, relate to them; he seeks less a snobbish status in the eyes of others rather than being emotionally in tune with them' (2001, xlii). 'Other-directedness' had two faces for Riesman: the need for constant approval by others accompanied the want for relating. Approval of the child and, through this, approving of oneself, became unequivocal goods of our times; spiral-like, it reinforced dependency on any approving group, regardless of which group this happened to be. Unsurprisingly, 'other-directed' parents doubted their parental skills and came to depend on other people's advice on how to bring up their children. This, in turn, eroded their parental authority. In Riesman's words: 'Increasingly in doubt as how to bring up their children, parents turn to other contemporaries for advice ... . Yet they cannot help but show their children, by their own anxiety, how little they depend on themselves and how much on others' (2001, p. 48).

Riesman was among the first sociologists to answer the question 'what are children for' in terms of a no-win situation. Parents were to lose in one way or another. The dilemma became even stronger once children were framed as 'knowledgeable individuals' in their own right, as in social constructivist family sociology which rejected notions of 'the' child, even of the 'child', as constructs made up by adults and emphasized the plurality of childhood(s) (Wyness, 2006, p. 119). It perceived children as competent actors and interpreters of their lives who pursued actions and interpretations that conflicted, above all, with those of their parents. By focusing on parents' shortcomings it empowered all sorts of experts and policies to intervene in parental affairs to secure the child's best interests. Put crudely, the social constructionist approach, i.e. perceiving children as parents' partners with an equal say and expertise, discredited the desire of parents to be the first and most important in making their children familiar with life and society at large (Koops, 2004).

A second dilemma exposed by family sociologists in the second half of the 20th century relates to what feminists such as Barrett and McIntosh (1982) coined the parochial inward-looking, 'anti-social' modern (bourgeois) family. They argued that the family represented particularistic private interests and thereby undermined the public spirit needed for community development and civil society. The argument grew stronger when other feminists questioned the very idea that the family cared for its members equally, given its structural basis in an age hierarchy and gender difference (Land & Rose, 1985; Balbo, 1987; Finch & Mason, 1993). The family, they maintained, assigned resources, also power, unequally and subjected the interests of weaker family members, mostly those of children and often their mothers once they became locked up in the private domain, to those of the more powerful ones. These critics raised awareness to potential conflicts between the interests of society at large and family members who gained or suffered from family life unequally.

The third dilemma was signaled during the 1980s, when sociologists eventually began to discuss the family in terms of 'plurality' and ongoing 'individualization' supported by expanding welfare state entitlements (Beck, 1983). The latter fostered a liable life course with clear-cut status and status sequences (Kohli, 1985), and since the late 1960s had provided an equally reliable safety net for those who did not – or failed to – follow established norms. The democratic welfare state created hitherto unknown opportunities for continuously living a life of one's own with or without a child or partner – in sum, it promoted individualization. The shift in sociological concepts reacted to far-reaching changes in family structure, gender roles and attitudes towards marriage or having a family.

In the 1990s, the contribution of families to their members and society was valued anew – in the wake of family change that revealed how precious as well as precarious caring relations for couples and generations could be, and in the extent to which families and family practices constituted crucial (non-market and non-state) resources for welfare states (Finch & Mason, 1993; Arber & Attias-Donfut, 2000; Knijn & Komter, 2004). As the number of one-person households expanded and work requirements were tightened, it became evident that having a family or caring for one's family helped prevent social isolation, promote social participation and offered a buffer against too many public demands (Daly & Saraceno, 2002). Family life did not automatically exclude those involved in family matters from public life, provided – as many sociologists nowadays maintain – families were 'democratized'. Family life and practices began to be framed on ideas of 'partnership', 'equal sharing' and respective negotiations (Giddens, 1998), and no more on hierarchy, hierarchical authority and 'compulsory altruism' (Land & Rose, 1985), as set out in Parsons' family and maternal model.

Family sociology therefore reflected the transformation, also weakening, of traditional ties. Riesman spoke of the dilemmas related to the decision about having children following from 'other-directedness' and peer orientation. Social constructivists exposed the declining capabilities of parents to introduce their children to the wider society, so extending the scope of 'individualization' and 'independence' to encompass children as 'autonomous' actors. Feminist scholars coined the family as an 'anti-social' oppressive institution in particular for women and children, while Beck and others stressed 'de-institutionalization' of the family and corresponding 'pluralization of social life-worlds' (*ibid.*, p. 63), emphasizing individualization. 'Individualization', 'family democracy' or 'equal sharing among partners' did not sit easily together in people's everyday lives, though. And 'individualization' and 'other-directedness' entailed special dilemmas for parents and parents-to-be. In this context, rhetorical action and related state policies gained (new) importance for the redesign of cash and care obligations between genders and generations as well as between (actual and future) families and society as a whole.

'CHILDREN' AND 'FAMILIES' IN DUTCH AND GERMAN POLICY DISCOURSES[3]

As defined by Lewis (1992), West Germany and The Netherlands had long been textbook examples of Parsons' family model and 'strong' male breadwinner states. Mothers' employment was low or part-time and childcare for small children was close to non-existent. In both countries, societal attitudes towards families and children, and related policies, seemed locked-in and hard to overcome. In The Netherlands, a unique mix of benefits for (lone) motherhood and status-maintaining employment-based benefits was combined with a, first communitarian now 'liberal', non-interventionist attitude towards family matters. In (West) Germany, family policy was founded on status maintenance via social insurance and marriage-related benefits. Recently, both countries have re-geared policies to boosting women's employment and raising institutionalized childcare; in sum, both have moved towards 'de-familializing the family' (relieving families of care obligations). They have also increasingly designed and applied measures to regulate parental practices. Why and how have they done so? Have they 'framed' family-related problems in similar ways? Do they apply similar arguments when turning to the issue of children? The next sections illustrate the uses of arguments in Dutch and German family policies. We begin with changing family *legislation* and related definitions of the 'family'; depending on their content and scope, such changes are tantamount to the transformation of family relations. A brief section scrutinizes the issue of pro-natalism – policies aimed at increasing the number and quality of children – in both countries. The remainder successively compares recently stipulated measures for Dutch and German families by focusing on cash benefits and services, including instruction and advice, and at the same time explores how these measures have been framed discursively in each country.

Legislation and Family Definitions

Since 1996, the Dutch government, in accordance with the sociologically inspired advice of the Dutch family council, defines a family as 'every living arrangement of one or more adults responsible for caring and raising one or more children' (TK, 2005–2006). By implication, it is not marriage but the presence of children that now defines a 'family', including same-sex parents, lone-parent families, adoptive families and divorced parents sharing childcare. This redefinition of the family preceded the 1998 family law reform, which recognized the equal rights of children born in different family forms (see also Knijn & Selten, 2002). A recent white paper, 'Gezinsbeleid', still outlines the Parsonian functions of the Dutch family, though under the recognition of the various family forms that can perform these:

> The family is a unique social structure and one of the pillars of a livable society. The family combines societal functions such as development, care for its members, care for other people, care for society, leisure, debate and dialogue. The uniqueness of the family

exists in the combination of these functions with unconditional bonding, commitment and love. Then the family is a safe spot for children as well as parents; a place where one can feel at home ... . Well functioning families are of crucial importance for society. (TK, 2005–2006, 30 512)

In German family law, a 'family' also consists of parents and their children; these can be biological or step-children, adopted or foster children. Up until quite recently, the Constitution and family laws closely linked 'family' and 'marriage', although various Constitutional Court rulings weakened the link. Lone mothers living with their child and non-resident fathers who were never married to their child's mother have become recognized as 'family'. Jurisdiction and related legislation have further expanded the notion of the family from a child-centered perspective. A 'child's family' pertains meanwhile to individuals who presently entertain, or did so in the past (before divorce or separation), longer-term close relations with the child, including grandparents, former partners of the parents and their children, provided a close relationship existed (Schwab, 2001, 2006). Same-sex couples have the right to register officially as a 'couple' (a minor form of marriage), yet do not have the right to marry or to adopt children (in contrast to The Netherlands), except in cases where children exist from former heterosexual partnerships. In both countries, therefore, the importance of marriage, as well as of residence (sharing a home) for what constitutes 'a family', has been successively weakened. Children have equal status and rights regardless of the marital status of their parents, and families are seen as 'multi-generational' as well as 'multi-local networks' (BMFSFJ, 2006, p. 30). Both countries now employ postmodern socio-logical definitions of the family as 'any group which consists of people in intimate relationships which are believed to endure over time across generations' (Cheal, 2002, p. 4), as of yet, mostly by re-interpreting ideas of 'kin', 'generations' and 'generational solidarity', and so far less by further deregulating marriage and family law. The German 2006 family report (p. 30) stresses that a family is more than a place where children live. Such a locally restricted definition, it argues, would deny the multiplicity of family relations which today merge families (in fact 'generations') with the wider society. The argument nicely illustrates the ongoing discursive (and normative) extension of what is to make up a family. German society, according to the report, is made up of concentric circles of 'solidarity' ('give-and-take') and largely populated by 'families':

Never before have so many age groups lived together in families at the same time, in some cases spread over a multiplicity of locations, but nevertheless in regular contact, and seldom before was there a healthier atmosphere between the generations. The family

is in the truest sense of the word the kernel where everyday solidarity is practiced. ...
Even if families are becoming smaller, more colourful and more mobile, we cannot
dispense with the give-and-take of everyday solidarity. New networks must be created to
be able to transfer the advantages of yesterday's large families to modern social
structures. (BMFSFJ, 2006, p. 3)

'Intergenerational solidarity' also comes into play, albeit implicitly, when
the report indicates that new sustainable family policies must pursue the
'goal of bringing more children into families, and more family into society'
(*ibid.*). To attain the first goal, 'families need to be relieved of more of their
burdens', 'to make it easier for young people to choose to have children and
to enhance families' economic stability, above all through their own gainful
employment', also by 'early promotion of children', so that people 'dare to
live as a family' (*ibid.*, pp. 4–5). 'Solidarity' in this context applies to parental
employment as an (to be enhanced) aspect of the generational contract; it
also pertains to norms of equality and partnership within families and equal
sharing between families, generations and society; finally, it points to
resources of older generations (not just kin!) who are expected more actively
to help younger ones to have children and stay employed. Dissolving the
'family' into multi-local networks of give-and-take, as well as the idea of
local communities as family networks/networks for families, answers aptly
to the sociological diagnosis of 'des-organizing' modern families or ideas of
'pluralization' and 'individualization'. The report regularly refers to such
concepts (e.g. BMFSFJ, 2006, p. 9), yet redefines families in ways (as 'multi-
local networks' including local communities) that help advertise new policies
of 'social integration' (Ostner, 2006). How should these ideas be combined
with family formation and investments in children? The 2006 German family
report, aware of declining birth-rates, frames such issues as 'promotion of
children' – a proposition that resembles pro-natalist propositions.

Arguing for Pro-Natalism?

The demographic data of our countries differ in some respects. Dutch
fertility rates have declined less dramatically than German rates (total
fertility rate (TFR) 1.7 vs. TFR 1.3 in 2003), though in both countries about
25 per cent of women aged between 36 and 46 with high educational status
have no children, and women increasingly often delay having children until
into their late twenties. Differences also exist: 30 per cent of German women
aged between 18 and 25 have children compared to only 15 per cent of Dutch

women in that age group (Forssén & Ritakallio, 2006). The attitudes of Dutch and German men towards children differ significantly. According to 2001 Eurobarometer data, the ideal number of children for German men is 1.38 (women 1.73). Dutch men and women both see more than two children as their ideal, albeit Dutch men want slightly fewer children than Dutch women do (2.07 vs. 2.08: see Knijn, Ostner, & Schmitt, 2006). Demographic trends are more seriously challenging in Germany than in The Netherlands. Is a (re-)turn to pro-natalism the answer? Can such a trend be observed more in Germany than in The Netherlands, and if so how is it framed?

Although The Netherlands had been familiar with pro-natalist ideas propagated by religious communities before World War II, politicians have steadily refrained from making use of pro-natalist measures. Being a country with a high population density, fertility has never been an issue in The Netherlands. Even now, Dutch politicians are not debating demographic changes with a particular stress on 'fertility'. Debates focus on the ageing society and on corresponding employment – not population – policies. Given that a very large part of the working-age population is not employed full-time, that unemployment among ethnic minority youngsters is very high, that women mainly work short part-time hours, that elderly workers retire early and, finally, that many potentially able workers depend on benefits, the Dutch government has responded to demographics by limiting early retirement and by introducing an 'activation policy' (Van Berkel & Hornemann Møller, 2002). Stimulating the current population to become or remain employed has higher priority than increasing the population as such. In addition, despite the relatively low support for parents and children, Dutch fertility nears the Danish and Finnish levels and exceeds the Swedish level. Rijken (2006) argues that the TFR of Dutch women is still at 1.7 children per women as a result of a combination of high average male wages, the availability of part-time jobs and the relatively low opportunity costs of children for the many Dutch women with relatively low educational attainment.

Dutch governments express some worry, though, about Dutch women who have their first child on average at the age of 29. However, once their first is born, they often have a second child shortly afterwards. Many women do not want a child before they have a stable job and can ensure good childcare. Other women who intend to become full-time housewives delay having children until they (and their partners) have saved enough money to buy a suitable house and can afford to withdraw from the labor market for several years. Abortion as the right not to have children has been well recognized in The Netherlands for decades and has remained an uncontested issue since the 1981 Abortion Act (*Wet Zwangerschapsonderbreking*; see Rademakers, 2002). Thanks to a very active and creative feminist movement that protested using the slogan '[Be a] boss in one's own womb' during the 1970s, the Dutch government officially tolerated, then legalized, formerly illegal abortion clinics.

Population policies had remained anathema in West Germany up to unification because of perverted pro-natalist measures and related 'negative eugenics' during the NAZI era, i.e. the 'elimination' of individuals of 'minor' or of 'no value' along racially and socially constructed lines. The 1949 (West) German Basic Law stipulated the privacy of marriage and family as a civic right, precluding any pro-natalist policies on the part of the state; family and social legislation strengthened women's personal dependence on a male breadwinner husband up to the late 1970s. The East German socialist regime expected women to be both workers and mothers virtually from the start, while the socialist 'provider state' took command of essential family functions, assuming a parental role and to some extent the role of the breadwinner husband. When birth-rates ostensibly fell from the late 1960s onwards, East German social policies became explicitly pro-natalist, however. In strict contrast to the NAZI regime, they were designed as 'positive' birth-enhancing measures and were never employed as 'negative' means of exclusion or elimination. Such policies stretched far beyond generous subsidies for children's food, clothes, upbringing and leisure time. One-year-long paid baby leave (for mothers only) in the 1980s, first for the second and third children, later also for the first child, was introduced to encourage women and couples to accomplish their desired number of children. Socialist East Germany steadily expanded childcare facilities (children aged 20 weeks and older were eligible) and increased grants for pupils and students in order to further relieve parents from paying for their children. From 1972 onwards, special programs supported student mothers (Grandke, 1979, 2001; Helwig, 1974; Trappe, 1995). Consequently, birth-rates increased and women's age at the birth of the first child decreased to an average of 23 years in 1989 shortly before unification. During the 1980s, between 80 and 90 per cent of women were full-time working and at the same time mothers of at least one child (Schulz, 1998, p. 145). When the wall came down in November 1989, the average East German family consisted of two medium-skilled parents and 1.7 children; both worked 43 hours in a 5-day working week up to the age of 65. In women aged 15–65 years, 82.3 per cent were employed. Pro-natalism provided specific opportunity structures for East German women: even mothers were not dependent on the income of a partner. Hence, women not only deferred marriage, they lived in consecutive partnerships, divorced, re-partnered and often married after the children were born. Pro-natalist measures went hand in hand, though with increasingly less cash and poor service provisions for the non-working elderly, among those many low-skilled impoverished women, or the disabled of all ages; disadvantaged elderly criticized pro-natalist policies as 'undeserved' (Schmidt, 2004, p. 92). On a macro-level, such measures contributed to the exhaustion of the socialist weakly productive economy; on the meso-level to the ongoing erosion of the legitimacy of the regime (*ibid.*). While discontent continuously rose, East German birth-rates began to fall again during the 1980s.

Negative NAZI legacies, East–West regime competition and the rise of Western feminism meant that pro-natalism had no chance of thriving despite the apparent decline of the West German birth-rate from the 1960s onwards to well below the replacement rate. Feminists, alluding again to Nazi times, and most Social-Democrats fiercely rejected any mention of falling birth-rates or the need for more children as 'reactionary'. The rebuff also followed ferocious debate about abortion – the conflict was provisionally settled by the 1975 abortion law ruling that abortions were not to be negatively sanctioned when carried out under strictly fixed and controlled conditions. Contrary to the Social-Democrats, the Christian-Democrats openly acknowledged falling birth-rates as a problem in the 1980s, coining them in terms of 'opportunity costs' in times of increasing options, but rejected GDR style population policies. Instead, they publicized a modified breadwinner model under the heading 'freedom of choice' ('Wahlfreiheit'): shorter working hours for parents, above all, part-time work for mothers and extended parental leave with income-tested flat-rate payments for either mothers or fathers. Considering the political hostility in West Germany towards even socialist style 'positive' pro-natalist ideas and practices, the return of pro-natalist discourses and measures, albeit small in scope, in unified Germany since the late 1990s is, on the face of it, surprising. Fifteen years after unification, older German legacies, as incorporated in socialist family policies, seem slowly to be succeeding in reframing the meaning of children in Germany. Another essay is needed to explain how this could happen.[4] Yet, we claim that unification has set Germany further apart from The Netherlands.

Meanwhile, pro-natalist ideas have entered the public debate in many European Union member states, including The Netherlands. Experts and politicians stress that women should have their children young: the younger woman and the more fertile years mean lower medical costs and the likelihood of second and third children. A few years ago a Dutch gynecologist, Ter Velde (1991), formulated the slogan 'a smart girl has her pregnancy in time' (Een slimme meid heeft haar zwangerschap op tijd), a slogan not fully repeated in a Dutch government campaign a few years later that said simply: 'a smart girl is prepared for her future'. So far, Dutch politicians have been reluctant towards explicit pro-natalism – more so than their German counterparts.

Child 'Poverty' as Family Failure, Children as Opportunity Costs: The Issue of Money

While Dutch and German discourses stress the give-and-take between generations, and Germany still legally obliges children and parents virtually to life-long support for each other, especially when in need of care, they also point to many family failures. In Germany, the main failure is marketed as 'child poverty', a concept that has many connotations, e.g. 'scarcity' of children, as presented by childless adults and small-sized families; scarcity of parents' resources for children and children's lack of resources, i.e. money, space, time, opportunities. 'Child poverty' as scarcity also alludes to qualitative shortcomings such as lack of stimulating environments, including parents. Dutch discourses are more ambivalent; parental failures, scarcity of stimulating environments and youth delinquency have been . framed for decades as a lack of cultural resources and have only recently been linked to child poverty. The material we studied for our Dutch–German comparison, i.e. the 2006 German Family Report, the 2002 and 2005 Reports on Children and Youth and the Dutch White paper on family life, question the educational competence of families in general, and of low-skilled non-stimulating people in particular. The OECD-governed PISA 2000 Assessment of Reading, Mathematical and Scientific Skills shamed Germany for its medium to low performance and, above all, for restricting upward social mobility of the lower classes and children of migrants, while in The Netherlands more attention is paid to average performance than to gaps between low-performing and high-performing children. Rare but repeatedly publicized incidents of severe child abuse (and murder) have also helped question families' positive impact on raising their children or, more generally, families' 'efficiency' for society in both countries. Efficient families avoid negative external costs for society as far as possible; if families fail, policies must regulate families' affairs in ways that force them to take into account related negative costs.

Arguing for a new 'sustainable' family policy, Bertram, Rösler, and Ehlert (2005) maintain that strong (West) German 'familialism' ('Hotel Mama') prolongs adolescence and hinders young adults from actively establishing a life of their own, including looking for paid work or finishing education. They explicitly advise the weakening of parental obligations for younger adults, thereby strengthening the latter's independence from their parents. However, they do not say how to attain this goal. In Germany, parental obligations – mostly financial – last until the age of 25 for children in education, for living-in children of any age who lack means, including the unemployed on the reformed job-seeker benefit scheme (Arbeitslosengeld II), in principle, forever. The same discrepancy between rhetoric and rule exists in The Netherlands: in the 1990s, the Dutch government by law increased the age of financial dependency on parents to 21 and denied social assistance to those below that age, including lone mothers. Current municipal measures even deny social assistance for those below the age of 27. Filial obligations also persist in Germany: While the German 2001 pension reform abolished the obligation on children to support their income-poor pensioner parents, they must still pay for the care of their needy elderly parents. Students (often their parents) have had to pay fees for their children's academic studies in most German Länder since 2006. Both countries now run activation schemes for unemployed family members on benefit, but do not otherwise encourage young adults' financial autonomy; in contrast, these reforms strengthen their dependency.

'Family failures', 'negative external effects' and the evolution of social-regulatory – in contrast to redistributive – policies are two sides of the same coin; Dutch and German family policies have shifted towards regulating efficiency. In the context of regulatory policies, 'child poverty', as lack of parents' financial resources, is to be met first by parents' employment efforts; and 'child poverty' pertaining to all sorts of qualitative shortfalls calls for a broad range of 'precautionary' welfare state provisions. In The Netherlands and Germany, such precautionary measures are being messaged as 'investing in children'. In what ways do they compensate the costs of having children?

The socialist East bore most of the costs in the bringing up children and thereby 'defamilialized', i.e. 'socialized', such costs. Unified Germany first of all expanded its cash transfers to families, e.g. child benefit for the first child from about €25 in 1990 to €135 after the Red-Green coalition had come into power in 1998, finally to €154 per month in 2002 and onwards. Between

1998 and 2002 the coalition increased family-related expenditure from 40 billion per year to more than 50 billion, i.e. by nearly 30 per cent within 4 years. Providing more money but few services for children has been criticized increasingly for its ineffectiveness, because it neither prevented child poverty nor boosted birth-rates (Ristau, 2005; Rürup & Gruesco, 2003; Gruesco & Rürup, 2005). The fifth family report (BMFS 1994) blamed German society for its 'structural thoughtlessness' as regards the 'positive external effects' of families. The blame might have contributed to increased spending, since the report perceived families as main 'producers' of human 'capital' – the latter term pertaining more to 'comprehensive capabilities' than to economic assets. As indicated, the seventh report questions the capacity and efficiency of families to deliver children of sufficient quantity and quality. In tune with other government papers, the report argues that marriage-related benefits gave not only married mothers but also childless wives the incentive to stay at home, and generally reduced women's labor market participation. German experts like their Dutch counterparts – pin down mothers' discontinuous and part-time employment and the rapid increase in child poverty rates in the 1990s. The income position of families with children in both countries declined rapidly in the 1990s; child poverty now reaches 9 to 13 per cent of all children (see Table 1). In The Netherlands and in Germany, this affects mainly children in non-working lone-parent families and children in migrant families. Current Dutch governments have

Table 1. Share of Children 17 Years and Under Living in Households with Equivalised Disposable Income Less than 50% of Median Income.

Country	2000	Mid 1990s	Mid 1980s	Population Total (2000)
Denmark	2,4	1,8	4,0	4,3
Finland	3,4	2,1	2,8	6,4
Norway	3,6	4,4	3,9	10,4
Sweden	3,6	2,5	2,5	5,3
France	7,3	7,1	6,6	7,0
Netherlands	**9,0**	**9,1**	**3,3**	**6,0**
Germany	**12,8**	**10,3**	**5,9**	**9,8**
Austria	13,3	7,3	5,5	9,3
Portugal	15,6	15,6	n.a.	13,7
Italy	15,7	18,6	11,5	12,9
United Kingdom	16,2	17,4	9.7	11,4

Source: OECD (2005) Society at Glance Data Chart EQ3.1

recognized the special needs of these families and have taken some measures to support families with children financially. Tax allowances introduced by previous governments for (one and two-earner) families with children, lone-parent families and compensation for childcare costs were increased in The Netherlands. Dutch children also receive free healthcare and free education until the age of 18 (formerly: 16). In Germany, children as well as non-employed wives were always exempted from contributions to statutory health insurance. Recent reform proposals recommend financing all children's healthcare costs and contributions, and also those of privately insured parents, through general taxes. However, despite high spending levels on families, German birth-rates have remained low (1.35 in 2001, among the lowest in the EU), while The Netherlands, despite ranking very low on spending on families, continues to have average birth-rates (1.7 in 2000) (Bradshaw & Finch, 2002; Rijken, 2006).

Obviously, births are not encouraged just by giving families cash. Cash has proved inefficient not only in that birth-rates have failed to increase, but also quality targets have been missed. The German Federal Government (since 2005 a coalition between the Christian and Social Democrats) has therefore:

> started to re-focus families' financial benefits in order to increase their effectiveness. A major project ... is to refine the previous child-raising benefit in line with successful examples in Sweden and other countries. The slump in income previously experienced after the birth of a child is hence largely avoided. Families receive support when they particularly need it. ... At the same time, a parental allowance offers an incentive for fathers and mothers to return to work faster than after the child-rearing phase than (sic!) was previously the case. ... Early promotion of children and better possibilities for gainful employment for mothers reduce poverty risks and help people to breakout of the poverty spiral. (BMFSFJ, 2006, pp. 4–5)

> Families in Germany ... experience an economic downward spiral: Family income is still high at the start of parental leave (due to full – 100 per cent – wage replacement during eight weeks of maternity leave), followed by a marked decrease when parents start to draw child-raising benefit, which is not linked to the previous income ... . (*ibid.*, 9)

The new parental leave ('Elterngeld'), in force from 2007 onwards, grants a 1-year wage replacement for one parent (14 months for a lone parent; but, for parents in partnerships, only if the second partner takes at least 2 of the 14 months of leave) of 67 per cent of former earnings up to a net income of €1800 per month (roughly an average young teacher's net income). 'Elterngeld' explicitly aims at higher qualified and better paid women (BMFSFJ, 2004; Rürup & Gruescu, 2005; critical: Leitner, 2005), and therefore smacks of selective pro-natalism. Policy-related elites have just launched a debate on how the child benefit (€154 per child) could be reduced in favor of free-of-charge public childcare. As with parental leave reform, retrenched child benefits will hit poorer families, and whether these families will be able to compensate for their benefit loss through low-paid employment and by being offered childcare is doubtful. The Dutch White Paper on family policy states things slightly differently:

> Current arrangements cover the costs of children better than they did in 2002. This does not mean that the allowances always cover all costs. This is not needed either: the government is of the opinion that parents themselves also have a financial responsibility for their children. (TK, 2005–2006, 30 512, p. 23)

So far, both governments have offered mostly tax reductions, child allowances, free (basic) education and healthcare to families in which work and family life have to be combined. They have asked (as in Germany), even obliged, primary schools to extend their opening hours – in the Dutch case, since 2007, from 7.30 a.m. to 6.30 p.m., which means that these schools are having to organize activities for children before and after regular school hours. In Germany, a child's right to publicly funded or subsidized (affordable) part-time childcare was established in 1995 and politicians are now calling for the right to free (!) full-time childcare after parental leave, when the child will be 12–14 months' of age. The 1995 law emphasized the older objective of enhancing the child's natural and social development, but stressed that the provision should be aimed at accommodating parents' needs as well as the choice between childcare and 'daycare mothers' (the law speaks of daycare 'persons') for very young children. In both Germany and The Netherlands there is a mixed economy of childcare. In Germany, the municipalities have to finance childcare with the support of the *Länder*, the individual states, while in The Netherlands childcare can only be provided by private companies (for profit or non-profit). In The Netherlands, a purchaser-provider split is being implemented; childcare centers have become fully privatized; fees are shared in a tripartite system in which each partner – employers, parents, the state (through tax reductions for low- and middle-income families) – pay 33 per cent of the costs. Both countries therefore have a diversity of institutions, rules and procedures in the supply of kindergarten facilities. Accordingly, childcare varies greatly in terms of quality, in who decides the amount to pay, in the definition of maximum or minimum payments (often a ceiling of 15–30 per cent of operating costs or costs for personnel divided by number of children), co-determination of parents (parents, provider, Youth Office), opening hours, and so on. In both countries, fees are graduated according to the number of children in the family; low-income parents get significant reductions and parents receiving benefits pay no fees. As stated above, for reasons of providing better education for children and other measures, politicians want to further extend affordable full-time childcare, indeed free-of-charge childcare at least for preschool children. In 2007, German parents are now able to claim more generous tax reductions for child-minders in their own home. While Germany has just established earnings-related 'Swedish style' parental leave, promoting a quicker return to the labor market, the 2001 pension reform significantly improved pension credits of part-time working parents. However, it is no longer certain whether these credits meet the objective of developing 'new life cycle models in order to realign and extend the time periods on training, work and family formation' (BMFSFJ, 2006, p. 9), since they encourage discontinuous employment of better-off married mothers, including those higher qualified. The 'life course saving scheme' recently introduced in The Netherlands encompasses parental leave, leave for care reasons, leave for additional education, and early retirement under a single scheme, and is almost completely individualized as well as privatized. Individual employees can save 12 per cent of their gross annual salary up to a maximum of 210 per cent, and once they have taken leave can again contribute to their savings up to this maximum in that year. Private insurance companies collect the savings, an employer's permission for taking leave is required, and employees maintain employment rights during their leave. The savings scheme is treated as deferred income, with tax due only when money is withdrawn for leave purposes, i.e. reduced by €183 for every year of participation in the savings scheme. Preferential tax treatment applies in the case of the still unpaid parental leave, with a reduction of income tax per household corresponding to 50 per cent of the gross minimum wage for the days taken. Consequently, employees earning twice the minimum wage or less are excluded from paying income tax when using this scheme for unpaid parental leave (TK, 2003–2004). When parents additionally take paid parental leave from their savings, this is at the cost of early retirement.

These policies reflect what politicians and social scientists have increasingly being pleading for; namely, a recalibration of the ways money for family policy is spent from marriage-based tax allowances to enhancing women's employment; from cash transfers for children to the funding of services and leaves. The new German political discourse on families acquired the heading 'securing sustainability'; 'sustainability' to be attained through an increased birth-rate, better balancing of work and family life, fighting child poverty, improving education, and, for smaller children, teaching parents how to bring up children properly (Ristau, 2005, p. 18).

Precautionary Measures – Teaching and Controlling Parents

As already mentioned, and in tune with Riesman's diagnosis of waning parental confidence, discourses on multiple family failures in West Germany preceded the policy shift. The 2002 Report on Children and Youth stated that the family, as hitherto known, no longer fitted the regular experience of children and youth (BMFSFJ, 2002, p. 57). Consequently, the importance of families, in general, the care they take and the socializing efforts they make for their members and for society as a whole, has been increasingly disparaged. Families seem to no longer guarantee children growing up beloved and happy. Children, it is said, need, above all, a good environment and not necessarily 'traditional' families (Schneider, 2002). The 2005 Report on Children and Youth (BMFSFJ, 2005) explicitly focuses on issues of caring for, bringing up and teaching children alongside as well as outside the family, and explicitly refers to the former socialist East as a model for early public socialization. It discusses at length how to prepare children for the break from home and from their mothers, who are now expected to stay in employment more continuously. These discourses and related measures tend to 'de-institutionalize childhood' while 'institutionalizing children' (Jensen & Qvortrup, 2004, p. 825) – a trend eased by notions of the family as 'multi-local support networks' as well as by efficiency arguments (lowering negative external effects).

The Dutch White Paper *Gezinsbeleid* introduces two instruments for supporting families, summarized as 'prevention' and 'intervention' and related precautionary provisions. *Prevention* is the strategy for creating good conditions for families in which to bring up children in combination with active citizenship. *Intervention* is needed for failed families, families that undermine and threaten children's rights and development. Here the Dutch government on the one hand recognizes the importance of families for society in accordance with the functionalist approach, and on the other is aware that families may harm their children, in which case the state will protect them. It reacts to or anticipates problems related to family diversity (partnership dissolution; lone-parent families), family isolation or the loss of close social networks ('des-organization') that can help in socializing the children, insecurity among parents about how to bring up a child, tensions between work and care; governments also answer for the problems of migrant families and their children (poverty, dropping out from school and social participation) and defective norms and values (in particular those of migrant families). The Dutch White Paper declares in the end:

> The government focuses mainly on creating conditions that help the family to function well. This means that parents can perform their role as educators well and can perform their other social roles at the same time. (TK, 2005–2006, 30 512)

German papers argue in similar terms.

Related policies are mainly intervention-oriented and focus on so-called 'families at risk'. Intervention projects include family tutors, at-home visits by social workers and volunteers, additional tasks for youth health centers and educational programs for parents. Most notable is the introduction of an *electronic child file* for every Dutch child containing instructions about child health and possibly also about school career, contacts with the police and justice and social work. Some German Länder also plan to introduce the measure. It has been highly disputed especially for reasons of constitutional rights in relation to data protection. Foucault's panoptic centre (waxworks) may be realized in The Netherlands with the argument that it will improve instruction for policy and management of interventions. In Germany, as well as in The Netherlands, in reaction to some striking cases of child murders by parents in the past few years, the Dutch government – in the German case, some Länder – has/have announced stricter rules for child protection, for supervision, for obligatory medical inspection, for better coordination of social work as well as for projects for parents of juvenile delinquents. The Netherlands is also developing a 'family security' policy. This is by way of a 'house ban' law that prohibits offenders from staying at their home for 10 days – a law passed in Germany in 2001 – and by a so-called *flexforce* of social professionals that should help to reduce waiting lists for children in need of help because of child abuse.

Additional support for schools and out of school education is provided in The Netherlands mainly in the extension of school hours (as mentioned previously, i.e. from 7.30 a.m. to 18.30 p.m.), but also in the education of personnel supervising children who remain at school during the midday interval with European money (ESF), the introduction of care advice teams and intervention tutors at schools that should supervise problematic children, guide them towards professional social work and prevent violence among schoolchildren. Programs for preschool education should prepare children well for primary school. After years of complaints by parents, professionals, pedagogical scientists as well as entrepreneurs, only very recently (in 2007) attention has been paid to the decreasing quality of

Dutch education. While many plead for better trained teachers, for quality control in childcare centers and for massive investment in Dutch schools, this White Paper proposes mainly investment in activities that extend school hours in order to facilitate parents' employment, in school security without improving education and in the preparation of migrant children for the Dutch school system. Values and norms was a manifesto item of the former administration, in particular of its Prime Minister Balkenende, part of whose program was the compulsory objective for (black) schools to promote citizenship and social integration. Special projects are introduced for the social binding of migrant parents, in particular mothers, i.e. to stimulate their independence and employment and to improve their language skills. Germany has recently started to catch up with Dutch measures on migrant children and their parents. Also part of the norms and values project is stricter control of the media, particularly in order to protect children from injurious television programs and Internet sites.

Germany is developing similar sophisticated measures under the heading 'new culture of family policy'. Families are increasingly assessed as in need of special advice and teaching. The government has launched 'local pacts' where communities, schools, firms, or all of these in combination, teach parents in 'Elternkursen' (courses for parents) and 'Familienzentren' (special family centers) about children's needs and how to help them overcome social disadvantage. Obviously, the public and the private have become increasingly merged.

TAKING STOCK: 'OTHER DIRECTED' ADULTHOOD AND FAMILY-RELATED SOCIAL POLICY

Our chapter tried to locate recent Dutch and German family policies. Family sociology helped us formulate three dilemmas young adults face during their transition to parenthood in an individualized culture that requires rational choices to be made. The first concerns lifestyle, i.e. whether one wants to enter parenthood or do away with parental responsibilities. The choice is complicated, since adulthood is no longer associated with entering parenthood. 'Other-directedness' has become an appropriate attitude as parents' authority has waned (by being publicly questioned), and also because parents regardless of their educational attainment and children are assumed to be equal partners. Second, private–public life dilemmas have resulted from the individualization – here isolation – of family life and the increased awareness-related dangers of personal relations that are largely governed by emotions, in particular, for children and women. Third, there is a growing dilemma between 'individualization' and 'institutionalization' resulting from the fragmentation of marriage-based families, from women's employment and from new public intervention into family life. We assume that discourses matter, especially if proposals for policy change target families and expect young adults to alter their preferences. Hence, we examined what concepts prevail in our societies' way of thinking on children? How have 'children' entered the public agenda in our countries?

A framework for policy discourse analysis as developed by Majone and Schmidt is a useful tool for describing family-policy-related actors' 'arguing' rhetoric in The Netherlands and Germany. Their rhetorical actions must appeal to the moral intuition and convictions of citizens by selectively activating ideas and values focusing on a particular value that cannot readily be denied.

As our analysis shows, some – not all – aspects of family-related policies are framed similarly in both countries. There is convergence in the framing of what exactly should be understood as 'family'. In both countries, the importance of marriage, as well as of residence (sharing a home), for what constitutes 'a family' have been successively weakened. Children have gained equal status and rights regardless of their parents' marital status. Families are seen as 'multi-generational' as well as 'multi-local' networks. In accordance with sociological theories, postmodern family definitions (Cheal, 2002; Wyness, 2006) have became virulent as legislation has redefined relations and obligations between genders and generations (e.g. in cases of divorce, single parenthood or unemployment). A family is where children live. Also in both countries, families are framed as productive contributors to society at large that deserve some, though not full, support. Families are expected to contribute effectively to society by parental employment and adequately educating their children. So far there are strong parallels in the framing of families in our countries and these frames appear to have incorporated the sociological analyses of past decades; the structure and composition of families are no longer restricted to a married breadwinner couple with children sharing residency; instead, generational, work and educational obligations are enforced.

Nevertheless, many young adults delay or defer starting a family, in particular the higher educated; many women in both countries still become housewives after giving birth or start working part-time; only a minority of children under school age attend full-time childcare; and the educational performance of many children in both countries does not meet international standards. So, in addition to the question 'how do family policies frame today's family?' we have answered the question 'how have current family policies framed the malfunction of families to meet the policy targets?', and followed this with an exploration of the policies introduced to counteract perceived 'failures'.

First, we stressed that a major difference between our countries concerns the decline of fertility rates, which is more dramatic in Germany than in The Netherlands; hence the accent on the failure to increase childbirth in Germany is stronger than in The Netherlands, although both countries have their (historical) reasons for limited pro-natalism. Second, the two countries diverge in their emphasis on such 'family failures' as child poverty and educational attainment, and therefore also in their emphasis on 'social investment' in those who promise 'returns' (Esping-Andersen, 2002). Third, we see similarities in discussions on qualifications to be parents as well as on women's employability and employment. Parents' capabilities as well as women's contribution to society's wealth are approached instrumentally; to avoid costs for society at large, parents need to be equipped for socializing their children and women for fulfilling functions as workers in the economy as bearers of society's children. In this context, the issue of child 'poverty' and fertility entered public discourses and policy, though much more so in Germany than in The Netherlands, where the focus is rather on risk prevention, both for society and for individual children, than on the numbers of children and their quality of life.

Despite the fact that both countries frame family failures differently, and in doing so blame families differently, some similarities in policy approaches can be identified that follow, although not logically, from our policy analyses. In both countries, legal rights to support for young adults, either from parents or from the state, have declined, which may stimulate parenthood less than employment. Childcare provisions are still patchy in both countries, and their quality hard to assess. Good quality childcare, where it exists, is also at risk of being sacrificed for quantitative goals such as augmenting the sheer number of places and hours despite newly introduced quality management procedures. While Germany surely lacks full-time facilities and childcare is expensive for Dutch parents, recent policy proposals tend to throw out the baby with bath-water and unnecessarily restrict parents' time with their children.

One main conclusion, therefore, is that policy discourse does not always result in coherent practical policies, and the instrumental attitude of the latter ignores the wishes of (to-be) families. Another conclusion is that family life is obviously less 'makeable' than policy makers tend to assume. For instance, even now fees for childcare are profitable for low-income parents, who get significant reductions; these parents seldom make use of childcare provisions. Also, the newly established earnings-related 'Swedish style' parental leave in Germany and the life course saving scheme in The Netherlands may reach the opposite result by encouraging discontinuous employment of the better-off married mothers, including those higher qualified. Therefore, the question remains whether and how social policies can meet dilemmas and uncertainties which shape young adults' ideas about having children. How then, if at all, can welfare states influence young people's attitudes towards having children?

If, indeed, young adults nowadays face the dilemmas we have outlined above, that is having to balance autonomy, emotional bonding and guiding newborns as equals within a confusing and increasingly diverse society on the one hand and behaving rationally, being cost aware and calculating on the other, politicians face an enormous socio-cultural, economic and demographic challenge. Reconciling work and family life, social investments, leave schemes and childcare policies are only part of the solution if good personal relations with kin and kids are felt to be important, if quality of life is in competition with careers and if social and economic security is experienced to be a precondition for family formation. Children are 'dear' for young adults in the full sense of the word. They may consider costs and careers, but neither lack nor plenty of means or opportunities explain attitudes towards having children. The ongoing discourse on costs and family failures, however, may further deter reluctant people from having and raising children. Others will perhaps make their decision on having children conditional on receiving public support. We said the 'cost' discourse in combination with the warning of risks and burdens can trigger more ambivalence and insecurity, hence initiate some vicious circles: telling young adults – women and men – about the threatening aspects of parenthood, blaming them for potential failures, while at the same time messaging that 'adulthood' comes along with work rather than with parenthood, will turn parenthood into an unattractive status. Instead, children should enter the public agenda in attractive ways, as welcome heirs of a good society, as the best reminder of our worth as human beings and as those who will keep our society alive and livable. The dilemmas of parenthood cannot be denied nor should they be presented as solvable by the state, but instead framed as a contribution to one's personal development and as the glue of social and generational networks.

NOTES

1. Our selection of cases follows a combination of two analytic approaches: the 'method of difference' and the 'method of agreement' (Skocpol & Somers, 1980, p. 184). The first approach assumes differences in policies and in the degree of policy change despite institutional similarities between our countries; the second approach presupposes remarkable differences between Germany and The Netherlands with regard to the foundations of their welfare states, but similar outcomes, similar family-related policies and arguments for policy change as a phenomenon to be explained. For each case, we identify in the end the crucial factors that help account for unexpected outcomes.

2. This is one of the best-selling books by a sociologist in American history, though Riesman can be criticized for his sometimes over-generalized and even teleological arguments.

3. The analysis of the Dutch 'framing' is based on recent social policy measures as well as on the White Paper *Gezinsbeleid* (Family policy, Tweede Kamer, 2005–2006). Several new measures are discussed, such as the Life Course Saving Scheme (*Levensloopregeling*), which represents a shift from collective to private insurance for leave of absence. The study of the German 'framing' relies on Federal Reports on Children and Youth (BMFSFJ, 2002, 2005) and on policy-related experts' proposals for 'sustainable' family policy reforms (BMFSFJ, 2002, 2004, 2006; Bertram et al., 2005; Gruesco & Rürup, 2005; Ristau, 2005; Rürup & Gruescu, 2003). It also uses official comments on family-related jurisdiction (Schwab, 2001, 2006).

4. After unification, the Christian Democrats continued to reject explicitly pro-natalist measures, whereas sections of the Social Democrats re-discovered long-standing notions of social engineering and 'reform eugenics' going back at least to the 1920s. These traditions had influenced socialist family policies in East Germany. The influence of OECD and European Union publications and reform proposals – not to mention the role of politically integer leftist experts like Esping-Andersen as policy advisers – might have been equally important in the rediscovery of the positive sides of pro-natalism and the ways of arguing for it. Its positive image was surely increased by the foundation of the Max Planck Institute (MPI) for Demographic Research in 1996 in Rostock, on the Baltic Coast of East Germany. In our view, the MPI was launched to renew demographic research and discourse not hindered by the burdens of the German past. It is indicative for the still existing trickiness of the population policy issue in Germany that the directors of the Institute's two divisions have been non-Germans, one of them the Swedish demographer Jan Hoem (2001–2004) (http://www.demogr.mpg.de).

REFERENCES

Arber, S., & Attias-Donfut, C. (Eds). (2000). *The myth of the generational conflict: The family and state in ageing societies*. London and New York: Routledge.

Balbo, L. (1987). 'Crazy quilts' rethinking the welfare state debate from a woman's point of view. In: A. Showstack Sassoon (Ed.), *Women and the state. Shifting boundaries of public and private* (pp. 45–71). London: Hutchinson.

Barrett, M., & McIntosh, M. (1982). *The anti-social family.* London: Verso.

Beck, U. (1983). Jenseits von Klasse und Stand? Soziale Ungleichheit, gesellschaftliche Individualisierungsprozesse und die Entstehung neuer sozialer Formationen und Identitäten. In: R. Kreckel (Ed.), *Soziale Ungleichheiten.* Sonderband 2 der Sozialen Welt (pp. 35–74). Göttingen: Schwartz.

Beck-Gernsheim, E. (1983). Vom Dasein für andere zum Anspruch auf ein Stück 'eigenes Leben'. *Soziale Welt, 34,* 192–207.

Bertram, H., Rösler, W., & Ehlert, N. (2005). Zeit, Infrastruktur und Geld: Familienpolitik als Zukunftspolitik. *Aus Politik und Zeitgeschichte, 23–24,* 6–15.

BMFSFJ. (2002). *Elfter Kinder – und Jugendbericht. Bericht über die Lebenssituation junger Menschen und die Leistungen der Kinder – und Jugendhilfe in Deutschland.* Bonn: Bundesministerium für Familie, Senioren, Frauen und Jugend.

BMFSFJ. (2004). *Bevölkerungsorientierte Familienpolitik – ein Wachstums Faktor.* Strategiepapier, Berlin: Bundesministerium für Familie, Senioren, Frauen und Jugend, BDI und IW.

BMFSFJ. (2005). Bericht über die Lebenssituation junger Menschen und die Leistungen der Kinder – und Jugendhilfe in Deutschland – Zwölfter Kinder – und Jugendbericht – (Deutscher Bundestag. 15. Wahlperiode. Drucksache 15/6014: 10.10.2005). Berlin: Bundesministerium für Familie, Senioren, Frauen und Jugend.

BMFSFJ. (2006). *Siebter Familienbericht.* Bonn: Bundesministerium für Familie, Senioren, Frauen und Jugend. [English summary version: Seventh Family Report. *Families between flexibility and dependability – perspectives for a life cycle-related family policy.* Statement by the Federal Government. Results and scenarios of the report drafted by the committee of experts]. Summary. [Internet: www.bmfsfj.de].

Bradshaw, J., & Finch, N. (2002). *A comparison of child benefit packages in 22 countries.* London: Department for Work and Pensions.

Cheal, D. (2002). *Sociology of family life.* Houndmills: Palgrave.

Coleman, J. (1990). *Foundation of social theory.* Cambridge: Belknap Press of Harvard University Press.

Daly, M. (2004). Changing conceptions of family and gender relations in European welfare states and the third way. In: J. Lewis & R. Surender (Eds), *Welfare state change: Towards a third way?* (pp. 135–154). Oxford: OUP.

Daly, M., & Saraceno, C. (2002). Social exclusion and gender relations. In: B. Hobson, J. Lewis & B. Siim (Eds), *Contested concepts in gender and social politics* (pp. 84–104). Cheltenham: Edward Elgar.

Esping-Andersen, G. (2002). A child-centred social investment strategy. In: G. Esping-Andersen (Ed.), *Why we need a new welfare state* (pp. 26–67). Oxford: OUP.

Esping-Andersen, G. (2005). Kinderen in de verzorgingsstaat bezien als maatschappelijke investering. In: J. Berghman, S. Klosse & G. Vonk (Eds), *Kind en sociale Zekerheid* (pp. 16–55). Amstelveen: Sociale Verzekeringsbank.

Finch, J., & Mason, J. (1993). *Negotiating family responsibilities.* London: Routledge.

Forssén, K., & Ritakallio, V.-M. (2006). First births: A comparative study of the patterns of transition to parenthood in Europe. In: A. Hatland & J. Bradshaw (Eds), *Social policy, employment and family change in comparative perspective* (pp. 161–178). Cheltenham: Edward Elgar.

Giddens, A. (1998). *The third way: The renewal of social democracy.* Cambridge: Polity Press.

Grandke, A. (1979). Die Entwicklung von Ehe und Familie. In: H. Kuhrig & W. Speigner (Eds), *Wie emanzipiert sind die Frauen in der DDR?* (pp. 229–253). Köln: Pahl-Rugenstein.

Grandke, A. (2001). Die Familienpolitik der DDR auf der Grundlage der Verfassung von 1949 und deren Umsetzung durch die sozialpolitik. In: G. Manz, E. Sachse & G. Winkler (Eds), *Sozialpolitik in der DDR: Ziele und Wirklichkeit* (pp. 317–336). Berlin: Trafo-Verlag.

Gruesco, S., & Rürup, B. (2005). Nachhaltige Familienpolitik. *Aus Politik und Zeitgeschichte, 6*(23–24), 3–6.

Helwig, G. (1974). *Zwischen Familie und Beruf: Die Stellung der Frau in beiden deutschen Staaten.* Köln: Verlag Wissenschaft und Politik Berend von Nottbeck.

Huinink, J. (2001). Entscheidungs – und Vereinbarkeitsprobleme bei der Wahl familialer Lebensformen. In: J. Huinink, K. P. Strohmeier & M. Wagner (Eds), *Solidarität in Partnerschaft und Familie* (pp. 145–165). Würzburg: Ergon.

Jensen, A. M., & Qvortrup, J. (2004). Summary – a childhood mosaic: What did we learn? In: A. M. Jensen, et al. (Eds), *Children's welfare in ageing Europe* (Vol. II, pp. 813–832). Trondheim: Norwegian Centre for Child Research.

Kaufmann, F. X. (1990). *Zukunft der Familie.* München: Verlag C. H. Beck.

Knijn, T., & Komter, A. (Eds). (2004). *Solidarity between the sexes and the generations.* Cheltenham: Edward Elgar.

Knijn, T., & Kremer, M. (1997). Gender and the caring dimension of welfare states: Toward inclusive citizenship. *Social Politics, 4*, 328–361.

Knijn, T., Ostner, I., & Schmitt, Ch. (2006). Men and (their) families: Comparative perspectives on men's roles and attitudes towards family formation. In: J. Bradshaw & A. Hatland (Eds), *Social policy, employment and family change in comparative perspective* (pp. 179–197). Cheltenham: Edward Elgar.

Knijn, T., & Selten, P. (2002). Transformations of fatherhood: The Netherlands. In: B. Hobson (Ed.), *Making men into fathers. Men, masculinities and social politics of fatherhood* (pp. 168–190). Cambridge: Cambridge University Press.

Kohli, M. (1985). Die Institutionalisierung des Lebenslaufs. *Kölner Zeitschrift für Soziologie und Sozialpsychologie, 37*, 1–29.

Koops, W. (2004). *Het kind als spiegel van de cultuur.* Utrecht: Universiteit Utrecht.

Kremer, M. (2005). *How welfare states care. Culture, gender and citizenship in Europe.* Dissertation. Utrecht University, Utrecht.

Künzler, J. (2002). Paths towards a modernization of gender relations, policies and family building. In: F.-X. Kaufmann, A. Kuijsten, H.-J. Schulze & K. P. Strohmeier (Eds), *Family life and family policies in Europe* (Vol. 2, pp. 252–298). Oxford: Oxford University Press.

Künzler, J., Schulze, H.-J., & Van Hekken, S. M. J. (1999). Welfare states and normative orientations towards women's employment. In: A. Leira (Ed.), *Family policies.* Yearbook of Comparative Social Research. Greenwich: JAI.

Land, H., & Rose, H. (1985). Compulsory altruism for some or an altruistic society for all? In: P. Bean, J. Ferris & D. Wynes (Eds), *In defence of welfare* (pp. 74–98). London: Tavistock.

Leitner, S. (2005). Rot-grüne Familienpolitik: Kind und Karriere für alle? *Blätter für Deutsche und Internationale Politik, 50*(8), 958–964.

Lewis, J. (1992). Gender and the development of welfare regimes. *Journal of European Social Policies, 2*, 159–173.

Majone, G. (1989). *Evidence, Argument and Persuasion in the Policy Process.* New Haven: Yale University Press.

Majone, G. (1993). Wann ist policy – deliberation wichtig? *Politische Vierteljahresschrift* (34, Sonderheft 24) 97–115

Nave-Herz, R. (Ed.) (1988). *Wandel und Kontinuität der Familie in Deutschland.* Stuttgart: Enke.

OECD. (2001). Balancing work and family life: Helping parents into paid employment. In: OECD (Ed.), *Employment outlook* (pp. 89–166). Paris.

OECD. (2002). Women at work: Who are they and how are they faring. In: OECD (Ed.), *Employment outlook* (pp. 61–125). Paris.

Ostner, I. (2004). 'What are children for?': Reciprocity and solidarity between parents and children. In: T. Knijn & A. Komter (Eds), *Solidarity between the sexes and the generations. Transformations in Europe* (pp. 167–184). Cheltenham: Edward Elgar.

Ostner, I. (2006). Paradigmenwechsel in der (west)deutschen Familienpolitik. In: P. A. Berger & H. Kahlert (Eds), *Der Demographische Wandel. Chancen für die Neuordnung der Geschlechterverhältnisse* (pp. 165–199). Frankfurt, a.M.: Campus.

Parsons, T. (1951). *The social system.* New York: The Free Press.

Parsons, T. (1964). *Social structure and personality.* London: Free Press.

Portegijs, W., Boelens, A., & Olsthoorn, L. (2004). *Emancipatiemonitor 2004.* Den Haag: Sociaal en Cultureel Planbureau.

Rademakers, J. (2002). *Abortus in Nederland 1993–2000.* Heemstede: StiSAN.

Riesman, D. (with N. Glazer and R. Denney) (2001/1961). *The lonely crowd.* New Haven/ London: Yale University Press.

Rijken, A. (2006). Fertility rates in Europe: The influence of policy, economy and culture. In: J. Bradshaw & A. Hatland (Eds), *Social policy, employment and family change in comparative perspective* (pp. 143–160). Cheltenham: Edward Elgar.

Ristau, M. (2005). Der ökonomische Charme der Familie. *Aus Politik und Zeitgeschichte*, 6(23–24), 16–22.

Rürup, B., & Gruescu, S. (2003). *Familienpolitik im Interesse einer aktiven Bevölkerungsentwicklung.* Gutachten. Berlin: BMfFSFJ.

Scheiwe, K. (1999). *Kinderkosten und Sorgearbeit im Recht. Eine rechtsvergleichende Studie.* Frankfurt a.M.: Vittorio Klostermann.

Schmidt, M. G. (2004). *Sozialpolitik der DDR.* Wiesbaden: VS Verlag für Sozialwissenschaften.

Schmidt, V. (2000). Values and discourse in the politics of adjustment. In: F. W. Scharpf & V. Schmidt (Eds), *Welfare and work in the open economy* (Vol. 1, pp. 229–309). Oxford: Oxford University Press.

Schmidt, V. (2002). Does discourse matter in the politics of welfare state adjustment? *Comparative Political Studies, 35,* 168–193.

Schneider, N. F. (2002). Elternschaft heute. Gesellschaftliche Rahmenbedingungen und individuelle Gestaltungsaufgaben – Einführende Betrachtungen. In: N. F. Schneider & H. Matthias-Bleck (Eds), *Elternschaft heute. Gesellschaftliche Rahmenbedingungen und individuelle Gestaltungsaufgaben. Zeitschrift für Familienforschung* (pp. 9–21). Sonderheft 2. Opladen: Leske + Budrich.

Schulz, G. (1998). Soziale Sicherung von Frauen und Familien. In: H. G. Hockerts (Hg.), *Drei Wege Deutscher Sozialstaatlichkeit. NS-Diktatur, Bundesrepublik und DDR im Vergleich* (pp. 117–149). München: Oldenbourg.

Schwab, D. (2001). *Familienrecht.* München: C.H. Beck.

Schwab, D. (2006). Ausgeträumt. *Frankfurter Allgemeine Zeitung, 23*(273), 8.

Skocpol, Th., & Somers, M. (1980). The uses of comparative history in macrosocial inquiry. *Comparative Studies in Society and History, XXII,* 174–197.

Ter Velde, E. R. (1991). *Zwanger worden in de 21ste eeuw: Steeds later, steeds kunstmatiger.* Utrecht: Oratie Universiteit.

Theil, S. (2006). Beyond babies. *Newsweek, 147*(September 4), 51–55.

TK. (2003–2004). Wijziging van de Wet Inkomstenbelasting 2001, de Wet op de Loonbelasting 1964 en enkele sociale zekerheidswetten c.a. (Levensloopregeling). Tweede Kamer, vergaderjaar, 29208, nrs. 1–3.

TK. (2005–2006). *Gezinsbeleid.* Tweede Kamer, vergaderjaar, 30512.

Trappe, H. (1995). *Emanzipation oder Zwang? Frauen in der DDR zwischen Beruf, Familie und Sozialpolitik.* Berlin: Akademie Verlag.

Van Berkel, R., & Hornemann Møller, Y. (Eds). (2002). *Active social policies in the EU. Inclusion through participation?* Bristol: Policy Press.

Van Praag, C. S., & Niphuis-Nell, M. (Eds). (1997). *Het Gezinsrapport.* Rijswijk: Sociaal en Cultureel Planbureau.

Van Setten, H. (1986). *In de Schoot van het Gezin.* Nijmegen: SSN.

Weeda, I. (1989). *Samen Leven. Een gezinssociologische Inleiding.* Leiden: Stenfert Kroese.

Wyness, M. (2006). *Childhood and society. An introduction to the sociology of childhood.* Houndmills: Palgrave.

PART II:
CHILDREN IN AN AGEING SOCIETY

CHANGES IN CHILDREN'S AGE AND GENERATION MOSAICS: CHALLENGES TO RESEARCH AND POLICY

Gunhild O. Hagestad

BACKGROUND: A DEMOGRAPHIC REVOLUTION

For much of history, children have constituted nearly half of human populations. The twentieth century marked a tidal turn in population composition for many societies. By the beginning of the current century, a number of societies had only 15% children under age 15 and nearly twice as high a proportion of individuals aged 60 and over (UN, 2007). Japan tops the statistics, having 28% old people and 14% children. With Japan as the only exception, the twenty "oldest" populations, with median ages of 39–42, are all in Europe. In sharp contrast, some countries in Asia and Africa have less than 5% of their populations aged 60 and over. Twenty-seven of these countries have median ages under 18. The lowest figure is found in Uganda, where the median is 14.8. In 2007, the proportion of children in the overall population of Africa is 41%, while individuals aged 60 and over constitute 5.3% (UN, 2007).

In many European societies, women can now expect to live more than 80 years. While more individuals reach a ripe old age, fewer children are born.

Childhood: Changing Contexts
Comparative Social Research, Volume 25, 113–132
ISSN: 0195-6310/doi:10.1016/S0195-6310(07)00004-X

The combination of mortality and fertility decline has dramatically shifted the balance between young and old, both on a societal and a family level. And yet, many aspects of this change remain unexplored.

Discussions of this demographic revolution have suffered from what I would call *generational myopia*. Consequences have typically only been seen in relation to certain age- and generation groups, whereas interdependence and interconnections across groups have been neglected. Population ageing has primarily been discussed in terms of consequences for old people, and to a much lesser extent for children. Often, it has been assumed that the old and the young are in competition for resources, and that the young become losers in ageing societies (e.g., Jensen, 2006; Preston, 1984).

In this paper, I first provide a brief overview of how age structures have been reshaped in modern societies and within family lineages. Second, I outline how we have experienced parallel and related changes in the organisation of daily lives and the course of lives. Of particular interest is the extent to which new institutional and spatial arrangements have led to changes in children's networks and socialisation experiences. In the third section, I outline some issues that need to be addressed in political as well as research discourse. Here, I suggest that rather than viewing old and young as competitors for resources, we instead see them as the *book-end generations* (Generations United), who may have more in common than is commonly recognised. First, however, some conceptual distinctions need to be drawn.

VERTICAL VIEWS: AGE AND GENERATION

The present discussion addresses three phenomena that are commonly assigned the term generation. First, there is what I prefer to label *age group* or *age category*: individuals who are in a given life phase, such as childhood, youth or old age. Second, there is *historical generation*, i.e. a set of birth cohorts that share certain characteristics. The third phenomenon is *position in a system of ranked descent* within the family. For this, I reserve the term generation. In many languages, the word child is used for two of these phenomena: it may refer to an age category or position in a family. In the second case, we often hear terms that sound like an oxymoron: adult children. The three concepts outlined above help us distinguish vertical connections between individuals with different anchoring in dimensions of time, most importantly historical time and biographical time/chronological age, but also in the rhythm of family time (Hareven, 1977). The three concepts raise important methodological issues. Not only in media presentations, but also in survey and sampling designs, it is often implicitly assumed that the three phenomena are "in step". For example, one encounters statements about "today's grandmother generation". In reality, grandmothers may range in age from the early thirties to the nineties and represent radically different historical experiences. They can be the oldest generation in a three-generational structure, or they may have two generations above them in a five-generation structure.

With regard to generations in the family, the problems of *anchoring* and *asymmetry* must be heeded (Hagestad, 2001). If we are discussing generational structures, it is of utmost importance to specify *whose* families we are focusing on: children, adults or old people. The structures look different from "the top–down" and "the bottom–up". For example, if we are interested in how common four- and five-generation units are, the figures will vary by where we anchor. We are here touching on the problem of asymmetry. While many lineages still are relatively "bottom-heavy", with more grandchildren than grandparents, altered fertility and mortality patterns have created increasingly symmetrical family lines, with about equal numbers of children and parents, and grandchildren and grandparents. Several authors have suggested that since parental and grandparental time, attention and material resources are finite entities, increasing symmetry of children and adults in family units leads to an intensification of ties, and each child receives more adult resources (e.g., Blake, 1989; Harper, 2005; Zajonc, 1976) than in more traditional, bottom-heavy structures.

An overview of current knowledge regarding generational structures of families will reveal that it is much easier to find information anchored in old people than it is to find similar data for children. The same goes for studies of contact and exchanges across generations. We know much more about how often old individuals see at least one grandchild than about how often children spend time with a grandparent. The underlying assumption seems to be that such cross-generational contact is more significant for the old than for the young, but this assumption has rarely been put to empirical tests. My own research, both in the United States and Norway, suggests that the reverse may indeed be the case. Asymmetry could be a part of this: A grandchild has only one maternal grandmother, but the grandmother may have six grandchildren. Possibly, the lack of knowledge about cross-age and generational ties of children also reflects privatisation, discussed below. The nuclear family home is the key arena for most children, and the key figure within it the mother. In the case of old people, the parent–child tie is still pivotal, but typically, the children also have children, and we cannot escape the need to consider at least three generations.

In contrast to studies of middle-aged and old people, research on children and their families tends to take a truncated, nuclear view, focusing on only two contiguous generations. We have quite limited knowledge about the wider cross-age and intergenerational ties of children, inside and outside the family realm. This is striking and unfortunate, since the most dramatic increase in the availability of vertical ties has occurred among the young. For example, among individuals who survived to old age a century ago, most had grandchildren, as is the case today. However, among young children, the proportion with a full set of grandparents increased seven-fold over the last 100 years (Uhlenberg, 1996).

A recent comprehensive European study of children's welfare, encompassing 13 countries, COST A 19 (Jensen, Kjørholt, Qvortrup, & Sandbæk, 2006) set out to be an exception by focusing on children in ageing societies, but most of the national reports pay limited attention to what altered age distributions actually mean for children's lives.

SHIFTING VERTICAL MOSAICS

Vertical Structures

As was outlined above, a number of European populations currently have about equal proportions of children and people over 65. By 2050, the old will outnumber children by a ratio of two to one in most of them. If fertility patterns remain unchanged, Italy may have four old people per child at that point. On the micro-level of the family, horizontal ties, *within* generations (to siblings, cousins) are shrinking and becoming increasingly age homogeneous, while vertical ties along generational lines are more durable, complex and heterogeneous than ever before in history. We have, indeed, witnessed a *verticalisation of family life*. Families with a generational structure that resembles a column, and top-heavy family lines, with more grandparents than grandchildren, are increasingly common. As Jensen et al. (2006) put it: today's children have more grandparents than siblings. From the perspective of children, a decline in family size and three-generation households has also lead to less age diversity in their households. However, beyond the household, young people have grandparents and great-grandparents available to an unprecedented degree. Thus, most children and youth in contemporary ageing societies have access to a restricted range of non-peers in their daily family life, but have a potential network of kin that is much more age-heterogeneous than was the case for children earlier. A brief caveat is necessary here. Some readers might miss a discussion of divorce and family reconstitution, as well as childbearing among single women. Space does not allow me to do justice to these topics in this brief chapter. It is important to recognise, however, that marital endings, remarriage and step-families are not historically new. The main change is that while in the past, mortality was the main cause of marital endings, divorce is now the main force behind reorganisation of children's families.

While no countries seem to have good historical data on the availability of grandparents in the past, Uhlenberg (1996, 2005) has used population parameters for the United States to estimate that in 1900, as few as 6% of 10-year-olds had all four grandparents living. He has further estimated that as late as 1940, only about 14% of 10-year-olds had four grandparents (Uhlenberg, 2007). By 1990, the proportion was 40%. This figure is strikingly similar to that emerging from a recent survey in Norway. In 2004, 41% of children aged 10–12 had a full set of grandparents (Hagestad, 2006).

Effects of Co-Longevity

Altered mortality patterns have also given links between grandparents and grandchildren an unprecedented *duration*, providing the potential for long-term, stable ties. At the time when the 1980 cohort of Norwegian children turned 16, more than a fifth had all four grandparents living (Jensen et al., 2006), and 95% had at least one living grandparent. A British study found that 80% of 20-year-olds had at least one grandparent (Grundy, Murphy, & Shelton, 1999). Data from the OASIS study, which includes urban samples of adults from England, Germany, Israel, Norway and Spain, showed that about one third of individuals in their thirties were still grandchildren (Hagestad & Herlofson, 2007).

Yet another result of lowered adult mortality is the role of middle-generation parents as mediators or gatekeepers for relationships between grandparents and grandchildren, widely discussed in studies of modern grandparenthood. Under conditions of high mortality, there was often no surviving mother to serve as a "bridge" or "kinkeeper". Of course, this position also opens the possibility of the middle generation making connections problematic between the young and the old, as has been often reported in studies of divorce and intergenerational ties.

With today's survival patterns, a substantial part of the grandparent role is to continue being a parent, providing support to adult children and their offspring. Consequently, many of the contributions made by grandparents to grandchildren are indirect, through the middle generation (Hagestad, 2006). Under high fertility conditions, there was often competition between the roles of parent and grandparent, as many families had children and grandchildren who were the same age. It is interesting to note that in contemporary patterns of marital dissolution and family reconstitution, men are more likely to have "old-fashioned" ties to descendants, both with regard to bottom-heavy structures and with grandchildren and children who are age peers.

MODERN LIVES: SEGREGATED AND PRIVATISED?

A view of children in ageing societies presents several apparent paradoxes. At a time when they are clearly outnumbered by adults in society, children may have daily access to a narrower spectrum of adults than in earlier historical times. Here, we need to move beyond demography and consider other types of social change. Two other trends that have reshaped the social worlds of children are highlighted here: the emergence of an institutionalised life course and the privatisation of childhood. As Jensen and Qvortrup (2006) note: contemporary childhood is both institutionalised and privatised.

Childhood in the Institutionalised Life Course

Starting with Cain (1964), and continuing with several other sociologists (e.g., Kohli, 1986; Riley & Riley, 1994) it has been argued that in urban-industrial, ageing societies, life scripts are structured into three main "acts", a tripartite life course. This tripartition emerged as states adopted rules using chronological age to prevent child labour, requiring children's school attendance and entitling older persons to pensions. Such structuring of biographical time is part of a societal division of labour, a process of "matching people and roles" (Riley, Johnson, & Foner, 1972). For individuals, the socially created life course has two somewhat competing functions: it both protects and constrains. The tension between protection and opportunity versus constraints emerged in a thought-provoking study of children in national constitutions (Boli-Bennett & Meyer, 1978). The content analyses revealed that in "old" states, education was presented as a *duty* linked to age. On the other hand, new nations in the developing world treated it as a *right*. Leisering (2004) notes that children constituted the first age group to be selected for welfare policies, through nineteenth-century laws aimed at preventing child labour. Laws stipulating mandatory schooling soon followed, and during the same century, retirement was introduced as a social institution for the old.

In the tripartite life course, the first segment is centred on preparation and education, the second on family building and work, and the last on retirement. Authors who have argued that the segmentation entails age constraints (Leisering, 2004; Riley & Riley, 1994; Settersten, 1999) suggest that age-group policies may give rise to age divisiveness and ageism. Recently, critical lenses have been focused on how the organisation of the life course is linked to age segregation, which in turn affects social networks and socialisation experiences, especially for the young and the old (Hagestad & Uhlenberg, 2005, 2006).

Age Segregation: Institutional, Spatial and Cultural

In my own work, I have recently explored how the segmentation of individual life trajectories leads to institutional, spatial and cultural *segregation* of persons who are in different age groups. Today, children and youth are channelled into day care and schools where they spend most of the day with a narrow band of age peers. Age segregation of spaces where routine daily activities take place is, to a large extent, a consequence of age segregation in social institutions. Institutional practices explain why the school environment for children and adolescents is so age homogeneous and why young and old people are seldom found in work environments. Recreational activities of young, adults and old also tend to occur in different locations, because age is used to organise them (e.g., youth clubs, children's choirs, senior centres). For adults, days are anchored in work settings that exclude the young and the old. Older people, who have limited access to school and work sites, are expected to live retired lives of leisure in their own separate arenas. In the United States, many popular residential communities for retirees explicitly exclude children from the premises. Last year, European press reported the development of such a community in Scotland. According to the reports, it has long waiting lists.

In the course of the 1970s and 1980s, sociologist James Coleman provided thought-provoking discussions of changing social contexts for children and youth. He argued that never in history before the twentieth century have the young been largely separated from the ongoing productive activities of society (Coleman, 1982). Like Lofland (1968), who spoke of "youth ghettos" surrounding residential colleges, Coleman argued that modern age-group structuring leads to spatial separation of age groups and historical generations. Institutional age segregation creates a situation in which parents' productive work – indeed, major portions of their adult lives – are carried out in settings where there are no children. In Coleman's view, this arrangement produces adults with less tolerance and understanding towards children, and children who do not get to know a variety of adults and observe their lives. Coleman chaired a Presidential Commission on Youth and presented its conclusions (Coleman, 1974). The report suggested that much because of age segregation, the transition to adulthood in North America becomes discontinuous, requiring skills, orientations and insights that the young person has not had opportunities to acquire.

In a recent address to sociological colleagues, Uhlenberg (2007) stated:

> Old people are rarely the care providers in pre-schools, the teachers in schools, the coaches of recreation league teams, or the counsellors at children's camps. If they thought about it, children, as they go about their daily activities, might well ask: "where are the old people?" But children probably do not think about it because it is so taken for granted that our social institutions designed to care for children largely exclude older people.

Changes in what we might call the ecology of childhood have roots in more than institutional and spatial segregation based on age. Additional changes, especially in urban public space, have intensified shifts in the landscapes and social worlds of children.

Beyond Age Segregation: Privatisation

New divisions of space is a central theme in a current discourse on privatisation of childhood (Conti & Sgritta, 2006; Jensen & Qvortrup, 2006), building on wider scholarly discourse on the separation of family and work, changes in boundaries between public and private space and individualisation. Recent work has concluded that these processes also affect children. Specifically, it is argued that more of children's lives are being constrained to their homes, and within their home, to their own private quarters – their bedrooms. One German scholar speaks of *Verhäuslichung* (Zinnecker, 2001), while a colleague uses Ariès (1978) metaphor of islands and speaks of *Verinselung* (Zeiher, 2001). In Ariès perspective, the automobile and television (spoken before the advent of personal computers!) have significantly contributed to a fragmentation of urban landscapes and human activities. He declares: "The urban conglomerate has become a mass of small islands – houses, offices and shopping centers – all separated from one another by a great void. The interstitial space has vanished" (Ariès, 1978, p. 233). He further argues that in the first part of the twentieth century, the new private family was kept in check by vital community life, both in urban and rural areas. In the second half, the individual home became a retreat: "People return to their homes, as turtles withdraw into their shells" (*ibid.*). Continuing his vivid imagery, Ariès states: "when a family leaves the house to do something that cannot be done at home, they go in a mobile extension of the house, namely, the car. As the ark permitted Noah to survive the flood, so the car permits its owners to pass through the hostile and dangerous world outside the front door" (*ibid.*, p. 234). Ariès links what he calls "overexpansion of the family role" to declining city communities.

In the recent studies on children in ageing societies, authors from several countries emphasise that privatisation is related to the loss of accessible and safe public space. In a statement quite similar to those made by Ariès, a respondent in an Italian survey (Tonucci, 1999, quoted in Conti & Sgritta, 2006) says: "Today the city is synonymous with traffic, noise, danger and people cannot wait to get back into their houses ... The home instead is their refuge and tranquility. It has become in effect the small city, but only because the real city has disappeared, it is dead" (Conti & Sgritta, 2006, p. 310). The respondent touches on major points in contemporary descriptions of public space: the fragmentation of city landscapes has made urban contexts *unfamiliar*; in the double sense of the word, traffic is hazardous, and mass media reports of child abductions and roaming paedophiles have created a climate of fear and insecurity. Even in rural areas, some of these fears prevail. Although traffic is different from that in cities, there are common reports that cars and large trucks travelling at high speed make roads unsafe for pedestrians and bicyclists of any age. Increasingly, children's mobility depends on transportation by car – often operated by mothers. In the United States, a popular "bumpersticker" has the inscription: "If a woman's place is in the home, why am I spending my day in the car?"

Conti and Sgritta (2006) raise an important point when they argue that a correlate of privatisation is the centrality of the mother. Both because of gender roles in family and work, and the prevalence of single motherhood in many societies, the mother becomes the central, if not the only, adult figure for a substantial part of the child's day. She is typically the person who takes the child to school or other age-specific settings, and she spends more time with the child in the privatised home than is the case for the father or other adults. Conti and Sgritta also suggest that when mothers in southern Europe are gainfully employed, the privacy is widened to include the extended family. In such extended care arrangements, grandparents are the pivots. The recent 10-country SHARE study (Survey of Health Ageing and Retirement in Europe), which includes Greece, Italy and Spain, confirms this generalisation (Börsch-Supan et al., 2005).

Authors in the 13-country report on children in ageing societies suggests that to fill the void left by unsafe public spaces, new alternatives have sprung up, such as protected places in which you have to pay for access (Rifkin, 2000). Examples include sponsored after-school play, fast food restaurants, sports or dance lessons. Another, and more central, set of alternatives is offered by new technology: television, mobile phones and a virtual space provided by the computer. All these new technologies are often accessible in the child's own room.

From an age segregation perspective, it is important to recognise that most of the limited access arenas, media worlds or virtual spaces on the World Wide Web offer products and programmes that are carefully tailored to specific age groups and do not present many reference point that transcend age- and generation boundaries. We are now touching on an important point: institutional and spatial segregation are tied to cultural segregation.

Cultural Segregation

Separation by age is reflected and reproduced in cultural contrasts. A central force in such separation is language, which draws us/them distinctions between age categories and marks differences in life styles. When we use words like "youth culture", we recognise distinct contrasts in language, as well as dress, food and music preferences. Marketing capitalises on such differences, and mass media have a commercial interest in maintaining them. Consequently, we find a wide range of magazines, television programs, web sites, and advertisements that target specific age groups and emphasise their distinctiveness, thereby maintaining cultural distance between age groups. Distinct contemporary communication styles are part of an apparent culture of age. Currently, young people who frequently use mobile phones for text messages have their own "SMS language", unintelligible to older outsiders. Of course, many of the cultural contrasts outlined here reflect the fact that when we separate by age, we also separate by cohort, i.e., individuals anchored in distinct historical periods. This is of central importance if we are interested in socialisation experiences, especially for the young and old.

Segregation and the Book-End Generations

A literature search on age segregation reveals that discussions of the topic rarely combine an interest in both young *and* old. Indeed, publications related to the separation of young people have quite a different perspective than those related to older people. The literature on age segregation of children and youth takes a "social problems" perspective, emphasising the *costs* of separation. On the other hand, literature on segregation of older people tends to emphasise *benefits* of separation, particularly residential. In the first case, one finds discussions of juvenile delinquency, troubled families and children with behavioural problems. The second stresses security, simplified service delivery and easy access to peers. My argument would be that there are a number of similarities in effects of age segregation for the young and the old, whom the organisation *Generations United* calls "the book-end generations". Both on a family and a wider community level, the two have some central things in common. Many of the themes surrounding segregation and privatisation apply to old as well as young. The old have also lost comfortable access to public space in the modern "island society". Conti and Sgritta (2006) point to communalities between the book-ends: "a solidarity and an understanding that can transcend age has sprung between two 'weak' segments of the population ... left on the sidelines, they seem to establish a deep understanding with one another based on having different, 'longer' times at their disposal than those of working adults" (p. 296). Being "on the sidelines" has several key aspects. Age segregation blocks opportunities for members of the book-end generations to meet, interact and discover what they have in common. As was implied by Coleman (1982), age segregation is an antecedent as well as a consequence of ageism. Indeed, it can be argued that both phenomena are part of a cycle of reproduction (Hagestad & Uhlenberg, 2005). Institutional, spatial and cultural arrangements maintain or increase ageism, which, in turn, maintains separation.

Segregation limits social networks and embeddedness for both old and young and makes a number of them vulnerable. In addition, it blocks essential socialisation for both groups.

Age and Social Networks

Networks play a key role in integrating individuals of any age into the larger society. Among network members, information and contacts are shared, support exchanged, ways of thinking and seeing the world are fostered, and identities are shaped and sustained. Given the crucial importance of networks, their age composition deserves attention.

A limited amount of research on adults has shown that outside the family realm, social networks are strongly age homogeneous (McPherson, Smith-Lovin, & Cook, 2001). To my knowledge, even less research has been done on non-kin adult ties of children. We simply do not know how many of them have key adult figures, who are sources of security, support and learning, outside the family, and how they became connected to them. My own work on Norwegian children suggests that often, ties to non-kin start with kin. Bonds develop with friends of parents or grandparents. Interestingly, very few children mentioned neighbours.

As was outlined above, the age homogeneity of non-kin social networks reflects how institutional and spatial age segregation restrict the age range in the pool of persons from whom network members can be recruited. Furthermore, because of cultural age segregation, people occupying very different age categories are viewed as having qualities that make them "not like us" and hence unattractive for potential relationships (Bytheway, 1995). Contact and cooperation over time may result in *recategorisation*, a process in which earlier "we/they" distinctions are blurred or eliminated (Anastasio, Bachman, Gaertner, & Dovidio, 1997).

Age and Socialisation

In his classic work on age and social structure, Eisenstadt (1956) noted that age is hierarchical: "the relations between different age grades are necessarily defined in authoritative terms and an adult socializing agent is the first prototype of authority that the child encounters" (p. 29). A similar view of socialisation can be found in Parsons' work (e.g., Parsons, Bales, & Olds, 1955), which describes adult "socialisation agents" in family and education.

Towards the end of the 1960s, two volumes (Clausen, 1968; Goslin, 1969) presented quite a different view. Here, socialisation was defined as a *life-long, reciprocal process*, starting very early in life. The perspective is well expressed in Rheingold's (1969) chapter title: *The social and socializing infant.*

Many authors began to stress that learning of any sort takes place through participation, not through one-way "transmission" from an authority or expert. Recently, Rogoff, Paradise, Mejia, Arauz, Correa-Chavez, and Angelillo (2003) have contrasted what they call *assembly-line instruction* "outside the context of productive, purposive activity" (p. 176) to what they call *intent participation*: "keenly observing and listening in anticipation of or in the process of engaging in an endeavor" (p. 178). They express concern about a shift from the latter to the former type of learning as a result of "historical changes connected with industrialization and child labor laws, which have contributed to compulsory extensive schooling and routine segregation of children from many mature settings" (p. 176). This quote could easily have been taken from Coleman's (1982) discussion of how blocking the young from observing adults at work deprives them of developing knowledge and skills that they will need later. Rogoff et al. recognise that "in the intent participation tradition, experienced people play a guiding role, facilitating learners' involvement and often participating alongside learners – indeed, often learning themselves" (p. 187). "Experienced people" need not be old. They might be 11-year-olds looking for cheap train tickets on the Internet or mastering text messaging, with intent participation by older adults! Those of us who are fortunate enough to have students recognise that through teaching, we learn. Indeed, a number of languages, including Norwegian, use the same verb for both.

Anthropologist Margaret Mead (1970) emphasised the need for intergenerational learning. She argued that in traditional, stable societies, the old have the best grasp of knowledge and skills needed to function as adult members. In modern, rapidly changing societies, on the other hand, the young have a grasp of much of what is needed to master everyday life. Here, she argued, the old need to learn from the young. Mead suggested that old people in changing societies who are not socialised by younger members become *immigrants in time*. The metaphor is an interesting one, since research has shown that in immigrant families, children often serve as interpreters and teachers for parents and grandparents. However, Mead (1974) also recognised that even in modern societies, the grandparental generation, who has witnessed massive changes, is essential for the development of the young, for example, in providing a sense of continuity and hope for the future.

All the authors mentioned above emphasise the importance of settings that facilitate *mutual socialisation* between young and old in ensuring that the young grow up with an awareness of history and cultural heritage and the old "keep up with the times". Thus, segregation deprives both young and old of essential teaching and learning experiences.

In most research on children and their grandparents, the focus has been on what grandparents *give*. Very little research has asked what grandparents *receive*. For example, do they learn from their grandchildren? In our recent interviews with Norwegian 10–12-year-olds, nearly all of them acknowledged learning from their grandparents: practical skills, knowledge about history. However, a majority of the children also said that they had taught the grandparents. The most commonly mentioned example was the use of cell phones and Internet, but the list also included such different skills as new dances, how to change tires, mastering slang, etc. Often, the children spoke with great pride about instructing their grandparents. Many similarly spoke of *helping* grandparents, typically with practical tasks. It may be quite significant that when their parents, members of the middle generation, were asked if their child provided help and learning opportunities for the grandparents, very few said that this was the case!

In the past, large families and relatively age-heterogeneous classrooms gave children responsibilities for non-peers. In today's individualised and privatised worlds of childhood, some children may experience a *responsibility void*, depriving them of the sense that they make a difference to others. In families, grandparents may be a substitute for siblings, both in the exchange of learning and help. Contact with older family members may also aid the development of empathy and patience. Research suggests that when individuals are encouraged to take the perspective of "the other", prejudice and impatience are reduced and new links are forged, as has been demonstrated in training for interactions with disabled persons (Galinsky & Moskowiz, 2000). Such findings would seem highly relevant for children's encounters with older individuals who are frail or disabled.

Beyond Family Generations

As we saw above, the family realm appears to be qualitatively different from other social arenas in providing stable, durable cross-age relationships, which are the source of embeddedness, support and socialisation.

A number of studies have shown that family ties across generations serve to mitigate age-cohort segregation and ageism. There is evidence that family relationships are central in promoting the knowledge of other age groups, and that older family members are judged less stereotypically and more positively than are old strangers (e.g., Caspi, 1984; Newman, Faux, &

Larimer, 1997). As a 7-year-old boy exclaimed: "That's not an old lady – that's my grandma!" The family is also an arena in which key socialisation experiences take place throughout the life course. To summarise, the family is central in counteracting the effects of societal age segregation. Indeed, it can be argued that in modern, ageing societies, it represents the *only* truly, age-integrated social institution.

However, it is unrealistic to think that families can carry the total responsibility for cross-age contact alone. Expecting kin ties to provide the core of age integration will restrict the range of styles, interests and resources available in cross-age interaction. It will also render many children and old people vulnerable because they are "at the mercy" of a restricted range of others in family systems. Having a reserve of adults, not only in intergenerational family ties, but also outside the family, may help fill potential gaps between what children need and what their household, kin network and welfare institutions can provide. Availability of kin in other generations is not universal – for the old or the young. Geographic mobility, psychosocial problems, lack of resources, and variability in family fertility and mortality patterns leave many individuals with a restricted range of potential cross-generational ties.

Beyond the family, strong efforts are necessary to create "spaces where young, middle-aged and older people from all walks of life can get to know each other enough to build mutual respect, develop cooperative relation-ships, and reignite the norm of human-heartedness" (Braithwaite, 2002, p. 332). Currently, such spaces are difficult to find. It will take strong and concerted policy efforts to establish and maintain them. Such efforts will also require a knowledge base, which is currently lacking. Researchers, policy makers and programme coordinators need to join forces to systematically plan, implement and evaluate efforts to facilitate age-heterogeneous networks.

TOWARDS A SOCIETY FOR ALL AGES: RESEARCH AND POLICY CHALLENGES

When the United Nations declared 1999 The International Year of Older Persons, the theme selected was "Toward a society for all ages". The con-ceptual framework and background papers were quite radical in their aim of combating institutional, spatial and cultural age segregation and recognising the interdependence of age groups and generations (Hagestad, 1998).

Few member nations have addressed the policy challenges posed by the organisation; few researchers have attempted to provide the knowledge needed to proceed.

While innovative programmes to promote and facilitate cross-age interaction have been launched in a number of countries (for overviews, see Generations United; Kuehne, 2003; Pennix, 2003), there have been few attempts to systematically evaluate the extent to which they have long-term effects on the forging of relationships. In programme development as well as research, the time dimension must be taken seriously. All too often, efforts aimed at cross-age interactions create brief and quite superficial interactions. To have school children sing carols in the old people's home at Christmas or inviting an old person for one session at the local school to talk about World War II will not do the job of building personal knowledge and viable ties.

Twenty-five years ago, Coleman (1982) proposed the creation of "age balanced organizations," i.e., systems that mirror the age structure of society at large, with nearly all persons spending some time in "productive work", and some time learning. There is a striking convergence between his recommendations, fuelled by concern for the young, and the Rileys' (Riley & Riley, 2000) visions of age integration to accommodate a new old age, which caught ageing societies unprepared. To my knowledge, no nation has directly addressed Coleman's challenge through social policy.

As researchers interested in age, we can begin to build a knowledge base needed by policy makers and NGOs. Demographers have provided the projections on age distributions. We now need to ask what *could* these shifts mean for children? Here, we enter "the sociology of the possible". In his recent address to colleagues, Uhlenberg (2007) states:

> Children are critically dependent upon adults to care for them, so changes in the level of involvement of old people with children could have important consequences. As the number of old people per child in the population doubles over the next several decades, should we expect the amount of time children spend with old people to increase? For example, if the average amount of time an old person spends interacting with children is the same in 2040 as it is now, would children in 2040 not spend twice as much time, on average, interacting with old people as they do now?

In an extension of his work on the age composition of adult networks (Uhlenberg & Gierveld, 2004), he comments that we need detailed data on how many older people interact with children not related to them by kinship, how much time they spend with non-kin children, what the interaction involves and what difference it makes to children and to old people. I would switch the "anchor" and say: We need new knowledge of children's vertical mosaics, inside and outside the family realm. How many adults do they have stable and regular access to? What do the children and the adults exchange? What is the significance of their ties? At what level of social context are intergenerational ties most effectively built and shaped: Society, through welfare policies for young and old? Community, through local policies, programmes and organisations?

Recently, a number of researchers have presented strong warning signals about widening inequalities among children (e.g., Esping-Andersen & Sarasta, 2002; Sørensen, 2005). Most of these discussions focus on financial resources, which in turn affect children's life chances. We now need to widen the focus to include children's social capital beyond the family realm. In an increasingly "top-heavy" age structure, who are the children "vertically rich" or "vertically deprived" with regard to ties that secure contact, support and learning across age and generation lines?

In the recent study of Norwegian grandparenthood, many children spoke of grandparents as a refuge, beyond their own, privatised household. Indeed, they did use a spatial metaphor: it is a *place* I always know I can go to! Such statements were made, even when everyday contact was dependent on cell phones or e-mail. On the other hand, about one out of five children did not feel that they had an intergenerational refuge – within or beyond kinship. Through further analysis, we hope to develop profiles of "vertically deprived" young people and map their distribution across family types, communities and welfare regimes. I invite colleagues to join us in such efforts!

REFERENCES

Anastasio, P., Bachman, B., Gaertner, S., & Dovidio, J. (1997). Categorization, recategorization and common ingroup identity. In: R. Spears, P. J. Oakes, S. N. Ellemer & A. Haslam (Eds), *The social psychology of stereotyping and group life* (pp. 236–256). Oxford: Blackwell.

Ariès, P. (1978). The family and the city. In: A. S. Rossi, J. Kagan & T. K. Hareven (Eds), *The family* (pp. 221–236). York, PA: Norton.

Blake, J. (1989). *Family size and achievement*. Berkeley, CA: University of California Press.

Boli-Bennett, J., & Meyer, J. W. (1978). The ideology of childhood and the state: Rules distinguishing children in national constitutions, 1870–1970. *American Sociological Review, 43*, 797–812.

Börsch-Supan, A., Brugiavini, A., Jürges, H., Mackenbach, J., Siegrist, J., & Weber, G. (Eds). (2005). *Health, ageing and retirement in Europe: First results from the survey of health, ageing and retirement in Europe*. Mannheim, Germany: MEA.

Braithwaite, V. (2002). Reducing ageism. In: T. D. Nelson (Ed.), *Ageism: Stereotyping and prejudice against older persons* (pp. 311–337). Cambridge, MA: MIT Press.

Bytheway, W. (1995). *Ageism*. Buckingham: Open University Press.

Cain, L. D. (1964). Life course and social structure. In: R. E. L. Faris (Ed.), *Handbook of modern sociology* (pp. 272–309). Chicago, IL: Rand-McNally.

Caspi, A. (1984). Contact hypothesis and inter-age attitudes: A field study of cross-age contact. *Social Psychology Quarterly, 47*, 74–80.

Clausen, J. A. (1968). *Socialization and society*. Boston, MA: Little Brown.

Coleman, J. S. (1974). *Youth: Transition to adulthood*. Chicago, IL: University of Chicago Press.

Coleman, J. S. (1982). *The asymmetric society*. Syracuse, NY: Syracuse University Press.

Conti, C., & Sgritta, G. B. (2006). Childhood in Italy: A family affair. In: A. Jensen, A. Ben-Arieh, C. Conti, D. Kutsar, H. M. Ghiolla Phádraig & M. Warming Nilelsen (Eds), *Children's welfare in ageing Europe* (Vol. I, pp. 275–333). Trondheim: Norwegian Centre for Child Research.

COST A 19. http://www.cost.cordis.lu and http://www.svt.ntnu.no/noseb/costa19

Eisenstadt, S. N. (1956). *From generation to generation: Age groups and social structure*. Glencoe, IL: Free Press.

Esping-Andersen, G., & Sarasta, S. (2002). The generational conflict reconsidered. *Journal of European Social Policy, 12*, 5–21.

Galinsky, A. D., & Moskowitz, G. B. (2000). Perspective taking: Decreasing stereotype accessibility and in-group favoritism. *Journal of Personality and Social Psychology, 78*, 708–724.

Generations United. http://www.gu.org

Goslin, D. A. (Ed.) (1969). *Handbook of socialization theory and research*. Chicago, IL: Rand McNally.

Grundy, E., Murphy, M., & Shelton, N. (1999). Looking beyond the household: Intergenerational perspectives on living kin and contacts with kin in Great Britain. *Population Trends, 97*, 19–27.

Hagestad, G. O. (1998). Towards a society for all ages: New thinking, new language, new conversations. *(UN) Bulletin on Aging, 2/3*, 7–13.

Hagestad, G. O. (2001). Adult intergenerational relationships. In: *Gender and generation programme: Exploring future research and data collection options* (pp. 125–143). New York and Geneva, Switzerland: UNECE and United Nations Population Fund.

Hagestad, G. O. (2006). Transfers between grandparents and grandchildren: The importance of taking a three-generation perspective. *Zeitschrift für Familienforschung, 18*, 315–332.

Hagestad, G. O., & Herlofson, K. (2007). Micro and macro perspectives on intergenerational relations and transfers in Europe. In: *Report from United Nations expert group meeting on social and economic implications of changing population age structures* (pp. 339–357). New York: United Nations Department of Economic and Social Affairs/Population Division.

Hagestad, G. O., & Uhlenberg, P. (2005). The social separation of old and young: A root of ageism. *Journal of Social Issues, 61*, 343–360.

Hagestad, G. O., & Uhlenberg, P. (2006). Should we be concerned about age segregation? Some theoretical and empirical explorations. *Research on Ageing, 28*.

Hareven, T. (1977). Family time and historical time. *Daedalus, 106*, 57–70.

Harper, S. (2005). Grandparenthood. In: M. L. Johnson (Ed.), *The Cambridge handbook of age and ageing* (pp. 422–428). Cambridge: Cambridge University Press.

Jensen, A.-M. (2006). Introduction. In: A. Jensen, A. Ben-Arieh, C. Conti, D. Kutsar, M. M. Ghiolla Phádraig & H. Warming Nilelsen (Eds), *Children's welfare in ageing Europe* (Vol. I, pp. 13–17). Trondheim: Norwegian Centre for Child Research.

Jensen, A.-M., Kjørholt, A. T., Qvortrup, J., & Sandbæk, M. (2006). Childhood and generation in Norway: Money, time and space. In: A. Jensen, A. Ben-Arieh, C. Conti, D. Kutsar, H. M. Ghiolla Phádraig & M. Warming Nilelsen (Eds), *Children's welfare in ageing Europe* (Vol. I, pp. 335–402). Trondheim: Norwegian Centre for Child Research.

Jensen, A. M., & Qvortrup, J. (2006). Summary – A childhood mosaic: What did we learn?. In: A. Jensen, A. Ben-Arieh, C. Conti, D. Kutsar, M. M. Ghiolla Phádraig & H. Warming Nilelsen (Eds), *Children's welfare in ageing Europe* (Vol. I–II, pp. 813–830). Trondheim: Norwegian Centre for Child Research.

Kohli, M. (1986). The world we forgot: An historical review of the life course. In: V. W. Marshall (Ed.), *Later life* (pp. 271–303). Beverly Hills, CA: Sage.

Kuehne, V. S. (2003). The state of our art: Intergenerational program research and evaluation (Part I). *Journal of Intergenerational Relationships, 1*, 145–161.

Leisering, L. (2004). Government and the life course. In: J. T. Mortimer & M. J. Shanahan (Eds), *Handbook of the life course* (pp. 205–225). New York, NY: Plenum.

Lofland, J. (1968). The youth ghetto: A perspective on the cities of youth around our large universities. *Journal of Higher Education, 39*, 121–143.

McPherson, M., Smith-Lovin, L., & Cook, J. M. (2001). Birds of a feather: Homophily in social networks. *Annual Review of Sociology, 27*, 415–444.

Mead, M. (1970). *Culture and commitment: A study of the generation gap.* Published for the American Museum of Natural History. Garden City, NY: Natural History Press.

Newman, S., Faux, R., & Larimer, B. (1997). Children's views on aging: Their attitudes and values. *The Gerontologist, 37*, 412–417.

Parsons, T., Bales, R., & Olds, J. (1955). *Family: Socialization and interaction process.* Glencoe, IL: Free Press.

Pennix, K. (2003). *De stad van alle leeftijden [A city of all ages].* Utrecht: NIZW Uitgeverij.

Preston, S. (1984). Children and the elderly: Divergent paths for America's dependents. *Demography, 21*, 435–457.

Rheingold, H. L. (1969). The social and socializing infant. In: D. A. Goslin (Ed.), *Handbook of socialization theory and research* (pp. 779–790). Chicago, IL: Rand McNally.

Rifkin, J. (2000). The age of access: The new culture of hypercapitalism, where all of life is a paid-for experience. New York, NY: Tarcher/Putnam.

Riley, M. W., Johnson, M., & Foner, A. (1972). *Aging and society* (Vol. 3). New York, NY: Russell Sage.

Riley, M. W., & Riley, J. W. (1994). Age integration and the lives of older people. *The Gerontologist, 34*, 110–115.

Riley, M. W., & Riley, J. W. (2000). Age integration: Conceptual and historical background. *The Gerontologist, 40*, 266–270.

Rogoff, B., Paradise, R., Mejia, R., Arauz, M., Maricela Correa Chavez, M., & Angelillo, C. (2003). Firsthand learning through intent participation. *Annual Review of Psychology, 54*, 175–203.

Settersten, R. A. (1999). *Lives in time and place: The problems and promises of developmental science.* Amityville, NY: Baywood.

Sørensen, A.-M. (2005). Family structure, gender roles and social inequality. In: S. Svallfors (Ed.), *Analyzing inequality.* Palo Alto, CA: Stanford University Press.

Tonucci, F. (1999). *La città dei bambini*. Bari: Editori Laterza.

Uhlenberg, P. (1996). Mortality decline in the twentieth century and supply of kin over the life course. *The Gerontologist, 36*, 681–685.

Uhlenberg, P. (2005). Historical forces shaping grandparent–grandchild relationships: Demography and beyond. In: M. Silverstein & K. W. Schaie (Eds), *Annual Review of gerontology and geriatrics* (pp. 77–97). New York, NY: Springer.

Uhlenberg, P. (2007). *Children in ageing societies*. The Matilda White Riley Award Lecture. Annual Meeting of the American Sociological Society New York City, August.

Uhlenberg, P., & Gierveld, J. (2004). Age segregation in later life: An examination of personal networks. *Ageing and Society, 24*, 5–28.

United Nations. (2007). *World population ageing 2007*. New York, NY: Department of Economic and Social Affairs/Population Division.

Zajonc, R. B. (1976). Family configuration and intelligence. *Science, 192*, 227–236.

Zeiher, H. (2001). Children's islands in space and time: The impact of spatial differentiation on children's ways of shaping social life. In: M. du Bois-Reymond, H. Sünker & H. H. Krüger (Eds), *Childhood in Europe. Approaches, trends, findings*. New York, NY: Peter Lang.

Zinnecker, J. (2001). *Stadtkids: Kinderleben zwischen Strasse und Schule*. Weinheim: Juventa.

GRANDCHILDHOOD IN GERMANY AND ITALY: AN EXPLORATION

Wolfgang Keck and Chiara Saraceno

Historically, tight relations between grandparents and grandchildren are a relatively recent phenomenon. The notion of "grandparents" entered into European languages sometime between the sixteenth and seventeenth centuries. Before then, parents of parents were mentioned as ancestors, but a family role was not acknowledged. Even when grandparents appear in biographic essays or in artworks, they are seen as old persons who are considered to be part of the family, but who live detached from the grandchildren and are not viewed as intimate relatives (e.g., Chvojka, 2003). Grandparenthood is a modern concept framed by the bourgeoisie family ideal of the eighteenth and nineteenth centuries, when life expectancy rose sharply and the age of women at marriage decreased (Göckenjan, 2000; Gourdon, 2001). As a consequence, the presence of grandparents became more likely, in particular for the matrilineal line (Chvojka, 2003). However, the "invention of grandparenthood" as a specific role for the parents of parents with children could fully develop only when childhood was acknowledged and protected as a distinct life stage with specific needs (Aries, 1962). In the process, the role of grandparents has been defined (Chvojka, 2003, p. 280ff.; Hugo, 2002 [1877]). Grandchildren, on the other hand, remained conceptually the passive recipients of this role, rather than active agents of it.

The tail end of the first demographic transition and the likely onset of the second transition in the second half of the twentieth century in Europe,

Childhood: Changing Contexts
Comparative Social Research, Volume 25, 133–163
Copyright © 2008 by Emerald Group Publishing Limited
All rights of reproduction in any form reserved
ISSN: 0195-6310/doi:10.1016/S0195-6310(07)00005-1

characterized by a radical change in the age-structure of both the population and kinship, have further fostered and intensified these trends. Demographic aging due to low fertility and increasing life expectancy has, in fact, changed both the configuration and the length of family and kinship relationships. More generations share a longer lifetime together, while the size of the younger generation is smaller. The outcome of this dual process is the so-called beanpole family (Harper, 2006, p. 346). The changing balance of the generations alters the range of intergenerational relationships available to each generation and particularly to children while growing up. It is also likely to affect the content and quality of the relationship between grandchildren and grandparents. Furthermore, increasing life expectancy, which modifies the duration of those relationships, contributes to the experience both of grandparenthood and of grandchildhood as veritable "careers" (Elder, 1985). With their different phases and turning points, marked by the somewhat opposite effect that the aging process has on the two generations, grandchildren grow up and acquire autonomy, competence and roles, whereas grandparents become older and frailer, and their roles become fewer and more limited.

Grandparenthood today may once again seem to be an unclearly defined role, as old images of grandparenthood inadequately fit both its different phases and the fact that many individuals are far from being old when they become grandparents (Gauthier, 2002). Many studies have examined what grandparents contribute to children and grandchildren and, to a lesser degree, how grandchildren affect their life circumstances (Attias-Donfut & Segalen, 1998; Denham & Smith, 1989; Kornhaber, 1996; Smith & Drew, 2002b). In contrast, surprisingly little has been done from the perspective of grandchildren, although their experience is as much, if not more, affected by the aging of kinship ties as that of grandparents (Hagestad, 2006). Grandchildhood as a specific dimension of children's experience and as a family role continues to be under-conceptualized and under-researched.

In this chapter, we specifically take the grandchildren's perspective, using a variety of sources, few of which have been developed with the children's point of view in mind. First, on the basis of the demographic and social research literature, we describe the context in which grandchildhood is experienced and the various shapes it takes across developed countries, particularly in Europe. Second, we distinguish specific modes of possible interaction and exchange between grandchildren and grandparents. Finally, we compare two countries – Germany and Italy – which differ not only in patterns of family formation and relevance of the kinship network, but also in recent demographic history as well as in welfare regimes with regard to the allocation of responsibilities among family and society in providing care and other forms of support. We show how the interplay of these various dimensions shapes distinct patterns of grandchild–grandparent relationships.

THE CHANGING CONTEXT OF INTERGENERATIONAL RELATIONSHIPS

The twentieth century witnessed dramatic changes both in the population and in the family/kinship age-structure, which affected the prevalence, length, and form of relationships between grandparents and grandchildren. Although most European countries share similar trends, there are considerable national peculiarities which have an impact on the experience of grandchildhood.

Demographic aging has been a central theme in public discourses and policy concerns for some time now. It is, however, framed mostly, if not solely, in terms of social policy dilemmas and economic threats (cf. Esping-Andersen, Gallie, Hemerijck, & Myles, 2002; Guillemard, 2000; Palmer & Gould, 1986), or in terms of intergenerational conflicts over societal resources (cf. Binstock & Quadagno, 2001; Esping-Andersen & Sarasa, 2002). The double trend of extended life expectancy and decreased fertility, however, changes foremost the age and intergenerational structure of family and kinship. In 1900, the number of children aged 0–14 in western Europe was about five times higher than the number of persons aged 60 and over. In 2000, there were over 1.5 times more elderly persons than children (European Data Service, 2007; Flora, Kraus, & Pfenning, 1987). The possibility of grandchildren having grandparents as a result of longer life expectancy is in turn partly reduced by the increase in the mother's age at first birth, particularly since the 1980s. For instance, in Germany, women's age at the birth of the first child has increased by 3.8 years from 1980 to 2003; in Italy, it has increased by 3.3 years from 1980 to 1996 (European Data Service, 2007). All in all, however, grandchildren of younger birth cohorts can expect to spend a longer period of their lifetime together with their grandparents than did their older cohorts (Grundy, 1999). This trend holds even for Germany, where the Second World War reduced dramatically the size of male cohorts who might theoretically be (older) grandparents as well as great-grandparents today (Engstler & Menning, 2005).

Because of the long-standing decline in fertility rates, the proportion of grandchildren to grandparents also has changed. A century ago, grandparents with more than a dozen grandchildren were not exceptional, whereas nowadays it is not uncommon for a child to have more grandparents than the other way around. The process is twofold. First, there are fewer grandchildren within each family unit, and, second, because of the reduced size of the parents' generation itself, grandchildren are distributed among fewer family units (Hagestad, 2006; Hondrich, 1999). If early twentieth-century grandparents could hardly keep in mind the names of their gaggle of grandchildren, today's grandparents may have to compete with each other to win the favor of a single grandchild.

Though they share common trends in demographic and social development, regions and nations in Europe differ substantially in the timing and degree to which these developments occurred and still occur (Coleman, 2005). Differences in timing and intensity in fertility patterns, age at marriage, life expectancy, and so forth affect the shape of generations and of generational and intergenerational roles for a long time, because their effects play out for a period lasting at least between 50 and 100 years.[1] Some examples illustrate how this process affects European countries differently. The issue of population aging emerged in France and Sweden at the beginning of the twentieth century, when other national populations were still young because of high fertility and reduced infant mortality (United Nations, 1956). Now France has one of the highest fertility rates in Europe. Age at birth of the first child has always been lower in the Scandinavian countries than in southern Europe. Thus, on average parents in the former countries become grandparents earlier and live longer with their grandchildren than those in the latter countries.

The two world wars also had a major influence on demographic developments, sweeping away a large share of men in specific birth cohorts, eliminating fathers and potential grandfathers. This outcome also led to a gender imbalance in the same and adjacent birth cohorts, which in turn had an impact on marriage behavior. Children born before or during the two world wars, for instance, were subject to a high risk of losing their fathers. Their children, therefore, had no or only one grandfather alive. In the United Kingdom, Benelux, France, and Italy, the First World War played a bigger role in substantially diminishing the male populations of those countries.[2] Austria, Germany, and Russia (USSR) suffered a particularly high rate of war dead in both world wars.[3] As a consequence, in these countries many children born after the Second World War never met some of their grandparents.

In addition to demography, other dimensions have an impact on the experience of being and having a grandparent/grandchild. One of the most important, which has long historical roots, concerns patterns of family formation and of kinship ties. According to John Hajnal's well-known thesis (1982), two broad areas may be identified in Europe on the basis of three criteria: prevalence of the nuclear, rather than the complex, family; degree of universality of marriage; and age at marriage for women. East of the ideal line that ran from St. Petersburg to Trieste, in what Hajnal called the Eurasian marriage pattern, the incidence of complex (stem or joint) households has been substantial for many centuries. Marriage was also virtually universal, and the age at marriage for women was lower than in western European countries. The complex household was nearly absent in western European regions and countries such as Scandinavia, the Netherlands, England, and northern France. It was present – mostly in the form of the stem family, as observed by Frédéric Le Play (1855) – in southern Austria, some parts of Germany, and the rural areas of northern and central Italy, but not in southern Italy. More recently, Sven Reher (1998) has pointed to an additional diversity in family structure: the relevance of embeddedness into kinship ties. In the Mediterranean countries, irrespective of the household structure (nuclear, stem, or extended), households have traditionally been embedded in a dense kinship network. These differences persist even today, notwithstanding the prevalence of nuclear households throughout Europe (Saraceno, 2007; Saraceno, Olagnero, & Torrioni, 2005). In Sweden, there were more elderly people living alone in the 1960s than there were in Italy in 1990 (OECD, 1994). Complex families are present more in eastern European countries than in western and Nordic ones. And in southern Europe, children and grand-children generally live closer to their parents and grandparents than children and grandchildren do elsewhere (Börsch-Supan et al., 2005). Because of this proximity between grandchildren and grandparents, contacts are more frequent in southern Europe, though this does not mean that they are more emotionally intense than in other countries (Ringen, 1987; Rothstein, 2001).

The different roles historically assigned to kinship ties and obligations in different parts of Europe interplay with the way in which welfare state arrangements in contemporary times implicitly or explicitly have institutio-nalized or ascribed these obligations, particularly in the area of financial support and care-giving. From this perspective, Mediterranean welfare regimes have been defined as regimes based on extended family obligations, thus having a high degree of "familialization" (Naldini, 2003; Saraceno, 2003), whereas Scandinavian regimes have been characterized as highly "de-familialized" and the Continental regimes as somewhat in between (Esping-Andersen, 1999; Etzioni, 1993; McLaughlin & Glendinning, 1994).

These different degrees of familialization have an impact on the behaviors of and exchanges between generations. This impact has been studied mostly with regard to support provided to the older generation. But there is also an impact on support provided to the younger generation not only by parents but also by grandparents, particularly in the form of childcare for young grandchildren (cf. Blome et al., 2008; Attias-Donfut & Segalen, 1998).

Whatever the welfare regime, the present cohorts of grandparents in western Europe are the main beneficiaries of the "glorious thirties," that prosperous period in Europe characterized by a growing economy and development of the welfare state (Alber, 1982; Therborn, 2000). On average, they experienced a lasting increase of wealth, which was secured in old age by expanded pension systems. These developments are accompanied by a longer healthy life expectancy due to better eating habits, overall improved living conditions, and improved health services. As a consequence, older people in western Europe are on average healthier and wealthier than ever before.[4] The situation of grandparents has changed from receivers of resources to givers of resources (Denham & Smith, 1989). Compared to their counterparts in the early twentieth century, today's grandparents have on average more capabilities to take over an "active" grandparent role (Höpflinger, Hummel, & Hugentobler, 2006).

Contrary to the above-mentioned developments which foster intergenerational relationships, some changes in living conditions and opportunities may affect negatively the relationship between grandchildren and grandparents. Many younger grandmothers are now in paid employment and might have the same difficulties in reconciling employment and family obligations as their daughters and daughters-in-law (Attias-Donfut, Ogg, & Wolff, 2005). Furthermore, retirement itself is increasingly conceptualized and anticipated as an active life phase with many opportunities for individualization. This development is supported by a growing economic market targeted to the "active young elderly." Although there are important class and cultural differences, "empty nest" parents and grandparents, at least as long as they are well and healthy, generally tend to live more autonomously and independently from their extended family than in the past (Lin & Rogerson, 1995).

Last but not least, the higher incidence of family dissolution changes in many cases the opportunity structure for developing relationships between grandparents and grandchildren. In case of divorce and separation, ties with the parents of the noncustodial parent – usually the paternal grandparents – risk weakening, while relations may become even tighter with the family of the parent with whom the child lives (Rossi & Rossi, 1990; Smith & Drew, 2002a). If the parents re-partner, and particularly if they have other children, children may gain step-grandparents. The relationship between step-grandchildren and step-grandparents, however, usually is characterized by fewer contacts. Step-grandparents often consider such a relationship less important than the ties to their own grandchildren, though there is wide variation in this respect, because step-grandparenthood is even less defined, as a family role, than step-parenthood (Hawker, Allan, & Crow, 2001; Sanders & Trygstad, 1989).

Another factor which might be perceived as a barrier between the older and the younger generations is rapid technological progress and social change. The image of old-fashioned grandparents became prominent in the nineteenth century, and was associated with the industrial revolution and urbanization in Europe (Höpflinger et al., 2006). Since then, the store of knowledge has doubled in ever shorter periods, and daily routines have become more and more connected to complex social and technological processes. The extent and speed of this change might make it difficult for the older generation to keep pace with the developments. Access to the Internet is one example of a possible technological divide between the old and the young, grandparents and grandchildren, particularly adolescent or young adult grandchildren with older grandparents. Precisely this divide, however, might offer grandchildren the opportunity to be those who transfer and not only receive knowledge. Interestingly, the scarce literature on the active role that grandchildren play with respect to their grandparents addresses to a large degree this specific aspect: grandchildren teach their grandparents how to use the computer or Internet (Brunowsky & Kubenz, 2006).

EXCHANGE PATTERNS BETWEEN GRANDPARENTS AND GRANDCHILDREN

Most studies focus on the grandparents' rather than the grandchildren's perspective. Moreover, even from this perspective, the exchanges between grandparents and grandchildren are often hidden within the exchanges between the former and their own children, that is, the grandchildren's parents. Such is the case, for instance, with the financial and other support that parents provide to their own adult children. This support, of course, affects the living conditions of grandchildren, but it is rarely, if ever, conceptualized as such. From the studies that focus on the grandparents' perspective and on exchanges between grandparents and their adult children, we can, however, gain some insight also on the exchanges and relations between grandparents and grandchildren. Studies generally distinguish between three types of interaction: direct, indirect, and symbolic (Denham & Smith, 1989).

Direct interaction comprises quite different exchange modes between grandparents and grandchildren. The most visible one is instrumental and material support in the form of the provision of money or care. But what grandparents do with and for their grandchildren when they interact directly is more comprehensive. When grandparents spend time with their grandchildren – even when this time is framed as generic "care" – they provide cognitive and social stimulation and represent observational models for the child (Kornhaber, 1985). For growing grandchildren, grandparents may be consultants and advisors. They can help with homework, discuss social and personal problems with them, offer emotional support, act as an intermediary between children and parents, and offer different opportunities to explore the world (Cochran & Brassard, 1979).[5]

Indirect interaction occurs when direct exchanges involve grandparents and grandchildren's parents. A large part of the cash flowing from grandparents downwards is not granted to the grandchildren directly, but does support their parents and therefore indirectly helps with the expenses for their children (Kohli, 1999). Analogously, when a grandmother helps the mother with household chores, indirectly she is allowing the latter to spend more time with her child, or in any case she is easing part of her workload and thus reducing time pressures in the child's household. Furthermore, grandparents can act as mediators in family conflicts (Denham & Smith, 1989).

The third aspect of grandparents' relation with their grandchildren is symbolic. The fact that grandparents "are there" and form a part of the family contributes to a different and in some sense richer family life. Grandparents take a specific position within the family which affects children's experience. In a study by Francois Höpflinger et al. (2006), the most frequently mentioned expectation towards grandparents is that they be available and have time for the grandchildren. "Being there" is considered important by 80% of the grandchildren and 97% of the grandparents. Grandparents, moreover, embody the family memory, its roots in the past, while introducing to younger family members the experience of aging not only as "growing up" but also of "getting old and frail." Their presence makes clear the multiple forms of obligations and membership (two sets of grandparents, two family histories) which constitute a family's and an individual's specific history. These aspects are important, particularly when both the grandparent and the grandchild careers may last many years and go through different phases, therefore requiring and enabling continual reflexive re-elaboration. Empirical evidence is scanty and is likely to be found more in memoirs and novels than in research. Yet, as Denham and Smith (1989) have pointed out, "intergenerational researchers concur that grandparents are more than their questionnaire or interview data can demonstrate."

Of course, not all of what happens between grandparents and grandchildren corresponds with this rosy picture. Grandparents are not always in the position to provide support; sometimes, in fact, they require support from their children to a degree that more or less negatively affects the financial resources or time available for their grandchildren. Bad feelings between grandparents and their children may affect negatively the relationship with their grandchildren. Grandparents may have a bad temper, or be emotionally distant or authoritarian persons. Grandparents, like all people, come in different sizes and shapes (see Attias-Donfut, 2001; Gauthier, 2002; Kemp, 2007). In a Swiss study, 82% of the interviewed grandchildren said they like their grandparents because of their positive characteristics. But 38% mentioned that they dislike their grandparents because of their negative behavior and morals (Höpflinger et al., 2006, p. 54).[6] Grandparents' authority is seen as interference and perceived as a form of distrust in the grandchildren's own abilities by 34% of the grandchildren.

Furthermore, grandparents might have a very different position in the family according to their line of relationship. Given the gender division of labor, conflicts over the proper way to organize family life are usually more frequent between grandmothers and daughters-in-law than between grandmothers and daughters or grandmothers and sons-in-law. This tendency may affect the intensity of the relationship with one or the other set of grandparents, and bring on a multiplicative effect: the privilege accorded to one set of grandparents may increase bad feelings or feelings of exclusion in the other. In contemporary societies, because kin-work and kin-keeping is mostly performed by women, kinship relationships are de facto skewed matrilaterally (Attias-Donfut & Segalen, 1998, p. 295; Smith & Drew, 2002a), though there may be local and ethnic subgroups where patrilaterality is instead the cultural norm, as in some Italian regions. Maternal grandparents, and particularly grandmothers, therefore, are generally given priority in contacts and emotional closeness (Dench & Ogg, 2001). The effect is reinforced in that grandmothers in the matrilineal line live on average longer with their grandchildren due to the lower marriage age and higher life expectancy of women. One might suggest that the dominant role of maternal grandmothers for grandchildren may contribute to reproducing over generations the kin-keeper position of women.

If we reverse the perspective, and look at what grandchildren provide for their grandparents and how their presence affects the latter's life and well-being, we are left with very scanty empirical evidence. At the research level, it appears that grandchildren have little to give their grandparents, even in the grandparents' own perception. Yet this apparent tendency is probably to a large degree a function of how the research itself is framed. Most research on intergenerational relationships is focused not only top-down and on two, rather than three, generations. It also is almost exclusively focused on issues concerning financial support and care-giving. Research risks losing grand-children as actors in the relationship altogether, unless they are in the role of carers themselves, which is rare, at least in Europe, if not entirely unusual (see Fruhauf, Jarrott, & Allen, 2006). This under-evaluation of grandchildren as actors and givers in the relationship with their grandparents, even when they are infants, is in sharp contrast with everyday narratives of grand-parents, which show how grandchildren add new dimensions and meaning to the life and experience of the former. This is true not only of family-centered grandparents, nor only of grandmothers. For many grandparents, the arrival of a grandchild, and a relationship with grandchildren as these grow up, opens up worlds of emotions, even in some cases allowing them to recuperate what they missed with their own children (Attias-Donfut, 2001; Herlyn, 2001). Generally, a more active and satisfying life might be the reason why grandparents have on average better health than do their contemporaries without grandchildren (Denham & Smith, 1989). Grandchildren are brokers of relationships not only between their parents and grandparents but also with a wider kin network. Children provide a common ground for communication, even when interests and values may differ.

ITALY AND GERMANY: TWO PARTIALLY DIFFERENT CONTEXTS FOR THE DEVELOPMENT OF GRANDCHILD – GRANDPARENT RELATIONSHIPS

In Germany and Italy, almost all children at birth have living grandparents, and nine in ten grandchildren still have at least one grandparent when they reach adulthood. In Italy, almost one half of grandchildren have living grandparents when they reach their thirties; in Germany, the figure is nearly

one-third. Grandchildhood in both countries seems to be universal, and a majority of young people have grandparents during their entire childhood (see Fig. 1).

The two countries differ, however, with respect to the number of grandparents that grandchildren have, and for how long. In particular, older cohorts of grandchildren in Germany have fewer living grandparents than their counterparts in Italy. We do not know for sure what the reasons for this difference are, but can offer two possible explanations. First, in Germany, older cohorts of grandchildren lack grandfathers because, due to the high death rates of men, the number of women aged 20–35 after the Second World War was 1.4 times higher than that for men, whereas in Italy the ratio remained balanced (1.05 women to every man; European Data Service, 2007). In Germany therefore, the marriage market was favorable for older men who could marry younger women. The age difference between spouses increased. Children, therefore, had relatively old fathers, and grandchildren were more likely to lose their grandfathers before birth or

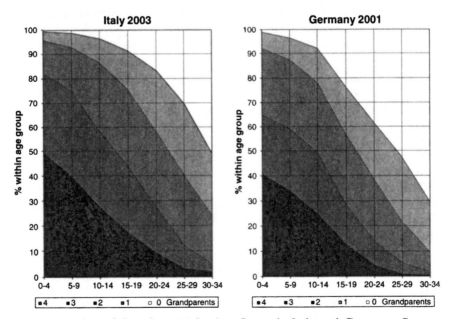

Fig. 1. Number of Grandparents by Age Group in Italy and Germany. *Sources:* For Germany, German Socio-Economic Panel 2001; for Italy, Famiglia e Soggetti Sociali 2003.

soon afterwards. Second, after the war, and for the same reason (gender imbalance in the marriage market), the rate of illegitimate births increased. From 1946 to 1952, more than 9% of births were out of wedlock in Germany, three times as much as in Italy (Flora et al., 1987). These children might not have known their father, or not have had contact with him. Hence, their children might not know whether they have a grandfather.

Other differences between the two countries that might affect the grandchild–grandparent relationship concern patterns of family formation and organization, on the one hand, and welfare state arrangements, on the other. With regard to the former, two dimensions seem to be relevant. First, in Italy children tend to exit the parental household later than in most European countries, including Germany, therefore prolonging well into adulthood habits of sharing and exchanging on an everyday basis. They also tend to live closer to their parents (Barbagli, Castiglione, & Zuanna, 2004; Börsch-Supan et al., 2005). Grandparents thus are more easily accessible than in other countries. Second, in Italy women's employment rate is lower than in Germany (42.7% in 2003 compared to 50%). But part-time employment among women is much more widespread in Germany than in Italy (23.8% compared to 7.4%; Eurostat, 2004). In both countries, women now in the grandparent generation are mostly out of the labor force, either because they retired early or, more often, because they never entered or exited the labor market when young. In both countries, the younger generation of mothers is predominately in the labor market, but at different rates and with a different intensity. Again, in Italy participation is lower (although with wide regional variations),[7] but intensity is greater, as mothers of young children mostly work full time. They therefore require care-provision arrangements that cover many hours a day. However, for children under age three, such arrangements are not always available through local municipalities or through the market.

Welfare state arrangements constitute another difference. The welfare regimes of both countries are structured by the idea of subsidiarity, which defines the family as the primary responsible unit for the welfare of its members. Yet in Italy legal family obligations to provide income support are much more extensive in terms of time and the range of relatives included, going well beyond the boundaries of the nuclear household (Saraceno, 2003). Furthermore, the Italian welfare state remains comparatively under-developed, particularly with regard to the provision of social services and protection from the risks of poverty (Ferrera, 1996; Leibfried, 1993). Care services both for the frail elderly and for very young children (under age three) are scarce, although there are wide regional disparities. Whereas

kindergarten usually is full time and is attended by about 90% of 3–5-year-old children, the elementary school often is part time and children must have their meals at home. Middle school (for 11–13-year-old children) is always part time. Thus, adult children are often called upon to provide care when their parents become frail, and grandparents (more often, grandmothers) are frequently called upon to provide childcare. Childcare services for the very young are scarce in Germany, too, particularly in the western regions, where women traditionally had a lower activity rate than in East Germany and where collective childcare still receives less social and cultural acceptance. Comparable with the situation in Italy, in Germany more than 70% of the schools offer part-time education only and do not provide lunch meals. Thus, both German and Italian mothers experience difficulties in reconciling paid and family work. In Italy, however, women experience greater difficulties because they mostly work full time. On the other hand, due to greater proximity to their or their partner's parents, they have easier (and culturally more legitimate) access to their help.

On the basis of these differences, we expect contacts between grandparents and grandchildren, as well as the experience of being cared for regularly by a grandparent, to be more frequent in Italy than in Germany, and thus to shape partially different modes and experiences of both grandchildhood and grandparenthood.

AN EXPLORATORY EXERCISE

Data and Methods

Looking at the prevalence and intensity of intergenerational relations from a grandchild's point of view poses several challenges. First, there is little information from the children themselves. Usually small children are not considered potential respondents, and even information from adolescents is often gained through their parents. Research on children, but also on adolescents and youth, rarely addresses the issue of their relationship with their grandparents. When it does, it is often restricted to the issue of care. This lack of data from the grandchildren's point of view might in part be explained as a consequence of specific methodological and conceptual difficulties in interviewing children, particularly young ones, or of legal restrictions in interviewing under-age respondents (Kränzl-Nagl & Wilk, 2000). In our opinion, however, it rather derives from the fact that research on childhood (and youth) and research on older people have developed in parallel with little or no interaction.

More specifically, there has been a focus on the relevance of intergenerational relations in research on the elderly and the middle generations, but no such focus in the research on children. Very few studies addressing the specific experience of grandchildhood have been conducted. Second, grandparents as partners in a possible relationship with their grandchildren are often lumped together as a category, without distinction between grandfathers and grandmothers, and between paternal and maternal grandparents. This tendency strongly reduces the informative value of the results. Third, information on the relationship may differ substantially depending on whether it is gathered from the grandparents' or the grandchildren's generation. Differences may concern both the quantity and intensity of exchanges and the meaning attached to them. In the first case, it is an issue not only of perception, but also of a different location in the exchange itself: the number of grandparents that a grandchild has differs from the number of grandchildren that a grandparent has. This difference in standpoint is one reason why data on relations between grandparents and grandchildren could deviate substantially across surveys, depending on whether grandparents or grandchildren are the unit of analysis. But also perceptions may differ (Hagestad, 2006). In the study by Höpflinger et al. (2006, p. 109), grandchildren attribute to the relationship with their grandparents nearly the same importance as their grandparents do. But in the same study, grandchildren more frequently than grandparents express the wish that contacts with the latter be reduced. Furthermore, the study reveals that attitudes towards the grandparents' role differ between the generations. Grandparents, in particular, see themselves as advisers and donors of money more often than grandchildren acknowledge. Fourth, most existing studies focus on contact and care. The few studies which address other dimensions and activities are not only rare, but quite heterogeneous in the conceptualization they use, the items they include, and so forth, thus strongly inhibiting any comparative effort.

In this exploratory study of relationships between grandchildren and grandparents in Germany and Italy, we privilege the grandchildren's perspective, and when the data allow it, we take dyads of grandchildren and grandparents as the unit of analysis. This exercise is admittedly partial, since in existing data sources grandchildren are neither the direct respondents nor the unit of analysis. Specifically, our analysis focuses on grandchild–grandparent relationships for grandchildren who are under 14 years old.

We used four large national surveys to analyze and compare patterns of contact – the only dimension of relationship that is fully comparable with available data taking grandchild–grandparent dyads as the unit of analysis: the Italian ISTAT survey on families and social conditions (Famiglia e Soggetti Sociali) conducted in 2003, the German Socio-Economic Panel (GSOEP) for 2001, and the German Family Survey (Familiensurvey) for 2000. In order to explore other dimensions of the relationship, such as care, emotional support, and play, we used the following, not fully comparable, sources: the European Social Survey (ESS) from 2004, the Italian ISTAT annual survey on living conditions (Aspetti della Vita Quotidiana) for 2005, and the German Childcare Study (DJI-Kinderbetreuungsstudie) for 2005.[8]

Contacts between Grandchildren and Grandparents

The main factor that influences the relationship between grandchildren and grandparents is geographical proximity. Proximity can be understood in two ways: either as a precondition which eases or complicates contacts, or as an aspect of intergenerational solidarity in case generations actively prefer to live close together (Bengtson & Roberts, 1991). Living in geographical proximity has been found to be the single most important factor for contacts and visits (Marbach, 1994). Fig. 2 shows the distance between young grandchildren and their grandparents for both countries. The general pattern from other studies is confirmed: generations live closer together in Italy than in Germany. In Italy, around two-thirds of grandparent–grandchild dyads live within the same community. In Germany, this is the case for only about every second dyad.

The figures on co-residence of grandparents with grandchildren are lower in our data, in particular for Italy, than in other studies (Blome et al., 2008; Attias-Donfut et al., 2005; Barbagli et al., 2004). One reason is methodological: in our case, the percentage figures are based on all grandparent/grandchild dyads, whereas most studies report the percentage on the basis of all grandparents or households. An example might help to visualize the difference. Consider a grandparent couple having two children who in turn have two children each. The grandparents co-reside with one child and two grandchildren. Considering dyads, we have eight combinations of the two grandparents with four grandchildren. In four of the eight constellations grandparents co-reside with grandchildren, in the remaining they live separate from them. If one takes grandparents as the base, 100%

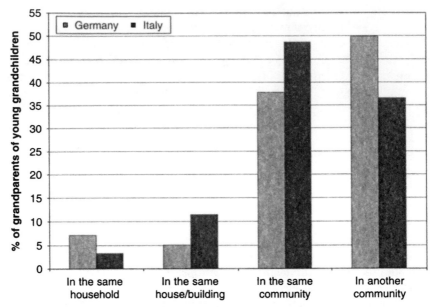

Fig. 2. Distance between Grandchildren Aged 0–13 Years and their Grandparents in Germany and Italy. *Note:* Full information is available only for those young children who live together with both parents, because the distance from parents to grandparents has been assigned to the children. *Sources:* For Germany, Familiensurvey 2000; for Italy, Famiglia e Soggetti Sociali 2003.

live with grandchildren; if one takes grandparent/grandchild dyads, only 50% co-reside.[9] The second important factor that explains the lower than expected rate of co-residence of young grandchildren with grandparents in Italy stems from patterns of family formation over the life course. Three-generational households in Italy mainly are formed not because the young, when they marry, remain in the parental household but because, when a parent becomes frail, or the marriage of an adult child ends, the two families merge. It is, therefore, more likely that a grandparent will live in the same household with his or her grandchild – if at all – when the latter is older than our target age-group.

According to the results on proximity, we expect that the frequency of contacts is higher in Italy than in Germany. Unfortunately, we do not have direct information on the contacts that grandchildren have with their grandparents from the grandchildren's perspective. In an attempt to find an alternative, we have looked at the face-to-face contacts between parents with young children and their parents, and have assumed that most of these

Table 1. Frequency of Face-to-Face Contacts between Parents and Their Adult Children Who Themselves Have Children (Aged 0–13 Years), in Percentages.

	Germany			Italy		
	Daily	Weekly	Less often	Daily	Weekly	Less often
Total	12.7	39.9	47.4	37.8	40.7	21.5

Sources: For Germany, Familiensurvey 2000; for Italy, Famiglia e Soggetti Sociali 2003.

contacts also involve grandchildren. Beforehand, we checked whether or not the existence of grandchildren makes a difference in the number of contacts. Controlling for the sex and age of adults in the middle generation, as well as the distance to their parents, we find for both countries that parents have significantly more contact with their own parents than do adults without young children. Grandchildren seem to constitute a bridge between their parents and grandparents (Haumann, 2006). Table 1 shows that contact rates are much higher in Italy than in Germany.

Differences are so great that they may not be attributed solely to the different patterns of proximity between the generations in the two countries, nor to the differences in availability of childcare services in the two countries. Daily face-to-face contact between parents and their parents happens three times more often in Italy than in Germany. Generations and family networks simply seem to be more tightly knit in Italy, confirming Reher's (1998) thesis of the long-reaching consequences of the historical relevance of kin in the Italian (and Mediterranean) family.

Regression analysis offers a more detailed image of what influences the frequency of contact between parents with young children and their parents (Table 2). The matrilateral privilege, based on women's kin-keeper role, is confirmed. In both countries, most contacts happen between mothers and their mothers. It is highly likely that, as a consequence, grandchildren have on average more frequent contacts with (and are given care more often by) the maternal than with the paternal grandmother. Because the contact with grandfathers, particularly when the children are very young, is largely mediated by the grandmother, grandchildren are also more likely to have more frequent contacts with their maternal than with their paternal grandfathers.

The age of the grandchild is also important. The younger the youngest child, the more contacts tend to occur between parents and grandparents. If the youngest child is 10–13 years old, contacts between his parents and

Table 2.   Clustered Ordinal Regression on Contact between Parents
with Young Children and Their Parents.

Dependent Variable: Contact Frequency (1 Daily, 2 Weekly, 3 Less Often)

	Germany		Italy	
	B	P	B	P
Distance: Ref.: Same household				
Same house/building	−0.42	0.206	0.47	0.010
Same community	3.17	0.000	2.39	0.000
Other community	5.04	0.000	4.68	0.000
Relationship: Ref.: Daughter/Mother				
Daughter/Father	0.33	0.000	0.17	0.000
Son/Mother	0.59	0.000	0.37	0.000
Son/Father	0.64	0.000	0.50	0.000
Age of youngest child: Ref.: child aged 0–2				
Aged 3–5	0.12	0.073	0.06	0.426
Aged 6–9	0.23	0.002	0.11	0.133
Aged 10–13	0.27	0.001	0.21	0.010
Pseudo R^2	0.214		0.203	
Number of observations	13,995		19,163	

Note: Other control variables are the number of grandparents and number of children within
the family unit.
Sources: For Germany, Familiensurvey 2000; for Italy, Famiglia e Soggetti Sociali 2003.

grandparents are significantly lower in number than in families in which the
youngest child is less than 3 years old. In Germany, the number of contacts is
also significantly lower for 6–9-year-old children than for the younger ones.
Two obvious explanations of this difference may be, first, that the interaction
between parents and grandparents is largely driven by the care-giving needs
of the small child, and, second, that as children grow older, they have more
activities and relationships of their own. In a German study, however,
grandparents report having the most activities with their grandchildren
during the time the latter are between 7 and 11 years old (Herlyn & Lehmann,
1998). This study does not contradict our findings, however. Rather, it
shows that relationships and forms of interaction change over time. The
more grandparents are involved in doing things other than providing care
for their grandchildren, the more they are likely to conceptualize this
activity as a specific relationship with them; whereas the provision of care
for very young grandchildren may be thought of primarily as a form of
support they give to their own children. For this reason, it is a pity that most

research not only on grandchildren, but also on grandparents, focuses almost exclusively on care as the only activity occurring between them.

Our data offer a partially richer insight, but they, too, are limited from this point of view. The following section sheds some light on the different modes of interaction. Given the data sources, we have no pretence of comparability in the following. We only wish to sketch the possible contours and contents of a relationship that needs to be explored in more depth.

What Grandchildren Do with Their Grandparents

Being Cared for

The almost exclusive focus on care as the activity characterizing the relationship between grandparents and young grandchildren is certainly reductive. Yet, cross-country differences with regard to being cared for by one's own grandparents point to more general differences in the degree of embeddedness in kinship networks. They also reflect differences in the experience of having multiple family care-givers as well as of intergenerational exchanges. A child who is more or less regularly cared for by a grandparent (usually a grandmother) learns early on to deal with issues of family variety (and diplomacy) – and even more so if the grandparents take turns in providing care.

The ESS provides some comparative information on childcare arrangements for families with children under 12. The share of parents who mention grandparents as the main care providers in addition to themselves ranges from 2% in Sweden to 60% in Italy.[10] On the basis of these data, Italy seems to be the land of grandparenthood in Europe. The country in second place, Hungary, follows at a distance of over 15 percentage points. Germany ranks in the lower mid-field, with around 25% of respondents mentioning grandparents. The data, however, are not completely convincing, for it appears that the Italian sample understood the question differently than the other samples: respondents do not seem to have perceived care services as possible "main providers."[11]

The data concerning older children are somewhat more robust, for all of these children are in school (which was explicitly not mentioned as a possible care provider) and it is more likely that all respondents have understood the question in the same way. German and Italian grandparents provide care to the 10–12-year-olds to a quite different degree: 27.9% of the 10–12-year-olds are cared for by their grandparents in Germany, 46.4% in Italy.[12] Although all of these children are in school for many hours a day, sometimes midday meals must be provided, homework must be supervised, and children must be taken to various activities. German/Italian differences in the recourse to grandparents, at least for this age bracket, may depend not only on proximity and general grandparents' availability, or on differences in school hours. They may also depend on the different perceptions that parents have of children's autonomy and on the belief that pre-teens may be left to their own devices, without the presence of an adult. Italian parents apparently feel less at ease in leaving a 10-year-old child alone at home for a few hours. In Germany, every third parent answers that older children manage alone, whereas in Italy only one in four parents responds that the child does not require care.

In any case, the fact that for one in four pre-teens in Germany and almost one in two in Italy, grandparents are perceived as the main providers of care when the parents are absent (or school is closed, or the child is ill) shows how important grandparents are both for the organization of a young household and in grandchildren's everyday life. This experience involves not only "care-giving" strictu senso, but having meals (and therefore developing dietary habits and table manners), doing homework, playing (even with friends, at home or on the playground), exchanging news, sharing emotions, being consoled or scolded, and acting as de facto messengers between the different family members.

We lack real comparative data on the exact amount of care provided by grandparents. The Italian source provides frequency information;[13] the German survey asks for the times of provided care for each day of the week prior to the interview. Even when we take into account these methodological differences, the general pattern of greater involvement of Italian grandparents is confirmed (see Fig. 3). In Germany, almost two-thirds of the children under seven receive care from their grandparents less than once a week, whereas in Italy only slightly over half of children under 7 are cared for by a grandparent less than once a week or never.[14] At the same time, almost every fourth grandchild in this age range receives care daily in Italy, a rare instance in Germany. This result confirms the findings of other studies, which point to the fact that in Germany grandparents do have an important buffer function when childcare is urgently needed, but that they seldom substitute maternal or service-based care provision (Blome et al., 2008; Templeton & Bauereiss, 1994).

What are the determinants for grandparents' availability to provide care? We applied an ordinal regression analysis to test the dimensions available in both surveys.[15] A higher or lower frequency of care-giving by grandparents depends on the situation of all three generations involved. From the

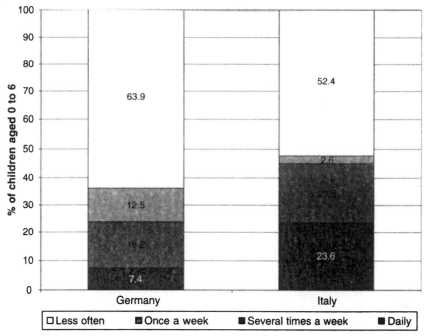

Fig. 3. Frequency with Which Grandparents Care for Grandchildren Aged 0–7 Years. *Note:* Data are the results of differently formulated questions. The Italian survey inquires about the different care frequencies directly and in general. In the German survey, respondents (the children's parents) are asked whether grandparents take care of the child for every single day of the week prior to the interview. We recoded the German responses to make them comparable to the Italian ones. Daily care includes instances in which a grandparent has looked after the child at least five times during the previous week. Several times a week comprises the range from 2 to 4 days care provision within that week, and once a week corresponds to having provided care one day. We exclude all cases for which respondents answered that this was not a regular week because of vacation, illness, and the like. We are aware that, because of the time limit (the previous week), there might still be an under-representation of actual care provided by grandparents in Germany. *Sources:* For Germany, DJI Kinderbetreuungsstudie 2005; for Italy, Famiglia e Soggetti Sociali 2003.

children's side, age and sex do not matter much in the first years of life. There is no significant difference between the groups (see Table 3). Exploratory analysis showed that use of a childcare service also does not make any difference, which may be somewhat surprising. Our data,

Table 3. Clustered Ordinal Regression: Frequency of Care by Grandparents for Children Aged 0–7 Years.

Dependent Variable	Care Frequency: 1 Daily, 2 Several Times a Week, 3 Once a Week, 4 Less Often			
	Italy		Germany	
	B	P	B	P
Child 3–6 years old (Ref.: 0–2 years)	0.04	0.754	−0.09	0.138
Child is female	−0.09	0.216	−0.02	0.651
Employment, mother: Ref.: Not employed				
Mother full-time employed	−1.08	0.000	0.15	0.097
Mother part-time employed	−1.05	0.000	0.05	0.381
Employment, father: Ref.: Not employed				
Father full-time employed	0.24	0.086	0.11	0.392
Father part-time employed	0.48	0.076	0.17	0.409
Nearest grandparent lives in the same community	−1.58	0.000	Not applicable	Not applicable
Number of grandparents	−0.32	0.000	Not applicable	Not applicable
Pseudo R^2		0.081		0.001
Number of observations		3,098		7,495

Sources: For Germany, DJI Kinderbetreuungsstudie 2005; for Italy, Famiglia e Soggetti Sociali 2003.

however, concern not intensity, but only frequency. A grandparent might therefore drop off or pick up a grandchild at the nursery or kindergarten. Moreover, in the case of children under age 3, use of a service is strongly linked to the mother's employment, whereas most children over age 3 are in a kindergarten. Given these complex interactions and possible colinearities, we decided not to consider the impact of childcare use. The most important difference between Germany and Italy concerns the association between the mother's employment and the grandparents' provision of care. Employed mothers in Italy receive much more care-giving support from the grandparents than do non-employed mothers. This differentiation does not occur in Germany, indicating the different responsibilities that grandparents have in the two countries. In Italy, grandparents substitute for missing or inadequate public childcare provision in order to ease the labor market integration of mothers. The tight intergenerational network is an important source of solidarity and helps mothers remain in the labor market. In Germany, grandparents do not care for their grandchildren more often when the mother is employed. If the latter wishes to remain in the labor market, she may count on either private or public services only. Because there are no relevant differences in the presence of public services for children under age 3 in the two countries, one might conclude that German mothers, particularly those in western Germany, have fewer "conciliation" resources than do Italian mothers. On the other hand, German mothers do have a greater tendency to work part time.

From the grandparents' side, again distance matters. The shorter the geographical distance between grandparents and grandchildren, the more likely it is that grandparents provide care more frequently. We lack information on proximity for those German grandparents who do not provide care. But if we take into consideration only those who do provide care, there is an increase in care frequency the shorter the distance is between grandparents and grandchildren (Bien, Rauschenbach, & Riedel, 2006). Second, at least for Italy, opportunities do matter. The more grandparents a child has, the higher are the rates of care by grandparents. This does not necessarily mean that each grandparent (grandmother) performs more care. Rather, care may be spread among a greater number of persons. As a matter of fact, between the 1998 and the 2003 surveys, the number of grandparents providing some care has increased in Italy, as has the total number of hours provided, but the intensity per person has decreased (ISTAT, 2006). In particular, the percentage of grandparents (grandmothers) providing care every day decreased, notwithstanding the increased percentage of working mothers among preschool children. This development points to changes both in the parents' and in the grandparents' generation: fewer grandmothers are willing to engage full time in care; more parents, in particular mothers, are looking for a mixed solution with respect to childcare. The percentage of children under age 3 attending daycare has in fact increased. Participation in extracurricular activities for school-age children also has increased (Ciccotti & Sabbadini, 2005).

Activities within Care and Beyond Care

When grandchildren are little, grandparents are mostly called upon because children need some supervision, if not outright care. But what do they do with their grandchildren when they provide care or supervise them? A caregiving relationship is always more than just tending and feeding. Very few studies have gone beyond the general issue of providing care and attempted to explore the spectrum of activities between the two generations. Furthermore, the information they offer is strongly shaped by the way the researcher first defines what activities and feelings might occur in this specific relationship. The richer the number of items proposed, the more varied the activities appear to be.

Activities depend on the age of the child. The more independent and self-reliant a child becomes, the more the activities involve partnership and cooperation between grandchildren and grandparents. The most important contribution offered by grandparents appears, however, to be some kind of service, even in the case of teenagers. In a German study, 70% of 10–18-year-olds mentioned that grandmothers cook for them (Zinnecker, Behnken, Maschke, & Stecher, 2002). Other instrumental support is less frequent. Only a minority of grandparents in Germany help adolescents and teenagers do their homework. In Italy, the picture is similar. The Italian 2003 Survey Famiglia e Soggetti Sociali asked who had the main responsibility concerning school-related activities. Grandparents play a minor role in dealing with these activities, which are perceived as being mainly the responsibility of parents, and mothers in particular. Fewer than 10% of grandparents are reported to be the main responsible person for taking children to school or back home, talking to teachers about school performance, or supervising homework.

Grandparents are often mentioned as persons who play with children. This play is most common for younger children. From the annual survey "Aspetti della vita quotidiana", which in 2005 had a specific module on children's activities, we find that around 41% of 3–5-year-old grandchildren play with their grandparents. Playing activities decrease with age: 28% of the 6–9-year-olds and 13% of the 10–13-year-olds play with their grand-parents. In all age brackets, grandmothers play more often with their grandchildren than do grandfathers. The difference is between two and four percentage points (see Ciccotti & Sabbadini, 2005). Percentages were slightly lower for the weekends, indicating once again that activities and relationships with grandparents are for many grandchildren a normal part of daily living, not something reserved for festivities and holidays. Play is an important dimension in shared activities between grandparents and grand-children in Germany, too. Taking into consideration the grandparents who are emotionally closest, grandchildren aged 10–18 years old responded that 29% of their closest grandmothers and 20% of their closest grandfathers play with them,[16] around one-third take them out on excursions, and 15% do handicrafts together with them (Zinnecker et al., 2002).

Another Italian survey, carried out in 2003 on a national sample of 7–11-year-old schoolchildren ("Osservatorio permanente sull'infanzia," 2004), found that 92.7% of children perceived their grandparents as affectionate (as against 4.7% who perceived them as distant), 82.3% declared that their grandparents understood them, and 76.2% believed that grandparents communicated their experiences. On the other hand, 40% (more boys than girls) perceived their grandparents as strict. Admittedly, these answer categories are very generic. But they do delineate an overall climate of affection and even intimacy between grandparents and grandchildren in this age bracket, which goes beyond being fed and supervised. The same holds true for Germany. The German "Kinderpanel", a study of 8–9-year-old children in 2003, reveals that more than 95% of them get along with their grandparents at least well, and every three in four grandchildren state very well. Grandparents are first and foremost described as "being there," available to console grandchildren when they feel bad, to support them when they have trouble with their parents, and to give advice (Zinnecker et al., 2002). Grandparents are perceived by grandchildren as a backup in troubled or uncertain times (Haumann, 2006; Höpflinger et al., 2006).

Older grandchildren viewed grandparents as interlocutors as well, not only for personal affairs but also for political and social matters. Every second teenager in the German study noted these discussions as an important activity. They may be triggered by reading the newspaper or by watching television together. Of German adolescents, 55% responded that they watch television with their closest grandmother, 27% with their closest grandfather (Zinnecker et al., 2002). "Watching television together" may, however, might also reflect weak interaction and communication between the generations.

CONCLUSION

Grandchildhood has become a longer and more intense life phase as a consequence of demographic and social changes. Although many scholars have examined the situation of grandparents and their relations and contributions to grandchildren, there is little research from the grandchild's perspective. Studies on children almost totally ignore this aspect of contemporary childhood. We argue that putting grandchildren at center stage might change our perspective in three ways. First, if we start from grandchildren, or grandchild–grandparent dyads, we have a different population from that obtained when we start from grandparents. Thus, the overall data on frequency of contacts and support between generations necessarily differ. Second, taking the perspective of grandchildren opens up a range of activities, as well as of hierarchies of importance, which are different from those prevalent when the focus is on the grandparents', or the parents', perspective. A grandparent or a parent may say that the former "provides care," whereas a child might point out that a grandfather tells stories or that a grandmother teaches her songs or bakes cakes with him. Third, the relationship should be conceptualized and researched as more symmetrical or at least bi-directional than is currently the case. Not only has most research focused on grandparents; it also has looked at them as pure givers, without examining patterns of reciprocity which, as reciprocity goes, may involve something more complex than a simple give-and-take. This tendency is partly the consequence of a focus on care-giving, which in turn offers a quite reductive image of care provision itself, underplaying the relational, cognitive, and identity-shaping processes that are involved in the care-giving relationship. The few studies available suggest that grand-parents – as "backstage figures" who are there and willing to communicate and support in times of need – provide an important experience for the overall development of children's cognitive and emotional skills. Grand-children give grandparents reasons to invest resources, time, and love. The modes of interaction are manifold: playing, entertaining, celebrating, going out on excursions, having discussions, telling stories, teaching, parenting, advising, caring, and helping. They are often intertwined with deep emotional relationships full of joy, sadness, anxiety, pride, hope, and confidence.

Unfortunately, the empirical basis available for developing our argument is poor, and even its comparability is limited. For this reason, we consider this study an exercise. With all its limitations, the analysis of contacts with grandparents and of patterns of grandparents' involvement in childcare in two countries with different family and kinship cultures, as well as partially different patterns of labor force participation among mothers and of welfare state arrangements, highlights the relevance of the presence of grandparents in both countries. It also provides some insight into a possible source of "diversities in childhood" even in the heart of Europe which has not been brought into focus so far. Research on grandchildhood is still in its initial stages.

NOTES

1. The shorter time span is estimated by adding the average age at first birth (ca. 25 years) twice, and the upper end is obtained by taking an age barrier of 100 years, which is still rarely achieved by grandparents.

2. The Spanish epidemic also killed many people during and immediately following the First World War.

3. In addition, specific groups within each country suffered additional destruction due to persecution or forced displacement. Such was the case for Jews in all countries under Nazi rule, for ethnic groups on the eastern border between Italy and Yugoslavia, for Germans fleeing Soviet rule after German defeat. In the Soviet Union, the kulak were subjected to this fate on a mass level.

4. Of course, this is a stylized image. Poverty ratios of elderly people still exceed the average for the overall population in the majority of European countries (Smeeding, 2005), and chronic illness and dependency on care among elderly people remain a prevalent concern both physically and financially (Theobald, 2004).

5. Not to mention the cases in which grandparents act directly as substitute parents, not only because of the death of the parents, but because of serious illness or parents' inability to perform their parental duties (see Peter, 2001; Uhlenberg, 2001).

6. Some young respondents were ambivalent and mentioned positive and negative traits, which is why the figures exceed 100%.

7. In 2005, 43.4% of children between the ages of 0 and 18 had both parents in paid work, compared to 36.3% in the mid-1990s. In the central-north regions, however, this figure was over 50%, whereas in the southern regions and the Isles it was below 30% (Ciccotti & Sabbadini, 2005).

8. The Italian ISTAT surveys "Famiglia e Soggetti Sociali" conducted in 2003 and "Aspetti della Vita Quotidiana" for 2005 both include almost 50,000 interviews of individuals in households. The German Socio-Economic Panel is a large-scale panel study including 12,000 households with around 23,000 individuals. The German Family Survey is a periodical survey with around 10,000 respondents. The German Childcare Study was launched by the German Youth Institute (Deutsches Jugendinstitut) in 2005. Overall, 8,000 parents with children under seven years of age were interviewed, providing information on around 10,900 children under age seven. The European Social Survey (ESS) is a biennial multi-country survey covering over 20 nations. The German sample comprises 2,870 cases and the Italian sample includes 1,529 cases.

9. Grandparents from the side of the other parent are not considered in this example.

10. The percentages do not reflect the fact that some of the children no longer have grandparents. Thus, they would be even higher if we could exclude those children from the base population.

11. The question concerned who was the main care provider, in addition to the parents. The alternatives included an ex-husband/ex-wife, some other family member, other unpaid childcare, paid childcare at home, free nursery or childcare, paid nursery or childcare outside the home, the child managing alone at home, and no childcare needed because the parents are at home. The high percentage of the Italian respondents who mentioned grandparents as the main providers, even when most 3–5-year-old children are in kindergarten, suggests that the question has been misunderstood.

12. According to the findings of the 2003 "Famiglia e Soggetti Sociali" survey, 32.54% of 10–13-year-old Italian children are cared for by a non-parental adult (usually a grandparent) at least a few times a week.

13. Caring rates in the Italian survey appear to be lower than in the ESS, which again raises uncertainties about the Italian ESS sample/responses. We would expect,

in fact, even higher rates, for in this case the question concerns any care provided by a grandparent, not whether the grandparent is the main care provider, as in the ESS.

14. We excluded those children who do not have living grandparents (1.5%).

15. Unfortunately, there is no information on the grandparents' age, health, or employment, which might be important. The same holds for an assessment of the closeness of relationships between grandparents and parents, as well as between grandparents and grandchildren. Moreover, the number of grandchildren that grandparents have – hypothetically an important determinant – is missing.

16. The survey asked the adolescents about activities that they do together with their "dearest" grandmother and/or grandfather. It is reasonable to expect that the grandparents who are emotionally closest are also those who undertake the most activities with their grandchildren. If all living grandparents were taken into account, the activity rates might decrease.

REFERENCES

Alber, J. (1982). *Vom Armenhaus zum Wohlfahrtsstaat*. Frankfurt: Campus.

Aries, P. (1962). *Centuries of childhood: A social history of family life*. New York: Vintage Books.

Attias-Donfut, C. (2001). La Fabrication des Grand-Pères. In: C. Attias-Donfut & M. Segalen (Eds), *Le Siècle des Grand-Parents*. Paris: Editions Autrement.

Attias-Donfut, C., Ogg, J., & Wolff, F.-C. (2005). Family support. In: A. Börsch-Supan, A. Brugiavini, H. Jürges, J. Mackenbach, J. Siegrist & G. Weber (Eds), *Health, ageing and retirement in Europe* (pp. 171–178). Mannheim: Mannheim Research Institute for the Economics of Aging.

Attias-Donfut, C., & Segalen, M. (1998). *Grand-Parents: La famille à travers les générations*. Paris: Edition Odile.

Barbagli, M., Castiglione, M., & Zuanna, G. D. (2004). *Fare famiglia in Italia*. Bologna: Il Mulino.

Bengtson, V. L., & Roberts, R. E. L. (1991). Intergenerational solidarity in aging families: An example of formal theory construction. *Journal of Marriage and the Family, 53*, 856–870.

Bien, W., Rauschenbach, T., & Riedel, B. (Eds). (2006). *Wer betreut Deutschlands Kinder? DJI-Kinderbetreuungsstudie*. Weinheim: Beltz.

Binstock, R. H., & Quadagno, J. (2001). Aging and politics. In: R. H. George & L. K. Binstock (Eds), *Handbook of aging and the social sciences* (5th ed., pp. 333–351). San Diego: Academic Press.

Blome, A., Keck, W., & Alber, J. (2008). *Generationenbeziehungen im Wohlfahrtsstaat. Lebensbedingungen und Einstellungen von Altersgruppen im Internationalen Vergleich*. Wiesbaden: VS Verlag für Sozialwissenschaften.

Börsch-Supan, A., Brugiavini, A., Jürges, H., Mackenbach, J., Siegrist, J., & Weber, G. (2005). *Health, ageing and retirement in Europe – first results from share*. Mannheim: Mannheim Research Institute for the Economics of Aging (MEA).

Brunowsky, H.-P., & Kubenz, M. (2006). *Opa – Das Kannst du auch! Mein Enkel erklärt mir den Computer*. Köln: BrunoMedia Buchverlag.

Chvojka, E. (2003). *Geschichte der Großelternrollen*. Wien: Böhlau.

Ciccotti, E., & Sabbadini, L. L. (2005). *Come cambia la vita dei bambini.* Firenze: Quaderno 42, Centro Nazionale di documentazione e analisi per l'infanzia e l'adolescenza.

Cochran, M. M., & Brassard, J. A. (1979). Child development and personal social networks. *Child Development, 50*(4), 601–616.

Coleman, D. (2005). Facing the 21st century: New developments, continuing problems. In: M. Miroslav, A. L. MacDonald & W. Haug (Eds), *The new demographic regime* (pp. 11–44). Geneva, New York: United Nations Population Division.

Dench, G., & Ogg, J. (2001). Grand-Parents par la fille, grand-parents par le fils. In: C. Attias-Donfut & M. Segalen (Eds), *Le Siècle des Grand-Parents.* Paris: Editions Autrement.

Denham, T. E., & Smith, C. W. (1989). The influence of grandparents: A review of the literature and resources. *Family Relations, 38*(2), 345–350.

Elder, G., Jr. (Ed.) (1985). *Life course dynamics: Trajectories and transitions, 1968–1980.* Ithaca: Cornell University Press.

Engstler, H., & Menning, S. (2005). Transition to grandparenthood in Germany: Historical change in the prevalence, age and duration of grandparenthood. Presented at the 7th European sociological association conference. Torun.

Esping-Andersen, G. (1999). *Social foundation of postindustrial economies.* Oxford: Oxford University Press.

Esping-Andersen, G., Gallie, D., Hemerijck, A., & Myles, J. (Eds). (2002). *Why we need a new welfare state.* Oxford: Oxford University Press.

Esping-Andersen, G., & Sarasa, S. (2002). The generational conflict reconsidered. *Journal of European Social Policy, 12*(1), 5–21.

Etzioni, A. (1993). *The spirit of community.* New York: Touchstone.

European Data Service. (2007). Eurostat Online Database. http://www.eds-destatis.de/de/database/estatonline.php

Eurostat, (2004). *Employment rate in the EU25 was 63.0% in 2003. Female employment rate stood at 55.1%.* Eurostat New Release 110/2004. Eurostat Press Office, Brussels.

Ferrera, M. (1996). Il Modello Sud-Europeo di Welfare State. *Rivista Italiana Di Scienza Politica, 26*(1), 67–101.

Flora, P., Kraus, F., & Pfenning, W. (1987). *State, economy, and society in Western Europe 1815–1975.* Frankfurt: Campus.

Fruhauf, C. A., Jarrott, S. E., & Allen, K. R. (2006). Grandchildren's perception of caring for grandparents. *Journal of Family Issues, 27*(7), 887–911.

Gauthier, A. (2002). The role of grandparents. *Current Sociology, 50*(2), 295–307.

Göckenjan, G. (2000). *Das Alter würdigen.* Frankfurt: Suhrkamp.

Gourdon, V. (2001). *Histoire des Grands-Parents.* Paris: Perrin.

Grundy, E. (1999). Household and family change in mid and later life in England and Wales. In: S. McRae (Ed.), *Changing Britain: Families and households in the 1990s* (pp. 201–228). Oxford: Oxford University Press.

Guillemard, A.-M. (2000). *Aging and the welfare-state crisis.* Newark: University of Delaware Press.

Hagestad, G. O. (2006). Transfers between grandparents and grandchildren: The importance of making a three generation perspective. *Zeitschrift für Familienforschung, 18*(3), 315–332.

Hajnal, J. (1982). Two kinds of preindustrial household formation systems. *Population and Development Review, 8*(3), 449–494.

Harper, S. (2006). *Ageing societies.* London: Hodder Arnold.

Haumann, W. (2006). *Generationenbarometer 2006*. Freiburg: Karl Alber.

Hawker, S., Allan, G., & Crow, G. (2001). La multiplication des grandparents. In: C. Attias-Donfut & M. Segalen (Eds), *Siècle des Grand-Parents* (pp. 167–186). Paris: Editions Autrement.

Herlyn, I. (2001). D'est En Ouest, Les Styles Des Grand-Meres Allemandes. In: C. Attias-Donfut & M. Segalen (Eds), *Siècle des Grand-Parents*. Paris: Editions Autrement.

Herlyn, I., & Lehmann, B. (1998). Grossmutterschaft im Mehrgenerationenzusammenhang. Eine empirische Untersuchung aus der Perspektive von Grossmüttern. *Zeitschrift für Familienforschung, 10*(1), 27–45.

Hondrich, K.-O. (1999). Generationskluft? *Merkur, 53*(598–608), 454–461.

Höpflinger, F., Hummel, C., & Hugentobler, V. (2006). *Enkelkinder und ihre Großeltern*. Zürich: Seismo.

Hugo, V. (2002 [Orig. 1877]). *L'art d'être grand-père*. Paris: Gallimard Poesie.

ISTAT. (2006). *Parentela e reti di solidarietà*. Roma: ISTAT.

Kemp, C. L. (2007). Grandparent–grandchild ties. Reflections on continuity and change across three generations. *Journal of Family Issues, 28*(7), 855–881.

Kohli, M. (1999). Private and public transfers between generations. *European Societies, 1*(1), 103–122.

Kornhaber, A. (1985). Grandparenthood and the new social contract. In: V. L. Bengtson & J. F. Robertson (Eds), *Grandparenthood* (pp. 159–171). Beverly Hills: Sage.

Kornhaber, A. (1996). *Contemporary grandparenting*. Newbury Park: Sage.

Kränzl-Nagl, R., & Wilk, L. (2000). Möglichkeiten und Grenzen standardisierter Befragungen unter besonderer Berücksichtigung der Faktoren soziale und personal Wünschbarkeit. In: F. Heinzel (Ed.), *Methoden der Kindheitsforschung* (pp. 59–86). Weinheim: Juventa.

Le Play, F. (1855). *Ouvriers Européens. Études sur les travaux, la vie domestique et la condition morale des populations ouvrières de l'Europe, précédée d'un exposé de la méthode d'observations*. Paris: Imprimerie impériale.

Leibfried, S. (1993). Towards a European social model? In: C. Jones (Ed.), *New perspectives on the welfare state*. London: Routledge.

Lin, G., & Rogerson, P. A. (1995). Elderly parents and geographic availability of their adult children. *Research on Aging, 17*, 303–331.

Marbach, J. H. (1994). Der Einfluss von Kindern und Wohnentfernung auf die Beziehung zwischen Eltern und Grosseltern. In: W. Bien (Ed.), *Eigeninteresse oder Solidarität. Beziehungen in modernen Mehrgenerationenfamilien* (pp. 77–115). Opladen: Leske + Budrich.

McLaughlin, E., & Glendinning, C. (1994). Paying for care in Europe: Is there a feminist approach? In: L. Hantrais & S. Mangen (Eds), *Family policy and the welfare of women* (pp. 52–69). Loughborough: University of Loughborough.

Naldini, M. (2003). *The family in the Mediterranean welfare states*. London: Frank Cass Publishers.

OECD. (1994). *Caring for frail elderly people: New directions in care*. Paris: Organisation for Economic Co-operation and Development.

Osservatorio permanente sull'infanzia. (2004). *5. Rapporto nazionale sull'infanzia e l'adolescenza*. Roma: Osservatorio permanente sull'infanzia.

Palmer, J. L., & Gould, S. G. (1986). Economic consequences of population aging. In: A. Pifer & L. Bronte (Eds), *Our aging society: Paradox and promise* (pp. 367–390). New York: Norton.

Peter, U. (2001). Élever ses petits-enfants. In: Attias-Donfut & Segalen (Eds), *Le siècle des Grand-Parents* (pp. 218–224). Paris: Editions Autrement.

Reher, S. D. (1998). Family ties in Western Europe: Persistent contrast. *Population and Development Review, 24*(2), 203–234.

Ringen, S. (1987). *The possibility of politics*. Oxford: Clarendon Press.

Rossi, A. S., & Rossi, P. H. (1990). *Of human bonding. Parent–child relations across the life course*. New York: Aldine de Gruyter.

Rothstein, B. (2001). Sozialkapital im sozialdemokratischen staat – Das schwedische Modell und die Bürgergesellschaft. In: R. D. Putnam (Ed.), *Gesellschaft und Gemeinsinn* (pp. 115–198). Gütersloh: Verlag Bertelsmann Stiftung.

Sanders, G. F., & Trygstad, D. W. (1989). Stepgrandparents and grandparents: The view from young adults. *Family Relations, 38*(1), 71–75.

Saraceno, C. (2003). *Mutamenti della famiglia e politiche sociali in Italia*. Bologna: il Mulino.

Saraceno, C. (2007). Patterns of family living in Europe. In: J. Alber, T. Fahey & C. Saraceno (Ed.), *Handbook of Quality of life in the enlarged European Union* (pp. 47–72). London: Routledge.

Saraceno, C., Olagnero, M., & Torrioni, P. (2005). *First European quality of life survey: Families, work and social networks. Conditions, European Foundation for the improvement of living and working*. Dublin: European Foundation for the Improvement of Living and Working Conditions.

Smeeding, T. M. (2005). *Poverty and income maintainance in old age: A cross-national view of low income older women*. Luxembourg Income Study Working Paper no. 398. Syracuse University, Syracuse.

Smith, P. K., & Drew, E. (2002a). Implications for grandparents when they lose contact with their grandchildren: Divorce, family feud, and geographical separation. *Journal of Mental Health and Aging, 8*(2), 95–119.

Smith, P. K., & Drew, L. M. (2002b). Grandparenting. In: M. H. Bornstein (Ed.), *Handbook of parenting* (pp. 141–171). Mahwah: SLawrence Erlbaum Associates.

Templeton, R., & Bauereiss, R. (1994). Kinderbetreuung zwischen Generationen. In: W. Bien (Ed.), *Eigeninteresse oder Solidarität. Beziehungen in modernen Mehrgenerationenfamilien* (pp. 249–280). Opladen: Leske + Budrich.

Theobald, H. (2005). *Social Exclusion and Care for the Elderly*. Discussion Paper SP I 2005–301. Wissenchaftszentrum Berlin für Sozialforschung, Berlin.

Therborn, G. (2000). *Die Gesellschaften Europas 1945–2000*. Frankfurt: Campus.

United Nations. (1956). The Aging of Populations and its Economic and Social Implications. New York: United Nations, Department of Economic and Social Affairs.

Zinnecker, J., Behnken, I., Maschke, S., & Stecher, L. (2002). *Null Zoff & Voll Busy. Die erste Jugendgeneration des neuen Jahrhunderts*. Opladen: Leske + Budrich.

CHILDREN'S WELFARE IN AGEING EUROPE: GENERATIONS APART?

An-Magritt Jensen

The debate on the implications of an ageing population has grown in most European countries in recent years. Books have been written, articles have been published and conferences have been organized to discuss ways of maintaining and protecting the welfare of the elderly. At issue have been questions such as how best to change the perception of old people from one of burden to one of resource, and how pension systems can be structured to survive the demographic shift. The issue of childhood, however, seldom enters the debate.

One main question posed in this article is how this broad social change, a decrease in the number of children and an increase in the number of old people might affect the material life conditions of children, their socio-spatial environments, and whether it will promote a climate of culture protecting the needs of the elderly rather than those of children? Across Europe, child poverty differs, as does the percentage of mothers in employment and the roles of the family and the welfare state. Through working more, parents can offer more to their children. At the same time, however, working mothers may fortify the perception that children *belong* to the family and undermine the perception of children as a common good. Does the quest for two parental incomes signify a private solution to a public issue? Will growing pressure from the aged result in a generational struggle for public resources? In the wake of an ageing population, are generations moving apart materially, spatially and culturally? Since we do

Childhood: Changing Contexts
Comparative Social Research, Volume 25, 165–189
Copyright © 2008 by Emerald Group Publishing Limited
ISSN: 0195-6310/doi:10.1016/S0195-6310(07)00006-3

not know the long-term consequences of ageing societies, these issues are discussed here, with children placed front stage.

The article builds on the work of the Children's Welfare Network involving European researchers under COST A19,[1] with examples drawn from the Network's country reports published in *Children's Welfare in Ageing Europe* (Jensen et al., 2004a).[2]

SCIENTIFIC APPROACH

The Children's Welfare Network was informed by the 'new social study of childhood' (Qvortrup, Bardy, Sgritta, & Wintersberger, 1994), with emphasis on the life conditions of children here and now. The basic question formulated in terms of a generational perspective was: Do children as a population group experience life conditions different from those of other population groups – the elderly, for example?

The Network puts emphasis on identifying research in which children were the unit of count in statistical data, national surveys and studies on everyday life, and also on employing generational comparisons where available. Having to rely on existing studies and national data, the work was bound to reflect country-specific conditions as well as the nature of the available data. Participants were actively encouraged to make use of research that included agency and structure, micro-issues and macro-issues, and qualitative as well as quantitative studies. A guideline for collecting information was developed, but it was clear from the outset that the information would vary, as would methods of data collection and definitions. We tried to turn this to our advantage in widening insight in national contexts.

We, therefore, searched for common childhood conditions and used national contexts as a source for broadening our understanding of the mechanisms of social change. The general insight from the collection of reports is of concepts and perspectives on childhood conditions. Discussions revealed that a feature described for one country was often relevant for several others. These common features, which we named as 'childhood mosaic' (Jensen & Qvortrup, 2004), included ageing societies, children's dependence on parental incomes and the emergence of virtual childhood as a specific feature of domestication. Although many nuances are country-specific, these 'mosaic pieces' capture elements of European childhood across differences.

AGEING SOCIETIES: SETTING THE SCENE

Despite the fact that the Network included countries with different cultures, religions and economic conditions, we found remarkable similarities in long-term demographic trends. Changes in fertility rates and consequent changes in population structure are common attributes of all countries. All general and country-specific trends point in the same direction in contributing to the ageing of society notwithstanding the differences in pace and intensity. Throughout Europe, fewer adults are living a life with children. Could an increase in childlessness indicate growing ambivalence about the value of children in society? (see Fig. 1).

Although the variation is strong, a glance at the long-term trend shows that all countries are experiencing a downturn in fertility rates. The common feature is that the motivation or ability to have children is lower in 2000 than in 1950. The literature contains ample explanations for this decline in fertility, two of which are prominent. Among the most basic elements provided in the theory of the first demographic transition is the general modernization of societies following industrialization. Children no longer constitute an economic gain for the family (Notestein, 1976). Following the first transition, provision for the elderly shifted from being a responsibility of the family

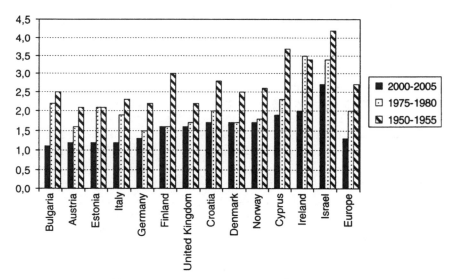

Fig. 1. Total Fertility Rates among Countries in the Children's Welfare Network, Sorted from the Lowest Value in 2000. *Source:* World Population Ageing, UN 2002.

to a responsibility of the public (McLanahan, 2004). The theory of the second demographic transition (Lesthaeghe, 1995) focuses on the fertility decline that began around 1950. As women have adjusted to the market economy and new family patterns have evolved, the costs incurred of having children have risen while they have remained primarily a private responsibility. The impact of these changes on children's material welfare is contradictory. While women's labour market participation may increase, and even strengthen, the financial resources available for children, the increasing fragility of marriage and partnership weakens children's access to an adequate income. McLanahan (2004) maintains that disparity between children increases as a result. The demographic response to the increasing costs of having children is unprecedented. In Therborn's words, declining fertility '... contained a unique historical turn to deliberate, peacetime below-reproduction fertility among the world's leading countries' (p. 294).

While all countries display a common trend towards lower fertility, the substantial country-specific variation in the pace of the decline can be described in three tempi: *forerunners* (1950–1975), *latecomers* (1975–2005) and *steady decliners* (1950–2005). Among the forerunners are the Nordic countries (Denmark, Finland and Norway)[3] symbolizing the second demographic transition, where education for women fostered their rapid entrance into the labour force and ideologies of gender equality. But also among the forerunners are countries in which fertility reduction was influenced by more general forces (Cyprus, Croatia and, less distinctly, Germany and the UK). Among the latecomers are Bulgaria, Estonia and Ireland. Two of these countries experienced political and economic transition from socialism to a market economy during the 1990s, and share their sharp fertility decline with most other countries in the Eastern European mould. The steady decliners are Austria, Italy and Israel. For Italy, the decline has accelerated in the recent past. It is beyond the scope of this article to identify countries according to their 'fit' with one or the other transition, but, as we can see, there is no clear geographical division in pace.

The present fertility levels among all countries are below the reproduction replacement level of 2.1 children on average per woman. Only Israel is above this line.[4] Without exception, fertility in 2000 is much lower than in 1950 and is presently the lowest in Bulgaria. Countries sharing these very low levels include Austria, Estonia, Italy and Germany, all with a fertility rate below 1.5. The most dramatic drops have been in Bulgaria, Cyprus, Ireland, Finland and also in Israel.

Fertility is about the ability to have children, as well as when to have them and in what number. Declines can result from postponement, from decisions to have fewer, or from childlessness – through choice or otherwise. The mechanisms of fertility decline have several direct impacts on the welfare of children in the family. For example, postponing parenthood implies older parents (and, we would expect more economic security), and fewer siblings implies less competition between each child for family resources. At the societal level, which is in focus in this article, the linkage between having fewer children and securing their welfare is a powerful mechanism in the ageing of society.

In all countries, the birth of the first child is now consistently postponed. The Children's Welfare Network explored this aspect specifically for Italy (Conti & Sgritta, 2004). Young people have difficulty entering the labour market at the same time, as the obligations of parenthood are perceived as a financial burden. Postponing parenthood eventually means that fewer children will be born on an average, since it can be more difficult for women to conceive as they get older. Most children, however, still grow up with siblings. In the case of Finland (as part of a general European trend), childlessness is rising and is among the highest in Europe (Sobotka, 2004).[5] One in every four women aged 35 has no children (Alanen, Sauli, & Strandell, 2004). However, there has been a recent trend towards having more children. Similarly, German children continue to grow up with siblings despite the fact that a growing number of adults seem to be choosing a life without children. Almost 30 per cent of all women now in fertile age in western Germany are likely to remain childless, and among women with higher education the proportion is even higher. Nevertheless, only 16 per cent of children have no siblings (Jurczyk, Olk, & Zeiher, 2004). In Denmark, where four out of five children have siblings, the proportion of single child is decreasing (Kampmann & Nielsen, 2004), as is the case in Norway too, where in 2002, 18 per cent of children had no sibling. In this country, childlessness remains at a modest level (13 per cent of women aged 40 have no children; Jensen et al., 2004b). Unlike most countries, Denmark and Norway have seen slightly rising fertility rates recently, and in the European context the levels are high.

Fertility development shows a general decline across all countries, although there are differences in the pace, level and mechanism, and often there are country-specific explanations. For some countries, researchers blame war or economic and political upheaval – such as the transition from socialism to market societies in eastern Europe. Others point to increased prosperity, such as in northern countries. Some researchers suggest that for their country the answer can be found in asymmetrical gender relations or in the inadequacy of welfare systems, as is the case in southern and central Europe.

The decline in fertility has taken place in combination with an increase in longevity, and these two processes have resulted in a shift in the age structure from younger to older age groups, as shown in Figs. 2 and 3.

The 'greying' of Europe (Fig. 2) illustrates the emerging marginalization of children as a population group (black bars) versus the rise in the elderly population (grey bars). In the year 2000, in the majority of countries there were more people 60 years of age and older than there were 14 years and younger. From a historical perspective, the percentage of children in the overall population is now completely different from what it was 50 years ago.

Fig. 3 demonstrates the change in population groups since 1950, sorted from the smallest to the largest total change. The change in the childhood population is negative for all countries, while the other end of the age range reflects a positive change. For example in Italy, at the beginning of the 1980s there were fewer than 60 elderly people (65 years and older) per 100 children (14 years or younger). Only 15 years later, there were 124 elderly per 100 children (Conti & Sgritta, 2004, p. 275). Bulgaria's situation can be described as 'a demographic collapse'. Over a 15-year period (from 1985 to 2001), the proportion of households with no children under 16 years of age increased from 60 to 70 per cent, while the proportion with two children

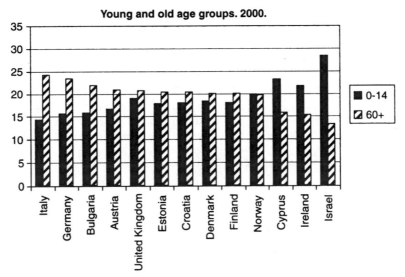

Fig. 2.   Proportion of Young and Old Age Groups in Populations of the Children's Welfare Network, 2000. *Source:* United Nations (2002).

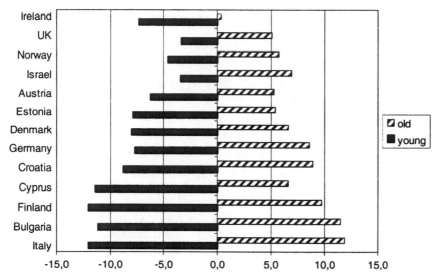

Fig. 3. Pace of Ageing among Countries of the Children's Welfare Network, 1950–2000 (per cent change). *Source:* United Nations (2002). Author's Calculations.

dropped from 18 to 10 per cent. In 1950, children (0–14 years) constituted 27 per cent of the population, and the elderly (60+) 10 per cent. Fifty years later, children comprised 16 per cent of the population and elderly 22 per cent (Raycheva, Hristova, Radomirova, & Ginev, 2004, pp. 472–477). The least pronounced ageing is found in Ireland, the UK and Norway. Ireland is different from other countries in that the change concerns almost only the declining share of children (about 7 per cent).

Israel has a young population profile (Fig. 2). Children comprised of almost 30 per cent of the population in 2000. Family size is relatively large. Almost 20 per cent of families have four or more children (Ben-Arieh, Boyer, & Gajst, 2004, p. 774). But Israel shares trends similar to those of ageing societies in other countries: declining childhood population and a rising percentage of elderly citizens (Fig. 3).[6] Countries are heading in the same direction, but the ageing of societies is most pronounced in Italy, Bulgaria and Finland, where three different paces – steady decliners (Italy), latecomers (Bulgaria) and forerunners (Finland) – indicate that while national contexts differ, they are all influenced by a common force, i.e. women having fewer children.

Given what – for most countries – are fairly remarkable demographic changes, the question posed by the Children's Welfare Network was whether any impact on children could be detected. Are children richer or poorer off than the elderly? What are the main factors associated with child poverty? Are generations moving apart?

AGEING SOCIETIES AND CHILDHOOD POVERTY

In his much quoted article *Children and the Elderly in the US* (1984), Samuel Preston argued that children were at a higher risk of landing in poverty than were the elderly, and that the disadvantage was on the increase as the population aged, since the elderly would be favoured in the struggle for public benefits. Some 20 years later, Preston's argument still holds for the US (Treas, 2000). Fig. 4 illustrates the proportion of children living in relative poverty among countries relevant to this study. Relative poverty is defined as households with an income below 50 per cent of the national median.

According to UNICEF (2005, p. 5) estimates, during the 1990s child poverty increased in most OECD countries (exceptions were the UK and Norway), particularly in Germany and Italy. This was also a period during which there was a decrease in the child population, an increase in the old age population and postponement of births (associated with improved economic conditions among parents). Fig. 4 illustrates the variation in poverty in the countries included in this analysis, with the percentage much lower in the Nordic countries compared to the countries of central and southern Europe. While in Italy, Ireland and the UK about 16 per cent

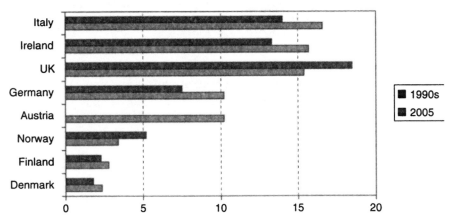

Fig. 4. Children Living in Relative Poverty[9] among Countries of the Children's Welfare Network, 2005 (in per cent). *Source:* UNICEF (2005, Figs. 1 and 2).

of children are poor, the level in Denmark, Finland and Norway is around 3 per cent. The figure does not include former socialist countries. Fig. 4 suggests a linkage between ageing and child poverty for some countries, but also that we need to go beyond the figures to broaden our understanding of the particular countries. Are the elderly given priority over children in the distribution of welfare resources in European countries and, if so, what are the consequences for children? To broaden our understanding, we need to go beyond the figures and see how this relationship is described in the particular countries.

Researchers of the Children's Welfare Network concentrated on exploring economic resources across age groups. In Italy, one of the countries most affected by an ageing population, children are poorer in terms of welfare than are their seniors (Conti & Sgritta, 2004, p. 301). Italy's expenditure on social protection (including benefits for children) is below the European average – and is a position shared by Ireland. Public spending on the elderly consumes 66 per cent of the total social spending (compared to a European average at 46 per cent). As summed up by the researchers: '... the high figure for Italy denotes a specific level of generosity towards the elderly' (Conti & Sgritta, 2004, p. 303). While tax/benefit policies have improved the economic conditions of children in other European countries, in Italy they have worsened the situation. The report concludes: '... in the southern European countries in general, and Italy in particular, the family, when not actually penalised, has been left alone to bear the burden of its members' needs' (Conti & Sgritta, 2004, p. 305).

Is the risk of child poverty increasing while the elderly are finding themselves better off? In Italy, child poverty is increasing – along with a decrease in the child population – while poverty rates among the elderly have decreased. Also in Germany, a shift in the generational distribution of poverty is reported: '... sociological poverty research has been pointing out a shift of poverty risk since the late 1980s, away from the traditional risk groups – such as older people, for example – to children and young people – or specific family arrangements with children – and has coined the rather unfortunate term of "infantilisation of poverty" to refer to the phenomenon' (Jurczyk et al., 2004, p. 708).

Several countries have drawn the same conclusion: children are at a greater risk of landing in poverty than are the elderly. This is the case in Estonia, Finland, Germany, Ireland, Israel and Italy, but is less conclusive in other countries. For example, the figures for Cyprus, Croatia and Norway do not show a clear trend in relation to childhood poverty compared to other population groups.[7] The poverty level of children in Norway is relatively low and stable at around 3–4 per cent. Poverty is more widespread among the elderly than among children (by the modified equivalence scale; see the discussion below). Still, public transfers from the welfare state (tax and income transfers) are substantially higher to the elderly than to children in Norway too. Family income remains the most important source of children's material welfare, supplemented with welfare transfers (Jensen et al., 2004b, p. 348). The observations made in our study are supported in recent research. For example, according to Lutz, Skirbekk, and Testa (2006, p. 186), population ageing 'almost universally tends to result in the hardest cut for the younger generations'.

The country reports varied in how much discussion was given to shifts in the generational distribution of poverty, as did the available data for each country. An important problem in comparing existing data on poverty between generations is the variation in measurements across time and across countries. Some countries have changed their scale of measurement over time, particularly in shifting from the traditional to the modified OECD equivalent scale.[8] The results from intergenerational comparisons are sensitive to choice of measurement; a general finding is that shifting to the modified OECD scale has changed the distribution of poverty between generations from the children to the elderly.

Fig. 5 illustrates the impact of the change in measurement for Norway based on two studies from Statistics Norway. One uses the traditional, the other the modified, OECD scale, but both include the year 1991 (Aaberge et al., 1996; Epland, 2001 in Jensen et al., 2004b, pp. 352, 355).

Comparing poverty levels as estimated by the traditional and modified scales for 1991 shows the effect of the scale change. On examining this figure, it can be seen that the changes in measurements have not had much of an impact on the incidence of poverty among children (6 and 5 percent, respectively). The main impact is in the intergenerational comparison. The new scale boosts the level of poverty among the elderly. Similar conclusions can be drawn from a comparison between the traditional and the modified OECD scales in Estonia (Kutsar, Harro, Tiit, & Matrov, 2004) and Finland (Alanen et al., 2004). Poverty among the elderly increased when the modified scale was used, while among children it decreased. For Austria, Beham, Wintersberger, Wörister, and Zartler (2004) concluded that while child poverty was at higher levels in the 1990s, a major shift in the generational distribution of poverty has taken place, along with modification of the OECD scales. Old age poverty is higher and childhood poverty

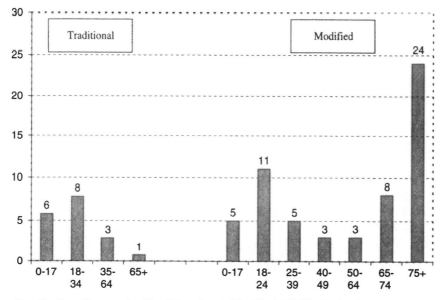

Fig. 5. Low Income by Traditional and Modified OECD Scales, Norway 1991.

lower. This is also the case for Cyprus, where only the modified scale is used (Kouloumou, 2004). Yet, '... it is [...] unclear to which extent this improvement with a view to child poverty is due to improvement in the monetary transfer system for families with children on the one hand, and to changed measuring instruments (e.g. a flatter equivalent scale) on the other' (Beham et al., 2004, p. 31).

Given these measurement problems, the jury is still out in some countries on whether there has been a balance in the relative incidence of poverty among children and the elderly. Conclusions concerning the incidence of poverty among children and the elderly depend greatly, in fact, on the instruments of measurement, and comparisons over time may be constrained because of changes. The question whether changes in the measurement instruments themselves are influenced by the ageing of societies was raised by several researchers. Will ageing societies further a common understanding of making the needs of the elderly more visible? No clear answer was given as to whether there was an ideological motive behind the shift, but the political message surfacing from the modified scale is clear; children appear to be less in need of public transfers than are the elderly when the modified equivalence scale is used.

CHILDREN'S DEPENDENCE ON
TWO PARENTAL INCOMES

Even though countries are very different in their economic, religious and cultural backgrounds, the sources of child poverty at family level are remarkably similar among the countries studied and can be summarized as:

- Age: Younger children are more likely to be poor.
- Sibling numbers: Several siblings means that children are at greater risk.
- Nationality: Children from ethnic minorities are more likely to be poor.
- Parental employment: Having a parent at home without a paid position increases risk.
- Parental relationships: Children of parents who are separated are at greater risk.
- Single-mother households: Living with the mother only increases risk.

One by one, these factors mirror the problems caused by reliance on mothers' additional income as a 'bulwark' against child poverty (Esping-Andersen, with Gallie, Hemerijk, & Meyers, 2002, p. 58). Children themselves reduce the likelihood of both parents being employed, since mothers are more likely to be at home or to have reduced working hours while their children are young or if they have several children. By being dependent on their mother's market activities, children, as stated in the Estonian report: '... "multiply" poverty by their existence' (Kutsar et al., 2004, p. 106). The situation is aggravated by the destabilization of families and the emerging trend of children living with single mothers. While having dual-earner parents offers protection against poverty, fathers are increasingly not living with their children – their income provision therefore being less secure. Furthermore, both education and family patterns are sensitive to an underlying class dimension. Higher educated mothers are more likely to be married and employed (with better salaries), while lower educated mothers are more likely to be single and less likely to have sufficient income (McLanahan, 2004). Marginal employment and single motherhood together increase the material disparities between children, but cultural traditions underpinning traditional male breadwinner families may also produce single-earner families. Ethnic minority parents may be single earners (although not single parents) owing to the combined factors of lower education, more children, traditional family norms and racial discrimination in the labour market. These families may experience unemployment for reasons linked to the labour market itself, but when parental income is unable to provide for their children's welfare, the role of the state gains in importance. It is exactly this role that is under pressure from ageing societies, but the impact varies from country to country. In sum, children's dependence on two parental incomes in combination with fragile family patterns increases the differences in their welfare. Some children are better off, while poverty among children lacking the required parental resources is aggravated.

Poverty risks are distributed differently across countries and social groups. Single-earner families vary widely across Europe, as do welfare systems. Two cases may serve as illustrations. In Bulgaria, 21 per cent of all children are brought up by one parent only: 17 per cent by the mother and 4 per cent by the father (Raycheva et al., 2004). In Norway, about 40 per cent of children born in the early 1990s were likely to live in a single-mother family for part of their childhood (Jensen et al., 2004b). Nevertheless, relatively few children in Norway are poor, while among Bulgarian children poverty is widespread. There are more reasons for this other than welfare systems. The overall wealth of these two countries, as measured by GDP, is widely different. In Norway, the phenomenon of street children, i.e. the situation of children with no or an absentee family and living on the street, is non-existent, while in Bulgaria it is substantial, as an after-effect of the previous regime's demographic policies and of the economic and social shocks of the transition period (Raycheva et al., 2004).

Children's accounts of poverty provide a clue to the difficult life situations beyond the figures. Mayhew, Uprichard, Ridge, Bradshaw, and Beresford (2004) give examples for the UK, a country with a high proportion of children living in poverty. Here, children describe three areas of particular concern: the need to have one's own money to spend autonomously; the need for 'appropriate' clothing for peer acceptance; and the restrictive effect of lack of transport on personal mobility. Being poor in a rich country is not easy, as illustrated by the many quotes. For example, one child says:

> Like when they went downtown and they were spending their money, I'd go downtown but not spend anything. If you're hanging around with people that are getting quite a lot of things from their parents and you are not, you feel you don't want them to know. That's the last thing you want them to know, and you're kind of like trying to keep it from them. (Girl, 15 years; Mayhew et al., 2004, p. 415)

Nicole, 13 years, explains:

> You can't do as much and I don't like my clothes and that. So I don't really get to do much or do stuff like my friends are doing ... I'm worried about what people think of me, like they think I'm sad or something. (Mayhew et al., 2004, p. 416)

Nicole lives in the UK, a liberal market society, but also a country where many children live in single-parent families or in families where the parents are unemployed. For children like her, the family is an indispensable source of welfare, and poverty levels are high.

Croatia has been at war for many years. Living through war means not only the fear of being killed at any moment, but also of experiencing difficulty in meeting the most basic needs. A 1999 study found that among young people (aged 17–18) living in war-affected areas, some 30 per cent were frequently worried about whether their family could cover the basic costs of living. In addition, 35 per cent of them did not have enough pocket money, 37 per cent stated that their family did not have enough money to pay the bills, 20 per cent that they could not buy clothes, while having a holiday was impossible for 61 per cent. The Croatian researcher concludes (Raboteg-Šarić, 2004, pp. 554, 555) that poverty touches more children during their childhood than is reflected by statistical data on poverty. Against this exceptional background of distress and high vulnerability, however, some of the perceptions of children experiencing poverty are similar to those found in countries not so devastated by war.

> For young people 'poverty is boredom'. Rural youth explained that without money they can't socialize with other young people, they are stuck with their family because of transport costs and because they cannot afford coffee in a café or any other form of entertainment. City youth explained that being poor means no goal, 'only mindless sitting around with friends'. (Raboteg-Šarić, 2004, p. 554)

Another former socialist country, Estonia, had poverty rates among children varying between 14 and 18 per cent of all children in 2002 (as measured by the modified and traditional equivalence scales, poverty threshold at 60 per cent of the median income). A study among schoolchildren (8th grade) confirmed a statistically significant impact of poor economic conditions as viewed by a child, from an economic, social as well as psychological perspective. Compared to their friends, children in poor families considered that they had less pocket money, could afford fewer necessities, and were unable to attend school events and hobby groups. Many children experienced social isolation. They felt they were less favoured by their teachers and classmates. They had little self-esteem and were less satisfied with their abilities. In sum, these children more often regarded themselves as being unsuccessful and unhappy than did children in a better economic situation. Children often stop telling their parents about needs the family cannot afford. As a result, their own feeling of deprivation grows (Kutsar et al., 2004, p. 108, 111).

Possibly, the worst condition is that of street children who have no or only tenuous links with their families. This phenomenon seemed to have disappeared in Europe, but immigration and the turmoil of the transition period have brought it back. Bulgaria is a case in point.

> The growth of the number of homeless children is an extremely painful and topical problem in Bulgaria. ... (the) number includes children spending most of the day on the street, where they earn their daily bread and then go back home at night, as well as children, who literally live in the street. The former ones either have no family or have left it for various reasons, including for being expelled by their parents. Parking lots, wayside pubs, markets, stations are the places usually inhabited by homeless children. They often move from place to place looking for food or running away from the police, which makes it difficult to establish their exact number. (Raycheva et al., 2004, p. 495)

So long as children are increasingly dependent on the income of their parents, there is a built-in moment of risk, due to the direct link between number of parental incomes, family structure and child poverty. In Germany, a growing polarization among children is already being noted, and is likely to surface in many countries through rising income inequality:

> Demographic factors such as the type of family (particularly lone parent families and families with many children), the number of unemployed or inactive adults in the household and the educational level of the parents or guardians are decisive for the concrete material situation and/or poverty of households. (Jurczyk et al., 2004, p. 711)

For Austria, Beham et al. (2004, p. 36) noted a remarkably strong correspondence between the number of children in a household and poverty. Using a set of international studies, the report concluded: 'All relevant studies agree that the risk of child poverty is predominantly connected with demographic (number of children/lone motherhood) as well as socio-economic (number of incomes in a household) criteria'.

Preston (1984) argued that the generational struggle for welfare transfers works through political priorities. The Children's Welfare Network has illustrated the impacts of mother's employment and changing family patterns in differing European contexts. In societies where two incomes have become a necessity, the growth in children living in single-income families embodies an economic risk for children in both traditional male-breadwinner and single-mother families. Changing family patterns expose children to new risks, as is done by traditional gender roles. For children, the welfare state is crucial. If families are susceptible to being unable to provide sufficiently for their children's welfare, the role of the state gains in importance, and it is this role that is under pressure from ageing societies. However, the impact varies among countries.

GENERATIONAL STRUGGLE FOR WELFARE RESOURCES?

In most countries, the welfare state intervenes to combat child poverty, but the levels of intervention differ. This may occur preventively – through relatively generous family transfers and the provision of services – or ex post, reparatively, when children are poor. The overall welfare state package varies greatly across Europe (see, e.g. Bradshaw, 2007), as does efficacy, combined with mothers' employment rates. In general, where children's material welfare is defined as a public responsibility through the welfare state, child poverty is lower. This is so in the Nordic countries, where child poverty is low, notwithstanding an increasing percentage of children growing up in single-mother families. In contrast, where children are seen as a private responsibility, more children are poor. This is the case in the UK and Bulgaria, countries with a high proportion of single mothers, but it is also true for Italy, where there are few children living with single mothers. The Italian case is actually a good example of how risks for children may arise from the very persistence of traditional, male-breadwinner, family and gender arrangements, not from their weakening, also given the lack of adequate child benefits:

> ... neither the employment of at least one of the parents, nor the greater stability of the family and the fact that the proportion of children born out of wedlock is very low – all conditions that would seem to constitute propitious circumstances compared with other countries – protect children and minors effectively against the risk of poverty. (Saraceno, 2002 in Conti and Sgritta, 2004, p. 301)

In countries such as the UK and Ireland, programmes have been launched specifically addressing poverty among children. In Ireland, high child poverty levels prompted a national strategy for the elimination of child poverty by 2007, resulting in a slight decline in the mid-1990s. But Irish children are still more likely to be poor than adults: in 1997, 26 per cent compared to 20 per cent of adults (50 per cent of the median income). Although the level of child poverty has declined in recent years, the condition of poor children has worsened (Devine, Nic Ghiolla Phádraig, & Deegan, 2004, pp. 219, 227). Similarly, since 1997, the anti-poverty strategy known as Opportunity for All has reduced the trend in child poverty in the UK (Mayhew et al., 2004, p. 408), but it still remains high (see Fig. 4 on p. 172).

Some countries stand out with particularly harsh descriptions of the economic situation of children, e.g. Bulgaria, Italy and Estonia. These are also countries where fertility has fallen to a very low level and where the pressure from an ageing society may be at its strongest. In contrast, Scandinavian countries have a relatively high and slightly increasing fertility in combination with high employment and fragile families. The welfare state has prevented this from resulting in more child poverty. But all over Europe children depend more on two parental incomes, while the elderly are provided for through the public purse. Ageing is likely to impact on this development. One possible route through which this can take place is by the spatial segregation of generations.

SPATIAL SEGREGATION, DOMESTICATION AND VIRTUAL CHILDHOOD

More adults are living with no children in their household. Urbanisation, traffic and the needs of modern societies have ushered children inside the home, engaging in the virtual reality of new technology rather than in face-to-face interaction. As a result of increased 'domestication', children are separated from an adult society in which a growing share of the population do not share their private lives with a child, and where the opportunity to meet other children in public spaces is on decline. As larger segments of the population have little or no direct interaction with children in everyday life, the social and cultural considerations of the needs of children may decrease, perhaps along with growing cultural divides between generations.

In a multitude of ways, children's everyday lives are constrained by common forces that are affecting their economic welfare and their access to socio-spatial environments. Parental employment is a prime force in structuring children's everyday lives, providing a framework for time use, use of space, sources of care and the interaction among family members. From the child's point of view, there may be a conflict between dependency on two parental incomes and access to time with parents. A particular problem lies with the increasing flexibility of the labour market, as described in the German report (Jurczyk et al., 2004). Only 15 per cent of the work force is now employed in 'standard working hours' (27 per cent about 10 years ago). People work in shifts, on weekends, overtime, part-time, or flexitime in an ever greedier labour market. The previously clear boundaries between working hours and leisure time are disappearing and those between work and family life have become 'blurred'. In a study of 8–10-year-olds, the uncertainty of working hours surfaced as a major problem, as expressed by one child:

> I never know when she comes home. When she has a business meeting and does not know in advance, she will come later. And I need to wait and can't arrange anything with my friends. I never can tell them to come, because my mother may not be at home. That's really vexing me. (Boy, 9 years; Jurczyk et al., 2004, p. 744)

And another child expressed:

> I may come home and mum's there, and another time I come home and mum's not there. Some time it's this way and some time that – I can't rely on anything. Then I look in on granny whether she is at home, but it would be best if I were at home. It bothers me that I don't know in advance and I get furious when things don't work out. (Boy, 10 years; Jurczyk et al., 2004, p. 744)

Children are unable to make plans because of uncertainties in parent work schedules. Many are allowed to play outside only while a parent is at home. They, therefore, have long periods of waiting inside until a parent arrives home from work. The solution, however, is not the parent stopping working. Children of non-working mothers constantly feel under observation and monitored, with their mother's constant presence robbing them of an opportunity to escape the family regime:

> It gets on my nerves when there's always somebody around. No matter what I do, my mother will always notice. I can't watch TV or eat when I want to. I told her to go to work for a few hours but she doesn't want to. (Girl, 11 years; Jurczyk et al., 2004, p. 743)

What children desire has been formulated by a 10-year-old girl:

> To leave free parts of time for yourself, to allow yourself from time to time for a break, ... to choose on your own on what issue you start. (Jurczyk et al., 2004, p. 763)

Studies of children's reactions reveal that parents' employment has a multifaceted impact on their welfare. German children described four desirable types of parental presence and absence: they want affection, proximity and activities shared with their parents, but also periods of time enjoyed autonomously. In situations of need, children see their parents' presence as a matter of course (Jurczyk et al., 2004, p. 743).

Similarly, Austrian children seldom complain about parental employment (Beham et al., 2004). They understand that their parents need to make money. Children appreciate family time but – perhaps surprisingly – too much time, rather than too little, with parents is more often reported as a problem: 'The children experience their parent's involvement into the planning of time schedules as too extensive and as a reduction of their own liberty and sovereignty' (Beham et al., 2004, p. 51). Children want access to their parents, but not unlimited time with them. These observations accord with the ways in which children in the UK view 'family time' (11–13-year-olds). Children listed the following features as important: ordinariness and routines of domestic life; availability of support when needed; time to be alone while also within reach of other family members; and being able to plan one's own time. Meeting these goals was constrained by busy lives in the family, but also by lack of space within the home (Mayhew et al., 2004, pp. 427–428). Several reports testified to a trend in which children no longer moved freely in public space.

Spatial segregation is not just the outcome of children's loss of control over space and time. Demographic developments also play a part in which children as a population group are alienated from adult society. In Italy, streets and public spaces are empty of children not only because of the low birth rate, but also because of parents' and grandparents' worries of what might happen to them outside (Conti & Sgritta, 2004). In the UK, a situation of children playing outside unaccompanied by an adult is becoming a marker of neglectful or irresponsible parenthood (Mayhew et al., 2004, p. 273). Children left alone at home, however, is also a problem. In Finland, this is labelled as 'crisis of parenthood' or a 'lone-child' problem (Alanen et al., 2004, p. 186). Traditional 'spaces in-between', such as the road to school, are reduced. In Denmark and Norway, where children's 'free play' and the ability to move freely outdoors loom large in adults' value perceptions of childhood, children are increasingly being taken to school in the family car – even over short distances. A Danish mother puts it this way:

> It is the way society functions – we drive our children too much, but we have to because you live so far from everything, and you are so busy and you have to get from one place to the other, and we have our cars. ... You are generally more anxious today, with the dark, violence, the street and everything. And the consequence is that they are ferried around by us – that's a pity. It is such a lovely freedom to ride your bike and feel the air on your face. (Mother of an 11-year-old boy; Kampmann & Nielsen, 2004, p. 542)

With children constituting a smaller section of the population and more people living with no children in the household, adult society contains more 'strangers and dangers'. The sum of varying forces is that the 'wild space' is being 'tamed' (Conti & Sgritta, 2004, p. 319). The virtual space is inducing children to accept being 'locked' inside the home. Adults are keeping children away from the dangerous outside with 'the helping hand' of new technology transforming the home into a 'golden cage'. TV, computer and mobile telephone have become means of control to keep the children away from outside dangers (Conti & Sgritta, 2004, p. 311).

Through virtual space, children are entertained and are able to communicate without the boundaries of the 'real' space. Several studies in Austria have shown that watching TV is a very important part of children's leisure time (7–15 years). Almost every second child has its own TV. The reasons children give for watching TV are: because they are bored (73 per cent), because they are alone at home (61 per cent), because of bad weather (68 per cent) or because no one has time for them (41 per cent) (Beham et al., 2004, p. 56).

Bulgarian children are another example of this development. Owing to parent work schedules, children spend a large part of their day alone at home, and are free to watch whatever they want on TV, on average three hours a day. Liberalization of the media market provides children who live in a household with cable TV (numbering more than 1 million out of a population of almost 8 million) access to more than 300 radio and TV programmes. A typical paradox, the report observes, is large quantitative supply combined with reduced quality, a lack of variety and limited choice. Imported film production (American as a rule, mostly cartoons) prevails (Raycheva et al., 2004).

Strikingly similar tendencies run across countries of children having a TV and/or computer in their own room, and spending an increasing amount of time using them. Family weekends watching TV, and a lack of local, non-commercial areas 'off-street', contribute to the feeling of boredom. These problems were particularly at issue for Ireland, Austria and the UK. However, the increasing amount of time devoted in front of a screen signifies the emergence of virtual childhood as a common feature of European children. Among the forces contributing to this development, the Children's Welfare Network has pointed at population development with increased spatial segregation and stronger pressures on everyday life caused by two parents in the workforce.

CHILDREN'S WELFARE AND AGEING SOCIETIES

Does ageing matter to children's welfare? Why should it matter, and in what terms? The first and second demographic transitions implied social changes with consequences for welfare, first for the elderly and then for children. McLanahan (2004, p. 623) makes a plea for supplying public resources in ensuring children' welfare: 'We did so for the elderly after the first transition, and children deserve no less'. To 'liberate' children from exclusive dependence on private, family-provision may prove difficult, however, since the ageing process in itself may be an obstacle.

One hypothesis of the Children's Welfare Network is that an ageing population might result in greater pressure and declining welfare resources for children. Perceptions of children's needs versus the needs of other age groups are subjected to public discourses and ongoing redefinitions, as we may have seen in the change in measurement instruments of poverty. The justification for providing for the elderly, who have already contributed to society during their lifetime, may be clearer than the justification for spending on children. Children are not necessarily seen as contributors to the social fabric, but often as an expense and a responsibility of their parents. Nevertheless, it is children who will provide for the elderly in the future; and too few of them are a challenge to society as such. Researchers have warned against increasing gaps in generational welfare (Preston, 1984). However, generational inequality is expanding in Europe and, consequently, Lutz et al. (2006) predict that ageing may accelerate.

Secondly, the impact of ageing populations does not necessarily work through direct links. It may operate in concert with other social changes such as an increase in maternal employment. The rise in female employment is caused by forces other than changing age structures, such as education and new gender roles. Nevertheless, the effect on children may accord with the claim that children are a private responsibility. At the same time, the influx of mothers into the labour market has been in parallel with an outflow of fathers from the family after parental break-up. Hence, the economic basis for children's welfare is both strengthened and weakened. As a result, a polarization of children's economic welfare is taking place (see also McLanahan (2004) for comparisons on the USA and Europe). Our work has shown that children themselves (through age and number) are at an increased risk of poverty just by being born. The 'child-risk factor' is at play in particular where mothers cannot add an extra income to the family, or where shaky family structures are not compensated by the welfare budget. In general, while providing for the elderly is more often seen as a public responsibility (although often at a low level), working mothers may undermine the claim of children to public economic transfers. In many countries, public services such as childcare have been part of a long-term political battle (as elaborated by Leira, 2002) resulting in strong resistance and persistent care deficits.

Our work confirms that where the welfare state takes a broader role in securing children's welfare, children fare better. In countries where families with young children have a societal security net through a welfare state, they are protected from direct poverty. Previous studies suggest that in the 'de-familising' and 'woman-friendly' welfare states of Scandinavia, public investment in children may partly modify ageing in society.

Third, the spatial separation of generations may perhaps be contributing to cultural climates in which children's needs are being downplayed. Children are increasingly segregated from the adult population outside the family realm. More adults spend a greater part of their lives with no child in the household. Children are increasingly excluded from public spaces, sequestered inside houses (both within homes and into age-segregated institutions such as kindergartens and schools) and out of sight of an increasing share of the population. We may ask whether age segregation could lead to a weakening of the collective consciousness of children as public goods.

The Children's Welfare Network raised the issue of the consequences of ageing societies, but the generational perspective turned out to be difficult to pursue. While the country reports describe a shift towards an ageing society, they also reveal that much remains to be studied if we are to understand whether and how this development may have an impact on childhood. Moreover, the marginalization of children from public concerns may not be the result of population ageing, but rather its cause. The high – financial and otherwise – costs of bringing up children, particularly for women, may curb the willingness to have any, or, at any rate, more than one. The ageing of society may be a reinforcing process if the needs of the elderly are given priority over those of children, which again increases the costs of children to parents. Consequently, ageing may cause changes in childhood conditions, but also be a result of a change in the position of childhood in society. Ageing of societies is a powerful process. If we are to grasp the mechanisms, the impacts on children's needs and experiences have to be considered. At its fundament, ageing is about children's position in the social structure, and as suggested by Ulrich Beck (1992, p. 116): 'the ultimate market society is a childless society'. But it is also true that a childless society has no future market.

NOTES

1. COST A19 started in 2001 and ended in 2006. The COST system is network-based, and has been administered under the European Science Foundation since 2003. It is financed by the European Commission. The COST system does not finance research. About 40–50 researchers from 20 countries took part. The list of countries for this study is presented in Fig. 1 (see p. 167). The Memorandum of Understanding, with its Technical Annex, gives the scientific justification and perspectives of an Action. For COST A19; see http://www.ntnu.svt.no/noseb/costa/ for the full document.

2. The separate country reports are available on the Internet at the address in footnote 1.

3. Sweden shares these features but is not among the COST country reports (Jensen et al., 2004).

4. A COST country, although not a European one.

5. A high level of childlessness is not a new phenomenon in Europe. At the beginning of the twentieth century, women in France, Germany and The Netherlands had a lifetime childlessness rate of around 25 per cent, while in Austria the level reached 32 per cent. Sobotka (2004) argues that childlessness in Europe is currently on the increase, most pronouncedly in England, Wales and West Germany. Among Northern countries, childlessness in Finland, presently and historically, is at much higher levels than in Denmark, Norway and Sweden.

6. In the remaining discussion, I focus on European countries, since Israel (also with less-pronounced ageing) differs in many respects that are not dealt with in this article.

7. Information on generational poverty is not provided for Denmark and the UK. In the Danish report, EU countries are compared according to a list of dimensions of deprivation. According to this list, Denmark scores much lower than Italy, the UK and Germany, and is below the average (3.58 versus 1.72) (Kampmann & Nielsen, 2004, p. 662).

8. In the traditional OECD scale, the first adult is given a weight of 1, and the second 0.7, while each child is weighted as 0.5. In the modified (new) OECD scale, the weight of children has been downscaled to 0.3, so that children count less in the distribution of income among family members.

9. Relative poverty defined as households with an income below 50 per cent of the national median. Austria has only data for 2005.

ACKNOWLEDGMENTS

I thank all the researchers involved in the Children's Welfare Network of COST A19. As the Chair of the Network, I greatly appreciated the enthusiasm and dedication displayed in the writing of the country reports for the publication *Children's Welfare in Ageing Europe*, which was done without financial support and often in the writer's free time. I also thank COST for financing the Network meetings, and the Research Council of Norway for additional financial support, all of which rendered this work possible.

REFERENCES

COST country reports:

Jensen, A.-M., Ben-Arieh, A., Conti, C., Kutsar, D., Nicghiolla Phádraig, M., & Nielsen, H. W. (Eds). (2004a). *Children's welfare in ageing Europe* (Vol. I–II). Trondheim: Norwegian Centre for Child Research.

Individual reports, all in Jensen et al., (2004). Page numbers in text refer to the printed report

Volume I

Alanen, L., Sauli, H., & Strandell, H. Children and childhood in a welfare state. The case of Finland (pp. 143–210).
Beham, M., Wintersberger, H., Wörister, K., & Zartler, U. Childhood in Austria: Cash and care, time and space, children's needs, and public policies (pp. 19–80).
Conti, C., & Sgritta, G. (2004). Childhood in Italy. A family affair (pp. 275–334).
Devine, D., Nic Ghiolla Phádraig, M., & Deegan, J. Time for children – Time for change? Children's rights and welfare in Ireland during a period of economic growth (pp. 211–274).
Jensen, A.-M. Introduction (pp. 13–18).
Jensen, A.-M., Kjørholt, A.T., Qvortrup, J., Sandbæk, M., Johansen, V., & Lauritzen, T. (2004b). Childhood and generation: Money, time and space. Norway (pp. 335–457).
Kutsar, D., Harro, M., Tiit, E.-M., & Matrov, D. Children's welfare in Estonia from different perspectives. (pp. 81–142).
Mayhew, E., Uprichard, E., Ridge, T., Bradshaw, J., & Beresford, B. (2004). UK: Children's welfare (pp. 403–457).

Volume II

Ben-Arieh, A., Boyer, Y., & Gajst, I. Children's welfare in Israel: Growing up in a multicultural society (pp. 771–812).
Jensen, A.-M., & Qvortrup, J. Summary. A childhood mosaic: What did we learn? (pp. 813–832).
Jurczyk, K, Olk, T., & Zeiher, H. German children's welfare between economy and ideology (pp. 703–770).
Kampmann, J., & Nielsen, H. W. Socialized childhood: Children's childhoods in Denmark (pp. 649–702).
Kouloumou, T. (2004). Children's welfare and everyday life in Cyprus: A family affair with intergenerational implications (pp. 591–648).
Raboteg-Šarić, Z. Children's welfare in the context of social and economic changes in Croatia (pp. 527–590).
Raycheva, L., Hristova, K., Radomirova, D., & Ginev, R. Bulgaria: Childhood in transition (pp. 469–526).

Other references

Beck, U. (1992). *Risk society. Towards a new modernity*. London: Sage.
Bradshaw, J. (2007). Child benefit packages in 22 countries. In: Wintersberger, H., Alanen, L., Olk, T., & Qvortrup, J. (Eds), *Childhood, generational order and the welfare state: Exploring children's social and economic welfare* (Vol. 1 of COST A19, pp. 141-160). Odense: University Press of Southern Denmark.

Esping-Andersen, G., Gallie, D., Hemerijk, A., & Meyers, J. (2002). *Why we need a new welfare state*. Oxford: Oxford University Press.

Leira, A. (2002). *Working parents and the welfare state. Family change and policy reform in Scandinavia*. Cambridge: Cambridge University Press.

Lesthaeghe, R. (1995). The second demographic transition in Western countries: An interpretation. In: K. O. Mason & A.-M. Jensen (Eds), *Gender and family change in industrialized countries* (pp. 17–62). Oxford: Clarendon Press.

Lutz, W., Skirbekk, V., & Testa, M. R. (2006). The low fertility trap hypothesis: Forces that may lead to further postponement and fewer births in Europe. In: *Vienna Yearbook of Population Research* (pp. 167–192) (special issue on 'Postponement of childbearing in Europe'). Vienna: Verlag der Österreichishen Akademie der Wissenshaften.

McLanahan, S. (2004). Diverging destinies: How children are faring under the second demographic transition. *Demography*, *41*(4), 607–627.

Notestein, F. W. (1976). Population – The long view. In: T. W. Schultz (Ed.), *Food for the world* (pp. 36–57). New York: Arno Press.

Preston, S. (1984). Children and the elderly in the U.S.. *Scientific American*, *251*(6), 36–41.

Qvortrup, J., Bardy, M., Sgritta, M., & Wintersberger, H. (Eds). (1994). *Childhood matters. Social theory, practice and politics*. Avebury: Aldershot.

Sobotka, T. (2004). *Postponement of childbearing and low fertility in Europe*. Doctoral thesis, University of Groningen, The Netherlands. Amsterdam: Dutch University Press.

Treas, J. (2000). Will social institutions mediate economic trends? *American Journal of Economics and Sociology*, *59*(1), 61–64.

UNICEF. (2000). *A league table of child poverty in rich nations*. Florence: Innocenti Research Centre.

UNICEF (2005). *Child poverty in rich countries 2005*. Report Card no. 6. Florence: Innocenti Research Centre.

United Nations. (2002). *World population ageing 1950–2050. Economic and social affairs*. New York: United Nations.

PART III:
DIVERSITIES OF CHILDHOOD

FIRST BORN IN AMSTERDAM: THE CHANGING MOTHER–CHILD SETTING

Cecile Wetzels

INTRODUCTION

One of the most important changes in the past few decades influencing the way in which early childhood is experienced in European countries is the dramatic increase of mothers with young children who are also active in the paid labour force. The Dutch case is exemplary of this change. Dutch women's labour force participation increased from internationally the lowest rate for married women at 7.3% in 1960, to 32.8% in 1987 and to 58.7% in 2005. The latter was above the average participation rate in the European Union (15 countries) (Statistics Netherlands, CBS, 2006). In addition, the proportion of employed mothers with children below the age of 6 more than doubled in less than a decade: from 26% in 1988 to 57% in 1996 (OSA, 1997).[1] In 2003, 90% of women in the Netherlands remained in the labour force after giving birth to their first child, although they worked fewer hours (Statistics Netherlands, CBS, 2006). Children who are born in the Netherlands nowadays, therefore, generally have a mother working in the labour market, who has to organise her time around the triple needs of care, income and professional demands. This substantial change from the situation still prevalent in the mid-eighties, is somewhat counter-balanced by changes in fathers' behaviour following the

Childhood: Changing Contexts
Comparative Social Research, Volume 25, 193–238
Copyright © 2008 by Emerald Group Publishing Limited
All rights of reproduction in any form reserved
ISSN: 0195-6310/doi:10.1016/S0195-6310(07)00007-5

birth of a child. While in most European countries fathers increase their labour force participation when they have a child (see e.g. Plantenga & Siegel, 2004), an increasing proportion of Dutch fathers on the contrary reduces it. 10% of first-time fathers reduced their working hours when their child was born in 1997, 13% did so in 2003 (Statistics Netherlands, CBS, 2006).[2]

Are these two trends homogeneous across all social groups? Dutch society in recent years has been experiencing, due to immigration, new forms of social and cultural differentiation in addition to the traditional ones. The proportion of children with an immigrant background has increased, and in 2004, more than half of the children born in Amsterdam had at least one parent or grandparent born abroad (O & S (2004)).

The purpose of this study is to improve our understanding of how parents of first-born children in the Netherlands take their decisions with regard to the combination of paid work and care. We hypothesise that these decisions are shaped on the one hand by human capital resources (education, language skills, autochthonous vs. immigrant background and so forth), culturally defined gender scripts and household structure and organisation (dual parent or one parent, presence or not of other adults), on the other hand by Dutch parental leave policies.[3] A number of existing studies have indicated that parental leave policies and the availability of part-time work are means for mothers to balance their paid work and family responsibilities (for a literature review see Del Boca & Wetzels, 2007). Little empirical work has however been conducted on the influence of the partner's employment status. Furthermore, there is no study known to us that investigates the effect of immigrant background on parental work patterns when children are born in a European country's setting.

This paper explores these issues in the Dutch context. Firstly, we assess parental paid work arrangements by different kinds of backgrounds with regard to the autochthonous/immigrant divide. With regard to the immigrant status, we distinguished between the mother, her partner and her parents. Unfortunately, our data do not provide information on the country of origin of the partner's parents. Secondly, we further flesh out, beyond the standard human capital explanations, what we would consider the influence of the family (the partner's employment status, the family's immigrant background and the importance of mother's mother opinion on breastfeeding) on women's employment and hours of paid work. In doing so, we shed light on the determinants of the mother's decision to care for her child herself or to share it with somebody else/a childcare service. This decision, in fact, affects whether or not both, or only one, parent(s) will try to combine paid work and childcare.

In our analysis, we focus on first infants born in the Netherlands in 2004. Therefore, all first infants' parents are making their employment and care decisions in the context of the Dutch welfare state, which has moved beyond the male breadwinner model prevalent in the mid-eighties as far as expectations concerning women's labour market participation are concerned, but without providing enough childcare services. We make use of unique and recent data from two surveys (a panel) on public health, which were conducted at two distinct points in a child's and mother's life: around 16 weeks of pregnancy and when the infant was between 3- and 5-months-old. The surveys were held in the public health project: "Amsterdam Born Children and their Development", which was carried out by the Amsterdam Medical Centre and the Amsterdam Municipal Health Service in 2003 and 2004, with financial support from the Dutch Scientific Council.[4]

This chapter is structured as follows. "The Dutch Context" presents the Dutch setting. Our hypotheses, which are informed by the findings of recent studies, are developed in "Hypotheses". "Methodolgy and Data" discusses the data and methodology used. Our estimation results are presented and discussed in "Results and Discussion" and our conclusions in "Conclusion".

THE DUTCH CONTEXT

Several researchers have emphasized that institutions influence the context in which labour market decisions are made (for a review, see Del Boca & Wetzels, 2007). In the Dutch context, the labour market is characterised by many male, and not only female, part-time workers. Since the developments in combining paid work and care for young infants are quite recent, we provide here an overview of their background.

In the Netherlands, in 1924, a female civil servant's wedding day was also the day she would lose her job. Only in 1973 did Dutch women gain the same protection that, for example, Swedish women secured in 1939 and Italian ones in the early fifties, namely legislation that made it unlawful for employers to dismiss a woman because of pregnancy, childbirth or marriage. Since then "the emergence (and persistence and growth) of the working wife in Holland" (Hartog & Theeuwes, 1985) has been spectacular in terms of participation rates. Yet, although having the same legal and social policy settings, several specific groups of women, especially mothers, in the Netherlands have significantly lower labour supply rates. Among these, there are women who were born in another country, or whose parents were born abroad. Family reunion, traditionally the main factor of ethnic minority[5] increase in the Netherlands accounted for 22% of all non-Dutch immigrants in 2001. It is however a decreasing phenomenon, whereas immigration due to family formation accounted for 15% of immigration, and is increasing (Hartog & Zorlu, 2004).[6] Zorlu (2002, Chapter 9) shows that – in Amsterdam in 1999 – the negative effect of having children on labour force participation was larger for Turkish and Moroccan families than for other immigrant groups. The gender gap in labour force participation is the smallest for Caribbean, followed by South European and Dutch women. For Turkish and Moroccan women, the gender gap in participation probabilities is respectively 0.497 and 0.302. Furthermore, the participation rates of second-generation immigrants do not differ from those of the first-generation, as indicated by the marginal effects of the variable "born in the Netherlands" across the sub-samples.[7]

In spite of the increase in labour force participation, the volume of full-time regular jobs in 1996 was the same as in 1970 – about 3.7 million people. The steady job growth in the early 1990s consisted entirely of part-time jobs. In 1996, 1.8 million people had part-time jobs and 0.7 million people had flexible jobs (Hartog, 1998).[8] Several factors can explain this (Visser, 2002, Gustafsson, Kenjoh & Wetzels, 2003). In the tight labour market of the 1990s, fear of labour shortages encouraged employers who were otherwise reluctant to accept part-time workers. Furthermore, public policies during the 1990s aimed at enabling men to take parental leave and work part-time in order to share care and paid work more equally, and thus keep both parents in the labour market when children are young.

The right to shorten or lengthen paid work hours was accepted in the Netherlands before everywhere else; and the country has gone much farther[9] than demanding that employers should "give consideration" to employees who wish to transfer between full-time and part-time work, as the 1997 European Directive on Part-time Work status states.[10] The employer should, in principle, agree to the request and is obliged to indicate any reason for disagreement. There is also a structural demand for part-timers in higher job levels in the Netherlands, which is larger than in other European countries. Furthermore, employers consider part-time workers as committed as full-time workers. With 39% of employed people in part-time jobs, the Netherlands is indeed far ahead of other European countries. It is also number one as regards the percentage of women working for pay less than 35 h per week (67.6%). In addition, part-time work in the Netherlands is much less limited to a particular group of women than in the UK, Germany and Sweden (Gustafsson et al., 2003). Nevertheless, in 1996, the greatest difference in the proportion of women working for pay less than 32 h per week was found between childless women (37%) and mothers (86%) (Wetzels, 2001). In 2005, only in 6% of two-parents households with a woman in the age 25–49 and small children both parents work for pay full-time. In similar households without children, the percentage of both partners working fulltime is 38% (SCP, 2006). Zorlu (2002, Chapter 8) found that in 1997 working for pay part-time compared to full-time and flexible jobs was more common among men and women in eight ethnic minority groups than in the ethnic majority.[11] More recent data, however, offer a different picture: in all main immigrant groups, if mothers with dependent children (age below 18) are employed, they are more often (19–32%) employed full time than the "fully Dutch" (11%) (Statistics Netherlands, CBS, 2005). These most recent figures also show that working between 20 and 34 h (long part time) is the popular choice of hours in all major immigrant groups, and varies between 35 and 48% compared to full Dutch (45%), and working between 1 and 20 h per week is most frequently chosen by the fully Dutch (44%). These data are similar to those found for other countries. For instance, Yerkes and Visser (2005) found that in the UK women from ethnic minority groups work more full-time than the ethnic majority. Tratsaert (2004) found the same for Belgium. There are, however, no statistics available on the choice of working hours for parents with an immigrant background before they have the first child and when the infant is very young.

A forerunner with regard to part-time and flexible work arrangements for both women and men, the Netherlands lag behind with regard to other kinds of conciliating policies. The Dutch pregnancy leave and maternity leave period is the agreed minimum of the EC directive in 1996. As of 2005, pregnancy leave is 16 weeks (100% paid). It starts 6–4 weeks prior to the expected delivery and ends when the child is about 3 months old. Each parent is entitled to an additional parental leave of 13 weeks. This leave may be taken part time and therefore it may be extended to about 6 months. However, in most cases the parental leave (different from the maternity leave) is unpaid.[12]

The Dutch conciliation policies as regards combining paid work and unpaid childcare started to develop in 1990. Especially since 1995, the Dutch ideal is parental sharing,[13] meaning that both men and women should share the available paid and unpaid work equally. The so-called Combination model pleads for a shift from the practice of the one-and-a-half model which developed during the 1980s and early 1990s, to the twice-three-quarter model, based on a 32 h paid work week. Parental sharing implies two things: part-time rather than full-time employment is the norm; and while women should not reduce all their caring activities, men should be more involved in caring.[14] Underlying this idea is that parents remain attached to the labour market for a substantial number of hours, and that they "temporarily" – when children are young – reduce their work hours in order to care for their child 1 day per week. Ideally, therefore, children should not be put in professional childcare for more than 3 days a week.

This model assumes that all households with children include two parents, that both parents work for pay a substantial number of hours before the first child is born and that when they have a child they partly substitute paid work with unpaid work, therefore renouncing a portion of their labour market earnings. The whole idea is presented in terms of change in labour market hours. However, parents who do not participate in paid work, or who work for very few hours before the first child is born, or who do not earn a high enough income to be able to "temporarily" renounce a portion of earnings, or who are the sole parent or the sole breadwinner, are not helped by this idea of parental sharing.[15] Furthermore, men are more easily persuaded to substitute a paid working day with an unpaid working day, if they start on an equal basis with their partner, if they know it is temporary and if their peer group is behaving similarly. Attracting men to care is however considered primarily as an issue of socialisation and conscious raising (Kremer, 2005). In the Netherlands in contrast to other countries, no additional measures were made to financially attract or force fathers to care, as in the Nordic parental leave schemes. Instead, ideological persuasion (using mass media and debate) and giving the opportunity to care (opportunity to work part-time, opportunity to take parental leave) seems to be the policy method.

Pleas for the ideal of parental sharing have not only been promoted as the alternative for full-time motherhood, they are also the opposite of full-time professional care. A strong consensus exists that young children should be taken care of by parents themselves: there remains a strong culture of self care (Plantenga, 1996, RMO 2006: 37).[16] Professional childcare facilities are increasingly available, but they are used on a part-time basis. Furthermore, this ideal of parental sharing is built on solidarity within couples in the Netherlands.[17] Conversely, vertical solidarity, dependency of adult children on their parents and vice versa, has been rejected. The ideal of intergenerational care was eradicated from social policy as early as the 1960s (Kremer, 2005). This has important consequences for childcare: grandparents are not supposed to be involved in caring for their grand-children. Although some grandparents care for grandchildren 1 day a week

(Portegijs, Boelens, & Olsthoom, 2004, Remery, van Doorne-Huiskes, & Schippers, 2000), the grandparents are not expected to care for grandchildren in order for mothers to work for pay. Only 12% of parents say they prefer care by the family (Remery et al., 2000).

The parental sharing of childcare is expected to start after the pregnancy leave period ends and the child is between 10 and 12 weeks old – non-parental institutional childcare is available for young infants from 10 weeks onwards – till the child is 4 years old when Dutch primary school starts.[18] But it is relatively expensive in the international context (Wetzels, 2005). In 2005, 22% of the parents used formal institutional care as the most important non-parental type of childcare when the child is below 1 year (Statistics Netherlands, CBS, 2006)[19] a percentage higher than that found in Italy, Germany and Sweden,[20] but well below that of France and in any case smaller than that of working mothers of young children.

International agreements on maternal health and infant's health have recommended exclusive breastfeeding up to 6 months (Yngve, Kylberg, & Sjöström, 2001). Dutch leave regulations, however, do not easily accommodate the possibility to fulfil this standard. A period of exclusive breastfeeding longer than 3 months might not be easy to reconcile with even part-time paid work, although employers are obliged to offer facilities for breastfeeding (Avishai Bentovim, 2002, Burgmeijer & Reijneveld, 2001; Grjibovski, Yngve, Bygren, & Sjostrom, 2005). Studies in the UK found that returning to work is the most common reason for ceasing breastfeeding between the ages of 4–6 months, whereas physical reasons were more common at earlier stages (for a review of studies in the UK see O'Brien, 2005; for a comparison of Ireland, Sweden and the USA see Galtry, 2003).

Very little evidence exists on how recent parents with an immigrant background actually act on the sharing parenting ideal. Firstly, almost every study analysing immigrant people in the Netherlands use data on the main ethnic minority groups (originating in Morocco, Turkey, Surinam and the Antillean Islands).[21] However, immigrants from these groups do not represent all immigrants in the Netherlands nowadays. In Amsterdam, for example, 60% of foreign-born women do not originate in these ethnic minority groups. 67% of all immigrant fathers with a Dutch-born wife whose parents are also Dutch born, do not originate in the ethnic minority groups defined by Dutch policy makers, and 25% of second-generation women do not originate in these categories (own calculations on ABCD data, in line with statistics of O & S, 2004). This means that we know extremely little about the paid hours of work before the first child is born for a very large proportion of parents who do not originate in the Netherlands.

Even less is known on how parents actually cope with parental sharing. O'Brien (2005) mentions that this is also true in the UK and elsewhere.

Secondly, the available cross section data on the labour supply of the ethnic groups defined by Dutch policy makers show that in 1998 Moroccan and Turkish female immigrants have much lower participation rates while having children younger than 4 years, as compared to women with the same immigrant background, but who still live at their parental home, and also lower compared to women who live with a partner but have no children yet (Hooghiemstra & Merens, 2003, Table 3.6–3.8). Since the data are cross sectional and we do not know how fast the behaviour of these particular groups change, we do not know whether the women still living with their parents or in childless couples will give up paid work when they give birth to children. On the other hand, the data show that Moroccan and Turkish immigrant women who participate in the labour market do so more in full-time jobs than the ethnic majority (Hooghiemstra & Merens, 2006, RMO, 2005), although the proportion working for pay full-time in these groups is decreasing (RMO, 2005).[22] In addition, a study using data in 1994[23] found that the proportion of women contributing between 50 and 100% to household earnings was higher in ethnic minority groups than for the fully Dutch (Ministry of Social Affairs and Employment 1997).

HYPOTHESES

Our aim is to further flesh out, beyond the standard human capital explanations, the influence of the family (including an immigrant background, the partner's labour force attachment and the importance of the woman's mother's opinion) on the decisions of women regarding labour supply and hours of paid work at two points in a family's life in the Dutch context: around 16 weeks of pregnancy and when the first infant is between 3 and 5 months old. We regard the situation at early pregnancy as one in which the woman has decided to work for pay without having childcare tasks.

Numerous studies have analysed female labour supply in the institutional context of Europe (see for a recent overview Del Boca & Wetzels, 2007) and of the Netherlands (see for a review Wetzels & Tijdens, 2002). Most studies have found support for the expectations of traditional, human capital theory. According to these, women with higher investments in human capital are more likely to participate in the labour market (Mincer, 1974). At the same time, the higher the income of the mother's partner, the less likely she is to be in paid work. Most studies, however, consider decisions concerning participation to the labour market as if they were individual decisions, and not – in the case of couples – as decisions negotiated within the couple (see also the discussion in Blossfeld & Drobnič, 2001). In our analysis, instead, we will consider the impact of the partner's (the child's father's) employment situation on the mother's decision whether to work for pay when having a child. We will also consider whether the impact is different when the father lives with the mother or instead lives elsewhere. 12% of all first-time pregnant women in Amsterdam did not live with their partner in 2004.

We analyse the probability that a mother will choose gainful employment and a certain category of work hours, controlled for her education by her partner's and family's characteristics. Specifically in the Dutch context, as described above, we expect parents who are employed to opt for equal role sharing of paid work (to maintain labour force attachment and reap the fruits of human capital investments) and of care for the first born after the period of maternity leave. Since the ideal of shared parenting is based on 32 h per week, we wish to understand women's choices for different categories of paid work also putting emphasis on different categories of "long part-time". Part-time jobs may still be perceived to have detrimental career effects in the long run (Russo & Hassink, 2005). This, especially around the birth of the first child, may become an issue as regards which category of hours the parents will choose.[24] Our first hypothesis, therefore reads:

H1. *The choice of working hours among parents who choose a two parents earning arrangement, is likely to be in line with social policies that encourage both parents to work for pay long part-time hours (four days a week) after pregnancy leave.*

Next, we aim to analyse the effects of immigrant backgrounds on the pregnant woman's and recent mother's decision to work for pay. Although previous work found that some immigrant mothers are less likely to participate, even if they are second-generation immigrants, very little research has taken the immigrant background of the partner into account. Some of the effects of an immigrant background on female labour supply will be related to standard human capital investments such as women's education level and the partner's labour force attachment and position, which may differ between immigrants and the "fully Dutch". It is also often mentioned in the literature that immigrants who have problems with the language in the host country are less likely to participate in the labour market. Moreover, previous studies define part time as including 20–34 paid work hours per week. This hours range includes both the long part-time Dutch social policies aim at, and also jobs with less than 24 h which in the literature are taken to indicate a weak labour market attachment. Therefore, we distinguish between less than 24 h of paid work per week on the one hand, and different categories of long part-time work on the other hand.

We propose to capture the effects of immigrant backgrounds in addition to the effects of investments in human capital and in language skills, in order to assess the effects of "being born abroad", and more specifically of having a non-Dutch cultural heritage. Our interest is to explore the effects of the gender and generation of immigration on the decision of a first infant's mother whether to participate in paid work, whether to work part-time after her leave and therefore whether to care full time for the child herself or to share this care with somebody else – a family member, a paid person an institutional service.[25] The immigrant background of the infant's parents is defined in contrast to a "full" Dutch background, which means that the parents of the infant, and the mother's parents, are born in the Netherlands. On the basis of existing literature on immigrant women's labour market participation, our second hypothesis reads:

H2. *The non-Dutch cultural background of the family affects women's decisions to work for pay; if the decision for paid work is made, women with this background choose short part time more often than the "full Dutch ones", and in contrast to the "long part time" policy ideal.*

If the mother's partner is born abroad we expect these effects to be similar or even reinforced, since the choosing of a non-Dutch born partner is seen as an investment in non-Dutch cultural background. If the mother's parents are born abroad but the mother is Dutch-born we expect weaker effects of non-Dutch culture than if she herself is born abroad.

Choosing between categories of working time and of patterns of combining, as well as sharing paid work and unpaid care may not only be affected by human capital and having an immigrant background but also by the influence of the grandmother on the woman's choice for paid work when pregnant and when the infant is very young. Very little is known on whether family members and, more specifically, the own mother's opinion affects the mother's choice to work for pay during pregnancy and when the infant is very young.[26] There is only some information on the general opinion towards employed motherhood.[27] There is a literature on breastfeeding practice and the effects of regular contact with grandparents and advice from grandmothers (Susin, Giugliani, & Kummer, 2005). As described above, especially in the Dutch setting, the older generation (grandparents) is not (expected to be) involved in the decision making on conciliation of paid work and unpaid care for children, and there are also no substantial financial transfers to adult children once they have completed their schooling. In general in the Netherlands, women are expected to make their decisions individually or jointly with their partner, without great influence of their parents. Previous studies have found that some immigrant groups, such as Moroccan and Turkish, have different expectations and standards as regards raising their children. For instance, they seem to stress more obedience, compared to full-Dutch parents whose goal is mainly to foster independence in their children. We may, therefore, expect that the opinion of the mother may be more important for immigrant than non-immigrant women. Whether the woman has an immigrant background or not, however, if the opinion of the mother as regards breastfeeding is very important to the woman, it is likely, as is found in sociological literature on immigrant families (but there is no quantitative evidence available), that the mother has an important say in the daughter's choices with regard to paid work when with a small child (e.g. Ewen, 1985, Orsi, 1985, Vermeulen, 1999). We, therefore, include in the analysis the perceived importance of the grandmother's opinion on breastfeeding, both when the woman is pregnant and when the child is 3 months old. We interpret it as an indicator of the degree of the new mother's autonomy (in relation to the older generation) in decision-making concerning participation to paid work. We see it as comparatively low if the perceived importance of the opinion of the mother's mother is high. We aim to analyse the effect of the mother's opinion on the woman's choices of employed motherhood controlled for woman's education, partner's labour supply, immigrant backgrounds, partner not living in and breastfeeding plans. H3 addresses this issue:

H3. *Mothers for whom their mother's opinion is very important as regards breastfeeding are expected to participate in the labour market to a lesser extent.*

We regard a plan to breastfeed as an indicator of the time the mother plans to be at home, caring full-time for the child. Since the pregnancy leave ends about 12 weeks after delivery, if the mother plans to continue breastfeeding, it will require more effort once she starts working for pay again. Therefore, we control women's labour market decisions for their intentions and breastfeeding behaviour. We expect that a pregnant woman who plans to breastfeed for a period of 3 months or less will be more likely to participate in paid work and return to paid work earlier after the end of pregnancy leave and most probably for a more substantial number of hours per week, compared to a pregnant woman with a plan to breastfeed for longer. Similarly, we expect that women who do not engage in breastfeeding when the infant is between 3 and 5 months old, or who breastfeed for a shorter period, will be more likely to participate in paid work and for longer hours.

METHODOLOGY AND DATA

We empirically analyse the mother's labour force and employment decision when she is pregnant with the first child and when the infant is 3–5 months old. In this section, we first present our data source, then we describe the empirical model and finally we show descriptive statistics of labour market involvement by immigrant backgrounds.

Data and Variables

Data were obtained from two surveys carried out within the longitudinal study called: "Amsterdam Born Children and their Development". The first sample (the ABCD pregnancy sample) comprised all pregnant women who consulted a primary care taker, or a midwife, or any health care institution. These women received a questionnaire in their own language, and if they needed assistance in filling it in, a free call could be made in their native language. In March 2004, 8,105 women who had started their pregnancies in 2003 returned a valid and complete questionnaire. The response rate was 67.8%.

Pregnant women who gave permission to follow-up the health status of the child received a second questionnaire 3 months after birth. This covered lifestyles, emotional problems and the health of the baby. In December 2004, 5,217 women returned the infant questionnaire, having filled it out when the child was 3–5 months old. After the exclusion of women who did not respond to one or more relevant questions, had a multiple pregnancy or used illegal drugs, our final sample consisted of 5,008 women (the ABCD-infants sample). Compared to the pregnancy sample, women of the follow-up sample were older, more educated, of lower parity[28] and more often of Dutch origin (Van der Wal, Eijsden, & van & Bonsel, 2006).

In our pregnancy-sample, we include women who are 34 weeks pregnant or less. The 34 weeks limit relates to the pregnancy leave in the Netherlands, which according to law has to start between 6 and 4 weeks before expected delivery. Thus, all selected women are in a stage of pregnancy in which they are regarded as potential labour force. We include only women pregnant with their first child,[29] since employment patterns change by birth parity in most European countries (Del Boca & Pasqua, 2005; Gustafsson, Wetzels, Vlasblom, & Dex, 1996; Gustafsson et al., 2003). This leaves our pregnancy sample with 4,527 observations. In addition, we include only first born in our infants' sample, which leaves us with 2,902 observations.

Dependent Variables

At 16 weeks pregnancy, the proportion of first-time mothers employed is 78%, which is in line with other research on national samples (Gustafsson et al., 1996). At this stage of pregnancy, 32% of mothers-to-be work for pay full-time, 35% work for pay long part-time, 11% work for pay short part-time, 5% of stopped working for pay because of pregnancy and 17% are not working for pay and have not worked for pay during pregnancy. At the time the first infant is (on average) 13 weeks,[30] the proportion of mothers who have started to work for pay is 42%, 19% work for pay less and 23% more than 24 h per week. Another 43% has the intention to start paid work soon, whereas 15% of the mothers have no intention to work for pay.

Independent Variables

Table 1 shows the characteristics of the two samples. Our control variables (the standard human capital variables, partner living-in, language skills) do not need further explanations. However, we will describe below the variables less common in labour market research.

To test our H1, we define, as Table 1 shows, several categories of working hours and changes of working hours. At pregnancy, the proportion of partners of the mothers-to-be in paid work is 81%. 70% of all partners work for pay full-time, 5% work for pay between 32 and 35 h per week and 6% work for pay in shorter part-time jobs. When the child is 3–5 months, the proportion of mothers' partners/fathers not in paid work is 9%, and 7% of the fathers started to work for pay after the first infant was born. Around half of all fathers (54%) do not change working hours, but a quarter of the fathers increases them, especially working for pay more than 40 h per week (18%). One of every five fathers, instead, decreases working hours, especially to 25–32 h per week (8%) after the first birth. Thus, fathers' changes in working time in both directions are substantial.

Only 47% of the children's sample is "fully Dutch" according to our definition: infant's mother is born in the Netherlands, mother's partner is born in the Netherlands and mother's parents are born in the Netherlands. This confirms the increasing ethnic and cultural heterogeneity of Dutch

Table 1. Samples' Characteristics, Means and Standard Deviation.

First Infant's Mother's Characteristics	Pregnancy Sample		Infants Sample	
	Mean	Std. dev.	Mean	Std. dev.
Dependent variables (%)				
Before*: Participation in paid work	0.78	0.417	0.85	0.360
Before*: Stops paid work because of pregnancy	0.05	0.224	0.04	0.185
Before*: In paid work <=24 h pw	0.11		0.11	0.309
Before*: In paid work >24 h pw	0.67		0.74	
Before*: In paid work 1>24&<36 h pw	0.35	0.478	0.40	0.490
Before*: In paid work full-time ≥36 h per week	0.32	0.465	0.34	0.473
After*: Not in paid work/no intention to start paid work			0.15	
After*: Intention to start work soon			0.43	
After*: In paid work <=24 h pw			0.19	
After*: In paid work >24 h pw			0.23	
Independent variables				
Personal characteristics (%)				
Age (years)	29.64	5.278	30.43	4.832
Low education[a]	0.13	0.336	0.08	0.267
Medium education[a]	0.33	0.471	0.30	0.459
High education[a]	0.53	0.499	0.62	0.487
Household characteristics (%)				
Does not live with partner	0.15	0.357	0.12	0.322
Has partner but does not live with him	0.12	0.329	0.10	0.297
Single	0.03	0.160	0.02	0.138
Weeks pregnant (weeks)	16.33	3.966		
Age infant-(weeks)			13.22	1.97
Family's immigrant characteristics (%)				
Difficulty speaking Dutch[c]	0.10	0.299	0.06	0.228
Born NL; P-born NL; her parents Dutch born[d]	0.45	0.498	0.54	0.498
Immigrant: her parents	0.04	0.187	0.03	0.174
Immigrant: one of her parents	0.05	0.220	0.06	0.233
Immigrant: partner	0.08	0.272	0.09	0.287
Immigrant: partner + parents	0.05	0.211	0.03	0.174
Immigrant: she + her parents	0.09	0.284	0.08	0.271
Immigrant: she and partner	0.22	0.414	0.14	0.348
Labour market characteristics (%):				
Partner in paid work >35 h per week	0.70	0.460	0.74	0.440
Partner in paid work 32–35 h per week	0.05	0.224	0.06	0.237
Partner in paid work 1–32 h per week	0.06	0.239	0.06	0.238
Partner not in paid work	0.15	0.362	0.09	0.282
After*: P-start to work			0.07	0.257
After*: P-in paid work 1–8 (no change of hours)			0.03	0.174

Table 1. (Continued)

First Infant's Mother's Characteristics	Pregnancy Sample		Infants Sample	
	Mean	Std. dev.	Mean	Std. dev.
After*: P-in paid work 9–16 (no change of hours)			0.03	0.157
After*: P-in paid work 17–24 (no change of hours)			0.04	0.184
After*: P-in paid work 25–32 (no change of hours)			0.04	0.195
After*: P-in paid work 33–40 (no change of hours)			0.34	0.475
After*: P-in paid work 41 + (no change of hours)			0.06	0.232
After*: P in paid work more h			0.25	0.435
After*: P in paid work less h			0.21	0.407
After*: P-in paid work 17–24 (less hours)			0.02	0.143
After*: P-in paid work 25–32 (less hours)			0.08	0.269
After*: P-in paid work 33–40 (less hours)			0.02	0.149
After*: P-in paid work 25–32 (more hours)			0.02	0.133
After*: P-in paid work 33–40 (more hours)			0.03	0.175
After*: P-in paid work 41 + (more hours)			0.18	0.387
Variables related to breastfeeding (%)				
Has plan to breastfeed	0.89	0.312	0.90	0.296
Plan for breastfeeding is 1–3 months	0.30	0.460	0.31	0.463
Plan for breastfeeding is 4–6 months	0.26	0.441	0.29	0.454
Opinion of the mother's mother is important[b]	0.21	0.404	0.15	0.353
Actual breastfeed[e]			0.84	0.363
Number of weeks breastfeeding (weeks)			10.89	5.45
N	4492		2902	

Data: ABCD 2003/2004 Pregnancy sample and Infants sample.
Before, at the time of pregnancy; After, at the time the infant is between 3–5 months old. P, Mother's partner.
[a]*A low level of education includes all education up to high school: a medium level of education (the base category in our analysis) includes high school plus two years, and a high-level education includes higher vocational training and a completed university level.*
[b]*Importance of grandmother's opinion is 1 if the answer to the question: how important to you is your mother's opinion on the choice between breastfeeding and industrial milk? Is: "A. Very important"; zero otherwise.*
[c]*Difficulty with language is 1 if the answer to the following question "Do you have a rudimentary knowledge of Dutch, which enables you to communicate? Is:" A. No, I do not speak Dutch; B. yes, but with a lot of difficulty", zero otherwise.*
[d]*We do not show the categories: Immigrant: mother's partner+one of mother's parents (1%) and mother born abroad with parents born in the Netherlands (1%), and even smaller categories.*
[e]*Actual breastfeeding is 1 if mother has started breastfeeding successfully, and 0 is not started breastfeeding or was not successful in breastfeeding.*

society. The remaining children are distributed as follows in the six categories we have developed in order to test our second hypothesis: (1) in 4% of cases both the maternal grandparents are born abroad; (2) in 5% of cases one of the maternal grandparents is born abroad; (3) in 8% of cases the mother's partner (the father) is born abroad; (4) in 5% of cases both the mother's partner and her parents are born abroad; (5) in 9% of cases both the mother and her parents are born abroad; (6) in 22% of cases both the mother and her partner are born abroad. See Table 2 for more details on the definition and the number of observations in our sample. The total proportion of first infants with at least one parent or one of the mother's parents born abroad (55%) corresponds with other statistics on Amsterdam (O & S, 2004).

To test our H3 we include a variable whether the opinion of their mother as regards breastfeeding is very important to the mother. One fifth of mothers indicate that this is so at pregnancy.

We include mother's breastfeeding plans and behaviour as control variables. Almost nine out of 10 women plan to breastfeed; two out of ten plan to breastfeed for less than or equal to 3 months, and 26% plan to breastfeed between 4 and 6 months. When the child is between 3 and 5 months old (on average 13 weeks), 84% of the women have breastfed, and on average they have been breastfeeding for 11 weeks.

Modelling the Parent's Employment Decision

We use multivariate analyses to model and estimate the effects of individual, family and institutional characteristics on our dependent variable: the mother's decision to participate in paid work and her categories of working hours. We estimate her decision twice: at the time of early pregnancy with the first infant and at the time the infant, according to Dutch law, is no longer considered dependent on the mother 24 h a day (10–12 weeks).

At (on average 16 weeks of) pregnancy, our dependent variable distinguishes between six possible employment states, namely domestic work only (non-participation during pregnancy up till now), non-participation at 16 weeks pregnancy but worked before the survey during pregnancy, three categories of part-time, and full-time work. Although the multinomial logit specification is often used for this type of a polychotomous dependent variable, this specification suffers from the need to assume the independence of irrelevant alternatives (IIA). This assumption results from the maintained assumption that the disturbances associated with the utility derived from each option are independent and homoscedastic. One way to relax

Table 2. Family's Immigrant Backgrounds, Single Motherhood (No Partner), Partner Living-in, and Work Status at Pregnancy of the First Child.

Definition of Family's Immigrant Backgrounds

First Infants' Immigrant Background	Born in NL=1 Not born in NL=0				% of Total	N
	M	P	GM	GF		
Parents and mother's parents Dutch born	1	1	1	1	45.32	2,255
Immigrant: mother's parents	1	1	0	0	3.63	163
Immigrant: one of the mother's parents	1	1	0	1	2.32	228
	1	1	1	0	2.62	
Immigrant: mother's partner	1	0	1	1	8.03	367
Immigrant: mother's partner + mother's parents	1	0	0	0	4.68	214
Immigrant: mother + mother's parents	0	1	0	0	8.85	396
Immigrant: both parents	0	0	0	0	22.02	995
Total						4,527

First Infants' Immigrant Background	Single Mother %	Partner Not Living-in Home %	Single Mother Not in Paid Work %	Partner Not Living-in Partner No Paid Work %	Partner Not Living-in Parents Not in Paid Work %	Mother is Sole Earner and Partner Not Living-in %	Partner Living-in Partner No Work %	Partner Living-in Parents Not in Paid Work %	Mother is Sole Earner and Partner Living-ir %
Parents and mother's parents Dutch born	0.1	7.4	0.1	1.1	0.3	0.8	4.2	0.4	3.8
Immigrant: mother's parents	2.5	29.5	1.3	14.7	11.0	3.7	10.4	7.4	3.0
Immigrant: one of the mother's parents	-	10.5	0	2.2	0.9	1.3	3.5	1.3	2.2
Immigrant: mother's partner		16.9	X	5.5	0.6	4.9	19.5	3.6	15.9
Immigrant: mother's partner + M's parents		21.8	X	10.9	6.6	4.3	21.9	11.9	10.0
Immigrant: mother + mother's parents	0.8	8.8	0.5	3.5	1.3	2.2	8.8	5.3	3.5
Immigrant: both parents		17.2	X	10.8	7.1	3.7	19.5	12.4	7.1
Total	0.3	12.4	1.4	4.9	2.7	2.2	10.3	4.7	5.6

Note: ABCD 2003/2004 pregnancy sample. We exclude 1.15% observations on mother's partner and one of mother's parents born abroad, 1.28% of the mother born abroad but her parents Dutch born, and all other immigrant backgrounds since they have below 1% of observations.
Key: M, First infant's mother; P, mother's partner; GM, mother's mother; GF, mother's father. X = single mothers have in many cases not provided information on the father of the child, therefore we can not provide the statistics.

the IIA assumption is to group the original alternatives into sub-groups and allow the variances to differ across the groups while maintaining the IIA assumption within the groups. This defines the nested logit model (Greene, 2000, and the Appendix A of this Chapter).

Suppose we subdivide the employment decision[31] (our dependent variable) into a three-level choice problem as depicted in Fig. 1. The first level consists of the decision of whether or not to engage in any kind of market work. The second level distinguishes between working for pay less than 24 h per week or more than 24 h per week for those who select to be active on the labour market, leaving the other branches unchanged. The third level distinguishes between working for pay less than 32 h (a 4 day working week that may be chosen if partners share care and paid work equally, and care for the child 1 day a week each, while using childcare by other persons 3 days per week), working for pay between 32 and 36 h per week and working for pay more than 36 h per week.

The nested logit model can be estimated by the full information maximum likelihood estimation, where the log-likelihood function is given by:

$$\ln L = \sum_{g=1}^{G} \ln P_g(ijk) \text{ where g indexes individuals in the sample.}$$

We apply a similar nested logit model for the mother's employment decisions when the first infant is between 3 and 5 months old. Fig. 2 presents the levels of decision making. We include, in the decisions made after first birth, the intention to work for pay soon and having started to work for pay.

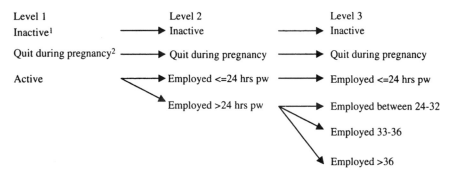

Fig. 1. Women Pregnant with the First Child: Choice of Labour Force Attachment. *Note:* [1]Inactive in this figure means not working for pay up until 16 weeks pregnancy. [2]Quit work in this figure means quit paid work during first 16 weeks of pregnancy because of pregnancy.

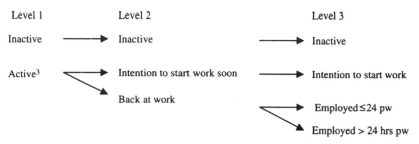

Fig. 2. Mothers of First Infant: Choice of Labour Force Attachment. *Note:* [3]Active in this figure means (intention) to be active.

Our explanatory variables aim to test the hypotheses in "Hypotheses": partner's labour supply and change in working hours, immigrant background and the importance of the grandmother's opinion to the mother. Our control variables are women's education level, partner living-in, language skills, breastfeeding plans and breastfeeding behaviour.

Heterogeneous Patterns of Parental Paid Work Arrangements and Immigration

In this sub-section, we describe the parental arrangement of first-born children in Amsterdam by their non-immigrant/immigrant backgrounds as described in Table 1. The proportion of children born to a single mother, with no partner either cohabiting or living elsewhere is relatively low in the whole sample (2.6%).[32] Surprisingly, the proportion of children born to a mother who has a partner, but her partner is not living-in the same household (on average 12.3%) is as high as 29.5% if both the infant's parents are born in the Netherlands, but the mother's parents are born abroad. The proportion decreases to 22% if the mother's partner is also born abroad. If the child's mother is born abroad, but the father is born in the Netherlands, the percentage of partners not living-in the household is lower than the average, at 8%.

A partner who is not sharing the household may not be able to fully share the responsibility for care, particularly if he lives abroad. But he may provide an income for the infant. On an average, 4.9% of children grow up in a household where the father is acknowledged by the mother as her partner, but he does not live with them and does not provide an income. In addition, 0.3% of children are born to mothers without a partner.

Therefore, there is altogether about 5.2% of children who are born in a household where the father is both physically absent and not providing. But the percentage of children whose father does not provide any income is higher in dual-parent households. 10.3% of first infants grow up in a household where the father is sharing the household but not providing an income, and 4.7% are born in a household with both parents present but neither has income from work.

Almost 15% of first infants born to couples born in the Netherlands, but whose maternal grandparents are born abroad, have a father neither sharing the household nor providing an income. 11% of the latter have none of the parents working for pay. The figures are lower for infants whose mother's partner and mother's parents are born abroad, and for infants whose parents are born abroad. Around 20% of fathers of first infants' who are born abroad and live with the mother and the child do not work for pay. Around 12% of first infants whose parents share a household and whose father and maternal grandparents are born abroad do not have any parental earnings. A similar proportion is found for first infants whose parents are both born abroad. Having parents with an immigrant background, therefore, clearly affects both the chances to have the father living in the same household and the financial conditions of the household, marking quite different material conditions for children since early infancy.

Since we are interested in the effects of the partner's labour market behaviour and its effect on the mother's labour market behaviour we exclude, in the further analysis, single mothers with no partner. Table 3 shows descriptive results by immigrant background of the mother's employment and her partner's employment during pregnancy with the first child. At pregnancy (on average 16 weeks), women's participation rates are high, also for women with an immigrant background, although the percentages of the latter are lower. Only one immigrant background shows a relatively low participation (44%): the mothers-to-be in couples where both partners are born abroad.[33] Also the distribution of the categories of working hours differs somewhat depending on the autocthonous/immigrant background, although part-time jobs are widely chosen options, and already before the first child is born women from all backgrounds hold part-time jobs.

The lower panel of Table 3 provides information on fathers. Again, the most pronounced difference between immigrant backgrounds concerns the partner's participation status than the working hours: 21% of first-generation partners of second-generation mothers with first-generation parents are out of work.

Table 3. Parent's Hours Supplied to the Market at 16 Weeks Pregnancy (First Child) by Immigrant Backgrounds.

First Infants' Immigrant Background		% First Infants' Mothers Not Working for Pay	% Working for Pay ≤24 h	% Working for Pay 25–32	% Working for Pay 33–36	% Working for Pay >36
Parents and mother's parents Dutch born	2,055	100%	5.41	10.44	25.41	19.81	38.93
Immigrant: mother's parents	163	100%	21.62	12.51	15.32	17.21	33.34
Immigrant: one of the mother's parents	228	100%	9.85	13.57	23.65	19.70	33.23
Immigrant: mother's partner	367	100%	10.41	10.78	26.39	17.47	34.95
Immigrant: mother's partner + mother's parents	214	100%	26.17	7.56	16.11	20.13	29.86
Immigrant: mother + mother's parents	396	100%	28.89	11.12	14.44	13.61	31.94
Immigrant: both parents	995	100%	55.45	8.84	8.05	7.27	20.39
Total	4,527						

Table 3. (Continued)

		% Mothers' Partners Not Working for Pay	% Working for Pay <= 32 h	% Working for Pay 33–36	% Working for Pay >36
Parents and mother's parents Dutch born	2,055	100%	3.95	11.32	13.47	71.28
Immigrant: mother's parents	163	100%	12.5	12.52	12.50	62.49
Immigrant: one of the mother's parents	228	100%	4.04	13.13	13.13	69.7
Immigrant: mother's partner	367	100%	17.05	13.25	9.09	60.61
Immigrant: mother's partner + mother's parents	214	100%	21.28	10.64	6.38	61.88
Immigrant: mother + mother's parents	396	100%	9.38	9.98	14.37	66.27
Immigrant: both parents	995	100%	20.64	10.38	9.97	59.01
Total	4,527					

Note: ABCD pregnancy sample 2003/2004. See note Table 2. Excluding single mothers.

Table 4. Parents' Hours Supplied to the Market when the First Infant is between 3 and 5 Months by Immigrant Background.

The Immigrant Background of First Infants			% Mothers not Working for Pay	% Not Yet, Intention to Start Soon	% Working for Pay 1–16	% Working for Pay 17–24	% Working for Pay 25–32	% Working for Pay 33–40	% > 40
Parents and mother's parents Dutch born	56.09	100%	6.73	43.74	7.42	14.83	18.50	7.55	1.22
Immigrant: mother's parents	2.77	100%	18.18	39.40	ns	ns	ns	ns	Ns
Immigrant: one of the mother's parents	5.94	100%	7.84	41.18	9.81	15.03	15.69	9.80	0.95
Immigrant: mother's partner	8.11	100%	12.32	48.77	6.9	10.34	15.27	5.42	0.95
Immigrant: mother's partner + mother's parents	2.92	100%	27.40	38.36	ns	ns	ns	ns	Ns
Immigrant: mother + mother's parents	8.25	100%	22.58	54.84	6.45	5.07	5.07	5.07	0.92
Immigrant: both parents	13.22	100%	46.48	32.72	5.5	3.36	3.98	7.03	0.92
Total	2,776*								

Table 4. (*Continued*)

			% Mothers' Partners Not Working for Pay	% Working for Pay 1–16	% Working for Pay 17–24	% Working for Pay 25–32	% Working for Pay 33–40	% >40
Parents and mother's parents Dutch born	56.09	100%	4.01	2.17	3.60	16.85	45.45	27.92
Immigrant: mother's parents	2.77	100%	9.23	ns	ns	ns	ns	ns
Immigrant: one of the mother's parents	5.94	100%	7.19	2.26	4.58	15.69	39.87	29.41
Immigrant: mother's partner	8.11	100%	15.75	8.4	2.46	13.30	38.42	21.67
Immigrant: mother's partner+mother's parents	2.92	100%	17.81	10.95	5.48	2.74	45.21	17.81
Immigrant: mother+mother's parents	8.25	100%	9.68	7.38	1.38	13.36	40.09	28.11
Immigrant: both parents	13.22	100%	14.98	23.56	3.36	4.89	35.17	18.04
Total	2,776							

Note: ABCD infants sample 2003/2004. Excluding single mothers.
* See note Table 2. Ns: not shown too few observations.

Table 4 shows descriptive results for the households at the time the child is between 3 and 5 months. The proportions of women who are not in paid work yet, but have the intention to start working for pay soon, vary between immigrant backgrounds from 32.7% (immigrant parents) to 54.8% (immigrant mother with Dutch-born partner), with Dutch first infants' mothers fairly in the middle with 43.7%. Since the proportions of those not in paid work and having no intention to start paid work differ, like during the state of pregnancy, between immigrant groups, we have quite striking differences between immigrant backgrounds and the number of hours they actually work for pay when the infant is 3–5 months old. The most important difference is between women who are born in the Netherlands and immigrant women: women born in the Netherlands work for pay more hours whether their partner (or parents) is (are) born abroad or not. The lower panel shows the participation rates and working hours of the mother's partner when the first infant is 3–5 months old, and reveals that the proportions of working hours' categories changed substantially, both: working for pay more than 40 h per week and working for pay less than 32 h increased in all immigrant backgrounds.

RESULTS AND DISCUSSION

This section analyses the mother's participation decision when she is pregnant (on average 16 weeks) and when the infant is between 3 and 5 months (on an average 13 weeks) old.

At Pregnancy with the First Child

As presented in Table 5, we estimate the probability of employment and working hours for parents with a nested logit model. The base category used in the first level of the nested logit model is "not employed", in the second level: short part-time employment, in the third level: working for pay between 24 and 32 h per week. The interpretation of the coefficient estimates is therefore based on how the relevant variable affects log odds of being employed or having stopped working for pay during pregnancy versus having never been active during pregnancy in the first level; being a short part-time worker (less than 24 h per week) versus a worker with longer working hours (more than 24 h per week) in the second level, conditional on choosing to be active in the first level; and choosing to be a full-time

Table 5. Parameter Estimates from a Three-Level Nested Logit Model of Labour Force Participation.

	First Level Active vs. Not Active up until 16 Weeks Pregnancy Coeff. [se]	First Level Quit before 16 Wks Preg. vs. Not Active up until 16 Wks Pregnancy Coeff. [se]	Second Level Employed >24 h pw. vs. Employed <= 24 h pw Coeff. [se]	Third Level Employed 32–35 h pw vs. Employed 24–32 h pw Coeff. [se]	Third Level Employed >35 h pw vs. Employed 24–32 h pw Coeff. [se]
Partner, but not at home	-0.32 [0.30]	-0.45 [0.22]*	0.06 [0.18]	-0.33 [0.18]	-0.19 [0.15]
Low education	-0.10 [0.33]	0.06 [0.19]	-0.02 [0.22]	-0.64 [0.25]**	-0.39 [0.19]*
High education	0.49 [0.24]*	-0.03 [0.19]	0.07 [0.13]	-0.03 [0.11]	-0.05 [0.10]
I*: Her parents	-0.89 [0.48]	-0.88 [0.40]*	-0.57 [0.32]	0.21 [0.32]	0.39 [0.27]
I*: One of her parents	-0.41 [0.46]	-0.96 [0.52]	-0.18 [0.24]	-0.03 [0.21]	-0.08 [0.19]
I*: Her partner	-0.48 [0.43]	-0.02 [0.36]	0.12 [0.21]	-0.13 [0.18]	-0.14 [0.16]
I*: Partner + parents	-0.61 [0.49]	0.43 [0.31]	-0.38 [0.31]	0.49 [0.28]	0.35 [0.25]
I*: She + her parents	-0.72 [0.35]*	-0.53 [0.27]	-0.47 [0.22]*	0.03 [0.21]	0.33 [0.17]
I*: She and her partner	-0.87 [0.31]**	-0.37 [0.22]	-0.46 [0.20]*	-0.08 [0.20]	0.29 [0.16]
Difficulty speaking Dutch	-2.26 [0.50]**	-0.81 [0.21]**	-1.47 [0.61]*	1.36 [0.60]*	2.22 [0.53]**
Partner not in paid work	-1.37 [0.39]**	-0.45 [0.23]*	0.41 [0.23]	-0.22 [0.21]	0.24 [0.18]
Partner works 32–35 pw.	-0.82 [0.51]	-0.55 [0.42]	0.91 [0.23]**	-0.73 [0.22]**	-0.87 [0.21]**

Partner works full time	-1.58 [0.42]**	-0.45 [0.17]*	0.86 [0.17]**	-0.14 [0.11]	0.41 [0.10]**
Opinion of grandmother	-0.63 [0.27]*	-0.42 [0.17]*	-0.01 [0.17]	-0.03 [0.16]	-0.08 [0.14]
Breastfeedplan: 0–3 mnths	-1.13 [0.46]*	0.41 [0.25]	0.79 [0.20]**	0.22 [0.13]	0.56 [0.11]**
Breastfeedplan: 4–6 mnths	0.14 [0.26]	0.35 [0.20]	0.10 [0.14]	0.07 [0.12]	0.13 [0.10]
(Incl. Value parameters)	0.82 [0.16]**				
	2.22 [0.28]**				
Log likelihood	-6221.20				
Number of Observations	25518				
Number of groups	4253				
LR chi2 (82)	2798.30				
Prob>chi2	0.0000				
LR test of homoskedasticity (iv = 1):chi2 (2) = 63.29					

Note: *Women 16 weeks pregnant with first infant. Netherlands*
Data: *ABCD 2003/4 Pregnancy sample. Excluding single mothers. See Table 1 for description of variables. Base categories: medium level education, "full-Dutch": infants' mother, her partner and her parents Dutch born, mother's partner working for pay less than 32 h per week; intention to breastfeed for longer than 6 months; no plan for duration of breastfeeding yet, no plan for breastfeeding yet.*
ı̅: Immigrant background of the first infant's mother, her partner and her parents. Works: in paid work.
Standard errors in brackets.
* Significant at 5%;
** significant at 1%.

worker (working for pay more than 36 h per week) or to be employed between 32 and 36 h in the third level, conditional on choosing to work for pay longer than short part-time hours (more than 24 h per week) in the second level.

Table 5 shows the estimations of the full model including the mother's education level, Dutch language fluency, partner characteristics (at home or not, employment type), immigrant background, importance of the opinion of the mother's mother and breastfeeding plans.[34] Our control variables show the following results. A high education level is significantly positive on being active in paid work (first level in Fig. 1). This is in line with numerous empirical results on the effect of investment in education and labour supply. There are no effects of education on the decision to quit paid work because of pregnancy. If the decision in favour of paid work is made, there is no effect of education on the decision to work for pay more than 24 h per week versus less than 24 h per week (second level in Fig. 1). This finding may be explained by the large availability of part-time work at all levels in the Netherlands (Gustafsson et al., 2003). If the decision to work for pay more than 24 h per week is made, low educated women are less likely to work for pay more than 32 h per week (third level in Fig. 1). This confirms expectations from human capital theory.

When the partner is not employed (as compared with the base category: a partner in part-time work), the impact is negative both on the likelihood of the employment of the mother and on the likelihood of her quitting employment, which indicates that the woman was less likely to be in employment at all during her pregnancy. However, there is no significant effect of a partner not being in paid work on the pregnant woman's decision regarding hours of paid work if she is in paid work. We do not find support, therefore, for the expectation that from an income perspective the woman is likely to provide the income if her partner is not providing for it. If the woman's partner works full-time, this has a significant negative effect on the mother's working for pay during pregnancy, that is, she is more likely not to be active during pregnancy. This finding suggests that, at this point in the individual and household life, the male breadwinner model may appear appealing. However, if the mother-to-be chooses to work for pay, then a full-time working partner has a positive effect on her working for pay more than 24 h per week; and if she chooses to work for pay more than 24 h per week, a full-time working partner has a positive effect on working for pay full-time. Thus, four distinct groups of couple's organization emerge during first pregnancy with regard to participation to work: non-worker couples (5.7%), male breadwinner couples (17.2%), female breadwinner couples (11.6%) and dual breadwinner couples (55.2%).[35] Of course, these four types, and particularly the first, cannot be interpreted simply as the outcome of choices, or values, but also of constrains.

We find support for our first hypothesis. If the mother's partner is, already at first pregnancy, working for pay between 32 and 35 h per week, the mother is more likely to work for pay more than 24 h per week. However, if she works more than 24 h per week, a partner working for pay between 32 and 35 h has a negative effect on her working for pay more than 32 h per week. These parents-to-be have, already before the first birth, organized their life to work for pay less than full-time but for still a substantial number of hours, but the woman is working for pay, on average, fewer hours than her partner (couples who are sharing but not fully equal).

Some specific effects of immigrant backgrounds remain in the full model presented in Table 5. As expected, women who have difficulties with the Dutch language are less likely to be engaged in paid work. If we account for the problems related to Dutch language fluency,[36] pregnant women born abroad (with a Dutch-born partner or with a foreign-born partner) are less likely to participate in the labour market at the time of first pregnancy, and if they do participate in the labour market, they are less likely to work for pay more than 24 h per week in line with H2. The likelihood of quitting a job because of pregnancy versus never having been active during pregnancy is negatively affected by the mother's parents being born abroad, that is, these women were not active at all during the pregnancy.

In line with our third hypothesis, the importance of the maternal grandmother's opinion has a negative effect on the mother's decision to participate in paid work at pregnancy: on being active versus not active up until 16 weeks pregnancy, and on quitting between getting pregnant and 16 weeks pregnancy versus not active up until 16 weeks pregnancy (if the opinion is important to the woman she is more likely not to have participated in paid work at all during her pregnancy up until 16 weeks). There is no effect of the importance of the grandmother's opinion on the woman's paid working hours if the woman participates in the labour market. This result remained unaffected if we excluded breastfeeding plans from the model.

Mothers-to-be who have chosen to be in paid work during pregnancy and have planned 1–3 months of breastfeeding are more likely to work for pay for longer hours (more likely to work for pay more than 24 h); but also, having chosen to work for pay more than 24 h per week, the shortest breastfeeding plans have a positive effect on full-time work as compared to working for pay between 24 and 32 h per week. This leads us to suspect that combining paid work and breastfeeding is not seen as a desired prospective option.

In an extension of the model in Table 5 (not presented here) we included information on whether the father originated in the Middle East and North Africa region (excluding Morocco) and whether the father originated in Morocco (Wetzels, 2007). We separated Morocco since: (1) within MENA, Morocco, stands out as an exception that conforms to the feminisation trend observed in the developing world (Moghadam, 1998), (2) migrants from Morocco have a longer history with the Netherlands than migrants from other regions and (3) we have sufficient observations for the country in our data set. The aim was to explore whether regions in which the feminisation of the labour force has less permeated in the developing world (Horton, 1999) and whether Morocco, would lead mothers matched with a father from this region to behave differently in the labour market while pregnant and having a very young infant compared to other mothers with the same immigrant background but with a partner originating in another region. The number of fathers originating from the MENA region was only 122 and almost all of these fathers were part of immigrant couples. The number of fathers from Morocco was 307, of which 63 with Dutch-born women, and 214 from immigrant couples. We found that a father from the MENA region and from Morocco makes the mother more likely not to have participated during pregnancy, and for Moroccan fathers, the mother was also less likely to participate in full-time work if she participated in paid work, whereas the significant negative effect of couples born abroad on participation was reduced, and second-generation women with a partner from other regions were significantly more likely to participate in jobs with 32–35 h and in full-time jobs, if they participated at all in the labour market. Other results remained unchanged.

When the Child is 3–5 Months Old

Table 6 shows the estimation results of the full model[37] at the time the infant is 3–5 months old. In the first level of the nested logit model, the base category used is not employed. In level two it is having the intention to start paid work soon. In level three, the base category is working for pay less than, or 24 h per week. The interpretation of the coefficient estimates is therefore based on how the relevant variable affects log odds of being employed or having the intention to start paid work soon versus no

Table 6. Parameter Estimates from a Three-Level Nested Logit Model of Labour Force Participation.

	First Level (Intention to) Work for Pay vs. No Intention to Work for Pay Coeff. [se]	Second Level at Work vs. Intention to Start Work Soon Coeff. [se]	Third Level Working for Pay >24 h pw vs. <24 h pw Coeff. [se]
Age 1st infant	−0.20 [0.06]**	0.13 [0.02]**	0.03 [0.03]
Partner, but not at home	−0.02 [0.33]	0.08 [0.18]	−0.53 [0.24]*
Low education	−1.05 [0.38]**	0.36 [0.22]	0.08 [0.32]
High education	0.67 [0.18]**	0.02 [0.15]	0.62 [0.14]**
I*:Her parents	−0.92 [0.50]	−0.14 [0.27]	−0.22 [0.38]
I*: One of her parents	−0.23 [0.40]	−0.02 [0.18]	−0.29 [0.24]
I*: Her partner	0.04 [0.31]	−0.41 [0.16]*	−0.27 [0.24]
I*: Partner + parents	−0.63 [0.46]	−0.32 [0.29]	0.24 [0.44]
I*: She + her parents	0.36 [0.32]	−1.03 [0.18]**	−0.34 [0.30]
I*: She and her partner	−0.32 [0.29]	−0.53 [0.18]**	0.06 [0.28]
Difficulty speaking Dutch	−0.95 [0.36]**	−0.50 [0.49]	1.35 [0.82]
Partner no job after first birth	−0.15 [0.39]	0.31 [0.35]	0.84 [0.30]**
Partner works >40 h pw. (no change)	0.06 [0.44]	0.16 [0.27]	0.09 [0.30]
Partner works 33–40 h pw. (no change)	0.50 [0.33]	0.11 [0.21]	0.04 [0.19]
Partner works 25–32 h pw. (no change)	1.05 [0.62]	0.08 [0.25]	−0.44 [0.34]
Partner works 17–24 h pw. (no change)	0.18 [0.80]	0.39 [0.40]	0.06 [0.51]
Partner works >40 h pw. (more hours)	0.61 [0.31]*	−0.20 [0.24]	0.18 [0.22]
Partner works 33–40 h pw. (more hours)	0.61 [0.48]	−0.21 [0.29]	−0.33 [0.41]
Partner works 25–32 h (more hours)	0.76 [0.63]	−0.24 [0.35]	−0.33 [0.52]

Table 6. (*Continued*)

	First Level (Intention to) Work for Pay vs. No Intention to Work for Pay Coeff. [se]	Second Level at Work vs. Intention to Start Work Soon Coeff. [se]	Third Level Working for Pay >24 h pw vs. <24 h pw Coeff. [se]
Partner works 33–40 h	−0.36	0.38	−0.04
(less hours)	[0.63]	[0.33]	[0.43]
Partner works 25–32 h	−0.24	1.04	−0.05
(less hours)	[0.70]	[0.24]**	[0.24]
Partner works 17–24 h	−0.79	0.47	−0.62
(less hours)	[1.07]	[0.47]	[0.59]
Opinion of the	−0.42	0.09	0.31
grandmother	[0.24]	[0.16]	[0.23]
Breastfeed [yes = 1, No = 0]	−0.24	0.19	−0.04
	[0.50]	[0.24]	[0.34]
Number of weeks	0.04	−0.04	−0.03
breastfeeding	[0.03]	[0.02]*	[0.02]
(Incl. Value parameters)			
	−0.25		
	[0.29]		
	2.91		
	[0.57]**		
Log likelihood	−3154.634		
Number of obs.	10,720		
Number of groups	2,680		
LR chi2 (77)	1121.07		
Prob > chi2	0.00		
LR test of homoskedasticity (iv = 1): chi2 (2) =	24.89		

Note: Mothers when first infant is 3–5 months old. The Netherlands.
Data: ABCD infants sample 2004. Excluding single mothers. See Table 1 for description of variables. Base categories: medium level education, "full-Dutch": infants' mother Dutch born, and her partner and her parents Dutch born, mother's partner working for pay less than 17 h per week. Key: I* Immigrant background of the first infant's family: the mother, her partner and her parents. Works: in paid work.
Standard errors in brackets.
* significant at 5%;
** significant at 1%.

intention to work for pay in the first level, being back at paid work versus having the intention to start paid work soon in the second level, conditional on having chosen to be(come) active in the first level, and working for pay more than 24 h per week versus less than 24 h per week in the third level, conditional on having been working for pay in the second level.

First, we discuss the control variables. As Table 6 shows, the age of the infant (between 3 and 5 months) has a significant negative effect on having the intention to work for pay, but a positive effect on the infant's mother being in paid work, if she has the intention to be an employed mother. It has no effect on working for pay for more hours if she is already at work.

We find that human capital has its expected effect on participation when the infant is between 3 and 5 months. The highest education level of the child's mother has a significant positive effect on having the intention to work for pay as opposed to not having the intention to work for pay. However, if the women have the intention to work for pay, then the mother's highest education level has no effect on actually working for pay as opposed to having the intention to start paid work soon. This could mean that there is no difference between medium and high-level educated mothers regarding the negotiation of parental leave (after the maternity leave, which ends 10–12 weeks after the birth of the child) with their employer.[38] For those who have started to work for pay when the child is between 3 and 5 months, a higher education level has a positive effect on working for pay more than 24 h per week versus working for pay less than 24 h per week. The low education level has only a significant negative effect on the participation decision (first level in Fig. 2).

The analysis in Table 6 aims to detect the effects of the partner's working hours adjustments after the first birth compared to before, as in H1. Somewhat unexpectedly, we find a significant positive effect of the partner's working hours on the mother's decision in favour of paid work (first level in Fig. 2) only for partners who increased their paid work hours and work more than 40 h per week. This leads us to expect that this particular group of parents is highly work oriented. However, the mother is more likely to have started paid work versus having the intention to start soon (second level in Fig. 2) if her partner works between 25 and 32 h per week, having reduced his work hours after the first birth. This decision, which is in accordance with the aims of Dutch public policies from the 1990s on parents' equal role sharing, appears therefore efficacious in supporting an early return of the mother to her job, offering evidence for our first hypothesis. We find no effects of (the changes of) the partner's working hours on the mother's choice to be in paid work more than 24 h per week versus less than 24 h per week, if she has decided to start working for pay. This latter choice to work for pay more than 24 h per week is significantly positively affected by her partner not being in paid work, and significantly negatively affected by her partner not sharing the household. Apparently, therefore, parents are more likely to be both in paid work when the child is very small either when they are both strongly work oriented or when they have an overall shared balance between paid work and family work.

If we account for having difficulties with the Dutch language, we find some support for our H2: three immigrant backgrounds (mother's partner is born abroad, the mother is born abroad and both child's parents are born abroad) affect negatively the decisions of mothers who have the intention to be employed and to be active in paid work when the infant is 3–5 months old (third level in Fig. 2).

The number of weeks of breastfeeding has a significant negative effect on choosing to start paid work versus having the intention to start soon, but not on working for pay more than 24 h versus less than 24 h, if the woman has already started to work. This seems to indicate that, as expected, a longer duration of breastfeeding is not compatible with starting to be active in paid work early.

CONCLUSIONS

This chapter has described parental paid work arrangements of a diverse group of first-time parents in the Dutch context, with a specific focus on parents having some immigrant background. The results indicate that in 2004 a substantial proportion of infant children has some kind of combination of dual working parents or a lone working parent. This proportion, however, as well as the specific combination, at least when the child is very young and the maternity leave has just expired, varies greatly on the basis both of the mother's education and of the characteristics and intensity of the parents' immigrant background. 78% of first-time mothers were in paid work during pregnancy. When the child was between 3 and 5 months (on average 13 weeks) old, half of the mothers who were born in the Netherlands and had Dutch-born parents were back at work, and 8% were even back in full-time work, and nearly one in five worked 3 or 4 days per week. This proportion was lower for mothers with some kind of immigrant background: when the child was 3–5 years old, one third of mothers with a partner and parents born abroad were back in paid work. If the mother herself was born abroad the proportion declined to 20%. These findings suggest that a substantial quota of Dutch and non-Dutch-mothers consider the period of maternity leave too short (for the well-being of their child). They, therefore, lengthen it even if in most cases it is not paid. While the behaviour of mothers at least in part point to the limitations of Dutch policy with regard to leaves, the behaviour of fathers offer more positive indications. The proportion of partners in part-time work after the birth of the first child in Amsterdam is quite substantial and unique in Europe, which makes a higher proportion of first born in Amsterdam who have a father earning on a part-time basis than there has ever been (for both "full-Dutch" and in most immigrant categories). The results of the nested logit model indicate that there is support for the first hypothesis that employed parents will combine paid work and childcare by working for pay long part-time in the Netherlands. Surprisingly[39] we also found that some parents arrange long part-time work already at pregnancy. Furthermore, only the partner's reduction of working for pay to 25–32 h per week after the birth of the first child, makes it more likely that the mother starts work when the infant is 3–5 months old.

There is also some support for the second hypothesis, which examined the impact of a family background in non-Dutch culture, which, we hypothesized, would lead to a weaker labour market attachment of recent first-time mothers. Controlled for human capital, partner living-in, partner's labour supply, language skills, importance of the mother's own opinion, breastfeeding intentions and behaviour, in the Dutch context, the mother's choice for employment at the time of early pregnancy with the first child and when the infant is between 3 and 5 months is negatively influenced by the woman being born abroad (both with a Dutch-born partner and with one born abroad). Furthermore, the choice to work for pay for more than 24 h per week is negatively associated with women born abroad. Controlling for all characteristics, we do not find a negative effect on labour supply and the hours of paid work for second-generation migrants, whether their partner is Dutch or foreign born. This means that our household data provide evidence that partner's characteristics do affect immigrant women's decisions as regards participation in the labour market, and therefore improve our understanding of young immigrant mothers' labour market decisions compared to previous research based on the aggregate 1997 data on individual women in the 18–64 age group analysed by Zorlu (2002). Our data also suggest that second-generation women behave differently from immigrant women in the UK and Belgium: countries which have high proportions of part-time work, but still much lower than the Netherlands, and which, especially the UK, have segregated labour markets for part-time and full-time jobs. In addition, when the first infant is 3–5 months old, a partner born abroad affects negatively Dutch-born mothers with Dutch-born parents who have the intention to be employed mothers to be in paid work when the infant is 3–5 months old.

Our nested logit models capture many control variables. Specifications of our model, leaving out the grandmother's opinion and the partner's labour supply, showed more statistically significant categories of immigrant background, especially second-generation women with a Dutch-born partner (the effect disappeared after including opinion of the grandmother) and with a foreign-born partner (the effect disappeared by including partner characteristics). Our study, therefore, indicates that most of the expected effects of immigrant backgrounds on the mother's decision to work for pay are determined by human capital, the partner's labour supply, the grandmother's opinion, and breastfeeding intentions and behaviour. However, being a female, first-generation immigrant has an independent – negative-effect, beyond human capital and other family characteristics, on the decision to work when pregnant and when the infant is 3–5 months old. Similarly, a partner born abroad has an independent, negative effect on the Dutch-born – with Dutch-born parents – mother's timing of her return to paid work. The differential findings for "full Dutch" parents and those with an immigrant background, therefore, do offer some ground for the hypothesis that different cultural and gender models may be at play. Yet, this may not be the full explanation, since having an immigration background may cause difficulties of its own in entering and remaining in the labour market due to their language and other skills. In this perspective, the fact that dual unemployed households, as well as households where the father is not providing and/or is also absent, are more easily found among parents with an immigrant background offers matter for concern for the well being of children, as well as of their parents.

Our testing of H3 was supported by our estimates. If the opinion of her own mother is important for the woman, she is less likely to participate in the labour market when pregnant, but there is no effect on her choice of working hours.

Additional research could provide insights into what benefits or risks children may encounter when both parents choose to work for pay full or part-time. Most importantly, while in this chapter we described and analysed the child's context by emphasizing the choices of the parents regarding paid work and the number of hours involved, we would need to understand the effects of these decisions on the outcomes of children via the choice of childcare. Based on the results of our study, however, it is safe to say that since highly educated mothers in the Netherlands are more likely to participate in paid work, not only their children will enter life without the strains of financial uncertainty. They will also have access to the best-quality childcare, even if it is relatively expensive (Wetzels, 2005, RMO 2006: 35). In contrast, since we find an independent, negative effect of being a female first-generation immigrant (with a Dutch and with a non-Dutch partner) on mothers' labour supply and the number of hours she works for pay before the first child is born and when the infant is very young, and fathers' labour supply and hours of work for first-generation immigrant women is also far lower, this would mean that their children not only will be more exposed to the experience of financial uncertainty. They will also have less access to high-quality non-parental childcare. There are far less opportunities for these children, while they are very young infants, to experience parental sharing of paid work and childcare based on father's reduction of paid work hours. Further analysis is needed to assess the implications of these findings on the outcomes of children. Data collection when the infant is older will hopefully give opportunities to fill this gap.

Our data have certain limitations. They do not provide information on whether parental leave has been taken and for how long and they do not provide information on the use of non-parental childcare. Furthermore, our results apply to Amsterdam, where, as in other major cities (Borjas, 2006), the proportion of immigrants is higher than in the rest of the country (Hartog & Zorlu, 2004). A comparison with other cities might show whether or not our results are affected by the labour market of the country's capital.

NOTES

1. The increase already appeared before the change in social policies to allow mothers to have a career in 1990. The Childcare Stimulation Act of 1990 is the first government action, which explicitly caters to the needs of the working mother rather than assigning priority to educational considerations for children.

2. RMO (2006: 31: Table 3.3. based on Statistics Netherlands Labour Surveys 2000–2002) reports that there is no difference according to education level for the fathers reducing working hours.

3. In this chapter I focus on the pregnancy leave, which in international comparison can be seen as part of parental leave. Pregnancy leave in the Netherlands ends 10–12 weeks after the birth of the child. Dutch parental leave may start after that if the parent has negotiated this leave with the employer. In most cases it is unpaid and it is maximum 13 weeks fulltime.

4. I thank Dr. M. van der Wal and Prof. Dr. G. Bonsel, coordinators of the ABCD-survey, to have given me permission to use the data for scientific research.

5. The term ethnic minority is used in Dutch policy not to indicate the number of people from a non Dutch ethnic origin, but also to indicate those whose socio-economic position is weak.

6. This could imply that more adults than children immigrate since the definitions of family reunification and family formation seem to consider different age groups. The increase in family formation mainly concerns women above 18, who marry an immigrant man who lives in the Netherlands. Family reunion mostly concerns family members such as wives and children who migrate to the Netherlands because they have a family history with an immigrant living in the Netherlands.

7. Zorlu (2002) controls in his labour supply model for age, age squared, education, gender, with children, without children and years since immigration.

8. Since the mid 1980s, unions in the Netherlands have been raising demands for part-time work and equalizing the employment conditions between full-time and part-time workers. Earlier, the women's movement had demanded short working days, but realizing that travel time would not be reduced, interest in part-time work has grown. Skilled women increasingly wanted to combine part-time work with family responsibilities. In addition, with a situation of high unemployment, women's incomes were needed by the family. Furthermore, employers began to recognize the benefits of part-time work in optimizing personnel strategies, for example, in the banking sector. Employers recognized that women's increasing skills made the costs of replacing these employees higher.

9. The Act on Adjustment of Working Hours (Wet Aanpassing Arbeidsduur), which went into effect in the Netherlands on July 1, 2000, gives those employed by firms with more than 10 employees the right to shorten or increase work hours on request if they have been employed for at least one year, and have not asked for a change in working hours within the past two years. Within four months prior to changing work hours, the employee should indicate the date that the new working hours take effect, the number of working hours, and the preferred distribution of working hours during the week. The hourly wage remains the same.

10. The 1997 European Union Directive on Part-time Work states: "Member states and social partners should identify and review obstacles which may limit the opportunities for part-time work" (European Union (EU), 1998). Furthermore, "employers should give consideration to requests by workers to transfer from full-time to part-time work and the reverse when such work becomes available."

11. Zorlu (2002), using Statistics Netherlands data in 1997 on the 18–64 age bracket, shows that 63 percent of Moroccan employed women work part time, 56% of Turkish women work part time, compared to 63% of Dutch women. The rate of working part-time is much more similar for Dutch and Turkish employed men: respectively 15%, of Dutch and 19% of Moroccan employed men were in part-time work.

12. In the Netherlands, leave indemnification is to be negotiated with the employer. For example, in the public sector, parental leave beneficiaries receive 75% of their wages. However, in the private sector, only few collective agreements (6% in 2000) include payment of the parental leave (replacement rate up to 30%). Only 40% of entitled mothers actually make use of their right to take parental leave. The percentage for the entitled fathers is much lower, 9% (Del Boca & Wetzels, 2007).

13. This ideal has been summarized and underlined in one of the most crucial policy papers of the 1990s, 'Unpaid care equally shared' (Commissie Toekomstscenario, 1995; Ministerie van Sociale Zaken en Werkgelegenheid, 1997).

14. Sharing unpaid care has received much attention in the Dutch debate. The first emancipation policy paper already stated that not only women should have choices, men too should be able to choose more freely (preferably care more). Rather unique for 1992, the central objective of emancipation policy was that men and women should not only be economically independent, but also 'care independent' (Kremer, 2005).

15. RMO (2005) reviews some recent statistics on the income of households as regards ethnic background in the Netherlands. Data on 2002 show that 25% of Surinamese couples with children and half of all Turkish couples with children are concerned about their financial situation, and several statistics show that indeed the income level of e.g. Turkish and Moroccan families in the Netherlands is lower than that of fully Dutch families. Furthermore, household income of Turkish and Moroccan families is 30% below the household income of two parent Dutch households. Data collected by Statistics Netherlands, CBS, 2004 report that households with young children of Turkish and Moroccan have a 20% lower household income than fully Dutch. Moreover, in 2001, 25% of all non-western immigrant couples with young children lived below or at the social minimum income, compared to 4% of "fully Dutch" (Statistics Netherlands, CBS, 2004).

16. The ideal of professional care is neither widespread nor robust. Social pedagogues and day care workers have not had a strong impact in the Netherlands either. The Netherlands takes a middle position as regards the staffing of state-subsidized services, with 4:1 staff ratios for the very young (0–1) and 6:1 for ages 1–4. Dutch day care workers are normally trained, but only for three years on a middle level (OECD, 2001).

17. Although the ideal of parental sharing has put fathers who provide unpaid care on the agenda, lone parenthood is very often left out of the discussion. Furthermore, non-working parents, or parents with very limited paid working hours, and or very insecure labor market position, like some immigrant groups on the Dutch labour market, will probably not be reached by this ideology, since it does not apply to their situation at all. The consequences for these parents and their children are rarely discussed.

18. Dutch primary schools consist of 8 grades covering the age groups of 4–12 year old children. Most Dutch children start school at 4, but compulsory schooling begins when children turn 5. Children are allowed to enrol in primary school the first school day after their 4th birthday, while enrolment is compulsory from the first school day of the month after the child reaches the age of 5 onwards. About 98% of the children start primary school before their 5th birthday. The program consists of 24 h per week during 41 weeks per year. The staff are certified primary

school teachers. The curriculum consists of structured learning activities, and typically children will have started to read and write by the age of six. Thus, differently from Sweden where children start elementary school at 7, and Germany where they start at 6, Dutch children start their schooling earlier.

19. Those parents who use formal child care also use it part-time. 40% use formal child care for less than 12 h per week, 25% use it between 12–19 h per week; 32% use between 20 and 27 h per week; using formal child care for more than 28 h per week is negligible.

20. In Sweden, almost no child under 1 year of age is in childcare since parents are entitled to a year leave, fully paid.

21. The main ethnic minority groups in the Dutch and especially in the Amsterdam labour market are: (1) former "guest workers' families", mostly from Morocco and Turkey, whose men were recruited for unskilled jobs in the 1960s; (2) after the decolonisation of Suriname in 1975, a large portion of Surinamese immigrants have chosen to settle in the Netherlands and especially in its capital.

22. Hooghiemstra and Merens (1999) mention that working full-time is negatively associated with having children, but that this association is less strong for ethnic minority groups. Unfortunately, they do not give further details or analysis.

23. Unfortunately, this particular statistic is not available in a more recent year.

24. Quite a number of studies have focused on the actual hours that parents work for pay, and the preferred hours working for pay in the Netherlands. Caution is however required in such analysis, since the analyses of actual behavior confronted with wishes using panel data have found that the changes in labour market behavior do not match with the wishes. Two results are worth mentioning that compare wishes among women with different characteristics: 1) Baaijens (2006) found that highly educated women with children in the household indicate to a lesser extent that they wish to reduce working hours than highly women with no children in the household. 2) There is an important distinction between salaried workers and hourly wage workers. Hourly wage workers are more likely to prefer an increase in working hours, whereas this is not the case for salaried workers (Yerkes, 2006).

25. We are aware that different countries of origin might share different gender models and particularly different ideas concerning women's participation to the labour market outside the household. Yet, it was not possible to disaggregate the data for the 832 specific countries of the mother's origin that are present in our sample. The most important countries of mothers' origin are the Netherlands (66.9%), European (EU-15) (6.1%), Morocco (5.4%), Surinam (4.0%), Turkey (2.8%), Ghana (1.7%), and Antillean Islands (1.2%), USA/Canada/Australia (1.3%), Middle-East (1.2%), and Latin America (1.2%).

26. Most of the literature analyses how certain attitudes of daughters are affected by mothers' attitudes and mother's behaviour. Here we are in search for how the attitude of the mother has an effect on daughters' behaviour (via daughters' attitudes).

27. Data concerning 2002, presented in Hooghiemstra and Merens (2006), show that 27% of the population older than 16 thinks that a woman should not work for pay at all when there is a child in the household of age 4 or younger. Furthermore, more than half of the Dutch female and male population have no understanding for mothers of under 4 year olds who work for pay full-time, whereas for fathers the figure is around 20%. Unfortunately, there are no statistics or explanatory research

on the general opinion and the grandparents' opinion as regards employment for pregnant women and for mothers of very young infants (younger than 4 months or younger than one year).

28. More first born children than second or higher order children.

29. The data provide information on previous births but not on the employment status and the partner's immigrant background for previous births.

30. Only 2.04% of the infants are 11 weeks at the time of survey. 34.32% are 12 weeks, 41.15% are 13 weeks, 10.98% are 14 weeks, 4.35% are 15 weeks, 2.57% are 16 weeks and the remaining 4.6% are between 17–22 weeks.

31. Our data lack information on unemployment and whether the parents are still in education. Teenage pregnancy rates are however very low in the Netherlands. And since the average age at pregnancy of the first child is over 29 years. We also checked whether the years of education and age give reason to think that the parents are in education, and we concluded that they are not. We use the words "choice" and "decision" here, since we assume the woman can decide on employment type herself. Therefore, we assume no restrictions on the demand side of the labour market.

32. We cannot distinguish clearly between different immigrant groups for single women, since only half of single women have indicated the father's country of birth.

33. This proportion is less than half (28%) for immigrant women with a Dutch born partner. However, the proportions are 26% for second-generation immigrant women with a first generation partner, and 22% for second-generation couples, compared to 5% for first infants' families with Dutch parents.

34. We performed the analysis for all women in the pregnancy sample and only for women in the pregnancy sample who also participated in the "infants' sample. The results hardly differ. In addition, we have estimated other specifications of the model in Table 5 (available upon request from the author). First, we estimated the model explaining the three levels of labour market engagement by mother's education levels only and partner not present. In addition to the effects of these variables in Table 5, mother's low education and partner not at home were negatively significant in the decision to work, mother's high and low education level were negative on quitting work, and mother's high education level and having a partner but not cohabiting were negative on working more than 32 hours per week, whereas mothers' high education was positive on working full-time. When we extended the model with the immigrant background of the couple, in addition to the results for these variables in Table 5, also women with a foreign born partner and foreign born parents were less likely to participate. Women with parents born abroad (and with a foreign born partner) were less likely to work for pay more than 24 hours vs. less than 24 hours, and the latter categories were also less likely to work full time if they were in paid work for more than 24 hours per week. When we extended the model with the importance of the opinion of the grandmother to the mother, the negative effect on participation in paid work of women with foreign born partner and parents disappeared. All other effects of immigrant background on mother's participation decision disappeared by including partner's labor supply, except for those mentioned in Table 5.

35. The data do not provide information on wages or income. The categories of breadwinner households are based on hours of paid work: male breadwinner is

defined as the father working and the mother not working (10.0%) and father working more hours for pay than the mother (7.2%); female breadwinner is defined as the mother working for pay and the father not (8.1%) and mothers working more hours for pay than fathers (3.5%); dual breadwinner (total of 55.2%) are defined as parents working for pay both full-time (25.6%), both long part-time (2.8%), the mother working for pay full-time with a father in a long-part-time job (0.9%), and a mother working for pay long-part-time with a father in full-time paid work (25.9%). There is a small category of 1.5% where parents both work for pay short part-time.

36. The language skills may also give an indication of time since immigration, a variable that is lacking in our data.

37. The model in Table 6 has been estimated explaining the employment decisions by education only, by education and partner's employment, by adding immigrant backgrounds, by adding difficulties speaking Dutch, by adding mother's opinion. These estimations are available upon request.

38. For example, they are more likely, because of educational matching on the marriage market to have a partner who provides for the income if the negotiated leave is unpaid or the paid leave does not pay enough.

39. This is surprising from a rational perspective. At 16 weeks pregnancy of the first child, there are no caring tasks yet for the child, and therefore, it seems irrational to have reduced paid working hours. However, firstly, there is a quota of childless couples where not both partners work full-time, thus the choice of working long part time hours may be a life style choice irrespective of the presence of a child. Secondly, couples may start bargaining with each other and with their employers the type of working hours before the child is actually born, in order to be settled in the routine when the child arrives.

40. In our case, all the explanatory variables refer to the individual's or first infant's mother's household's characteristics rather than to the alternatives she selects so that the same explanatory variables show up at all three stages. Since each potential alternative is specified as a separate observation in the nested logit model, it was necessary to re-specify all the explanatory variables as interactions between the original explanatory variables and the relevant alternatives at each level, thus leading to different vectors of explanatory variables at each level.

REFERENCES

Avishai Bentovim, O. (2002). *Family-friendly as a double-edged sword: Lesson from the "lactation-friendly" workplace*. Working Paper, 46. Centre for Working Families. University of California, Berkeley.

Baaijens, C. (2006). *Arbeidstijden: Tussen wens en werkelijkheid*, Doctoral Thesis, Universiteit Utrecht, Utrecht.

Blossfeld, H.-P., & Drobnič, S. (Eds). (2001). *Career of couples in contemporary societies*. Oxford: Oxford University Press.

Borjas, G. J. (2006). Native internal migration and the labour market impact of immigration. *Journal of Human Resources, 41*(2), 221–258.

Burgmeijer, R. J. F., & Reijneveld, S. A. (2001). *Motieven om te stoppen met borstvoeding: Gegevens uit de PGO-peiling Jeugdgezondheidszorg 1997/1998 in vergelijking met de gegevens uit de literatuur. TNO-PG rapport/JGD/2001.051.* Leiden: Instituut voor Toegepast Nauurwetenschappelijk Onderzoek, Preventie en Gezondheid.

Del Boca, D., & Pasqua, S. (2005). Labour supply and fertility in Europe and the U.S. In: T. Boeri, D. Del Boca & C. Pissarides (Eds), *Women in the labour force: An economic perspective.* Oxford: Oxford University Press.

Del Boca, D., & Wetzels, C. M. M. P. (Eds). (2007). *Social policies, labour markets and motherhood: A comparative analysis of European countries.* Cambridge: Cambridge University Press.

European Union (EU). (1998). *The part-time directive.* Publication no. L014. European Union, Brussels, 20 January, pp. 9–14.

Ewen, E. (1985). *Immigrant women in the land of dollar: Life and culture on the lower east side, 1890–1925.* New York, NY: Monthly Review Press.

Galtry, J. (2003). The impact on breastfeeding of labour market policy and practice in Ireland, Sweden and the USA. *Social Science and Medicine, 57*(1), 167–177.

Greene, W. (2000). *Econometric analysis* (4th ed.). Upper Saddle River, NJ: Prentice Hall.

Grjibovski, A. M., Yngve, A., Bygren, L. O., & Sjostrom, M. (2005). Socio demographic determinants of initiation and duration of breastfeeding in North West Russia. *Acta Paediatrics, 94*(5), 588–594.

Gustafsson, S. S., Kenjoh, E., & Wetzels, C. M. M. P. (2003). Employment choices and pay differences between non-standard and standard work in Britain, Germany, the Netherlands, and Sweden. In: S. Houseman & M. Osawa (Eds), *Non-standard work in developed economies: Causes and consequences.* Kalamazoo, MI: W.E. Upjohn Institute for Employment Research.

Gustafsson, S. S., Wetzels, C. M. M. P., Vlasblom, J. D., & Dex, S. (1996). Labour force transitions in connection with child birth: A panel data comparison between Germany, Great Britain and Sweden. *Journal of Population Economics, 9*(3), 223–246.

Hartog, J. (1998). *So, what is so special about The Dutch Model?* Report for the International Labour Organization. ILO, Geneva.

Hartog, J. & Theeuwes, J. (1985). The emergence of the working wife in Holland. *Journal of Labour Economics,* 3(1) (part 2) (January, Supplement: Trends in Women's Work, Education and Family Building), S235–S255.

Hartog, J., & Zorlu, A. (2004). *Economic effects of migration (in Dutch).* AIAS working paper 2004/26. Report commissioned by the Ministry of Finance. The Hague.

Hooghiemstra, E., & Merens, A. (2003). *Variatie in participatie: Achtergronden van arbeidsdeelname van allochtone en autochtone vrouwen* (pp. 38–55). Den Haag: Sociaal Cultureel Planbureau.

Hooghiemstra, E., & Merens, A. (2006). *Sociale atlas van vrouwen uit etnische minderheidsgroepen.* Den Haag: Sociaal Cultureel Planbureau.

Horton, S. (1999). Marginalization revisited: Woman's market work and pay, and economic development. *World Development, 27*(3), 210–255.

Kremer, M. (2005). *How welfare states care culture, gender and citizenship in europe.* Doctoral dissertation, University of Utrecht, Utrecht.

Mincer, J. (1974). *Schooling, experience and earnings.* New York: National Bureau of Economic Research.

Ministerie van Sociale Zaken en Werkgelegenheid en Centraal Bureau voor de Statistiek. (1997). *Jaarboek emancipatie, arbeid en zorg.* Den Haag: VUGA.

Moghadam, V. (1998). *Woman, work and economic reform in the Middle East and North Africa.* Boulder, London: Lynne Rienner Publishers.

O & S. (2004). Research and statistics. *Statistical yearbook.* Municipality Amsterdam.

O'Brien, M. (2005). *Shared caring: Bringing fathers into the frame.* Equal Opportunities Commission Working paper 18. Equal Opportunities Commission, Manchester.

OECD. (2001). *Starting strong – early childhood education and care.* Paris: OECD.

Orsi, R. (1985). *The Madonna of 115th street: faith and community in Italian Harlem, 1880–1950.* New Haven: Yale University Press.

OSA (R. Kunnen, W. Praat, M. de Voogd-Hamelink, & C. M. M. P. Wetzels). (1997). *Labour Supply in 1997.* OSA report, 25. The Hague: Organisatie voor Strategisch Arbeidsmarktonderzoek.

Plantenga, J. (1996). For women only? The rise of part-time work in the Netherlands. *Social Politics, 3*(Spring), pp. 57–71.

Plantenga, J. & Siegel, M. (2004). *Childcare in a changing world.* Position paper, part I, European Childcare strategies, Prepared for the conference 'Childcare in a changing world', Groningen, October 23–24, http://www.childcareinachangingworld.nl/downloads/position_paper_part1.pdf

Portegijs, W., Boelens, A., & Olsthoom, L. (2004). *Emancipatiemonitor 2004.* DenHaag: SCP/CBS.

Remery, C., van Doorne-Huiskes, A., & Schippers, J. En als oma nu ook een baan heeft? De toekomst van de informele kinderopvang in Nederland. *NIDI-Rapport nr. 57.* Den Haag: NIDI, Mei 2000. p. 121.

RMO (M. Distelbrink & N. Lucassen en E. Hooghiemstra). (2005). Gezinnen anno nu. *Rapport fvoor de Raad voor Maatschappelijke Ontwikkeling,* Den Haag. September.

Russo, G., & Hassink, W. (2005). *The part-time wage penalty: A career perspective.* IZA discussion paper no. 1468. Bonn: IZA.

SCP (E. Hooghiemstra & M. Merens). (2006). Ch. 6: Voltijdswerkende moeders, in investeren in vermogen. *Sociaal Cultureel Rapport 2006.* Den Haag: Sociaal Cultureel Planbureau.

Statistics Netherlands, CBS (Centraal Bureau voor de Statistiek). (2003, 2004, 2005, 2006).

Susin, L. R. O., Giugliani, E. R. J., & Kummer, S. C. (2005). Influence of grandmothers on breastfeeding practices. *Rev Saude Publica, 39*(2).

Tratsaert, K. (2004). Nieuwe Belgen in loondienst in Vlaanderen: gewogen en minder vreemd bevonden? In: Steunpunt WAV-SSA, *Reeks De arbeidsmarkt in Vlaanderen, Jaarboek Editie 2004.* Leuven.

Van der Wal, M. F., van Eijsden, M., & Bonsel, G. J. (2006). Stress and mood disorders during pregnancy and excessive infant crying. Paper presented to the first annual Amsterdam Born Children and Their Development Conference. Amsterdam, March 31.

Vermeulen, F. (1999). *Een breed perspectief, Het Amerikaanse onderzoek naar Italianen in New York als model voor een historische benadering van de Marokkaanse gemeenschap in Nederland.* Master thesis, Department of Social History, University of Amsterdam, Amsterdam.

Visser, J. (2002). The first part-time economy in the world: A model to be followed? *Journal of European Social Policy, 12*(1), 23–42.

Wetzels, C. M. M. P. (2001). *Squeezing birth into working life, household panel data analyses comparing Germany, Great Britain, Sweden and the Netherlands.* Aldershot: Ashgate Publishing.

Wetzels, C. M. M. P. (2005). Supply and price of childcare and female labour force participation in the Netherlands. *Labour, 19,* 171–209.

Wetzels, C. M. M. P. (2007). *Feminization of the labour force in the country of origin and immigrants' labour supply around first childbirth in the Netherlands.* Research paper, University of Amsterdam.

Wetzels, C. M. M. P., & Tijdens, K. G. (2002). Dutch mothers' return to work and the re-entry effect on wage. *Cahiers Economiques De Bruxelles, 45*(1), 169–189.

Yerkes, M. (2006). *Women's working preferences in the Netherlands, Germany and the UK.* AIAS Working paper 06/43. University of Amsterdam, Amsterdam.

Yerkes, M. & Visser, J. (2005). *Women's preferences or delineated policies? The development of part-time work in the Netherlands, Germany and the United Kingdom.* AIAS Working paper 06/45. University of Amsterdam, Amsterdam.

Yngve, A., Kylberg, E., & Sjöström, M. (2001). Breastfeeding in Europe – rationale and prevalence, challenges and possibilities for promotion. *Public Health Nutrition, 4*(6A), 353–1355.

Zorlu, A. (2002). *Absorption of Immigrants in European Labour Markets. The Netherlands, United Kingdom and Norway.* Doctoral thesis, Tinbergen Institute: Tinbergen Institute Research Series 279, Amsterdam.

APPENDIX. NESTED LOGIT MODEL

Under the nested logit model, the IIA assumption is maintained within the alternatives of each decision, but can be relaxed across decisions.

Suppose that each alternative at the second level is associated with a level of utility given by:

$$U_{ijk} = \beta' X_{ijk} + \alpha' Y_{ij} + \gamma' Z_i + \varepsilon_{ijk} + \varepsilon_{ij} + \varepsilon_i \tag{1}$$

where Z_j, Y_{ij} and X_{ijk} are vectors of explanatory variables specific to the first-, second- and third-level choices, respectively and ε_i, ε_{ij}, ε_{ijk} are independent and identically distributed error terms with Weibull distribution.[40] The probability that an individual will choose alternative *ijk* in the third stage is given by:

$$P(ijk) = P(k|ij)\, P(j|i)\, P(i) \tag{2}$$

where the conditional probability $P(k|ij)$ will depend only on the parameter vector β'.

$$P(k|ij) = \frac{e^{\beta' X_{ijk}}}{\displaystyle\sum_{n=1}^{N_{ij}} e^{\beta' X_{ijn}}} \tag{3}$$

We define the inclusive value for the second-level options j as:

$$I_{ij} = \ln \sum_{n=1}^{N_{ij}} e^{\beta' X_{ijn}}$$

so that the second-level conditional probabilities $P(j|i)$ are given by:

$$P(j|i) = \frac{e^{\alpha' Y_{ij} + \tau_{ij} I_{ij}}}{\sum\limits_{m=1}^{M_i} e^{\alpha' Y_{im} + \tau_{im} I_{im}}} \qquad (4)$$

Similarly we define the inclusive value for the first-level options i as follows:

$$J_i = \ln \sum_{m=1}^{M_i} e^{\alpha' Y_{im} + \tau_{im} I_{im}}$$

yielding the following unconditional first-level probability $P(i)$:

$$P(i) = \frac{e^{\gamma' Z_i + \delta_i J_i}}{\sum\limits_{l=1}^{L} e^{\gamma' Z_l + \delta_l J_l}} \qquad (5)$$

By substituting Eqs. 3–5 into Eq. 2, we obtain an expression of how the probability of each level-3 alternative depends on the explanatory variables and the model parameters.

CHANGING CHILDHOODS: MIGRANT CHILDREN AND THE CONFRONTATION OF UNCERTAINTY

Nadina Christopoulou and Sonja de Leeuw

INTRODUCTION

'Being a refugee means learning from your children instead of teaching them yourself'. These are the words of a 43-year-old writer from Turkey, father of three. He is a refugee in Greece, where he works as a tailor. Language, the tool of his trade, is what he can no longer use, even for his own children. In contrast to her father, 12-year-old Boran, who is fluent in both Greek and her mother tongue, sits beside her father and translates what he says, and at the same time explains how frustrated he feels that he cannot communicate with the people around him.

Boran was a member of the research group of CHICAM (Children in Communication About Migration), an EU-funded research project which studied media and digital technology as a platform of expression for children (9–14 years old) of migrant backgrounds and as a means of promoting social inclusion.[1] The research groups that were set up in six European countries consisted of children who had migrated either as asylum seekers or as labour migrants. Although we are well aware of the

Childhood: Changing Contexts
Comparative Social Research, Volume 25, 239–264
Copyright © 2008 by Emerald Group Publishing Limited
ISSN: 0195-6310/doi:10.1016/S0195-6310(07)00008-7

increasingly problematic use of the category 'migrant', which is unable to differentiate between newly arrived ethnic migrants who were forced to fly and those who have been in the new country for several years either as asylum seekers or labour migrants, we have chosen to use the term migrant as a general and inclusive category, in order to envelop all the types of migrating experience that the children involved in our research had. CHICAM included both refugee and migrant children because the project sought to explore different experiences of dislocation and resettlement bound up with migration (de Block, Buckingham & Banaji, 2005). It thus addressed a typical kind of migration experiences, namely those of children who risk disempowerment in several ways.

When Boran first joined the CHICAM club, she introduced herself through an act of mediation, by translating the meaning of her name (and perhaps giving a hint of her character) to the others: 'Boran means hard rain'. The very conditions that may be disempowering for the father, namely the loss of language, the sense of homelessness and longing, together with the feeling of cultural disorientation, may at times contribute to an empowering experience for his daughter Boran. She uses language not only as a tool of expression but also as a tool of mediation across different cultures, languages and generations.

The aim of this paper is to shed light on the changing roles that migrant children take on as mediators between their family and the society of the receiving country and on the inventive use of all the available resources. Migrant children are charged with double roles, on the one hand keeping the family values under the strains of a new environment, while on the other hand learning the circumstances of the reception country and introducing them to their family. They take on the burden and the challenges of adaptation often more arduously than the adults. As a result, they swiftly develop a double agency 'commuting' between two cultures, transgressing and subverting, converting meanings, confronting differences and searching for similarities, thus creating a 'third space' (Bhabha, 1994), which allows them to define themselves anew and to make the unknown inhabitable.

In studying socialization processes, the focus has been mainly on the adult world without taking into consideration the social worlds of children (Jenks, 1982, 1996). Yet, as Hirschfeld points out, children do not just learn and reproduce culture but they also create and produce it (2002, p. 624). Despite their high proportion in the ever-increasing populations of migrants, children have until recently been of secondary importance in relevant literature. Displacement signifies a broader change in the experience and the conceptualization of childhood, thus creating the space for transformations within the core of the family, either when it is migrating together or when it breaks for the purpose of migration. As a result, children are confronted with the burden of coming to terms with new cultural realities from early on and are bound to take on responsibilities often disproportionate to their age. Instead of being recipients of culture within a fostered environment, they are called to become active cultural agents negotiating and translating values and meanings, not only earlier but also in more trying circumstances. It is thus crucial to take into consideration 'the different historical, social and cultural contexts within which childhood is situated' (Knörr & Nunes, 2005, p. 9). Even when migrant children are taken into account, the focus is mostly on the trauma and the experience of loss and displacement that they have been through and less on their creative capacity as social agents (Erny, 2003; James & James, 2004). In integrating a view of agency in migrant children, light has to be shed on the empowering experience that the process of migration may entail. This is what we will try to highlight in this paper, looking at the changing roles of childhood in the process of migration. Our point is that loss, trauma and insecurity are often accompanied by an increasing sense of involvement and a growing responsibility, which enables migrant children to cope better with the new environments that they confront.

We argue that being a child and being a migrant creates a condition of double marginality. The other side of this seemingly debilitating situation is, by reflection, the development of a double agency. Migrant children become the first envoys and representatives of their family into the new society, while at the same time by swiftly mastering the rules of the latter they bring them into their household. Migration breeds uncertainty and destabilization, commanding a reshuffling in the roles and responsibilities of individuals and families. As all given structures are challenged in the sudden reversals of fortune that the shifting routes of the journey bring along, a vast space of possibility opens up where migrant children claim diverse roles. Uncertainty in their immediate surroundings motivates them to look for certainty in themselves and in the use of their own resources, confidence in their own skills and abilities, together with a determining will and the capacity to network, to create links and build bridges (Christopoulou & de Leeuw, 2004).

Migration alters childhood experience significantly and in irreversible ways. Nothing remains the same after the getaway from the land of origin, including the familial and social bonds. Relations within the family are redefined: adults start perceiving children differently while the children also start perceiving themselves differently. The necessities of living and the forces beyond the control of the individuals require a reassessment of roles and actions. Things that may have seemed inconceivable in the previous order of things within the family life (i.e. child labour) start appearing feasible and at times indispensable. As a result, migrant children do not just become acculturated through a predictable process, acquiring cultural knowledge and learning existing cultural codes, within a known and safe environment. They in fact create new codes along with the existing ones, and produce cultural knowledge by mediating between different cultures and establishing a hybrid foundation upon which they can build their lives in their new surroundings (see Toren, 1993; Hirschfeld, 2002; Erny, 2003).

The social nexus within which children take the first steps of socialization ceases to exist. The basic vocabulary of their social life, the ways in which they have learned to perceive the world around them and to make meaningful connections, are shaken. In the same way that they can no longer rely on their mother tongue alone and have to learn a new language, the reality in which they eventually have to make a living requires the command of a new vocabulary. Not only that, but also those usually responsible for the passing on of knowledge, namely the parents and grandparents, are either far away or no longer in a position to fully undertake the responsibility of passing on knowledge, as they are also faced with uncertainty. As a result, notions of home and family belonging alter and stretch in order to accommodate new relationships and interdependencies (see Christopoulou & de Leeuw, 2004).

That is not to say that migration on its own right determines agency. James and Proutt (1990, p. 4) have shed light on the importance of childhood agency in all social contexts, claiming that children 'must be seen as involved in the construction of their own social lives, the lives of those around them and of the societies in which they live. They can no longer be regarded simply as the passive subjects of structural determinations'. The creativity of children in the process of social reproduction is particularly pronounced in circumstances of rapid change (Erny, 2003). Migration makes the issue of agency more pronounced in practical terms, as the children themselves are called into the social milieu earlier and often by force, and are expected to actively engage in it despite lack of other resources.

Why are the children 'forced' out of the protective shell of the family? Because, to begin with, for a variety of reasons, the family itself is forced out of its own shell, its roots, its homeland. What sets off the trajectory of migration is often the same as what threatens the very existence of the family nest, challenging the ability of the parents to provide for the survival and the security of their children. From the very beginning of the migration experience, this conceptualization is shaken if not altogether abolished. Poverty, fear or persecutions have already threatened the foundation of family life and social existence, if not shattered it altogether. The notion of the safe home environment and the parents as providers may have often been distorted long before the decision to migrate is made.

This notion breaks even further along the migration route. The uncertainty of the journey itself and the ambiguity of its outcome have a demoralizing effect and undermine the confidence of the family. The inability of the parents to protect their own offspring in the course of the journey, where all the family savings are passed on to illegal traffickers and invested in the passage to the West, let alone the future debts that may bind them even after the arrival in another country, be it the one they initially wanted or a different one, unsettles family hierarchies and makes all the family members interdependent, getting involved in the day-to-day concerns and the struggle for survival.

Migration, even when it may be a situation arising out of some sort of deprivation, also involves an element of choice. The decision to migrate, to move away from the familiar environment and seek to create a 'home' in an unfamiliar setting is a purposeful activity. Furthermore, the reasons behind the decision to migrate are always multilayered and complex. In most of the children's narratives about the journey and the decision to leave the homeland usually for an unknown country, there is always a project for the future: either the one articulated by the parents or one of their own making. Even when migration is forced, as it is for example in the case with the majority of asylum seekers, there is an investment in what the future may hold which makes the risks sustainable.

No family migrates as a whole, with all the components that make up family networks in the country of origin. In fact, given the diverging routes of migration and the vast variety of migrant experience, all that may be said with some certainty is that every migrant family is a broken family (Christopoulou & de Leeuw, 2005, p. 113). Even when the nuclear family remains together, the extended family network is almost always disrupted. As a result, displacement in terms of spatial shifts is paired by a discontinuity, dislodgement in terms of family memberships and notions of belonging. What is lost or left behind is not just the home in the material sense of the domestic abode and the homeland, but also the people that make up the family together with the social network around it.

Yet, all this may at the same time strengthen the familial bond. The difficulties of the journey and its determining experience turn it into a literal 'rite de passage' such that all the family members travelling together undergo together. The passage to the West signifies the passage to a new 'era' in the family life and relations. What has been experienced by the family members who are travelling together – the difficulties, the anxiety, the fear, the frustrations as well as their inability to provide for and protect one another, together with their inevitable reliance on one another – may bring them closer and fortify their links. The journey itself mediates the family experience to such an extent that the links among those travelling together may even become stronger than the links with those left behind. Often, people whose fortunes converge along the way or in the reception country, facing the unknown together, interweave with ties stronger than blood ties.

THE RESEARCH

The data and observations that we draw upon are based on research with migrant children in six European countries in the context of CHICAM in which the present authors participated as researchers in Greece and the Netherlands, respectively (see de Block, Buckingham & Banaji, 2005; Christopoulou & de Leeuw, 2005). CHICAM focused on the social and cultural worlds of migrant children. The project aimed to explore and develop the potential uses of media and communication technologies as means of empowering these children and enabling them to realize their potential. Four themes have been defined to investigate the relationship between media, migration and childhood. These are: family and social relationships, school relationships and media literacy. In terms of methodology, CHICAM was conceived of as a form of 'action' research: during the project, six media clubs were set up in the respective countries (UK, Italy, Sweden, Germany, the Netherlands, Greece). In each club, a researcher and a media educator worked with migrant children in order to make visual representations of their lives and their experiences in their new locations, comprising 10–12 children. The media club involved practical media work done by the children over a long period of time; the research work was designed as ethnographic research. It involved participant obser-vation and keeping a field diary as an ongoing tool for data collection and analysis; interviews with the children (group, individual, formal, informal) and with the families of migrant and refugee children as well as with representatives of schools and the community; portfolios of the ongoing club media work; video recordings of activities and the research process; and final video productions.

From the start, the CHICAM club was set up as a place where children with diverse migrant backgrounds (refugees, second-generation immigrants) were given the possibility of using media in a creative and dynamic way to express their experiences of childhood and where 'imagination' was both stimulated and given shape. Media is a visual artefact and, as such, is a very powerful instrument to shape and articulate experiences. We have addressed the experiences of migrant children, while at the same time explored the common grounds in terms of youth culture. This was pursued mainly through specific media educational tasks, such as making a family picture show or drawing a family tree, which helped to discuss different experiences that children had lived through. Another example that illustrates the specific media educational context of CHICAM is how we stimulated the children to explore and articulate their migration experiences by asking them to think of the aspects of continuity and traditions that are most important in their family and to draw these as a basis for animation.

We motivated children to develop authorial and artistic voices by giving a specific task and at the same time encouraging them to articulate their own views while working. Each child had his or her own motivation to join the club and to stay. All the individual needs could be accommodated because we worked with different forms and changing production units, as the club work was product-oriented. By making productions, the kids created a particular media space for themselves. As CHICAM confirms, media stimulates the process of self-representation. The productions they made (both about their past and about their present life) became new artifacts for them that confirm identity and help to fantasize about the future. The CHICAM club provided a productive space and was therefore relevant for children who do not easily have access to 'free spaces'. Making movies about authentic and personal experiences was of great importance for the children in terms of personal empowerment. CHICAM offered room for the children to create their own cultural and social space, framed by their experiences both as children and as migrants. This is not to say that the experiences of the children were the same, regardless of their migrant background and their country of settlement. Differences are apparent both in Greece and the Netherlands, where the present authors actually did the research (Christopoulou & de Leeuw, 2004, 2005). In Greece, the club was accommodated by the Greek Council for Refugees in Athens, while in the Netherlands the media club took place at a so-called 'black school' with 80–90 per cent immigrant pupils, located in a town in one of the southern provinces. Differences that we found indeed had their origins in the different reasons for migration. These will be addressed below at points that in our view are relevant for an understanding of how the children negotiated their identities through their social interactions. Nevertheless, CHICAM also confirms that many problems and experiences the children explored were shared across the clubs (de Block, Buckingham & Banaji, 2005). This paper will thus be based on the common research findings of CHICAM as a whole. As we want to show some of the original empirical data, the specific examples used here are from the Dutch and Greek media-club members. The media productions made by the children as well as the production process that was observed and recorded generated the data based on which this chapter draws its observations.

THE REVERSAL OF ROLES

The children are fast learners and pick up the influences and the codes of the new society easier and earlier than their parents. They acquire cultural knowledge swiftly, efficiently and 'exceptionally well' (Hirschfeld, 2002, pp. 615 and 624). They explore the world in the new country with the same curiosity and vigour that they would in the country of origin, if not more. Each new mental acquisition and skill is greeted with enthusiasm and with a significantly less critical and/or dismissive eye, and does not entail the arduous negotiation in which the parents may engage. In this process they are more flexible than adults, as they are more willing to stretch boundaries and bend rules for the sake of exploration. Furthermore, due to their overall mobility as children, and also due to their less defined and demanding roles, they have more access to public spaces. The street, the playground, the neighbourhood and, most importantly, the school are major areas of socialization and mingling.

As a consequence, roles are often reversed in migrant families. What is usually expected from adults in a family, i.e. in terms of material and practical responsibilities, may at large become the task of the children. Children may even take up part of the educative role of the parents, either through educating them into the ways of the new society (Erny, 2003), or through contesting the rules and values promoted by parents. Parents may remain the keepers of the old culture, preserving memory and passing on knowledge, habits and values. They may even strive to reinvent the latter, and make them relevant to the new context within which they are currently situated, so as not to become void of meaning. Under the pressures of the new environment, family relations are tense, while roles and rules are challenged. This may be temporary and may not happen in all cases, but it nonetheless sets the context within which the family has to find a place for itself.

Their easier access to the new society enables children to be more easily accepted by the locals than adults. As we observed in our research, migrant children enter the houses of the locals even in contexts where adults would never be accepted to do so. As a result, they often receive positive encouragement to take on the task of mediation in day-to-day situations, resolving conflicts and misunderstandings, and often handling difficult and sensitive cases. Ahmed and Masud, two Syrian Kurds living in central Athens, aged 10 and 12 years, respectively, are already skilful negotiators: they are particularly sociable and extrovert, knowing all the neighbours by name, often addressing them in familial terms and engaging in elaborate social interactions. While their mother is a traditional, scarf-wearing Muslim who speaks no Greek and spends her day in the house looking after the needs of a multimembered family, and their father is a hard-working artisan who is also politically active in the Kurdish community, the children have taken on the task of connecting the family to the Greek world: they bring into the house local friends and go back and forth between their houses fetching offerings and treats. The material exchanges are often accompanied by descriptions and explanations that open up a channel of communication between the household and the outside world. The parents, who are generous and hospitable, support and encourage this sociable behaviour. Yet, it is the children who become the live wires and actually perform the socialization rituals that point to practices shared between the two cultures.

As a result, together with the new codes that children pick up through their socialization process, they also build a set of common references with people outside their family. Sharing a celebration, attending a ceremony or partaking in simple daily rituals go beyond the mere acquisition of cultural knowledge and become the ingredients of active social relationships, while at the same time they are more accessible to children than to adults. The common experiences shared with others and the sense of belonging together through alliances beyond the family, the language, the religion and the ethnic origin create a sense of multiple belongings and the basis for the construction of hybrid identities (see Bhabha, 1994).

Taking on adult roles may, in some cases, imply the direct involvement of children in the labour market. They start working in order to support themselves and their family, or just to contribute to the family income. Mozde, an 11-year-old girl from Afghanistan in the Greek club, goes to school. But, during the year at the media club, she also works in a street kiosk, the small family business that her parents keep. She does not clearly refer to her working responsibilities nor do her parents admit it openly when discussing with teachers and social workers. During an interview at her workplace, she does admit that, being the elder child, she has to give a hand to her parents who are faced with a variety of problems and responsibilities. What started as a temporary engagement (during the period her parents had to attend Greek classes in the process of having their migration papers sorted out and could not afford to employ a worker) ends up lasting significantly longer and becoming ever more demanding. Mozde takes on her new tasks dutifully and relieves her parents from some of their burdens. She is very skilful, well behaved, polite and diligent. She does not complain about being alone and getting bored. She has a small TV installed inside the street kiosk that she watches. Moreover, being able to contribute to the family life makes her happy, satisfied and proud of herself. The parents at first do not consider it inappropriate, and perceive it as a contribution to the family life and as a private issue, not to be discussed outside the family. The situation changes only when teachers and social workers caution them, as it has started affecting Mozde's school performance as well as some aspects of her social life.

The issue of child labour is a complex one to be dealt with, and we are tackling it only to the extent that it cannot be ignored as part of the reality that migrant families face. As a versatile issue on its own right, it demands closer attention, taking into consideration factors such as the diverse practices of childhood and the barriers between childhood and adulthood across cultures. Who is a child and who is an adult, together with the responsibilities that each role entails vary largely across cultures. Gender issues also determine the different roles and expectations: when young Balkis actively engages in the preparations of finding a suitable husband, her cousin Stivan who has approximately the same age is more preoccupied with finding a proper job that will cover his own expenses in Greece and at the same time provide for the needs of his family back in Iraq. For our purpose, it suffices to mention that, overall, in the countries where the current migrant populations originate, firstly, adulthood is reached earlier for both genders in comparison to the West, and secondly, children are perceived as much more embedded within a social network and holding a responsibility towards their family and community, as opposed to a construction of childhood focusing on individual rights, which is prevalent in the West. As a result, children are expected to enter in a negotiation with the social world around them earlier and in more diverse ways.

Even in situations where child labour is not involved, the degree of responsibility of children within the family is significantly raised. There are cases where the burdens and duties may not be as obvious, but rather manifest themselves in latent ways. The following extract from an interview with a 13-year-old girl from Iraq regarding school, demonstrates the diversified tasks that a young refugee girl accomplishes in her daily life outside school and her multiple roles within the family.

Researcher: ... Why don't you go to the proper school then?

Balkis: Oh, it's all the same ... I will still be with smaller kids, you know, because of my Greek ... It's so boring.

R: But your Greek is very good. You are fluent.

B: No ... There is no point.

R: Isn't it more boring to stay at home all day?

B: No.

R: Come on ...

B: OK sometimes it is ...

R: What do you do at home all day?

B: Watch TV ... And now that my mother was sick there was a lot to do and help her ... also errands, shopping, stuff ... Then take Chuchu to school and back ... Sometimes play with my aunt's baby. And also play with Stivan and the other kids in the neighbourhood ...

R: Do you spend a lot of time with them?

B: Yeah ... But most of them go to school.

R: So?

B: So I meet them in the afternoon or in the evening ... and we hang around and talk.

R: Well, see? You can still hang around with your friends and go to school at the same time ...

B: Hmmm .... No, not really. There is so much else to do. And it is more difficult for me because of the language.

R: Your Greek is excellent, you know that, and if you go to school it will be even better. It's a pity to give it up ... (....)

B: But what's the point? I mean we are not planning to stay here forever ... We will eventually go to the United States when our papers are done. So I don't really need Greek.

Balkis lives in Athens with her mother and two brothers. Her father lives in the US, where he works in restaurants. The mother used to work at a perfume factory but gave up the job due to health problems. The elder brother is 18 years old and works occasionally in the vegetable market, while he recently had trouble with the police. The younger brother is 8 years old and goes to school where he does very well. They await family reunification, hoping to be able to leave Greece soon and move to Detroit, US. Meanwhile, Balkis does not go to school but only attends English classes occasionally. She does not attend school for a variety of reasons. The ones that she chooses to mention first are related to the lack of effective entrance classes for foreigners, to the subsequent low placement and to the inevitable age differences with the classmates. As a result of this she experiences language frustration. Furthermore, school becomes boring as it seems to be addressing younger ages and concerns. This is not just her personal feeling that she is communicating, but in fact the experience of the majority of migrant children, and has to do with the deficiencies of the Greek educational system.

When asked about how she spends her day in the house, Balkis refers to TV. What may at first sound like boring and undifferentiated time spent within the household, acquires for her a different dimension. In other interviews, she mentions how much she enjoys it and takes pride in watching 13 TV series and soap operas. She commands a definite expertise on the subject, something that makes her popular among her age-peers as well as various adults of her social circle. She is the one to be asked anytime someone misses a detail or an episode, as well as the one who has the overall picture of each series, as she follows these uninterruptedly. The TV for Balkis, who uses her media knowledge as a socialization strategy, is a source of authority.

Behind this however, Balkis appears to have a structured day full of activities, obligations and responsibilities: she takes her younger brother back and forth to school, runs errands and does the shopping, and helps with household chores. Due to her mother's bad health, she often does a lot more than that: she takes over the household responsibilities and the day-to-day care of the two brothers. Although this is seen as temporary, it happens quite often and seems to have become the norm rather than the exception.

Balkis has also become her mother's right hand. She accompanies her to hospital and to the social services where she acts as a translator. Her task is not only to transfer information from one language to the other but also to make it understood both ways, explaining attitudes to health issues or different types of treatment. She also does most of the handling of their papers concerning their migration to the US, whereby she has learned to deal efficiently with public services on the one hand and illegal in-betweens on the other. She is the one to communicate with the teachers of the younger brother with respect to his school progress, while at the same time, when her elder brother had problems with the police, she was the one to speak with them on behalf of the family. By not speaking Greek at all, her mother has remained outside the ongoing daily concerns and has allowed Balkis to take over. The same holds true for the father, whose contribution to the family may be financial (sending money from abroad) and moral (expressing his wish to reunite). In practice, however, he is absent from the daily life of the family, the management of which is accomplished mainly by Balkis.

For Balkis, family obligations take precedence over the need for education. She presents school as time-consuming, competing with family needs and undermining socialization. Gender issues are also at play here, as education is valued for the younger brother but not for Balkis, who is seen by the family as a woman-to-be who should be preparing for adulthood and marriage instead of pursuing education. Balkis also presents education as irrelevant to her due to the temporary character of their stay in the reception country. Greek language is not a desired skill as it will be of no use further on the journey. Greece is perceived as a transit country on the way to America where all the family problems are expected to be resolved once the father takes over. This is the story in which the family has invested and what they keep telling themselves as time passes and their papers do not come through.

What emerges from our observations is that migrant children take on new roles both practically as well as abstractly, materially as well as culturally. Those roles, as the cases and the examples mentioned above illustrate, are largely characterized by novelty and multiplicity. Children take on new responsibilities as well as new rights. Having to perform tasks often beyond their knowledge, capacity and skills, they must adapt faster, and thus become quick learners, as they are under pressure to contribute to the well being of the whole family. In order to achieve this, they take on a multiplicity of tasks fulfilling different roles simultaneously, often going beyond the age barrier.

In the beginning, they may be perceived as replacing the parents in various functions due to their flexibility and faster learning. Yet, they soon surpass the mere replacement role, which they often master much faster than the parents, and may even perform it better than the latter ever could. In this way, the temporary becomes permanent, and the replacement endures. They perform their new role and in fact fill the gaps and fulfil the parental needs and expectations. What determines the role of the child as replacing an adult and its degree of temporariness, has a lot to do with the expectations of the parents related to the migration journey, as well as the desire invested in the process. The reasons that set them moving in the first place also play a major part in the process of adaptation. They often affect the degree of integration of the family as they dominate the domestic discourse.

Migrant children often take on adult roles on what is presumed to be a temporary basis, upon the expectation that those will soon be taken on again by the parents themselves, once the latter acquire the essential degree of cultural competence necessary in the new society. In some cases, this never happens, or by the time it happens, in a slower and more arduous than the initially imagined process, there is no chance of reversing to the previous order. By that time, the children have already developed their own competencies, have tried out different strategies and have experienced the power that decision-making and knowledge give, and it is no longer possible to regress.

CHILDREN AS MEDIATORS

Children swiftly become competent in double agency and become the mediators between the family and the new society (Christopoulou & de Leeuw, 2005). They are the ones who transfer the knowledge of the new society into the private space of the household, while at the same time they take on the task of representing their parents as well as their cultural values and habits into the public spaces that they primarily inhabit, i.e. the school or the neighbourhood. However, in order to do this, the parents (as the ones immediately responsible for the family's reversal of fortune) have to obtain a degree of access and to acquire a degree of cultural knowledge, even if it is only in order to be able to 'translate', explain and qualify their cultural values. This cannot be done as a simple transfer, but has to enter a dialogue and reestablish itself through a new terminology and, often, new meanings. Developing their arbitrating skills between two different cultures, the children become the channels through which this becomes possible. As a result, they enter from early on into a negotiation, which is critical for the redefinition of the family in the process of settling down in the reception country. Once the roots are cut off and symbolic meanings are reconsidered, they develop the capacity to shift between contexts and to assess their circumstances. This gives them the ability to learn from a young age on how to make choices. These choices are often forced and they may also imply a dismissal: something new may be found, something old may become revalidated and something else may be discarded. In this way, the children are able to engage in a cultural negotiation more actively than they would probably do in their country of origin.

As Balkis' case illustrates, facing the situation of migration and being confronted with uncertainty, children find themselves negotiating between the family and the new society. This applies to many dimensions of life both inside and outside the family. Sustaining a busy social life and an extensive social network, while at the same time looking after her mother and brothers and keeping the household – all these are only some aspects of the multifaceted tasks and responsibilities in the life of Balkis. Undoubtedly, some would have still been there if she was a young woman in Iraq; yet, the specific congruence of roles and responsibilities that she faces is the result of her migrating past and the pressures of living under her particular circumstances in a country which is neither that of her origin nor that of her eventual destination.

Balkis' case also articulates how the experience of childhood of refugee children drastically differs from that of their age-peers. Their way towards maturity comes earlier and in irreversible ways. Does this simply make them no longer children – or does it point towards a darker yet more complex construction of childhood under the strains of the contemporary history, which has shaped it? There is more to say about this, which goes beyond the purpose of this chapter. However, the CHICAM research made clear that this is not necessarily the case (de Block, Buckingham & Banaji, 2005; Christopoulou & de Leeuw, 2005). To put it differently, the CHICAM club offered the children a place where they could play out their experiences of migration involving feelings of loneliness and uncertainty beside the active and confident struggle for survival and their 'identity' as a child. Migration entails loss and suffering but is at most a creative activity (Flusser, 2003, p. 3). Flusser conceptualizes the notion of homeland not as an eternal value but rather as a function of a specific technology. Still, whoever loses it suffers. 'This is because we are attached to heimat by many bonds, most of which are hidden and not accessible to consciousness. Whenever these attachments tear or are torn as under, the individual experiences this painfully, almost as a surgical invasion of his most intimate person (Flusser, 2003, p. 3). According to Flusser, heimat is often confused with home. Being without a heimat, though always living somewhere, migrants by definition encounter a new place, other people, other habits, cultures and symbols. Exile then is to be viewed as a challenge to creativity. 'Exile is an ocean of chaotic information [...] If he is not to perish, the expellee must be creative' (Flusser, 2003, p. 81).

Migration allows for active engaging with the new society, as this requires to get rid of the burden of uncertainty and to learn to understand the new rules of communication, in terms of language, codes and symbols. The role of language is determining in this process of identity building. For the majority of migrant children, linguistic practices have a shifting character, speaking their mother tongue at home, and another new language in the public sphere outside the household. Language is a strong tool to develop a new sense of identity, to get connected to new communities, and is therefore one of the first things migrant children need to start with. It is also very important for their acceptance as children among other children. Rana from Syria, who had been living five years in the Netherlands when joining the CHICAM club, thinks she does not yet speak Dutch well enough. She is trying hard though. In an interview, she indicates to what extent language, for her, opens up the perspectives of a possible future in which status and standing are important:

> My favourite language is French, I know some words in French. But I like Arabic too. The Arabic of Damascus. Damascus is the capital of Syria. And of course I like my own language, Aramaic.

Her friend Masja does speak a bit of Russian and German (because the family first stayed there after fleeing), but she prefers to speak English (the global language) and her mother tongue, Kurdish Armenian. Beaugarçon's mother speaks French (the official language of Congo). The family however speaks Lingala, and a more private language keeping the rituals: children are allowed to speak this language among each other but not with older people. Older people however can address children using the private language. For all families, language seems to be an important tool in building the notion of continuity in family life as it is here and now, but also for some children language represents possible ways of being mobile, of finding their place in a global world, which confirms their position as mediators and as the ones to be able to adapt to new cultural codes.

In defining their place as children within the family and outside the family, we have observed how the children in the CHICAM club feel challenged to negotiate between the demands of the family traditions and rules and the demands of the outside world. Also, we have noticed some differences here that can be traced back to the different reasons for migration. Yet for all families, family life and religion seem to be very much connected. However, the migrant families tend to withdraw from traditions mainly defined by religion, whereas refugee families are trying to get connected as much as possible and as soon as possible to the new world, without losing their own family traditions. A Syrian girl in the Dutch club mentioned how sharing the religious rules of family life to her was important to experience the feeling of belonging to a community:

> Easter is coming up and as usual I will help my mother baking pastries. You know what we do; we decorate a basket and fill it with food and presents to bring to other Syrian families. I have to fast, but that is no problem for me at all. I want to do that.

At the same time, her parents very much got involved in the school, as was also true for other refugee families. They expressed great thankfulness for having the children there. Education for the children is not only seen as an investment in the future but also as an instrument of integration. According to the Dutch headmaster P.:

> They fled from a country where living has become impossible for them. They are forced to look at the future. This is very different from the situation in migrant families. They come from a safe country where they often go back to, where they have built a second house and where they will return. This perspective makes it less urgent to integrate and as a result education in the Netherlands is less important for them.

Originally Catholic, the school celebrates Christian holidays; at the same time the children are allowed to stay at home to celebrate the end of Ramadan.

The act of mediating is a function that migrant children take on by way of surviving. Following Flusser (2003, p. 3), they should not be seen as outsiders but as 'vanguards of the future (...) no longer pitiable victims whom we need to help to regain their lost heimats [homelands] but rather models whom we should emulate if we have the requisite courage'. Migration thus involves a constant process of negotiating the notion of homeland, which in the first place means negotiating cultural identity.

HYBRID IDENTITIES

Ethnicity is one of the constituting elements of cultural identity. It recognizes the place of history, language and culture in the formation of identity with reference to origin. Everybody therefore is ethnically positioned. Ethnicity concerns explicitly a common history, shared historical memories, one or more elements of a common (felt) culture, a link with a homeland and a feeling of solidarity with at least several members of the group. In the context of migration, this is the issue rather than nationality (Kostoryano, 2003, p. 72).

Hall (1996, p. 447), in his essay about shifts in black cultural policy, distinguishes between the dominant notion of ethnicity connected to nation and 'race' and a non-essentialist notion of ethnicity, recognizing 'that we all speak from a particular place, out of a particular history, out of a particular experience, a particular culture without being contained by that position as ethnic artists or filmmakers. We are all in that sense, ethnically located and our ethnic identities are crucial to our subjective sense of who we are'. Ethnicity no longer is an absolute, fixed position, rather it should be conceived as a social construction of relational differences. Here too, a non-essentialist approach of ethnicity is preferred, though, as Hall states, the essentialist and non-essentialist approach go hand in hand, as most people do have a dual discursive competence (Baumann, 1999) which helps them to deal with identity in different ways. Building upon the non-essentialist notion of cultural identity, Homi Bhabha (1994), as mentioned previously, suggests the notion of the third space, a process of hybridity away from the politics of polarity and the politics of cultural binaries. It develops as an integral part of cultural dialogue, as in Bhabha's view cultures are only constituted in relation to others and otherness, if in ignorance. The process of cultural hybridity gives rise to something different; it is a space, which enables new cultural practices, without truth claims (Bhabha, 1990, p. 213).

This notion of hybridity is only partly useful when discussing the experiences of refugee families and their children. In entering a new country, people do encounter a new culture, of which one cannot disconnect oneself. However, the dialogical relation to the new culture is very differently performed, depending upon the position of the family in the new society and of each of the family members within and outside the family. The notion of hybridity does not consider the need to keep old certainties and the need that people feel of perceiving themselves as constant and stable persons, not to mention the efforts put into this notion of stability. It is clear from the data of the CHICAM research that the children articulated a differentiated encounter with the new society and that they were indeed entering a third space, playing out their identities over the multiple roles they were taking on while at the same time yearning for a feeling of belonging firmly rooted in old contingencies, if reconstructed (de Block, Buckingham & Banaji, 2005; Christopoulou & de Leeuw, 2005).

One of the key aspects in children's lives is friendship, the development of relationships to peers. These are important in terms of identity construction as a child or an adolescent. For migrant children, there is the additional notion of getting connected to a new world for which new 'friends' and new relations outside the family are crucial. Several children in the CHICAM club indeed had to make new friends again and again because of the transfers that are inherent in the life of an asylum seeker. Their families fled a country where life was no longer possible for them, keeping little or no contact with family and friends in their countries of origin, because this would have been too dangerous. Therefore, friendships with children in their own country were not maintained. Moreover, not many children in the clubs came from the same country, sharing the same religion and speaking the same language. It is within this context that their obvious high standard for their friendships and loyalty to their friends that our data reveal, should be read.

Refugee children indeed have a more exceptional position, even though some of them have lived in the new country for many years. Before they came to the small town of Roosendaal in the south of the Netherlands, the children in the Dutch CHICAM club lived in a centre for asylum seekers, and moved around quite a lot. Many families only had temporary residence permits, which made their future in the Netherlands uncertain. The dynamics within the group and the interviews with the children showed that the experience of being a refugee was crucial in the forming of friendships.

Two cases from the Dutch club illustrate this: Rana from Syria describes her friendship with the Armenian Masja as 'different'. She feels different, more familiar, with her than with other girls: 'No one else in class understands what it means to be an asylum seeker'. Rana is unable to explain, but from the moment she saw Masja she wanted her to be her friend. She plays with two Turkish girls too, but she does not invite them over to her house, and her mother does not know them. Masja visits her at home. 'My mother knows her, she talks to us, eats with us, I play with her and she sits next to me'. Her friendship with Masja is 'ten percent more'. Masja feels exactly the same. Their shared experience of the centre for asylum seekers forms the basis for their friendship.

The feeling of sameness is strongly developed in Kambooye and Beaugarçon, if grounded differently. They are of different faiths, Muslim and Catholic, but they are both from Africa. They have established a bond because the other children often react negatively to the fact that they are black. Kambooye and Beaugarçon felt excluded because of this, and soon found support in each other. Kambooye tells that he used to be bullied a lot: 'In Kindergarten, I was the only brown kid. There are two in the class now, so it is normal'. By the second one, he means Beaugarçon. The two have been very close from the moment Beaugarçon joined Kambooye's class, because they need each others' support. We have also noticed how Kambooye shared his food with Beaugarçon, who often does not get enough food from home.

We have also observed how the needs of the parents to build bridges to the new society are projected onto the desired peer relations of their children, which confirms the idea of children being seen as mediators by the parents. Basically, the children are left free in their choice of friendships. However, small restrictions and preconceptions are apparent. Kambooye's mother, for example, is unhappy about the fact that the school the children attend is a so-called 'Black School', meaning that the school has a large number of minority children. The same holds true for Elias's Iraqi mother. She feels it is important for her son to socialize with native Dutch children as much as possible. The family's desire to integrate manifests itself in the preferred friendships for their children.

The children in the Dutch and Greek club have very different family histories, which were hard to address, especially in terms of how they 'remember' the family. Generally speaking, they do not bring the family history into the school or the club, nor do they discuss it among friends, as it is at the same time obvious and personal to the children. Overall, the conceptualization of family history is a defining factor in the construction of identity. How the children build hybrid identities in relation to their perception of 'family', and their place within it became visible in how they imagined a family history. An example from the Dutch club illustrates the role that media can play in the reconstruction of a family history, offering the children concrete background stories which are crucial in their experience of who they are: a Congolese boy who had no autobiographic memories of Congo used existing pictures to construct a family history that contained both true and invented stories. Imagination is a key word, as the pictures triggered his fantasy about a past life about which he has heard his mother talking a lot, but which was not yet internalized and therefore not yet part of his personal identity. In using media (reworking the pictures into a family picture show, with commentary personally spoken and dubbed), it was possible for him to link the past to the present life and thus create a narrative to tell about his family history as a continuous story in which the 'there' and 'here' are linked. We noticed this link also on a different level. He represented himself as an average teenage boy (i.e. in terms of clothes) who does not hide his African background, using tribal icons in his drawings and wearing family jewellery: an African chain that his uncle gave his father, and his father passed on to him. On one of his video diary tapes he plays a sort of an African king, putting a curtain on by way of a cloak, dancing. Past and present lives have not only converged into a complete family history, but also in a more indirect way, convergence is revealed in acts of self-representation.

USING MEDIA AS TOOLS OF INCLUSION AND EMPOWERMENT

CHICAM aimed to identify how new media and communication technologies can be used to promote inclusion, both social and institutional, by building bridges between migrant children and members of the host societies. Also, it was an ambition through the use of these technologies to raise the voice of migrant children in decision-making at local, national and European Community level in relation to policies that directly affect their social and economic well being. This is basically about empowerment, about increasing their social inclusion and public participation. As the EU funded CHICAM, and the CHICAM findings were assumed to inform EU educational and cultural policies, the notion of inclusion and of citizenship was important throughout the research. Though the latter may seem beyond reach, in making media productions, in reflecting upon these through active discussions and in exchanging productions with other clubs and commenting upon these as productive audience, authorial voices were developed, a preliminary condition for citizenship.

Wiener (1997) offers a useful approach to citizenship, using the concept of 'fragmented citizenship'. Identity represents the notion of belonging, together with the more legal aspect of nationality, which represents your official place. We acknowledge that in the global world, where you are does not automatically equal with where you feel at home. That is exactly why the notion of belonging is crucial. Other aspects of citizenship support this, such as rights (to vote, to move, for protection) and access (to welfare provisions) (Wiener, 1997, p. 549). For refugee families, the notion of fragmented citizenship is an everyday experience, as waiting for a residence permit (legal belonging) can be at odds with participation in the new society as migrants and residents at the same time. Refugee children need to deal with these tensions. In the CHICAM club, media proved to be empowering instruments in coping with the obvious uncertainty and the challenge to create a future perspective.

In the media clubs, the children had access to communication means, to modern media enabling them to articulate their everyday life experiences and to explore creative ways of communication. This was important in terms of media education, but was also supportive in giving them a place, a position in the public arena, which is dominantly formed and defined through media. Media is not a neutral resource. In making media, the children created a position from where they could speak. Their productions thus reflected both how they see the world and how they see themselves positioned within this world. As a matter of course, they used the available communication means also to present themselves in a certain way, either focusing on what is shared by youth culture such as teenager style, or emphasizing ethnic accents in their present lives. For the children, the media club developed into a common social place. Making media offered a space for establishing common ground while at the same time differences and struggles for power were played out over the definition of particular spaces where they could represent themselves in a more complete way.

As we have pointed out before, the children worked in all genres. Yet, some genres in particular allowed for more individual voices. The children found several sources of inspiration for (self)-representation that were capable of overcoming language barriers across geographic boundaries while at the same time offering the possibilities of personal contributions. We have observed how the children articulated both teenage style and individual (subcultural) style. The sources of inspiration that turned out to be especially appropriate for the children regarding this double address were rap, animation and performing scenes. One example of these is how in the Dutch club they 'staged' themselves on a picture. The children had to think of a possible future profession and were asked to bring props to the club that could express this, so others could tell. They worked precisely as if they were in a professional photo studio and they liked to perform this way, feeling 'bigger' than they actually were. Performing is presenting oneself; it helps to become more secure; here the camera literally was a mediator between the children and the social world. In that respect, performing helps to develop personal empowerment, meaning self-representation in terms of self-esteem, power and self-respect that could be articulated because their personal qualities, skills and knowledge were addressed.

Making media had an additional impact, as all school teachers were surprised by the skills that each of the children displayed, especially by their creativity and by the fact that most of them achieved much better in the CHICAM club than they did in class. The productions made in the CHICAM club did reveal quite some other aspects of the children and brought out talents that the teachers had not noticed before. School to some extent reduces the creative skills and ambitions of the children. Through the media productions, teachers began to see pupils in a different way, noticing aspects that apparently were never addressed in classroom and could neither be developed.

The children themselves were very proud of their work in the CHICAM club, and the day after the club they liked to talk in their own classes about what they had made in the club. This was empowering in a personal way. It was further intensified during 'official' presentation of the club work. During these presentations, the children very much presented themselves as media producers, as children who were given instruments (and thus a voice) to communicate their experiences, their desires, fun and joy within the context of CHICAM. In front of an audience, their roles as media producers were recognized. In our view, presenting to a public audience is an important aspect of personal and interpersonal empowerment in the sense of recognition and acknowledgement by their direct social environment making up the actual audience. Interpersonal empowerment thus strengthens personal identity, being one of the conditions of social inclusion. Making media productions means raising your voice, not only within the diaspora community, but also in the public arena. By making media, the children obtained the right to articulate their own identity in all its complexities. This is an important step towards active citizenship, developing the need to be involved in and contribute to social debates and decision-making and eventually to full picture citizenship, in case a residence permit is given.

CONCLUDING REMARKS

Migrant children develop competence in double agency, learning to live betwixt and between both cultures, that of the country of origin and that of the reception country. Furthermore, those with direct migration experience, having lived through the difficulties of the journey, may carry the burden of the separation trauma and the uncertainty of what has followed, but also come equipped with a heightened instinct of survival as well as a sense of accomplishment. The experience of the journey strengthens them and builds confidence in their own ability and faith in their own skill. When confronted with difficulties in the subsequent stages of settling down anew, they may revert to what they have already accomplished and draw from it the strength and reassurance that will motivate them to try harder. What for other children comes from the positive encouragement of parents, teachers and social networks, for migrant children it often resides within themselves, in their own repository of experience. The difficulties confronted along the way in the early odysseys of migrant children are also sources of empowerment, and each time a knot is severed, the 'freedom to judge, decide, and act becomes greater' (Flusser, 2003, p. 5).

The ability to draw upon this experience in order to invent tools, to utilize all the resources available to them and to set out strategies makes migrant children active agents within their social environments. The degree of agency corresponds to the ways in which they have been able to engage with the new society and to develop feelings of belonging and inclusion. According to Berry, Phinney, Sam, and Vedder (2006), integration ('the best of both worlds') turned out to be the most helpful strategy for most migrant youth in terms of being well and feeling well as articulated by the youth itself. Integration involves speaking the original language and the national language, as well as an orientation towards the new society without denouncing their own background. Integration though is not obvious. It rather illustrates how difficult it is for young people to negotiate between different worlds, to deal with the requirements and pressures from both the new society and the own group, mainly represented by the family. This is even more true when it comes to refugee children who, by definition, encounter great uncertainty when arriving in the new country due to the incompleteness of the family and the new roles they are forced to take up as a consequence, while facing uncertainty from the new society, as it is not clear from the beginning whether they will be given permission to build a new future and home.

In using media, however, as the experience of the CHICAM project demonstrates, the children obtained control over instruments of communication and expression through which they could not only imagine a new future but also reflect upon their present state, marked by uncertainty and the urge for survival. Film and television are an important aspect of youth culture. An audiovisual medium is appealing and ranks highly in the cultural hierarchy that children maintain. The magic associated with film and television greatly enhances the appeal of these media to children. Within the context of migration and displacement, the use of media enables them to subvert and at the same time make use of various existing classifications and to explore different aspects of citizenship as discussed above. By giving instruments to the children and then listening to what they say instead of asking them to tell what it means to be a migrant, the children were addressed as people who are able to contribute to the discourse on multiculturalism in the wider society, while at the same time media use helped to them to represent themselves as children. Media thus became the tool to express both modes of acculturation and shifting identities at the same time.

Thus, at least for children, media can be regarded a useful instrument for 'rites de passage'.

In her influential study on children's minds, Margaret Donaldson concluded that children are 'not plants with only one 'natural' way of growing. They are beings of richly varied possibilities, and they are beings with potential for guiding their own growth in the end. They can learn to be conscious of the powers of their own minds and decide to what ends they will use them' (Donaldson, 1978, p. 122). In this process, they certainly need aid, support, and most importantly, opportunities. Migration may deprive them of an overall supportive environment, tested, impermeable and well composed, but it opens up to them not only a world of many risks and hazards but also of opportunity. Migration, 'although a creative activity, also entails suffering, just as action often originates in suffering' (Flusser, 2003, p. 3). In that sense, migration may not be a 'natural' context within which children grow. It may cut roots, but it creates wings. In its volatile and unpredictable course, migration is a painful yet a creative process that entails loss but at the same time it is a motivation for children to draw upon a wide span of skills and resources in order to interact with and enrich their social environments.

NOTE

1. CHICAM as a research project ran from 2001–2004 and was co-ordinated by the Institute of Education, Centre for the Study of Children, Youth and Media, University of London. See http://www.chicam.net

REFERENCES

Baumann, G. (1999). *The multicultural riddle. Rethinking national, ethnic, and religious identities.* London: Routledge.

Berry, J. W., Phinney, J. S., Sam, D. L., & Vedder, P. (2006). *Immigrant youth in transition: Acculturation, identity and adaptation across national contexts.* New York: Lawrence Erlbaum Associates.

Bhabha, H. (1990). Interview with Homi Bhabha. In: J. Rutherford (Ed.), *Identity. Community, culture, difference* (pp. 207–221). London: Lawrence and Wishart.

Bhabha, H. (1994). *The location of culture.* London: Routledge.

de Block, L., Buckingham, D., & Banaji, S. (2005). *Children in communication about migration.* Final Report. The European Commission, Community Research.

Christopoulou, N., & de Leeuw, S. (2004). *Home is where the heart is: Family relations of migrant children in six European countries.* The European Commission, Community Research, Children In Communication About Migration (CHICAM) Deliverables 11 and 12.

Christopoulou, N., & de Leeuw, S. (2005). Children making media: Constructions of home and belonging. In: J. Knörr (Ed.), *Childhood and migration: From experience to agency* (pp. 113–135). Bielefeld: Transcript Verlag.

Donaldson, M. (1978). *Children's minds.* London: Fontana.

Erny, P. (2003). Einleitung. In: W. Egli & U. Krebs (Eds), *Beiträge zur Ethnologie der Kindheit. Erziehungswissenschaftliche und kulturvergleichende Aspekte.* Ethnopsychologie und Ethnopsychoanalyse (Vol. 5, pp. 5–20), Münster: Lit Verlag.

Flusser, V. (2003). *The freedom of the migrant: Objections to nationalism.* Chicago, IL: University of Illinois Press.

Hall, S. (1996). New ethnicities. In: D. Morley & K.-H. Chen (Eds), *Critical dialogues in cultural studies* (pp. 441–449). London: Routledge.

Hirschfeld, L. (2002). Why don't anthropologists like children? *American Anthropologist, 104*(2), 611–627.

James, A., & James, A. (2004). *Constructing childhood: Theory, policy and social practice.* New York: Palgrave Macmillan.

James, A., & Proutt, A. (Eds). (1990). *Constructing and reconstructing childhood: Contemporary issues in the sociological study of childhood.* Basingstoke: Falmer Press.

Jenks, C. (1982). *The sociology of childhood: Essential readings.* London: Batsford.

Jenks, C. (1996). *Childhood.* London: Routledge.

Knörr, J., & Nunes, A. (2005). Introduction. In: J. Knörr (Ed.), *Childhood and migration: From experience to agency* (pp. 9–21). Bielefeld: Transcript Verlag.

Kostoryano, R. (2003). Transnational networks and political participation. In: M. Berezin & M. Schain (Eds), *Europe without borders. Remapping territory, citizenship, and identity in a transnational age* (pp. 64–85). Baltimore, MD: John Hopkins University Press.

Toren, C. (1993). Making history: The significance of childhood cognition for a comparative anthropology of mind. *Man (N.S.), 28,* 461–478.

Wiener, A. (1997). Making sense of the new geography of citizenship: Fragmented citizenship in the European Union. *Theory and Society, 26,* 529–560.

DIVERSE CHILDHOODS: IMPLICATIONS FOR CHILDCARE, PROTECTION, PARTICIPATION AND RESEARCH PRACTICE [*]

Andy West, Claire O'Kane and Tina Hyder

INTRODUCTION

Researchers have been known to complain that practitioners do not listen to their findings or recommendations, and have emphasised the importance of evidence-based practice. In the late 1980s and early 1990s, research concerning children produced a shift leading to a new sociological paradigm of childhood. This paradigm parallels the United Nations Convention on the Rights of the Child (CRC), produced at the same time. Both productions emphasise common themes, which in the principles of the CRC are expressed as non-discrimination, children's participation and the best interests of the child. Sociological frameworks and the CRC were brought together in the growing movement to 'child-rights programming' (CRP) taken up by many UN and international children's agencies since the turn of the twenty-first century.[1]

[*] An earlier version of this paper was presented at the *Childhoods* conference in Oslo in 2005.

Childhood: Changing Contexts
Comparative Social Research, Volume 25, 265–292
Copyright © 2008 by Emerald Group Publishing Limited
All rights of reproduction in any form reserved
ISSN: 0195-6310/doi:10.1016/S0195-6310(07)00009-9

CRP highlights the roles and practices of governments, other agencies and individuals as duty bearers for children's rights (see Theis, 2004). An essential part of CRP is research on children's circumstances before any proposed intervention, to identify where rights are unfulfilled and who are the relevant duty bearers. An understanding of the local constructions of childhood, power and diversity should be part of this, but is not always done when analysis is subjective. Analysis of children's circumstances needs to be holistic: how different aspects of children's lives are connected, and how breaches and fulfillment of rights impact each other. Children's participation is important in this process, including their involvement in analysis and identification of violations of rights.

Analysis of children's circumstances has often included the relation ship between policy and children's and young people's participation (see Crimmens & West, 2004 for examples). A sociological understanding of local ideas about childhood is needed if attitudes towards children and harmful practices are to be identified, which means a diversity analysis must be included. The ways in which children's participation in programming can be developed also depend on local circumstances and understandings of childhood. But attention to local constructs of childhood can pose tensions with a blanket application of universal child rights. The unifying key might be the CRC principle 'best interests of the child' which, if properly interpreted, would require information gathering and local understandings of children and childhood. But making and implementing decisions on the best interests of the child is still potentially difficult. Which measure should be used if children's rights are apparently in conflict with local practice? In some cases this should be easy, where children are harmed emotionally or physically, but in other cases simplistic superficial analyses and use of rights can be damaging; for example, the debates over working children and child labour, and where the notion that children should not work is inadequate in dealing with situations where it is necessary for survival, and prohibition would lead to worse circumstances. A more subtle approach, questioning what the work is (alongside the hothouse labour of school, testing and examination pressures experienced by many children); and what work is safe and unsafe for children at different ages and abilities, from the perspectives of children as well as adults, and ensuring protecting children from harm and exploitation, might be more in their best interests. But to reach this point of understanding, before the complexities of decisions (by whom – with children?) and their implementation (by whom – with children?), requires an engagement with local understandings of diversity, with children and with children's views.

These tensions are more than academic debates. Have research and new studies of childhood influenced the practice of governments and non-government organisations working with children? The translation of research into practice requires more than publication, and here lies a twist in the tale, for while researchers feel research results are not taken up, many academic institutions are failing to respond to the findings of research and the implications of the sociological paradigm and children's rights.

In terms of protection, recent work through practice and research has established a linkage between diversity, participation and child protection, particularly through the understanding and promotion of children's resilience. This linkage has important implications, which should be explored, understood and applied by governments, welfare services, non-government organisations and other duty bearers who have responsibilities to fulfil children's rights. The ways in which diversity, participation and protection are connected, and how to engage with the variations entailed, are a component of work being developed in Save the Children[2] in understanding the processes and methods of protecting children. This paper draws on some findings from the recent work of Save the Children highlighting connections between – and complex dilemmas relating to – research and practice. Main components of processes necessary to engage practitioners and children in understanding and responding to childhood diversity are outlined. These processes involve adults looking at their own understandings of childhood, local models and categories of childhood, and children's involvement in research and practice.

Save the Children UK (SCUK) is an international non-government organisation committed to fighting for children's rights and supporting practice and policy work in countries across the world. SCUK asserts the basic concept that all humans, including children, have universal, indivisible rights to life with respect and dignity, but also recognises the importance of understanding individuals and groups within their wider, cultural, socio-economic and political context. Therefore, it is critical that programme work is informed by an understanding of diversity of childhoods in local context. Such understanding must be informed by the views of children. Conflicting views concerning childhood, participation and protection need to be sensitively explored and built upon to ensure practice and policy developments that are in children's best interests.

CHILDHOOD, DIVERSITY AND PROTECTION

Diversity and the Social Construction of Childhood

The new paradigm of childhood has three main tenets:

1. that childhood is a social construction, it is an interpretive frame for understanding the early years of human life, and that biological immaturity rather than childhood is a universal and natural feature of human populations;
2. that childhood is a variable of social analysis and so cannot be separated from other variables such as class, gender, ethnicity etc.; and
3. that children must be seen as actively involved in the construction of their own lives and the lives of those around them (Prout & James, 1997, pp. 3–5).

The first two concern diversity. First, the idea, definition and expectations of childhood vary between cultures. Second, even within a culture children are not a homogeneous unit, with variations such as age, gender, ethnicity, class, wealth, disability etc., as these ideas are structured and explained in different societies, influencing children's individual experiences. Third, since children are social actors, they affect the world around them from birth (for example, in causing different reactions of other children and of adults). As they grow, they develop different relationships with other children and adults, and take action in their social world. These three tenets resonate in principles of the CRC, for example, to non-discrimination, to best interests of individual children and to children's participation.

The sequencing of these three ideas develops its implications for practice work with children. Variation of childhood across cultures means that there is no objective, natural state of childhood or path along which children's development should occur: the ideas of what children should do and be capable of doing at different ages depend on local customs and perceptions of childhood. It means there is no 'standard' child that can be used as a measure for childhood globally or even within societies. The ideal of a child and childhood is constructed within a culture, and generally defined and upheld by particular powerful groups. Taboo behaviour in one culture can be accepted or sought after behaviour in another. Such variation also implies that local ideas of child protection, what is it that girls and boys need to be protected from, will also differ across societies, cultures and even localities. For example, different ideas of the cosmos, spirit world, of how harm can occur to humans and so on. It also means that children must be involved and consulted in decisions on their lives and environment, not only because children are the experts (Ennew, 2004, p. 24) but also because it promotes their resilience (for example, see West & Zhang, 2005; Boyden & Mann, 2000), which should be a prominent feature in child protection.

Variation across Space and Time

Ideals of childhood not only differ between cultures, but also change over time. The nineteenth–twentieth century dominant, monolithic, Western model of childhood was challenged from the 1980s (see James & Prout, 1997; James, Jenks, & Prout, 1998; Jenks, 1996). The model is inconsistent, encompassing children as both innocent and as evil: the mechanics of explaining this dichotomy illustrate the fluidity of particular notions of childhood, how they are rooted to specific places and times, with only broad notions lasting over longer periods. This model shows how conceptions of childhood are also linked to ideas of protection.

A notion of childhood as a period of innocence and time for play, developed in industrial Europe in the nineteenth century, partly in response to the appalling conditions of life in industrialised cities. Problems included young children working in dangerous and exploitative conditions, such as coal mines and mills. Increased recognition of the exploitation and abuse of children in Britain in the nineteenth century led to the formation of the National Society for the Prevention of Cruelty to Children in the 1880s and the 1889 Prevention of Cruelty to Children Act empowering the police to take action against parents. By the end of the nineteenth century, 'the main components of child protection law that exist today [in the UK] were in place' (Corby, 1993, p. 19).

This example of the development of a social construction of childhood and consequent development of non-government organisation, social activism, legislation and then practice shows the impact and effect of childhood constructions that are later taken for granted. It indicates how ideas about childhood are related to ideas of protection, which can then become institutionalised in law and practice, and provide a baseline from which future behaviour is measured or constrained. Practice ideas about the care of children and their needs can become static and not pay attention to social change. Systems for childcare are caught in time and, once established, can be difficult to alter. They can remain the norm even when they have become inappropriate over time or by dispersal to places with different traditions.

Diversity within Societies

The spread and dominance of this model has obscured the depths and extent of diversity in childhood around the world. Children are not a homogenous group, even those living in small community. Children's experiences are different, for example, taking age and gender as variables, the lives of a 7-year-old boy and a 14-year-old girl. When other factors are added in, such as disability, class or social status, wealth (such as a disabled 12-year-old boy of low status and in poverty, a non-disabled 16-year-old girl with wealthy parents), it is evident that children's rights cannot be discussed in isolation, but through the particular circumstances of particular children. Age is of special significance for perceptions of childhood, and especially ideas of transition to youth and adulthood. Some understanding as to which categories are significant in a particular society is needed. Concepts of disability and gender issues are well known, but there are many others equally important, such as ethnicity, skin-colour, caste, class, religion etc.

Cultural ideas of, and attitudes to, disability vary. For example, 'The Massai [of Kenya] do not regard people with a disabling condition as a single unified category toward whom they relate by a standardised set of behaviours' (Talle, 1995, p. 56). Cultural norms have an impact on children's development. For example, learning to communicate through picking up children and speaking for them in order to encourage them to talk (Gottlieb, 2000). The Ifaluk (in Micronesia) believe that children under the age of 2 years cannot understand anything said to them, so there is no point in talking to them (DeLoache & Gottlieb, 2000; Le, 2000; Lee, 2001). Forms of communication are often taken for granted or assumed, for example, speaking and hearing are *the* means of communication. This widespread cultural practice places deaf children at significant disadvantage. 'Whether deafness is congenital or acquired, it is often not diagnosed in China before age two or three, when parents realise their child is slow to speak' (Callaway, 2000, p. 32). Because it takes a couple of years for diagnosis, although some deaf children are abandoned, 'deaf children are less likely than those with visible disabilities to be abandoned or neglected in infancy' (*ibid.*). Here, two cultural practices come into play: attitudes towards deafness and the practice of abandonment.

In China, some disabled children are abandoned, and children's residential homes mainly look after disabled boys and girls, and non-disabled girls. Gender differences are evident here, because apart from disabled babies, it is the non-disabled girls who are abandoned. But diversity within country means that residential homes in the north-west have roughly equal numbers of non-disabled boys and girls. In many societies, a preference for boys for various reasons (such as the 'dowry' costs of marrying their daughters in India, performing cremation ceremonies in Bali, looking after parents when they are old or caring for ancestors in patrilineal societies such as China) leads to discrimination against girls. Mistreatment, abuse and neglect of girls (such as being fed less, female abandonment or infanticide) remain too well known in many places in the world, despite legislation, policy and practice.

Social Actors with Evolving Capacities

Recognising children as social actors is an additional aspect of diversity, and raises another dimension. Children are not 'adults-in-waiting' or empty vessels waiting to be filled, but human beings having influence on the world around them. This challenges the notions implicit in models of childhood that conceptualise adults as 'beings' and children as 'becomings' (see Qvortrup, 1994). In some societies, restrictions on children achieving full social status until a certain age is marked in law, but this derives from children's powerlessness. It is spuriously based on ideas that children lack competence, rather than evidence of them suddenly gaining competence on a particular birthday.

Increased research on children's lives around the world has brought attention to children's evolving capacities (Lansdown, 2005). The new Disability Rights Convention makes provision for recognition of children's evolving capacities. That even young children can make sensible and wise decisions is apparent from research, their participation in various activities, and the survival of some in difficult circumstances such as living on the street. Understanding of children's evolving capacities has found that while some children cannot do some things, for example, because they are too small, children generally have greater capabilities than adults recognise. Development of capacity is not standardised because of diversity of circumstances and cultural expectations of individual children. Physiological changes in the brain, and sexual development, generally occur over a period before humans become 18 years old, but the timing varies from person to person, and the expression of those changes varies by culture as well as individually (Greenfield, 2000). Because of adult conceptions of age as a dividing line, age is an important area of diversity within childhood.

Power and Discrimination

One reason why children's agency is little recognised is that children are usually in a less powerful position than adults (both status and physical power), a general form of discrimination. Prejudice, discrimination and oppression are often associated with gender and racism. New forms of prejudice arise as societies change, for example, around migration and HIV/AIDS. Certain categories of children provoke discriminatory responses. For example, the term 'street children' is poorly defined and of little analytical use, but has popular resonance (see West, 2003). Local constructions of 'street children' vary, and so do responses – between extremes of locking them up as a social problem, through charitable provision to engaging with them on the streets – empowering them as citizens (O'Kane, 2003b). Responses to children in conflict with the law also vary, although with less sympathetic approaches evident among the general populace. Children taken into the care of the state face stigma and discrimination in both the West (West, 1999) and the East (personal communication; West & Zhang, 2005). Within these groupings, there are further differences: older street girls are especially vulnerable to sexual exploitation, and seem to disappear from the streets when past a certain age in some places (for example, parts of China).

Issues of sexuality are not acknowledged in many societies, particularly in connection with children (see Taylor, 2005), but are a site demonstrating complexities of diversity, protection and participation. Children's sexuality is a difficult topic to raise, partly because of the construction of childhood innocence (contradictory to reality experienced by many children), and the placement of sexuality in the 'adult' world. Yet the CRC age definition of up to 18 years encompasses older children – young people – who are likely to and do engage in sexual activity. In some (western) societies, this is evidenced by the number of teenage pregnancies, the cause of occasional moral panic, especially when conception and birth is under the age of consent. Sex and marriage of children under 18 years in other societies has been practiced, regarded as traditional, but now, for example, in South Asia, it is the subject of campaigns against child-brides.

Apart from the complexities of age, consensual sex between peers, early birth, marriage, non-consensual sex including rape and abuse has an impact on children's life experiences and futures. The complexities of protection include boys and girls, rape and abuse in the home even from a young age and by trusted, close family or friends, forced selling of children's sex by controlling adults, and children selling sex themselves as means of survival on the street. An early 'sexualisation' of children may affect individuals in different ways, emotionally and physically. Child protection concerns in the area of sexuality derive much from local, cultural constructions, including notions of the child/young person as representative and possession of the family and its honour.

Emerging Diversities

Cultural diversity is popularly associated with a plethora of 'traditional', rural and small-scale societies, threatened by a homogenisation through globalisation of businesses, technology and population movement. Yet, these changes contribute to increased diversity as new forms of difference and identity emerge.

Domestic and international migration contributes to changing constructions of childhoods, including through migrants' experiences of discrimination. Migrants usually move from poorer rural areas to cities, and constructions of childhood are different in each place. Migration is better seen as one strand in population movements, some of which are safe and some dangerous, some voluntary and some involuntary, some through deceit and some not, and all especially affecting children. Some children and young people migrate independently and purposefully for economic reasons, some run away, some are trafficked and some are left behind when parents migrate. The opportunity of movement contributes to and exacerbates vulnerability created by abusive and harmful lives in families and communities. The question of who moves, and how, concerns diversity. Problems arise for the most powerless who migrate to seek opportunity and become commodities – another impact of discrimination. During awareness-raising work on diversity, it was realised that in parts of southern China, deaf girls are particularly vulnerable to being trafficked.

HIV/AIDS epidemics are creating new forms of discrimination, with children orphaned or with family infected by HIV. Constructions of discrimination depend on local ideas. In some places, discrimination rests on the idea that infected people must have been involved in immoral behaviour. In central China, the HIV epidemic was caused by blood-buyers' bad practices and unsterilised equipment. Even so, infected individuals are blamed as lazy, for earning easy money through selling blood instead of working, and so responsible for their own infection. Problems of poverty underlying blood-selling are ignored. Children find that they are also blamed: 'Children know that when people know a family member is infected with HIV, the whole family is affected, and that they cannot find a job in the future and no one will want to marry them' (West & Zhang, 2005). The operation of discrimination is circular, and means that individuals lose humanity and are blamed for the aspect of identity or circumstances that underpin their experience of discrimination.

Implications for Protection

While children are not a homogenous group, the notion of protection also varies. From what do we want to protect children? Because of the complexities involved, the CRC introduced basic rights. Local constructions of childhood involve ideas of protection, which are prevalent in popular discourse: problems from which children need to be protected are reported frequently in newspapers. Examples from one newspaper offer what might be seen as generally agreed problems. The *Bangkok Post*, of 1st October 2004 carried stories involving countries in Asia, the Pacific and Britain. The front-page report, 'child-porn swoop nets police and teachers', involved 160 people in Australia. Inside stories also focused on sex abuse, including 'Bangladesh policeman hanged for rape and murder of a 14 year old girl in 1995'; 'at least half a million South Asian boys and girls are working as prostitutes despite government attempts to curb a child sex trade fuelled by Internet pornography'; 'The trial of seven Pitcairn Island men … began … with the Mayor the first to face charges of rape and underage sex'. Other stories took a less sensational tone. A photograph of 'life on the streets' was captioned 'a disabled Bangladesh child lies down as his sister begs' noting 30th September as the National Girl Child Day in the Child Rights Week.

   Different issues concerning protection of children from sex emerged in a story 'Tanning cream for pre-teens?' published two days earlier (Boycott, 2004). This involved magazines for teenage girls, marketing surveys showing 'most 7–10 year olds in the UK are using make-up' and commercial survey reports concluding that cosmetic companies could improve marketing by placing cosmetic vending machines in schools. The story suggested: 'Claims that youngsters are being forced to express their sexual identity long before childhood is over have provoked rows and moral panics in recent years'. The Archbishop of Canterbury (a senior British church leader) was reported as having criticised consumerism for its 'corruption and premature sexualisation of children'. The NSPCC (a major British NGO) was reported as stating that 'children should be free to enjoy childhood without due pressures' but 'young girls have always experimented with make-up and the dressing up box. This should only really cause alarm if a child feels that its something they are uncomfortable with but forced to do'. But this 'dressing-up-box' explanation is specific to a particular time and place, associated with a Western middle-class construct of childhood, and does not translate to other childhoods.

These examples raise questions about what is meant by childhood and, implicitly, by protection. The tensions over childhood are evident – what should it be like when it is over. How to reconcile younger children's interest in 'adult' behaviour such as make-up, associated with expression of sexuality in the newspaper, with protection from sex? How to reconcile childhood as a time of young girls dressing up with young girls begging and undertaking childcare? The detail of protection services required in different places must deal with perceptions of what children need to be protected from.

MOVING FORWARD

Adult Understandings: From Research to Practice

Constructions of childhood involve ideas of whether children need protection, from what, and how. While the CRC provides an international benchmark, the nature of protection services also depends on local views and conditions as well as policy, cost and staffing available. However, adults frequently do not take diversity of local circumstances into account. It is still not unknown for highly qualified medical or social experts from one country to promote inappropriate interventions in another. For example, at a conference in China in 1999, European and American doctors presented complex therapeutic approaches to child abuse, based on Western psychological models, in a country where the recognition of child abuse is minimal, and the provision of basic protection services is non-existent. No discussions followed the lectures, which some said reinforced the perception that child abuse is a Western problem. This sort of problem is bound up with the broader question of developing protection responses that take account of the local constructions of childhood and legislative/social frameworks. The export of ideas will not necessarily fit with local conditions, and can lead to ineffective provision, possibly exacerbating children's problems. Examples of this include attempts to ban 'child labour' in some countries, where working of children is necessary for family's or children's survival, and where a ban has led to children working in worse circumstances. The idea that all child work is a problem, based on a particular construction of childhood, while alternatives that some forms of work contribute positively to children's development, have not been recognised. The issue is that of children's working conditions and rights.

While child rights are increasingly discussed and promoted, are the sociological developments in thinking about constructions of childhood being used? If so, how, especially in connection with children's rights? What is their relationship to practice, what effect has the new paradigm of childhood had? How is research transferred into practice? Discussions and anecdotal evidence suggest that it is not being used, and that there is a tendency to begin programming from a perspective of services rather than an analysis of childhoods and issues. This problem might be linked to a reluctance to talk with children and involve them in decision-making, or take account of their views, despite the advances made in children's 'participation work' around the world.

In some international, national and local organisations for children, adult staff spends most of its time in discourse with or training other adults such as teachers, health providers, parents, community leaders and government officials. Engagement with children is limited, or left for a few 'specialists', usually lower-graded staff. Distance between decision makers and children, especially when organisational emphases on fund raising and future planning come to the fore, often increases despite rhetorical pronouncements of participation.

The implications of not understanding and taking account of diversity and participation, the basic tenets of the 'new' sociology of childhood, are significant. In many cross-cultural settings in countries where welfare policy and social work is undeveloped, work with children has drawn much from Western theory and practice. But the new sociology implies that there are problems where the monolithic Western construction of childhood is nodded towards and underlies imported ideas, but actually sits alongside other local and competing models that are, in effect, in everyday use.

Moving Forward in Practice

The 'new' sociology of childhood has been included in the policies of some organisations for children (SC, 1994). However, disseminating these ideas, and particularly linking them to and understanding what they mean for practice, requires action with staff working with children. It also means that services and organisations for children must regularly consult with them in order to develop and maintain an understanding of children's views, diversity and protection. In order to begin to understand the impact of diversity on practice (especially child protection), workshops with children and adults to explore concepts and experiences of childhood have been devised. These build on existing work in different countries, by some Save the Children staff, exploring ideas of childhood to improve policy and practice for vulnerable children. Preliminary workshops with adults and children in Asia and Africa are drawn on in discussions below, principally from China, Mongolia, Myanmar and Nigeria. Further work is needed on explorations of local meanings of protection, to link up diversity with the implementation of protection and with duty bearers for children's rights (see SC, 2006).

This experience suggests that work on understanding the ways in which diversity, participation and protection are connected, and how to cope with the variations entailed, requires a number of approaches. First, an understanding of personal attitudes and views towards childhood, and how these relate to the social or dominant categories of children and protection that are in local use, is required. Second, the participation of children is a component highlighted as important in addressing diversity, which means that children's views on vulnerability and their involvement in practice and research should be taken up. Third, following on from children's participation, practice, policy and organisational responses to findings from children's research and consultations are needed. While a fully developed programme of training and practice engaging adults and children is still needed, the separate elements have been tested, and show the importance and effect of translating research into practice.

Self-Attitude/Understanding Self

The first step is understanding our own and local perceptions of childhood. What it means to be a boy or girl, what is expected of them at different ages, constraints on sexuality, views on disability, different ethnicities, forms of social status. Children's work and educational roles must be understood, along with the significant social categories and grounds for prejudice, discrimination and oppression. Workshops with adults included exploration of different childhoods and constructions of different categories of childhood, such as street children, children in conflict with the law and others. An important aim was to enable participants to understand their assumptions about children, their models of children's behaviours and roles, and their expectations of children.

Workshops in Myanmar were held with national staff from different sector projects, many of whom principally worked with other adults.

They looked at the terms used for boys and girls, children and young people, and their meanings. Ages were linked to these terms and expectations of children so named or categorised. These ideas of childhood were built on by looking at the lives of children in urban and rural areas, both conventional and unconventional, boys and girls. Reflection on these constructions with participants suggested that these are adult perceptions of children, largely based on memories of their own childhood and are linked to adult views of how children should be – an ideal model. The idea of change in childhood emerged through adults' discussions of children's current behaviours. The workshops on diversity and change were an important part of preparation for adults to begin talking and working with children.

Workshops in Nigeria (Nicolson, 2004) were held with adult staff from a range of local organisations, to consider how to make the groups they worked with more inclusive of marginalised children. Adult participants began by exploring their own childhoods. For several of the participants, this was found to be a very difficult exercise, partly because 'it became evident ... that many of us could have been labelled as "vulnerable" in our own childhoods'. This problem has been found elsewhere: there are risks in focussing on experiences of childhood because of the memories that may be raised or awoken. The processes of doing this have also been found to be beneficial, but the availability of support for individuals in reflecting on their childhoods also needs to be discussed. Such support needs to fit with local, cultural conditions, for example, of public displays of emotion. This issue also links the local forms of protection and how they too are embedded in cultural constructions.

Both of these workshops point to how ideas about childhood are drawn largely from main social constructions rather than either personal experience of one's own childhood, or an understanding and empathy with contemporary childhood. In Myanmar, as in Mongolia, participants constructed childhoods based on standard models, but through facilitation identified that childhood had changed since they were a child. Explorations of personal childhoods in Nigeria highlighted experiences that many 'would rather forget' but also brought up the importance of not labelling children: not using the categories in common use.

Categories of Children and Vulnerability

In Nigeria, participants undertook a childhood mapping exercise to explore perceptions and assumptions that people hold of different childhoods.

In this case, assumptions included that a child from a rich family must be happy and free from abuse, and that a child who is orphaned is automatically assumed to be destitute and hopeless. This exercise high-lighted the need of not using labels for children, such as 'street hawker' or 'AIDS-affected orphan' to identify a child. Participants concluded that 'it is important to know each child, talk to them, and listen to them, in order to understand their realities and vulnerabilities'.

Workshops in east Asia with staff responsible for running government street children centre, explored who is a 'street child'. The outcome initially looked rather depressing for the children, with lists of attributes and behaviours that were largely perceived as bad. What participants initially constructed was a composite that was based on stereotypes. But the list of attributes was reviewed and reversed, because although there were initially very few 'good' elements, in fact many of those seen as 'bad' could, in other settings or conditions, be seen as commendable. For example, children's enterprise and skills of survival were often not appreciated, and there was a tendency to see them as bad or immoral because they were out of school, because they mistrusted adults, and because they worked on dirty jobs. The key to these workshops was discussion on constructions of children and street children, and unpicking existing assumptions held by adults.

Workshops with adults in Nigeria began because agencies found difficulties in ensuring that their children's groups were inclusive, and wanted to ensure their work affected the lives of the most-marginalised children, and included explorations of vulnerability. The notion of vulnerability in childhood has been the subject of increasing attention, particularly because it has also been used in the construction of a new category of children – 'OVC'. This term is in common use as a shorthand for 'orphans and vulnerable children', usually where there is a severe HIV/AIDS epidemic. Although many practitioners have argued that the term is not very helpful or clear and is stigmatising, it continues in use. Some organisations refuse to withdraw the term, saying they have spent a lot of time persuading the government to set up 'OVC Committees' (personal communication). Yet, at the end of the workshops in Nigeria, participants suggested that the term 'OVC' is a particularly stigmatising and unhelpful label.

This raises a linked issue, concerning the development of what become categories of children by international and national agencies. The difficulties of using labels such as 'street children' because of imprecise definitions, led to the development of terms such as 'children in especially difficult circumstances' and 'children in need of special protection'. The acronym 'orphans and vulnerable children' was an attempt to highlight the problems experienced by children who were affected by HIV/AIDS but who were not orphaned. In reality, these categories can only be defined locally, but in practice they rarely are, leaving adult practitioners with a label that is not explored, has no particular meaning and which is often stigmatising.

Realisation of this problem by adults through workshops is more powerful and effective than reading a document. Awareness of problems and the need for change offers potential for understanding the importance of diversity and putting it into practice. The widespread use of the term 'OVC' particularly among HIV/AIDS practitioners has shocked many, and the way it was created and spread could provide a useful case study of the development and use of a specific construction of childhood, and how this provoked a series of responses that are particularly associated with protection. The term seems to have been in existence for few years, but it has already created an attachment amongst some workers, who have got used to it and do not want to change (personal communication). The use of such labels is also implicitly encouraged where agency managers want simple and popularly powerful messages for fund-raising purposes. But these labels are still used as a basis for research.

Understanding the nature of vulnerability requires an examination of local meanings and interpretations of phrases in common use. But apart from engagement with adults on this, children can also express definitions of vulnerability. Given the importance of change, and that childhood now is not the same as adults recall of their own experiences, it would seem crucial to understand children's perspectives on vulnerability. This is linked to the overall importance of taking account of children's views.

Children's Views

Workshops with children have also explored childhood experiences and difference, particularly in the development of children's participation. These have included children defining attributes of vulnerability in their communities. Children have also identified their issues, which begin to create images of local models of childhood, and which indicate problems, for example, through adults' assumptions, and misunderstanding how children are affected by adult behaviours. In the processes of identifying their own issues and preparing to take action in response, children need an understanding not only of themselves but of their local communities, which involves recognising diversity (see O'Kane, 2003a).

The importance of understanding children's views has led not only to increased involvement of children in research, but also to children and young people conducting their own research. Practice in this area of facilitating children's own research is over 10 years old. In 2003, 10 children and young people from residential care homes in five provinces of China participated in a workshop to develop their own research. They were aged 12–18 with one aged 22, five female and five male. They began sharing their experiences of life in residential and foster care, and went on to develop research questions and interview schedules, and then conducted research with other children when they returned home. Their research was to compare foster care and residential care, to contribute to government discussions on shifting away from large-scale institutional care. Four of them presented their findings at a national conference run by the Ministry of Civil Affairs. On the whole they found foster life offered better care, except less opportunity for education because placements were largely in rural areas. Their work and presentation so impressed the Ministry that the staff developed plans to (and did) include children in subsequent delegations to evaluate new standards for foster care.

The strengths of children's research have been found elsewhere, for example, in Bangladesh and in England. In Bangladesh in the late 1990s, the street children (aged 12–17) conducted their own research and organised a press conference on their findings, and later other groups of children looked at life in rural areas, girls living in urban slums and life in detention centres (see Zeng, Yang, & West, 2004). These projects began by demonstrating that children had capabilities, views and opinions, and adults learning how to work with them. The projects moved on to using this method as the main way of finding out about children's lives, and highlighting the need to respond to those circumstances and to children's perspectives and findings. Adults involved in the early projects, even those familiar with street children, rural life, girls and their issues, were surprised by some of the points raised.

In England in 1995, 10 children and young people who had lived in residential and foster care conducted research on leaving that 'care'. Their findings from a 3-month project, with 80 3-hour interviews, parallelled the main points of a 3-year academic research project on the issue. But the children's and young people's project supplemented it with useful insights on the processes of support, health and other issues. For example, they highlighted that care leavers especially wanted emotional support as much as the 'practical' forms of support (such as advice on budgeting) offered by social workers.

Recent work, for example in China, has included children defining vulnerability in their localities. This has also revealed differences in perceptions from those of adults, particularly when placed alongside children's own research. For example, children living in high-prevalence HIV/AIDS areas, where a great many adults have died and many children have been orphaned, drew out different perspectives to those expected by adults. Children did not see the effect of HIV/AIDS as being the only cause of problems. They also highlighted not being able to go to school, disability, homelessness and separation from family, and children with emotional problems and no friends. While children emphasised the importance of education, which would be agreed by adults, they described complexities in their social world that affected education, and talked of how they were worried about the future.

These approaches provide a different way of understanding children's circumstances, and rationales and methods of interventions and services required. Yet, adult perceptions of protection needs are likely to create and emphasise on categories differently, particularly in terms of hierarchies of intervention needs. Children in a high prevalence HIV/AIDS area in central China, from their experience and in their research, reported severe and widespread problems of discrimination against adults and children with HIV/AIDS in their families. The problems included school teachers. Adults did not expect such discrimination in a high-prevalence area because they thought the incidence of HIV/AIDS was so great as to create a levelling. But problems of discrimination required specific interventions for children's lives to enable them to attend school and improve their lives in the community.

This work highlights not only the importance of engagement with children and understanding their perspectives, but that children are sensitive to diversity of childhood experience. The work also demonstrates children's skills and capacities in articulating their views, consulting other children and conducting research, if processes are used that take children seriously and respect their ideas and opinions. The work also highlights differences in the views of adults and children, and the importance of devising interventions that at least are based on discussions with children rather than adult assumptions.

Differences between Adults and Children

Adult assumptions about the best interests of children are challenged by engagement and research with and by children. In central China, in very high-prevalence HIV/AIDS affected/infected areas, increasing number of orphans have led to concerned adults placing children in orphanages. Yet, children are clear they prefer to stay in their villages and in contact with surviving relatives, especially grandparents, and friends. They report problems where they do not get on with the limited number of careers assigned to them in orphanages and that children run away to return to and visit grandparents. Research by children here has led to different interventions to enable children to remain in villages, but requires new support mechanisms and acceptance of forms of living such as child-headed household that many adults find hard to accept. Responses here by Save the Children have included the development of children's centres and small group homes. The question of best interests of children is the main principle of the CRC but necessarily involves children's views.

One issue frequently raised by girls and boys, in different settings and contexts, is violence by adults. Bullying by other children is a problem, but children report, fear and hate being beaten by parents, teachers, religious officials and others. They said that being beaten puts children in difficulties and makes them vulnerable. When children (aged 11–16 years), affected by HIV/AIDS in a high-prevalence area in north-west China with an increasing number of orphans, conducted their own research with other children, they also discussed ideas of vulnerability as well as raising issues of concern to them (see Chen, 2006). They considered that the conventional definition of orphan as having one or both parents deceased, could be extended. For children, the key issue was of being without parental care, which included children living in reconstituted families with a step-parent who did not care for them, children who were left behind when parents migrated and children whose parents abuse them.

Adult perceptions of this issue are often different, regarding who is at risk and what that risk is. Assumptions over who is vulnerable to violence, either at home or outside are unhelpful. Categories of childhoods are problematic, in masking the reality for children, for example, assumptions (above) that rich children have happy childhoods. A group of well-off American missionary women in southern China were reported as discussing over coffee what they hit their children with, and how effective it was. Adults' attitudes about violence towards children depend on their models of childhood. The language used such as discipline, punishment, etc. provides some indicators, or the word 'smacking'[3] and so on. Physical violence is built into some childrearing practices, past and present, from whipping (north America, seventeenth century) to a 'light slap to the head' (eastern Europe, present) (Reese, 2000, p. 53; Delaney, 2000, p. 139).

Touching the head in this way would be regarded as appalling in much of South East Asia.

For some years in China, the increased number of 'street children' has been explained as due to poverty and children's desire to see the bright city lights: that children are at fault for leaving home. Following on from research by chidren in residential care, it was then possible for some children in government Street Children Centres in 2004–2005 to do a short piece of research. From this, they instead raised a different explanation for children leaving home. Many children were running away from violence at home. When they presented their findings at a national conference, on the same platform as the Vice-Minister of Civil Affairs, it was perhaps the first time this was so publicly acknowledged. The implications are that a different approach to 'street children' and their protection is needed, and a part of that must include addressing adult perceptions. New research on the situation of 'street children' in China has since been commissioned, and assessments involving children themselves are being conducted, but the issues around abuse and differences between adults and children have only just been opened.

The problem of violence and the importance of understanding children's views was the subject of an international project in south-east and east Asia and the Pacific 2005–2006 (Ennew & Plateau, 2005; Beazley, Bessell, Ennew, & Waterson, 2006). This adult-initiated research involved working in partnership with child respondents from eight countries. The research demonstrated not only the significance and breadth of the issue, but that rigorous research involving children that is both quantitative and qualitative is possible, challenging the view that such research has to be both led and conducted by adults. Any understanding of these issues, the forms of violence and punishment used, would not be possible without engaging with children, who were also able to discuss the effects on them.

Benefits for Adults and Children

Important findings from this type of workshop included the importance of raising awareness of change in the experience of childhood over time, and the risks involved in relying on memories of one's own childhood as guidance for practice now. This work emphasised the importance of understanding children's lives through children, and children's perceptions of childhood. Some of these notions of change in childhood (implicit in adults' reflections) compare with research in England showing a tendency of adults in succeeding generations to think that modern children are behaving worse than they did when they were younger, as did their parents (see Pearson, 1984).

Training workshop activities were also devised to work with children, and at the end participants found that they felt more capable and skilled in such work. Participants also thought that the exercises drew them closer to the feelings of being a child, and they should be able to relate better to children. Participants reported that the workshops made them 'realise that weaknesses can be turned into strengths and that those people that listened to us in times of difficulties and challenges inspired us' (Nicolson, 2004). This finding concerns processes that develop children's resilience, but also had positive impacts on the lives of adults themselves. A greater consideration of diversity and practice with children's participation provided adults not only with more understanding of childhood and children, but also confidence in their work and a better understanding of purpose, as in workshops with NGO staff in Myanmar and Mongolia, which were followed by experiential work consulting children.

Processes of work with children that are participatory, and exploring serious issues with them have been found to promote children's resilience, and so have the implications for undertaking these activities as part of the development of child protection. Bringing together girls and boys from different backgrounds has also been found to have contributed to this development of resilience, as well as enabling a better and shared understanding of a variety of children's lives. For example, children from urban schools and children from nearby villages met during preparation for a forum, and shared some of their views and life experiences. Here, the urban children found out about a severe HIV/AIDS epidemic in their area that was orphaning large numbers of children in villages, but about which they knew nothing. The work with children from villages with the HIV/AIDS epidemic demonstrated different effects on girls and boys, and differences in the impact on age. The work also showed the variety of different childhoods in a comparatively small locality, and the variety of responses required to begin to address issues of protection: these ranged from anti-discrimination work to support for children through centres and small group homes (see West & Zhang, 2005; West & Chen, 2005).

Thus, involvement of children in research and the identification of problems is a means of developing children's resilience. One means of protection is strengthening children's capacity for resilience, as well as strengthening family and community structures for protection. Work with children affected by HIV/AIDS has found that children's participation in processes where they are taken seriously, treated with respect, consulted and had fun contribute to the provision of psycho-social support and promote children's resilience (West & Zhang, 2005). Children as a resource for their own protection, the importance of participation and its links to resilience not only challenge ideas of protection of children based on some constructions of childhood, but also argue for children's increased involvement in design and delivery of services and practice.

Practice Developments and Issues

A number of practical issues emerge from this work: the need for agencies (and individual staff) to move beyond labels; tensions between different perspectives of adults and children (and between adults and between children), which are outcomes of, and complicated by, power; difficulties of paying attention to children and responding holistically – the ethics of determining what is the best interest. All these issues may be summarised by emphasising on process and reflective practice – thinking about the means and nature of engagement, what is happening and changing responses accordingly.

Perhaps, the biggest difficulties concern organisational structures, which make it easier for adults to make decisions, to sort out needs and interventions, to plan in advance, and not to take account of childhood diversity, children's views, or incorporate them. Organisational planning, fund-raising and other requirements, particularly run over several years, which delineate work content and sequences in advance, are not responsive to childhood diversity and change, nor do they include new groups of children and their views. Targeted outcomes are prioritised over process, despite the benefits of participatory processes that involve children making decisions that may shift these adult-planned outcomes.

Thus, process of incorporating diversity and participation becomes incremental: working with staff to facilitate their engagement with children, and subsequently consulting children and responding to their views. The range of issues raised by children requires a holistic response, at least in terms of protection. Education and health projects cannot easily ignore child-protection issues that may emerge. Integrating sectoral work in one locality is being tried in parts of China to enable a holistic approach to children and the issues they raised through research. This approach brings additional tensions in terms of different perspectives and priorities of staff and agencies involved. However, non-government organisations call upon government and other agencies to involve children and to work together, and need to be able to demonstrate practice themselves.

CONCLUSION

An understanding of childhood is fundamental for any cross-cultural work, but also essential for working within one society, and challenging preconceived notions on childhood amongst duty bearers. It means that assumptions cannot be made about children's lives and childhoods, and preconceived ideas need to be rethought, especially in relation to the most marginalised and excluded groups of children in society. Our own models of childhood are not universal.

Different cultures have different roles and expectations for children who will consequently have different behaviours. There are different ways of raising children, different attributes that are valued and which have to be taken into account in rights-based work. Second, children's capacities are not standardised. Children have abilities to participate in decision-making about their lives from a young age, and contribute to the life of their families and communities. Children work in a variety of occupations in many parts of the world. All this means that children should not just be the objects of projects, but should participate in the development of programme work including, and perhaps especially, in emergencies. Due account needs to be taken of diversity and evolving capacities in such participation, and clearly the potential degree of involvement of a 15- or 17-year old is going to be different to that of a 2-year old, but this is why recognition of diversity and application of responses is so necessary. 'In emergency situations, response to the urgent care and protection needs of children is sometimes undertaken without a full understanding of the cultural norms regarding their care. This can lead to inappropriate measures which may undermine existing coping strategies and leave children poorly protected' (Tolfree, 2004, p. 37).

In developing effective child-protection policies and programmes, an understanding of local perceptions of childhood and how they relate to child development, child care, protection and participation are crucial to developing viable, sustainable options in the best interests of the child. Existing research (Boyden & Mann, 2000) indicates that children rooted in their own culture retain many positive values and assets despite prolonged deprivation or adversity. We need to focus on the strengths and resilience of children and communities to search for, understand and value diversity, and to value children's views and then respond. Such an approach will lead to richer, more innovative, responsive programming for children living in varied contexts and will contribute towards reducing inequalities (SC, 2006).

A tripartite approach, using links between diversity, participation and resilience for children's protection is essential and offers a way forward. The tendency to see models of childhood as static needs to be challenged and change needs to be recognised. The fluidity of ideas as people move, communications develop and cultures increasingly come into contact increases, rather than decreases, the importance of issues of diversity. Linear, staged models of life, childhood, youth, adulthood and old age are not helpful in reducing children to a set of 'becomings' rather than 'beings'.

Working on issues of diversity in practice now has some increased urgency because of the complexities of differences in childhoods undergoing rapid change. The Internet has been found to provide new ways of abusing children. Such technology is rapidly changing childhood cultures for many, while movements of children around the world are bringing new experiences and vulnerabilities. Making assumptions about children's lives and child-hoods is even more untenable, but the process of sharing experiences, perspectives and ideas needs to be positive in order to combat stigma and discrimination towards the better fulfillment of children's rights.

All this has implications for research and researchers. Adults need to rethink their categories of children when undertaking research as well as when planning and implementing interventions. While research is an essential component of CRP, for protection it needs to take account of children's rights, diversity and children's participation; understanding power is a key to this exploration. Researching protection has increasing importance because of the recognition of failure of protection systems and the need for new approaches in both 'developed' and 'developing' countries. While conceptualisation of protection is one starting point, there is a need to recognise and question at least four elements: (1) the homogeneity of childhood that is implicit in many discussions; (2) how children's own views are best taken account of in research as well as interventions; (3) how children can participate in research as well as in practice, services, projects and other interventions; and (4) the links between research and practice and how these can be developed.

The integration of research and practice is important if each is to benefit from the other. Researchers need to be more involved with the outcomes of their work in addition to making recommendations. The divide between research and practice needs to be bridged (as is so often rhetorically proclaimed). How is research best translated with practice and how are adults – especially those working with children – and children themselves, involved in understanding and applying findings? How is social change responded to and practice change effected?

Deconstructing childhood and categories of children is important for researchers. So too is the involvement of children in research and dissemination of and response to findings. Two of the big challenges here are the protection of children in research, and ensuring power and influence of children's views. It is often difficult to reconcile completing frameworks and understandings, especially when large power differences are involved, and when material conditions make effective interventions extremely difficult. Power relations need to be recognised and strategies developed to address imbalances between adults and children during and following research. Agencies have increasingly recognised that abuse can and does occur in unexpected circumstances, in locations presumed to be safe. This has resulted in many academic ethics committees effectively having a blanket prohibition on involvement of children in research, or even adult researchers talking to and working with children. Yet, this clearly runs counter to academic findings of children as 'social actors' and the importance of children's participation beyond responding to questions.

Strategies to promote ethical participatory research practice with children with safeguards to ensure their protection are required. Involving children as well as adults in efforts to identify and respond to risks will be beneficial. Limits to children's participation need to be explained clearly so that false expectations are not raised: including if policy developments will take years or there are insufficient resources to respond to children's suggestions.

Dealing with rights, diversity, children's participation and protection cannot be achieved by blanket approaches. It denies both diversity and competence of children. It effectively promotes older dominant Western models of childhood in denying the reality of children's (under-18-years old) involvement in work, sex and making decisions. Children's protection from harm, exploitation and abuse is of crucial importance. Increasing recognition of the importance of children's evolving capacities means that adults need to understand this in local contexts and listen to what children say about their changing protection needs over time. Academic researchers and practitioners in children's organisations need to respond to this through engagement with the broad practice of working with children. The CRC provides standards, principles and benchmarks for quality of work. Research itself is also a matter of work with children and outcomes of children's lives. It is, after all, non-discrimination, participation and the best interests of children that should be the guiding principles and the best means of understanding and engaging with diversity in childhood.

NOTES

1. For example, UNICEF, Save the Children Alliance, Plan International.
2. Save the Children was founded in European countries in 1919. It is an international alliance with country members from all round the world, and working in over 110 countries.
3. 'Smacking' is used by proponents of the physical punishment of children to suggest it is not unreasonable. It covers up a range of implements and methods and obscures the violence employed. Children's views are rarely sought (but see Willow & Hyder, 1999; Beazley et al., 2006).

REFERENCES

Beazley, H., Bessell, S., Ennew, J., & Waterson, R. (2006). *What children say: Comparative research on physical and emotional punishment.* Bangkok: Save the Children Sweden.

Boycott, O. (2004). Tanning cream for pre-teens? *The Nation* (Bangkok), *28*(September), p. 8.

Boyden, J., & Mann, G. (2000). Children's risk, resilience and coping in extreme situations. Background paper. Consultation on Children in Adversity, Oxford, September 2000.

Callaway, A. (2000). *Deaf children in China.* Washington: Gallaudet University Press.

Chen, Q. (2006). *Listen, secrets! Research by children affected by HIV/AIDS in Xinjiang and Yunnan.* Beijing: Save the Children.

Corby, B. (1993). *Child abuse: Towards a knowledge base.* Buckingham: Open University.

Crimmens, D., & West, A. (Eds). (2004). *Having our say: Young people and participation – European experiences.* Lyme Regis: Russell House Publishing.

DeLoache, J., & Gottlieb, A. (Eds). (2000). *A world of babies: Imagined childcare guides for seven societies.* Cambridge: Cambridge University Press.

Delaney, C. (2000). Making babies in a Turkish village. In: J. DeLoache & A. Gottlieb (Eds), *A world of babies: Imagined childcare guides for seven societies* (pp. 117–144). Cambridge: Cambridge University Press.

Ennew, J. (2004). Children's participation: Experiences and reflections. In: Z. Zeng, H. Y. Yang & A. West (Eds), *Child participation in action: Concepts and practice from east and west* (pp. 19–48). Beijing: All China Women's Federation.

Ennew, J., & Plateau, D. P. (2005). *How to research the physical and emotional punishment of children.* Bangkok: Save the Children.

Gottlieb, A. (2000). Luring your child into this life: A beng path for infant care. In: J. DeLoache & A. Gottlieb (Eds), *A world of babies: Imagined childcare guides for seven societies* (pp. 55–90). Cambridge: Cambridge University Press.

Greenfield, S. (2000). *The private life of the brain.* London: Penguin Books.

James, A., Jenks, C., & Prout, A. (1998). *Theorising childhood.* Cambridge: Polity Press.

James, A., & Prout, A. (Eds). (1997). *Constructing and reconstructing childhood: Contemporary issues in the sociological study of childhood* (2nd ed.). London: Falmer Press.

Jenks, C. (1996). *Childhood.* London: Routledge.

Lansdown, G. (2005). *The evolving capacities of children: Implications for the exercise of rights.* Florence: Innocenti Centre.

Le, H.-N. (2000). Never leave your little one alone: Raising an Ifaluk child. In: J. DeLoache & A. Gottlieb (Eds), *A world of babies: Imagined childcare guides for seven societies* (pp. 199–220). Cambridge: Cambridge University Press.

Lee, N. (2001). *Childhood and society: Growing up in an age of uncertainty.* Buckingham: Open University Press.

Nicolson, C. (2004). *A meeting to understand better the issues facing children who are more vulnerable. Kaduna.* Save the Children Internal Report.

O'Kane, C. (2003a). *Children and young people as citizens: Partners for social change.* Kathmandu: Save the Children South and Central Asia.

O'Kane, C (2003b). Street and working children's participation in programming for their rights: Conflicts arising from diverse perspectives and directions for convergence. *Children, Youth and Environment 13*(1), retrieved January 2008 from http://cye.colorado.edu

Pearson, G. (1984). *Hooligans: A history of respectable fears.* London: Routledge.

Prout, A., & James, A. (1997). A new paradigm for the sociology of childhood? Provenance, promise and problems. In: A. James & A. Prout (Eds), *Constructing and reconstructing childhood: Contemporary issues in the sociological study of childhood* (2nd ed.). London: Falmer Press.

Qvortrup, J. (1994). Childhood matters: An introduction. In: J. Qvortrup, M. Bardy, G. Sgritta & H. Wintersberger (Eds), *Childhood matters: Social theory, practice and politics.* Avebury: Aldershot.

Reese, D. (2000). A parenting manual, with words of advice for puritan mothers. In: J. DeLoache & A. Gottlieb (Eds), *A world of babies: Imagined childcare guides for seven societies* (pp. 29–54). Cambridge: Cambridge University Press.

SC (Save the Children). (1994). *Towards a children's agenda.* London: Save the Children.

SC (Save the Children). (2006). *Tools for exploring diverse childhoods: Implications for child protection.* London: Save the Children.

Talle, A. (1995). A child is a child: Disability and equality among the Kenya Maasai. In: B. Ingstad & S. R. Whyte (Eds), *Disability and culture* (pp. 56–72). Berkeley, CA: University of California Press.

Taylor, M. (2005). Schools accused of abandoning thousands of gay children to classroom bullies. *The Guardian* (London), May 9.

Theis, J. (2004). *Promoting rights-based approaches: Experiences and ideas from Asia and the Pacific.* Stockholm: Save the Children Sweden.

Tolfree, D. (2004). *Whose children? Separated children's protection and participation in emergencies.* Stockholm: Save the Children.

West, A. (1999). They make us out to be monsters: Media images of children and young people in care, with assessments by children and young people in care. In: B. Franklin (Ed.), *Misleading messages: The media, misrepresentation and social policy* (pp. 253–268). London: Routledge.

West, A. (2003). *At the margins: Street children in Asia and the Pacific.* Metro Manila: Asian Development Bank.

West, A., & Chen, X. M. (2005). HIV/AIDS and vulnerability, education and participation: Issues of rights, responses and children in or out of school – A growing divide in China. Paper presented at Children and Youth in Emerging and Transforming Societies – Childhoods 2005 Conference, Oslo, 2005.

West, A., & Zhang, H. (2005). *A strange illness: Issues and research by children affected by HIV/AIDS in central China*. Beijing: Save the Children/Fuyang Women's and Children's Working Committee.

Willow, C., & Hyder, T. (1999). *It hurts you inside: Children talking about smacking*. London: Save the Children/National Children's Bureau.

Zeng, Z., Yang, H. Y., & West, A. (Eds). (2004). *Child participation in action: Concepts and practice from East and West*. Beijing: Save the Children/All China Women's Federation.

CHILDHOOD: A HOMOGENEOUS GENERATIONAL GROUP?

Maria Carmen Belloni and Renzo Carriero

METHODOLOGICAL PREMISE AND RESEARCH APPROACH

This paper reports several findings of a survey on children aged 5–13[1] years focusing on their daily lives. The aim was to test the assumption, claimed in New Childhood Sociology, that children are a generational group so strictly dependent on adult society that they have little autonomy in their daily behaviour. Moreover, although they are a social group that is different from that of adults, they are so diversified internally that it seems more appropriate to speak of diversified childhoods (James, Jenks & Prout, 1998; James & Prout, 1990; Qvortrup, 1991; Hengst & Zeiher, 2004). Our first objective in this paper was therefore to improve the rather scarce knowledge of children's everyday lives in post-industrial Western societies and then to analyse to what extent these were connected with those of adults. Finally, we wished to detect the degree and patterns of differences in the children's lifestyles.

Towards this end, we used a time-use methodology and data. In this approach, time use is a means of detecting and assessing the activities performed during the day, the relationships they involve and the scenarios (places and situations) in which they occur.[2] In our case, time is considered both as an indicator of the generational structure in which children and adults are related, and of the cultural and normative framework in which

Childhood: Changing Contexts
Comparative Social Research, Volume 25, 293–324
ISSN: 0195-6310/doi:10.1016/S0195-6310(07)00010-5

children accumulate their experience within society in general. As an indicator, time, measuring behaviour during the day, can outline a general picture of relationships, range of decision-making, autonomy in actions and so on. In cultural/normative terms, time constitutes the social background against which behaviour occurs and decisions are made. Indirectly, it also points to hierarchies of relevance within the various activities performed by/imposed on children. From this point of view, the rules regarding the social organisation of time – basically the timetable principle and its local fulfillment – represent the system of opportunities and constraints in which, through adults, children participate in society.

In this paper, we will concentrate on the discussion of the results of time-use diaries by children in elementary and middle school, which is on children aged 7–13 years.[3] In order to represent their daily lives outside of school, according to three different kinds of days (weekdays, Saturdays and Sundays), each child was given three diaries to complete. In accordance with the standard methodology of time-use studies, time spent at school was measured in total and included in the category "school".[4] This is why children's leisure activities and social relations in school have not been considered in the following analysis.[5] Besides diaries, each child also completed a questionnaire, offering information regarding events beyond daily routines (e.g. vacations, activities not performed on a daily basis) and attitudes, perceptions and aspirations. Here, we will not use systematically this second type of information. In addition, each family also completed a questionnaire illustrating the characteristics of the family's and the parents' participation in their children's lives. This allowed us to understand in what overall time and social organisation were the children involved.

In our analysis of children's lives as embedded in the general system of social times, we have focused particularly on leisure, relationships and places. We hypothesise, in fact, that, given the highly structured and homogeneous characteristic of school time, differences between children and childhoods are more likely to appear in these three dimensions, due to both cultural and social class differences. We hypothesise, in particular, that, together with age, gender and ethnic structure also cause different uses of non-school time.

TIME AND TIMETABLES

For children, the experience of everyday time represents the process through which, in structuring daily activities, they acquire the temporal norms that regulate the society they live in. The timetable system thus establishes and generates the rules to which children must adapt from their earliest years, and, as these are internalised, they allow individuals to establish priorities in their choices, thus becoming an instrument of orientation in social behaviour. Activities structured in this way can be measured by calculating the amount of time spent for each of them, and where they are placed in the daily schedule. This permits us to consider how children's time is structured, and the possibilities of autonomy for children in our system of social organisation, including the opportunity to express needs different from those of adults.

From an analysis of children's days, it is immediately apparent that children's times largely mirror adult times, based on the power of the *timetable* as a structuring principle of social times. However, this does not mean that children are unable to create autonomous spaces,[6] which they achieve by negotiating the rules set down by adults. The degrees of rigidity of these rules depend on the activities performed and the temporal-organisational framework to which they apply.

The strong regulatory power of timetables is most visible with regard to school. Starting with infant school, it represents the biggest organising principle and constraint in the structure of a child's day and this becomes even more obvious during elementary and middle school, when school time is highly visible both in terms of its position within the day's activities, and the amount of time it occupies. It is in fact the pivot time for all other activities, including those linked to physiological needs and those which are freely chosen. This is true above all for elementary school children. School time for them is a compact block (8 hours, comparable to adult working hours) extending until late afternoon (4:30 p.m.).[7] For middle-school children, school time is shorter (6.5 hours on average), and, in the afternoon, more differentiated and fragmented between returning home for lunch and resumption of afternoon school or extracurricular activities.[8] The daily time budget (Table 1) illustrates the high proportion of time that children spend in school.

The school timetable structure, in its two variants (full-time or predominantly morning), has two sides, depending on whether it is viewed from the adult's or child's standpoint. In terms of family organisation, school is both a resource and a constraint. On the one hand, it relieves the family of the responsibility for care and supervision of children for a large portion of the day, with a duration resembling that of a standard working day. However, it does not coincide exactly with most people's working hours, which usually extend until evening,[9] and this is a major problem in

Table 1. Time Spent in Different Activities on Weekdays (in Hours and Minutes). Elementary and Middle Schools.

	Elementary School	Middle School
	Mean	Mean
Sleeping and eating	11:23	10:45
School and courses	8:19	8:02
Shopping and housework	0:09	0:20
Religion	0:11	0:06
Playing and videogames	1:00	0:39
TV	1:02	1:57
Other leisure	1:07	1:53
Travelling	0:49	0:58
Total	24:00	24:00

family organisation, often holding back women who wish to enter the labour market, or orienting them towards activities with compatible working hours. From a child's standpoint, school represents a temporal continuum rather than fragmented time, within a context of stable relationships and rules. Nevertheless, they spend a good part, if not most of the day, in an institutional dimension, where most relationships are only partially free, and usually under the supervision of adults outside the family. School timetables force families and children to respect deadlines, which are usually unavoidable and inflexible. In a social system which is becoming increasingly flexible, school is still the most rigid "time giver" (Sansot, 1981). The interviews with parents show that, faced with these constraints, families adopt – and thus children are subjected to – various forms of conciliation and adaptation strategies. One of the main constraints on family organisation is the hours of entering and leaving school. Usually, especially when children are not old enough to go to school or remain at home alone, it is the mothers who adapt their timetables to the school's requirements.[10] In other cases, families adopt cooperative strategies, in which it is usually the fathers who take the children to school in the morning, with the grandparents going to meet them in the afternoon.[11] It is not difficult to imagine how the sense of dependency in children is reinforced by always having to rely on adult figures (often variable and interchangeable) for the simplest and most habitual routines. When adult time constraints are more rigid and it is not possible to reconcile work and school starting times, children must be dropped off at school early.[12] For a significant number of children (15–20%, in our research), therefore, the "working" day starts half an hour or even an hour earlier. This means an earlier wake-up time (between 6:00 and 7:00 a.m.) and the habitual experience of waiting for the school to start, a sort of suspended time during which children are supervised and protected from danger, but are not participating in any "real" time, defined as such by the actual start of lessons. Thus, the school timetable introduces children to the awareness and experience of two kinds of opposite times: those dictated collectively (as it will happen later in the working world), belonging to the public sphere, and those more closely linked to the private sphere, and more dependent on individual choices and needs.

The normative power of adult's time – resulting, for children, from the mix of school time, parents' work time and domestic organisation time – is clear in how different activities and times are structured in the three days observed (weekdays, Saturdays and Sundays) (Fig. 1).

The most remarkable readjustment concerns the changed biorhythms. When the school timetable is not imposed, the body's natural rhythms take over. On Saturdays and especially Sundays, children sleep late in the morning and sleep more hours altogether. Elementary school children get up between 9:00 and 9:30 a.m., middle school ones whenever they want (at 10:00 or even 11:00–11:30 a.m.)[13] more directly respecting their own biorhythms (more time is also dedicated to eating and to personal care). As most infant school children (70%) confirm in the interviews, holiday means being able to wake up on their own instead of being woken up. Besides, all other times (activities) are modified. Playing (not in an institutional frame) is more pervasive, TV watching is not only more pervasive as well, but even more extended in the night (till 10:00–11:00 p.m., prolonging the social time with parents, as it is confirmed by data on the time use of adults).

LEISURE TIME

Speaking of children's leisure implies taking the similarity between children's and adults' time for granted. This is untrue. The concept of leisure is defined historically by the division of labour and the separation between paid time and time characterised by free choice, gratification, attention to self and restoration of physical and mental energies.[14] Thus, in attributing the availability of leisure time to children, we also attribute a substantial dualism to their time, between that subjected to strong social regulation (mainly school, comparable to work; Saporiti & Sgritta, 1990), similar to that of adults, and that characterised by self-determination.

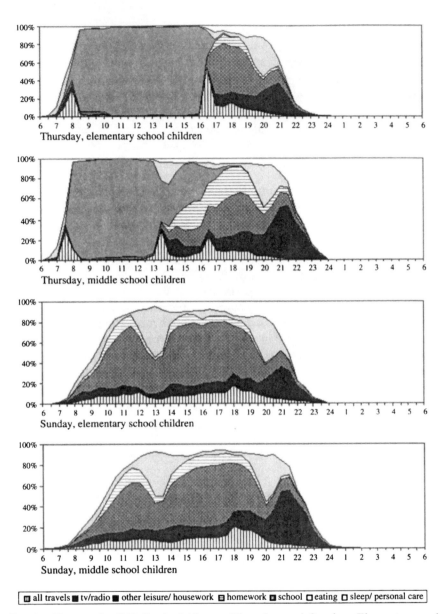

Fig. 1. Daygraph of Daily Activities on Thursday and Sunday. Elementary and Middle Schools.

Children's leisure time, however, is subjected to a further mediation by adults. Children's leisure should therefore be considered as "free" time[15] rather than as a full free-choice time. This does not mean denying children's capabilities and opportunities for decision-making. It only means that their choices must pass through two levels of constraints: those regarding them directly (mainly originating from school) and those deriving from the constraints that their parents must deal with and the priorities they set. Moreover, a correct understanding of children's leisure time must consider that the child/adult relationship is based largely on "supervision"[16] by adults, essentially through school and family.[17]

A first constraint for children lies in the amount of leisure time available and in the resources – relational or otherwise – they can bring to it. The range of possibilities is already defined by the choice of school by parents. The criteria that guide them in choosing their children's school, as it emerges from the parents' questionnaires (Table 2)[18] essentially depend on family organisation, and show that children's preferences with regard to friends are not among the most important reasons.

This is not without consequences for children's daily lives. The amount of free and leisure time, the group of friends and the chance to spend time with them, and the link with their own neighbourhood will depend on the choice of the kind of school.

Another constraint is the choice, especially common among families of upper and upper-middle class, to enrol their children in extra-school courses (sport, music etc.). How should we consider these choices made by parents even for very young children?[19] What do these activities represent for children, leisure or contracted time?[20] The ambiguity is obvious, and lends itself to reflection, as pointed out by Lareau (2000) when she compares the hectic and tight schedules of American middle-class children with the relatively unstructured and appointment-free schedules of working-class children. Parents often opt for extra-scholastic/extracurricular[21] activities

Table 2. Parents' Motivations in Choice of School (in Percentage).

	Organizational Problems	Quality of the School and Services Offered	Possibility of Social Relations
Infant school	93.3	3.3	6.1
Elementary school	78.2	15.9	5.5
Middle school	68.6	24.4	6.6

Note: Total superior to 100, questions being multiresponse.

due to organisational reasons (particularly those that take place at school and actually represent an extension of school time). In some instance, however, the reason is that parents want their children to learn skills they consider important in advance. For children, this time is regulated and hetero-directed and the activities actually represent obligations; although we cannot rule out that they may also be sources of amusement. In any event, the attitude of children towards these activities[22] seems quite clear, and shows that these are generally not considered as true and proper leisure activities. Infant school children do not even mention them with particular interest. Elementary- and middle-school children claim that they prefer games organised by themselves rather than those organised by adults. However, as we mentioned earlier, one of the main constraints on children's leisure is inflexibility with respect to its amount and placement in the day's structure. The amount varies considerably according to the day, as Table 3 illustrates.

Here, we must focus mainly on the variation in the amount of time between the different days of the week. The imbalance in leisure between weekdays, Saturdays and Sundays is influenced by the fact that all the activities performed during school hours are measured together[23] and therefore within school, recreational activities do not appear. But we should not ignore the fact that during the recreational time allowed within school time, these activities occur in an "institutional" framework, which gives them a different meaning and that they cannot be considered in the same way as outside-school leisure activities. In any case, the long school day strongly reduces the availability of "free time" for children.[24] Two and a half hours of leisure on weekdays for 7- or 8-year-old children is really not very much. And the time outside of any kind of regulation is actually even less, considering that these hours may include organised activities outside the school.[25] Among pre-adolescents in the third year of middle school, the imbalance in leisure time is particularly noticeable in the increase of sport or other physical activities on Saturdays and Sundays.

Without embarking on an analytical discussion of the content of children's leisure time, we will limit ourselves to focusing on a few leisure activities that are particularly affected by the organisation of other daily activities.

Television

Watching TV is generally the main resource that children turn to, especially when, as on school days, leisure and free time are limited. All respondents

Table 3. Children's Leisure Time, by Day of the Week and School Class (in Hours and Minutes).

	Thursday				Saturday				Sunday			
	2–3 elem.	4–5 elem.	1–2 middle	3 middle	2–3 elem.	4–5 elem.	1–2 middle	3 middle	2–3 elem.	4–5 elem.	1–2 middle	3 middle
Socialising	0:07	0:07	0:12	0:18	0:22	0:28	0:33	0:46	0:21	0:24	0:37	0:34
Sport	0:22	0:27	0:33	0:39	0:56	1:08	1:07	1:38	1:02	1:23	1:14	1:37
Play	1:02	0:45	0:26	0:12	3:05	2:06	1:16	0:36	2:40	2:05	1:26	0:31
Computer	0:05	0:09	0:14	0:25	0:15	0:21	0:21	0:40	0:11	0:17	0:19	0:32
Television	0:54	1:11	1:50	2:11	1:44	2:22	2:37	2:32	1:30	2:09	2:30	2:50
Total	2:30	2:39	3:15	3:45	6:22	6:25	5:54	6:12	5:44	6:18	6:06	6:04

showed an interest in it. Even the youngest respondents (aged 5) demonstrate knowledge of programmes and schedules (TV as second "time giver" in daily time!). Time spent in watching television varies from a minimum of 1 hour to a maximum of 3 hours daily, increasing with age and on non-school days. Television fulfils a number of functions, as indicated by its uses and by children's own comments. It represents a *filler*, a *habit* and a *time organizer*. Some examples taken from interviews, questionnaires and diaries support this interpretation, for example, the claim that one watches television "when there's nothing else to do", or before going to school (especially common among very young children: 70% of cases), or "during afternoon snack time".

Another characteristic of television is that it represents a *background noise*, a presence that often accompanies other activities. This is very apparent, for example, in very young children's drawings of dinner time, when the box representing the TV is always present, often occupying a dominant position in the dining area. This function also emerges from time-use diaries, in which watching television during meals is very common and represents almost the only occasion on which children appear to perform more than one activity simultaneously.[26]

Another function is that of *catalyst* in family relations, due to the poor compatibility between school and working hours, which leads to family relations being concentrated in the evening. There is, in fact, a peak in television watching from 8:00 to 10:00 p.m. for elementary school children, and from 8:00 to 11:00 p.m. for middle school. This naturally carries a price. The first is loss of sleep (20 minutes less sleep for each extra hour of evening television). Moreover, children watch a good deal of television programmes, which are not specifically intended for them (what adults consider suitable for children). The question remains as to whether children watch television in order to participate in adult life, to imitate their behaviour, share a common time or because they are actually interested in those programmes (which represent a point of access to the life and world of adults).

Television, however, is not always capable of bringing the family together. Young children's drawings sometimes show children alone in the evening, in front of the television in their bedrooms, while the adults are sitting at the table in the kitchen (about 10% of cases). TV is sometimes given a *babysitting* function, especially during critical moments (for example, in the morning before school), or when no one else can look after the child, or when adults are engaged in something else.

Finally, children indicate television also as a *pastime* and a source of *recreation*. Particularly, the youngest children express strong affection for cartoon characters or for what they define as "their" programmes, to the point where these become a regular "appointment" and a vehicle for relations with friends or with adults. Hence, television watching is also a leisure-time choice; questionnaires and interviews reveal that children are able to orient themselves among the various programmes and decide, and therefore choose, the ones that interest them (for example, for elementary- and middle-school boys, football games involving their favourite teams).

Play

A few explanations regarding the "play" category are needed to prevent superficial and inaccurate interpretations of the data. In our research, we defined "play" as the set of recreational behaviour and activities that have been explicitly indicated as playing in diaries. This does not exhaust, of course, the recreational/playing meaning that can be given, especially by children, to different kinds of activities (Huizinga, 1944)[27] or the playing dimension embedded in different kinds of activities. It follows that we cannot accurately establish the amount of playing (what *children* consider the amount of *their* playing), which is therefore undoubtedly under-estimated. We only measured what is explicitly indicated as "play". This is linked to another difficulty in interpreting the amount of play. We have to consider that, as children get older, the way in which they indicate recreational activities changes. Elementary-school children tend to give a generic definition of "play" to most of their recreational activities, regardless of their content or of the people with whom the activities are performed. Middle-school children, instead, tend to indicate play through the activities performed and the people they are with at that time.[28] Hence, we must be careful in assessing the amount of time dedicated to play at various ages.

Table 3 clearly highlights a steady decline of explicit play as children get older and a slight increase of other leisure activities (except TV watching). The increasing amount of time spent playing computer games with age shows an actual transfer of part of the "traditional"/indefinite playing activities into the new/technological ones; but it is not sufficient to explain the smaller amount of playing time in the older children. It remains unclear, therefore, whether "play" extends to other activities performed in the presence of friends and/or recorded as "staying with friends", or whether it actually diminishes with age.[29] Table 4 shows that the amount of play time actually decreases as children get older. If we consider children who did not

Table 4. Play Time and Videogames among Children Who Were/Were Not with Friends (in Hours and Minutes and in Percentage).

	Children Who did Not Spend Time with Friends			Children Who Spent Time with Friends	
	Play	Videogames	Total play	% Play time	% Videogames
2–3 elementary	0:58	0:06	1:04	36	2
4–5 elementary	0:48	0:08	0:56	23	2
1–2 middle	0:26	0:13	0:39	12	4
3 middle	0:12	0:26	0:38	4	4

spend time with friends, their "traditional" playing time contracts from about 1 hour a day to only 12 minutes. The "technological" playing time increases significantly from elementary to middle school, but the total time devoted to play diminishes. The percentage of time devoted to play on the overall time spent with friends decreases as well, while the time spent with friends generally increases with age.

What conclusions can we draw from this? The definition of play certainly changes with age. But the overall time devoted to playing decreases, leaving space for other activities and other kinds of relationships. Moreover, as age increases, so does the amount of time spent playing alone (with increased time for videogames, without friends present).

Sport

Some final considerations regard sport or other physical activities,[30] which Table 3 shows as occupying a fairly limited proportion of children's leisure time (especially when compared to television watching): between half an hour and a little over an hour and a half. Some preliminary clarifications are needed here as well. Firstly, the times are undoubtedly underestimated, since physical activities often cannot be separated from other kinds of activities performed by children. Moreover, these activities may be partly included in play (e.g. ball games, hide and seek). However – of greater interest to our observations on children's opportunities for autonomy – sport often includes many of the extra-scholastic courses that we have considered as ambiguous time between leisure and contracted time. Given how common these courses prove to be, sports activities, above all on weekdays, might lose the character of full leisure. This hypothesis is also supported by the times these activities take place especially on weekdays, usually in late afternoon between 6:00 and 8:00 p.m. Sport activities increase with the age of children and can be related, moreover, to the progressive achievement of autonomy. On the other hand, the variation in time dedicated to sport on the different days of the week illustrates, once again, how heavily the constraints of school and connected activities also affect this part of children's leisure time.

The most popular sports appear to be the four or five ones that are most visible in the mass media (basketball, football, volleyball, swimming, tennis) and that are of most interest to adults, contrary to the findings of the questionnaires, according to which children practised 50 different kinds of sports (almost all of which are practised in extra-scholastic courses). This discrepancy between the number of sports occasionally and systematically practised might offer some evidence to the adults' remarkable intrusion even in this type of children's leisure choices.

RELATIONS WITH PEERS AND ADULTS, WITH SPACES AND PLACES

The long duration and compactness of the school timetable make school, in our societies, the most important framework for children's various and varied relationships. At school, children find peers with whom they can share experiences and rules of relational life, as well as having to deal with adult figures who do not belong to their family. According to James et al. (1998), the main constraint for children is that here they cannot express themselves in a completely "spontaneous" way, as their relationships, however varied and rich they may be, are developed in contexts which are highly regulated and under adult control. But school also represents a good opportunity to develop a real intergenerational child culture (Corsaro, 1997).

Outside school, on the other hand, participation in peer groups is severely limited due to the difficulty of arranging meetings. Since children cannot easily move autonomously in urban spaces, relationships are outside of their decisional power: they depend on the availability or willingness of family members or other adults to accompany them to places designed for children (parks, sports centres etc.) or to each other's homes. Obviously, the younger the child, the greater the dependence on adults. Parents, prevalently mothers, especially of very small children, arrange the relationships of their children in places they can easily reach; it is no coincidence that public parks are favourite spots (18.5% of our infant school sample), while their own home or other people's homes are less popular (4.4%).

In elementary school, the dependence on adults in meeting other children is still evident (Table 5). At this age, less than half of children, on weekdays, are able to establish relationships with friends outside the school and then only for a very limited time (three quarters of an hour on weekdays). This time increases on Saturdays and Sundays (an hour more), but because of the dependence of children, the relationship opportunities remain the same. Greater opportunities are enjoyed in middle school, due partly to the reduced school timetable (an hour more on weekdays) and partly to greater opportunities for leaving the house alone (about three quarters of children are able to do so on weekdays and about an hour more on Saturdays and Sundays). Children, however, decrease their contacts with friends on Saturdays and Sundays. This is another confirmation of the role of adults in shaping children's option in the use of time. Saturdays and Sundays are more "family days" than weekdays. Therefore, children have less freedom and opportunities to be with their friends, even if they have more "free time". This corresponds to a strong "privatism" and "familialisation" of extra-scholastic time. Home is actually the space where most relations develop, and consequently most waking time is spent with, or in the presence of, figures belonging to the family nucleus (parents, and occasionally grandparents, siblings, cousins).

This does not mean that children always experience problems in seeing their peer groups. School, as we said, is the most important social channel,

Table 5. Time Spent with Friends and Siblings, in Hours, Minutes and Percentages of Participation (Doers), by Day of the Week and Order of School.

		With Friends		With Family Peers (Brothers/Sisters/ Cousins)		Total with Peer Group	
		Elementary	Middle	Elementary	Middle	Elementary	Middle
Thursday	Mean	0:43	1:16	1:35	1:44	2:19	3:01
	% Doers	45.7	75.9	65.9	67.8	81.5	91.8
Saturday	Mean	1:47	2:28	3:40	2:42	5:27	5:10
	% Doers	45.7	59.2	71.0	66.1	84.8	87.7
Sunday	Mean	1:40	2:14	3:11	2:46	4:51	5:01
	% Doers	44.3	61.3	67.9	65.5	82.7	87.3

Note: Excluding time spent at school, at church classes or sleeping; adults may be present.

although supervised. Sibling groups are the other great opportunity that children have to stay with peers, mostly for those in elementary school. Children, in fact, can generally spend more hours with siblings than with friends, and this is especially true when their dependence on adults is greater. On the whole, we can say that there is a significant difference between only children and others, mainly in elementary school, as regards the opportunity to stay with peers. The former seem to be more deprived as regards the relationships with peers and are more dependent on adults.

Focusing on the adult figures of parents, relations with mothers and fathers are not balanced, both in terms of the amount of time spent together and in the actual activities performed. Children are closely connected to their mothers, both for the more "instrumental" duties (going to and from school and extracurricular courses, domestic chores), and for those more closely linked to care, sociality and control.[31] There are also clear gender differences. As we can see in Table 6, girls and boys do not perform the same activities with their mothers and fathers. Even though girls and boys share domestic episodes with their mothers and fathers, when the girls are in the presence of their mother they participate in more domestic episodes than boys regardless of the parents' educational level or whether the mother is employed. Thus, through the different activities performed with one or the other parent, images and norms of gender roles are transmitted. Generally speaking, we can say that boys and girls are not equal in their relationships with their parents: girls perform more domestic activities with their mothers than boys do, whereas girls and boys perform different types of activities with their fathers.[32]

Apart from family members, there are several other significant adult figures with which children are used to having relationships and spending time. They are mostly educational figures. School teachers are undoubtedly

Table 6. Episodes with Mother and Father in the Day (in Percentage).

	Episodes with Mother			Episodes with Father		
	Non-domestic	Domestic		Non-domestic	Domestic	
Elementary school						
Girls	93.6	6.4	100.0	95.5	4.5	100.0
Boys	96.0	4.0	100.0	96.4	3.6	100.0
Middle school						
Girls	88.6	11.4	100.0	93.2	6.8	100.0
Boys	93.6	6.4	100.0	93.6	6.4	100.0

central figures, not only in children's education, but also in connecting them with the adult world and introducing them to "in public" relations. There are, however, also other popular figures. A first group consists of "specialists", that is teachers of various disciplines in extra-scholastic courses. These are quite common among the children we analysed, although more among children of higher social status. Among these specialists, a particular subgroup consists of teachers of religious classes, with whom almost all children enter into contact during elementary school when preparing for the various religious events that in Catholicism, but also Protestantism and Hebraism, mark the passage into adolescence. Another group is that of "educators", belonging to the recreational sphere and operating in leisure-time facilities for children, of which a relevant subgroup is religious or lay figures in parish recreational centres, frequented mainly by children from middle and lower social classes and immigrants. Generally speaking the relationships of children with the adults are strongly characterised by the presence of a large group of specialised and differentiated figures.

Before concluding this general overview on children's social relationships, let us briefly discuss how these can be considered an indicator of children's autonomy. The starting point is the hypothetical over-presence of adults, as we can deduce from the limited time that children spend with peers. Here, we consider the possibility of both being alone, and with others – adults and/or children – in performing activities. The category "alone", however, is not an easy concept in order to interpret the results and it is actually ambiguous. It might mean that the respondent is not interacting with others – although there may be somebody else present in the same place, presumably fulfilling a supervisory function or perceived as such – or that nobody is present.[33] As regards children specifically, it can mean being lonely, lacking in relationships, poor social skills or on the contrary being autonomous, not subject to supervision and therefore having responsibility. We limit ourselves here to simply stating the problem, which would need targeted research and additional data analysis, and to presenting some general results.

As Table 7 illustrates, children spend only a small part of their time alone (obviously excluding hours of sleep). This increases with age and on Saturdays and Sundays, proportionally more among children of elementary school than among the others. A similar pattern can be observed for the time spent with groups of peers without adults. Time spent with adults, whether with or without other children, does not differ significantly during the week between children of elementary and middle school, taking account of differences in school hours, although elementary school children do spend

Table 7. Children's Relational Time, by Day and by People (in Hours and Minutes).

	Thursday				Saturday				Sunday			
	Alone	Only with children	With children and adults	Only with adults	Alone	Only with children	With children and adults	Only with adults	Alone	Only with children	With children and adults	Only with adults
Elementary	1:03	1:08	9:48	2:04	2:08	2:42	4:12	4:12	2:02	2:20	4:24	3:42
Middle	2:48	2:00	8:18	1:54	3:18	3:18	4:16	2:48	3:00	3:00	4:00	2:28

Note: Excluding time for sleep and personal care.

more time with adults. On Sundays and especially on Saturdays, the experience of being with adults, but not with children increases significantly, particularly for elementary-school children.

How can these results be interpreted? They appear to confirm the general hypothesis of dependence of children on adults, which is greater when the children are smaller. On the whole, children have a limited temporal space without the presence of adults. During the week, this can be attributed mainly to the long hours spent at school, but even on Sundays, the majority of waking time is spent within the sight of an adult, and largely without other children present. This is particularly true for younger children. On Saturdays, the day dedicated to the family's organisational activities (particularly to the weekly shopping),[34] the younger children, who cannot be left alone (without supervision), presumably usually accompany their parents in these activities. On the other hand, opportunities to spend time exclusively with peers are limited and are also concentrated mainly on Saturdays. On Saturdays both elementary- and middle-school children spend the longest amount of time with adults (without other children). Sundays seem rather dedicated to activities with (or in presence of) adults and peers together. Thus, the character of the week appears marked not only by the difference between more or less contracted time, but also by a remarkable difference in the balance in the relations with adults and with peers.

Let us now use another field of experience, space, as a further indicator of autonomy of children (Valentine, 2004). The biggest limitation for children, in contemporary society and especially in cities, appears to be spatial. Table 8 illustrates the main kinds of places where children spend

Table 8. Time Children Spend in Different Places, by Day and Type of Place (in Hours and Minutes).

	Indoor, Domestic	Commercial, Entertainment	Study, Religious, Sport	Outdoor Places	Car	Other Means of Transport
Thursday						
Elementary	4:24	0:06	8:18	0:47	0:20	0:03
Middle	6:46	0:06	6:48	1:06	0:20	0:10
Saturday						
Elementary	9:26	0:50	0:23	1:35	0:41	0:02
Middle	8:48	0:50	1:23	1:42	0:37	0:09
Sunday						
Elementary	8:30	0:19	0:39	2:10	0:50	0:06
Middle	8:24	0:27	0:36	2:06	0:42	0:09

Note: Excluding time for sleep and personal care.

their time, constrained by school timetables and extra-scholastic activities, and their dependence on adults for a large number of outdoor activities .

The data in Table 8 show that opportunities to spend time outdoors are very limited. Children's time is spent mainly indoors and/or in institutional spaces (home, school, venues of extra-scholastic courses, commercial spaces[35] generally under adult supervision (parents or educators). Even most of Saturday and Sunday is spent within the domestic walls; very little time is spent outdoors. A fairly significant percentage of children (20–25%) do not spend any time at all outdoors during the day[36] particularly during the week (considering that the time outdoors includes travel to and from school, if performed by foot, and it is often limited to that). Acquisition of territorial knowledge is further thwarted by the fact that children move around mainly by car, particularly on Sundays (and often for travelling to and from school). Gender differences emerge in the different places frequented. Girls, starting in elementary school but to a greater degree in middle school, are more oriented towards the use of domestic spaces (during middle school, approximately 1 hour more than boys on Sunday) and less to outdoor spaces (approximately half an hour less than boys).

ONE OR MULTIPLE CHILDHOODS?

According to the New Childhood Sociology, especially to the "structural" current (Qvortrup, 1999), children should be considered and studied as a permanent group (although its members change continuously), which is different from other age groups in society (i.e. young people, adults, elderly) and quite homogeneous internally. At the same time, childhood is never the same across time and space: as society changes, so does childhood. This claim was similarly advanced by the French historian Ariès (1960). The "culturalist" current inside childhood studies (Corsaro, 1997; James et al., 1998) recognises also the fundamental unity of children as a group with respect to other social/age groups. Nevertheless, they point out differences among children that cannot be hidden and that should be uncovered, looking at gender and social background.[37] Much more comparative research is needed to test claims about the diversity/unity of childhood(s). In this perspective, Ben-Arieh and Ofir (2002) suggest that time-use studies might contribute significantly to such an endeavour and more generally to childhood research.[38]

Our study is not comparative. Yet, since Torino is a city which has experienced for some time substantial immigration from outside the EU and includes immigrant groups that have settled and have families and children who attend school (particularly infant and elementary), it is possible to compare children belonging to cultures other than the Italian one and to different social/family backgrounds. Data on daily activities and social relations can therefore help us to see whether children share a substantially common childhood or experience quite different childhoods.[39] First, we will compare Italian and immigrant children.

An important *caveat* is necessary before discussing the analyses: in our sample, immigrant children are not themselves a homogeneous group. Indeed, they are very different. They come from almost all of the continents and world regions. The most represented come from Romania, China, Morocco, Peru and Albania. The problem is that altogether they are little more than a hundred and hence we can only compare them as a unique group to Italian children. It is a great simplification. Yet, we believe this is still a good opportunity because it allows us to assess whether native and immigrant children share a common life or, on the contrary, exhibit very different lifestyles, whatever their respective origins.[40]

In the fourth section of this chapter, a question was introduced concerning the issue of control vs. autonomy. Looking at children's social relations and the important indicator represented by "trips with the peer group only", we gained the impression that immigrant and Italian childhoods are quite different types. In this case, we think that control and autonomy are two faces of the same coin. Immigrant children experience a daily life of greater separation from the adults' world than the Italian ones. Hence, in this sense they are more autonomous. Immigrant children are also much more likely to make trips on foot or by bicycle in the company of their friends, without adults (Table 9). This is the best indicator of autonomy, among those available, because it tells us about their knowledge of the urban environment and their capacity for movement. Thursdays and Saturdays are the days on which the difference between the two groups is best appreciated (possibly because of trips from/to school). On the other hand, looking at contacts with mothers and fathers, separately or together, it seems that "native" children are more present in the life of their parents than the immigrant ones.

Similarly, time spent alone or with peers shows quite interesting differences between Italian and foreign children. The former reported less time spent alone and less time spent in the company of peers without the presence of adults, whereas the latter did just the contrary. It seems that immigrants have more opportunity to meet friends and, at the same time, do more activities without any person present.[41]

Table 9. Trips with Peers and Relational Time of Immigrant and Italian Children in Turin, by Day of the Week.

	Thursday		Saturday		Sunday	
	Italian	Immigrant	Italian	Immigrant	Italian	Immigrant
Trips with peers (% of doers)	28.6	45.4	10.1	28.6	7.8	15.9
Time with mum (not dad)	1:26	1:04	1:55	1:29	1:30	1:14
Time with dad (not mum)	0:25	0:17	1:01	0:32	0:55	0:31
Time with both parents	0:46	0:32	2:03	1:13	2:13	1:36
Time alone	1:51	2:46	2:37	3:35	2:22	3:32
Time with peers only	1:27	2:18	2:57	3:37	2:34	3:34
Time with adults and peers	9:07	7:59	4:15	3:57	4:31	2:33
Time with adults only	2:03	1:29	3:38	2:17	3:11	2:14

Table 10. Regression Models for an "Average Day" (Time in Minutes).

	Model 1		Model 2	
Dependent: Time alone				
Constant	122.6	0.000	78.7	0.000
Immigrant	58.2	0.000	44.4	0.000
Male child			1.1	0.847
Middle school			89.3	0.000
One-parent household			−3.1	0.721
Dependent: Time with adults and peers	B	Sign.	B	Sign.
Constant	468.1	0.000	511.3	0.000
Immigrant	−68.5	0.000	−53.1	0.000
Male child			−15.4	0.047
Middle school			−67.1	0.000
One-parent household			−28.3	0.021
Dependent: Time with peers only				
Constant	109.0	0.000	83.1	0.000
Immigrant	54.8	0.000	45.3	0.000
Male child			4.5	0.406
Middle school			45.4	0.000
One-parent household			14.4	0.095

The above results should be controlled for factors that may affect the relationship between time spent with peers (or other people) and immigrant condition. Multivariate analyses show the results are robust and remain substantially unchanged after controlling for some individual and household characteristics. A few examples may help us to understand to what extent the relationship is confirmed. Table 10 shows regression models of time spent alone, with adults and peers, and with peers only.

The first model for each dependent variable includes the "immigrant" variable only (as a dummy). The associated coefficient indicates the average difference between Italian and immigrant children in time spent, for example, with peers. The second model adds three control variables: sex, age (in terms of school level) and family structure (two- or one-parent household).[42] We expected to find a coefficient for the "immigrant" variable significantly different from zero, net of control variables. More precisely, we expected positive differences between immigrant and native children in terms of time spent alone and time spent with peers only, and a negative difference on time spent with adults and peers. As it can be seen, the effect of the immigrant condition is always significant; it does not change sign and remains substantially strong with respect to the basic model.

However, the overall meaning of these results is not so clear. In fact, there are at least two competing interpretations. The first leads us to think that in post-industrial societies the relation between childhood and adulthood takes on the form of control/supervision by the latter over the former. According to this interpretation, immigrant children from different cultures would be under a lesser control of their parents and more treated as capable persons at a younger age. This would be confirmed by the fact that, on average, immigrant children spend more time alone, more time with their peers and less time with only adults or adults and peers together (see Table 11). These findings foster the idea of greater separateness between the adult world and childhood among children coming from third-world cultures. This contrasts with Ariès (1960) and much anthropological research that suggests that it is precisely in modern Western societies, contrary to pre-modern or less developed ones (i.e. immigrants' societies), that children and adults live increasingly separate lives, with childhood being considered a stage of life completely different from adulthood (and to

Table 11. Time Spent in Leisure Activities, by Day of the Week.

	Thursday		Saturday		Sunday	
	Italian	Immigrant	Italian	Immigrant	Italian	Immigrant
Sport	0:25	0:21	0:45	0:23	0:51	0:29
Playing	0:38	0:27	1:51	1:24	1:47	1:18
Reading	0:10	0:05	0:21	0:16	0:18	0:17
Watching TV	1:26	2:04	2:13	3:05	2:08	2:56

be kept as such). The finding, according to which Italian/Turinese children spend more time under the supervision of parents and adults in general, even when they are engaged in activities with peers, is consistent with that view, because it simply confirms the thesis of the institutionalisation of childhood. But the fact that immigrant children spend less time with parents (or adults in general) and more time with peers defies that thesis. Indeed, under a general hypothesis of greater integration of children into adults' lives in the third-world, less-developed societies, we would expect quite the contrary.

The last point brings us to the second interpretation of these data. Parents of immigrant children, living in a foreign country, face different constraints compared to those experienced in their countries of origin, and they often have considerable difficulties in daily life (longer working hours, especially unusual hours, housing problems etc.). This may be one of the main reasons they let their children do "their things among themselves", without too many concerns about control and supervision. This does not necessarily imply that parents do not have such concerns. It simply means they have other priorities or cannot do otherwise. It would also explain why we do not observe the expected greater integration of immigrant children into their parents' lives. Unfortunately, the data do not allow us to distinguish between interaction and co-presence in children–parent (adult) relations, and so we have to limit ourselves to stating the hypothesis.[43] Nonetheless, we believe the findings regarding trips and time spent with peers without (reported) supervision of adults is of major interest because it reveals the existence of a significant difference between Italian and immigrant childhoods. Theoretical literature from the New Childhood Sociology (James & Prout, 1990; James et al., 1998) suggests interpreting it from the perspective of increasing control over and institutionalisation of children's lives in post-industrial societies, where – we would argue – immigrant children would represent "outliers" or "deviant" cases.

Relational time is not the only "divide" between Italian and immigrant children. Comparing patterns of leisure time, we see differences suggesting that immigrant kids are disadvantaged: their leisure time is poorer in terms of cultural and cognitive stimuli. Immigrants spend more time watching television, do fewer sports activities, play less and are less likely to read (see Table 11). The differences are confirmed, and in some cases highlighted by multivariate analyses.[44] Immigrant childhood appears less privileged compared to that of natives. This finding leads us to ask whether the immigrants' condition is more similar to that of the least advantaged Italian children or it is something of a rather different sort.

In order to answer the above question, we first looked at Italian children, to ascertain whether differences can be found with respect to the socio-economic background. Then we compared immigrant children with those among the Italians that were less privileged. Basically, we estimated regression models to assess differences among Italian children according to social class, using parents' level of education and other child's and family's characteristics (as in the models of Table 10) as control variables. The results from this first step show that differences do exist as far as leisure patterns are concerned, but do not emerge for relational time.[45] Children from blue-collar households tend to watch more television and do less sport (this feature is shared with children of self-employed workers but holds to a greater extent for the children of blue-collar households), holding parents' education, child's sex and age and family structure (as an example see Table 12) constant. Reading as a pastime is not an activity that is evenly spread among children of different social classes. Working-class children are likely to read less. However, once we control for parents' education, the differences disappear. We also found that children from blue-collar families do slightly more "autonomous" trips (with peers) than children of other social classes. It seems that class is an important factor in shaping children's daily lives, in line with the findings of ethnographic works (Lareau, 2000).

In the second step of our analysis, we compared Italian blue-collar children with immigrant children and found mixed evidence: immigrants still watch more TV than Italians (a 20-minute difference) but do not engage

Table 12. Regression Models of TV Time among Italian Children, Minutes on an "Average Day".

	Model 1		Model 2		Model 3	
	B	Sign.	B	Sign.	B	Sign.
Constant	74.7	0.000	155.5	0.000	111.8	0.000
Social class (ref. cat.: upper class)						
White collars	15.5	0.036	7.1	0.339	10.0	0.158
Blue collars	48.9	0.000	18.2	0.084	23.4	0.019
Self-employed workers	32.2	0.000	9.7	0.341	9.1	0.342
Mother's years of education			−3.9	0.000	−3.2	0.001
Father's years of education			−1.3	0.196	−1.1	0.258
Male child					11.2	0.020
Middle school					48.2	0.000
One-parent household					8.3	0.465

in less sport or read less. They are also quite similar regarding the "auto-nomous" urban mobility indicator. With regard to relational time, we found that immigrant and Italian children do differ (see Table 10), but the latter are not internally differentiated by social class: in this case, blue-collar Italian children do not follow different patterns from other social classes. Hence, as far as social relations are concerned, the relevant difference is between native and immigrant children. These data suggest that there are, as a matter of fact, partly diverse "children's worlds" across social class and particularly along the native/immigrant divide. There appears to be a mutual re-enforcement between differences owing to social class and differences owing to the immigrant experience. Immigrant children appear active explorers of the city: they discover its space-time dimensions more by themselves, without adult supervision, than their Italian peers. And they appear more often left to their own resources, but also possibly perceived as more capable to fend off for themselves. But outside what they can do by their own means, they appear to have fewer of the resources – books, sports, trips and so forth – that today form part of the children's curriculum.

CONCLUSIONS

In this paper, we have illustrated some of the main features of everyday life of children in a western European city. As regards the structure of daily schedules, childhood seems to be very similar to adulthood. Time is split between compulsory activities and leisure, and based on a precise timetable. School, as a prevailing part of the day, can be compared with the time adults spend at work. However, childhood differs from other age groups in terms of what we can refer to as the "double level of dependency". That is, they first depend on the social organisation of time and second on adults as a social group who has the power. The amount of time dedicated to various kinds of activities (social times) performed by children reasonably reflects the rigidity of children's time and the scarce possibility of diverging from prescribed schedules. As a consequence, although children may be considered a separate and even segregated social group, they cannot easily perceive themselves and behave as such, since they have little opportunity to develop autonomous relationships and activities even when they reach physical independence. The (little) time spent with friends supports this argument.

In summary, we can say that in our analysis we found various distinctive characteristics of childhood as conceptualised by the New Childhood Sociology: institutionalisation, dependency, weak possibility of self-reliance, fragmentation and isolation of the components of the group. In accordance with the more "structural" approach of this corpus of studies, we also analysed differences in childhood.

The most important difference, generally speaking, appears linked to age and concerns the relation between institutionalised and non-institutionalised time. Elementary-school children have a longer institutional time than the middle-school ones. This is correlated not so much to the biological–psychological development of children over the years as to the social–normative function of school, which separates what must be considered "first" childhood from "pre-adolescence". This is particularly true, in a city like Torino where the elementary school is organised on a full day basis, while pre-adolescence is de facto perceived as less in need of full-time supervision. In other cities, where the full-day organisation of the elementary school is less available, these age-group differences might not be so clear, while differences might emerge between same age children attending schools with different time schedules. Gender differences are not evident to the same degree in all of the activities performed, but they start from early childhood, and are transmitted through family behaviour and increase with age. Girls develop their activities and relationships more often than boys within closed spaces. They seem more restricted in their ability to move in public, open spaces. They are also involved more often in domestic chores, particularly when they are with their mothers. Only children appear more isolated (poor relationships with peer groups) in a children's world that is heavily dominated by school and family and is more dependent (from adults). Last but not the least, more than social class, a clear difference emerges between native and immigrant children. Immigrant children are more separated from adults, while they are closer to their peer groups: they spend more time alone and with their peer groups. As regards autonomy/control, they are more autonomous than Italian children: they show a greater ability to move alone or with friends outside the home. As regards leisure, they have lower cultural resources, reflected by the small amount of time dedicated to sports or cultural entertainment and the large amount of time spent watching TV. A comparison with the subgroup of Italian children belonging to blue-collar families revealed similarities in terms of autonomy and cultural consumption. But native children from blue-collar households are similar to all other native children with regard to time spent with adults and particularly parents.

We believe that these preliminary results constitute a sound basis for further analysis into the structure of everyday life and the culture of children, utilising time-use data.

NOTES

1. The research was carried out in March 2003 and was mainly financed by the city of Torino, in collaboration with the Department of Social Sciences of the University of Torino. The population analysed consisted of 721 children from the second to fifth year of elementary school and 708 from the first to third year of middle school belonging to 13 school complexes and 6 infant schools around the city of Torino, in northern Italy. In addition, 280 children (aged 5–6 years) from 6 infant schools, were also interviewed. All the schools were specifically chosen to represent areas of different social composition. The methodologies adopted were: time-use diaries, questionnaires and drawings (only for infant school children). The data illustrated here represent the first elaborations; further elaborations are underway. The research group consisted of Carmen Belloni, who was also the coordinator, Renzo Carriero, who was mainly responsible for processing time-use data, and Francesca Zaltron, responsible for the part relating to infant school children. The various research phases were discussed with the school teachers, who also distributed the instruments for data collection to the children.

2. We adopted the standard time-budget methodology. The tool used was the time-use diary, in which children noted, in their own words and for 24 hours a day and in succession, the duration of the activities performed (principal activities) and activities performed simultaneously if present (secondary activities), the locations where the activities took place, and the people present or interacting. Post-codification of the short narratives allowed statistical elaboration (Szalai, 1972). For methodological problems relating the time-use diary in childhood analysis, see Belloni and Carriero (2007).

3. For the pre-school group, information on their daily lives was gathered through questionnaires to parents, interviews to children and drawings by the same. The questionnaire ascertained the temporal position of several macro-activities before or after school, which were then discussed in the interviews with children aged 5 years. These children were also asked to draw pictures of dinner time on a weekday and on a holiday, in order to obtain an image of sociality and relationships inside the family. For a discussion about the problems in the sociological interpretation of drawings, see the research report (Belloni, 2005).

4. In the time-use studies, job and school are considered as a whole, in line with the research goals to study the out-of-job/school everyday life.

5. Hence, it is quite obvious that, excluding time spent at school, children often have limited time to spend in informal settings and social contexts, especially at elementary school when most children (at least in Torino) attend on "full time" basis (from 8:30 a.m. to 4:30 p.m.).

6. In our research, this emerges more directly from interviews with children in infant school, but also, more indirectly, from some questions on the survey addressed to children in elementary and middle school and their organisation of daily time.

7. Also, infant schools in most Italy and particularly in the Center-North have the same length, although there may be more flexibility in entrance and exiting hours.

8. In Italy there are different kinds of schooltime. Generally, in elementary school there are three options: full time (from 8:30 a.m. to 4:30 p.m. and from Monday

to Friday), normal time (from 8:30 to 12:30 and from Monday to Saturday) or integrated time (from 8:30 to 12:30 and from Monday to Friday; in this case there are two or three days of school in the afternoon). In middle school, the normal time is from 8 a.m. to 1 p.m. from Monday to Saturday, but many schools organise afternoon activities (sport or extracurricular courses). The supply and the times vary according to schools. The school time in the infant school is more flexible and can extend till 6 p.m. (especially in the private schools), but it can finish early in the afternoon too. In Torino, the elementary schools are generally full time or at least integrated time, and the middle schools offer a lot of afternoon activities. As regards infant and elementary schools, a flexible entrance is allowed.

9. A research project on time use conducted on the whole of Torino's population, in parallel with the research on children's time illustrated here, revealed that work is usually prolonged until as late as 7 p.m. (Belloni, 2007).

10. As our research shows that a majority of mothers work, we can assume that their choice of work is influenced by this constraint.

11. This is especially true for children in infant and elementary school. However, we also observed that a large number of children are accompanied to and from school even in middle school, whether for organisational reasons (speeding things up in the morning and sharing family responsibilities, especially when it is the father who is involved), or to protect children from urban dangers.

12. In order to help resolve families' timetable difficulties, schools (especially infant and elementary) provide flexible entry times, so that children are supervised by additional personnel besides teachers until school activities begin.

13. This difference provides clues about time rules that families are forced to adopt depending on the constraints they are subjected to. Beyond slight differences in sleep needs among children of different ages, presumably younger children (elementary school), considered as needing supervision, are more habitually involved in family organisational activities, concentrated on Saturday, and are thus more often forced to respect adult rhythms. Middle-school children, who can be left alone, have more opportunities to follow their natural waking/sleeping rhythms.

14. We refer essentially to Dumazedier's definition (Dumazedier, 1962).

15. Although we consider this expression more correct, for convenience we will use after the term "leisure".

16. The concept of "surveillance", here used in relation to the control of time, refers to the association between control and power described by Foucault (Foucault, 1975), although, where children are concerned, it must be interpreted with reference to a more complex group of functions, including appeasing adult feelings of responsibility and probably also of guilt (especially among mothers) at having to perform other activities that are very time consuming.

17. Time-use diaries frequently record the presence of adults (supervisory function) without there being any interaction (relational and care function).

18. Similar results emerge in the question about the choice of school: full time or only morning.

19. In our research, for example, 45% of 5-year-old children already attend extra-scholastic courses in sport or corporeal expression.

20. According to Åas, contracted time is time devoted to work/educational obligations. The other kinds of time are: necessary time, committed time and free time (Åas, 1978).

21. Sometimes, we cannot distinguish between extracurricular (activities organised in the school but not compulsory) and extra-scholastic activities (followed courses in sport disciplines, arts, foreign languages etc.).

22. These considerations summarise data from interviews with infant school children and from the questionnaires accompanying the time-use diaries of elementary- and middle-school children.

23. As we said, in the diaries, the time spent at school is measured altogether as "school". Therefore, this also includes children's play activities during recreation, during intervals or even "stolen" during lesson time.

24. Obviously in middle school, where there is no full time, but where there can be different courses in the afternoon, total school time is less but more variable.

25. From time-use diaries, it is not always possible to determine whether play activities (e.g. playing soccer) are performed in institutionalised contexts, such as a soccer club, or are performed in an informal, unstructured setting. In future data analysis, we will try to make more precise estimations (although exact calculations are not possible) regarding the importance of the two settings of activities.

26. Here we refer to analyses of national data on the practice of multitasking. The performance of more than one activity contemporaneously, very common among adults (an average of seven multitasking episodes daily), is more limited among children (averaging 4.5 episodes daily). As regards children, the multitasking analysis shows that, in 37% of cases, the primary activity is accompanied by television and other media, whereas in 52% of cases it is superimposed on social activities ("socialising").

27. That is a common problem in time-use surveys, related to the subjective meaning attributed by the individuals to their activities, but in this case the possibility of misunderstanding in coding is greater.

28. Obviously, the change in term indicates a change in the meaning attributed to the activities performed; however, this will not be discussed here.

29. The amount of time spent with friends is underestimated, since, as we have said, we do not record the time that children spend with peers while at school. Also, in this case the nature of relationships changes, taking place in an institutional setting. For further analysis of the steps taken to correctly interpret the "play" category, see the report mentioned above (Belloni, 2005).

30. The "sport" category includes both sport in the strictest sense (whether practiced independently or in the form of organised courses) and activities such as going for a walk or "spending time at the park".

31. In many cases there is an adult (usually the mother) in the house, performing her own activities, without there being interaction with the children. This, together with the practice of never leaving the children alone (unsupervised), supports the hypothesis that, in our society, the adult/child relationship is defined largely in terms of control.

32. In the recent years we can find a little greater participation by the fathers in childcare, but with a preference for leisure-relational activities (Sabbadini, 2005; Saraceno, 2005).

33. The time-use diaries cannot determine whether there is effective interaction or merely the presence of another person. Moreover, children's accounts are not always homogeneous: sometimes they indicate the presence of an adult even if he or she does not occupy the same space, sometimes not.

34. This emerges clearly in the national survey on time use and the parallel survey on Torino in 2002–2003.

35. In this table, the categories are aggregated. For example, given the scant amount of time involved, the category "commercial, entertainment" includes both commercial spaces and snack bars, restaurants etc. The category "study, religious, sport" includes school spaces, spaces for religious functions or formation, and spaces for sport courses (mainly gymnasiums, swimming pools etc., but also to some extent outdoor spaces). Nevertheless, this information is sufficient for our discussion.

36. Also, in this case the data do not report in detail the amount of time spent at school, and therefore underestimate the use of outdoor spaces during school time. Outdoor time in school is however necessarily limited to the interval between lessons and spent, if at all, in generally small schoolyards. More important opportunities to be outdoors, though not habitual, are outings to museums or other places of interest in the city.

37. James et al. (1998) individuate a similarity between the emergence of women's and children's studies, as the acknowledgement of new social actors (groups) worth studying in their own.

38. For a general purpose of comparison, readers can see Sandberg and Hofferth (2001) who show trends in children's time with parents in the US between 1981 and 1997. The authors found that children's time with their parents has not decreased despite strong change in the population's structural characteristics. On the same topic, see Yeung et al. (2001). Hofferth and Sandberg (2001) also analysed children's time spent in various activities using data from the 1997 CDS-PSID survey. By means of regression models, they show the impact of various individual and household/parents' characteristics on different sorts of time use, finding significant impact of ethnic membership on developmental-related activities (reading, playing, doing sports, watching TV etc.).

39. It is also likely that childhoods differ across time, but this is a rather difficult issue to explore with the standard tools of sociological research. Nonetheless, we compared children's use of time across 24 years analysing data collected with the same methodology (time-budget diaries) in 2 years (1979–2003) (see Carriero, 2005).

40. Another technical problem arises from lower response rate of immigrant children's parents who refused to provide background information to a greater extent than Italian parents. This is of concern in multivariate analysis due to listwise deletion of cases with missing information.

41. As already mentioned above, it is not clear what is the correct meaning to attach to the term "alone": it might be loneliness or autonomy (no need to be supervised).

42. Other important controls (parents' education level, parents' job status) have not been included because of very low response rate among immigrants.

43. Knowing what adults do when directly interacting with children would help us to disentangle the meaning of the data on relational time.

44. Data are not shown. We estimated logistic and linear regression models, like those presented in Table 10.

45. The only exception is time spent with both parents: middle-class children seem more involved with their parents than upper-class children. It might be an effect of standard and shorter work hours, more spread among parents of the former.

REFERENCES

Åas, D. (1978). Studies of time use: Problems and prospects. *Acta Sociologica, 21*(2), 125–141.

Ariès, P. (1960). *L'enfant et la vie familiale sous l'ancien régime.* Paris: Plon.

Belloni, M.C. (Ed.), (2005). *Vite da bambini. La quotidianità dai 5 ai 13 anni,* Torino: Archivio storico della città di Torino.

Belloni, M. C. (Ed.) (2007). *Andare a tempo. Una ricerca sul tempo della città.* Milano: Angeli.

Belloni, M. C. & Carriero, R. (2007) *Il tempo dei bambini,* in ISTAT (2007). *I tempi della vita quotidiana. Un approccio multidisciplinare all'analisi dell'uso del tempo,* Roma: ISTAT Collana Argomenti n. 32. Available at http://www.istat.it/dati/catalogo/20070807_00/

Ben-Arieh, A., & Ofir, A. (2002). Time for (more) time-use studies: Studying the daily activities of children. *Childhood, 9,* 225–248.

Carriero, R. (2005). How children's use of time has changed over 24 years in a large Italian city. Paper presented at the IATUR Annual Conference, Halifax, Canada [see www.iatur.org].

Corsaro, W. (1997). *The sociology of childhood.* Thousand Oaks, CA: Pine Press.

Dumazedier, J. (1962). *Vers une civilisation du loisir.* Paris: Seuil.

Foucault, M. (1975). *Surveiller et punir.* Paris: Gallimard.

Hengst, H., & Zeiher, H. (Eds). (2004). *Per una sociologia dell'infanzia.* Milano: Angeli.

Hofferth, S., & Sandberg, J. (2001). How American children spend their time. *Journal of Marriage and the Family, 63,* 295–308.

Huizinga, J. (1944). *Homo ludens.* Basel: Burg-Verlag.

James, A., Jenks, C., & Prout, A. (1998). *Theorizing childhood.* Cambridge: Polity Press.

James, A., & Prout, A. (Eds). (1990). *Constructing and reconstructing childhood.* London: Falmer Press.

Lareau, L. (2000). Social class and the daily lives of children: A study from the United States. *Childhood, 7,* 155–171.

Qvortrup, J. (1991). *Childhood as a social phenomenon: An introduction to a series of national reports* (Vol. 1). Vienna: European Centre.

Qvortrup, J. (1999). *Childhood and societal macrostructures.* Working Paper 9. Child and Youth Culture, Department of Contemporary Cultural Studies, Odense University.

Sabbadini, L.L. (2005). Essere padri in Italia. Tempi di cura e organizzazione di vita. Paper presented at the Conference ISTAT "La paternità in Italia", Roma, 20 October.

Sandberg, J., & Hofferth, S. (2001). Changes in children's time with parents: United States, 1981–1997. *Demography, 38,* 423–436.

Sansot, P. (1981). *Les donneurs de temps.* Albeuve, Suisse: Castella.

Saporiti, A., & Sgritta, G.B. (1990). *Childhood as a social phenomenon.* National Report. Italy.

Saraceno, C. (2005). Paternità e maternità. Non solo disuguaglianza di genere. Paper presented at the conference ISTAT La paternità in Italia, Roma, 20 Oct.

Szalai, A. (1972). *The use of time. Daily activities of urban and suburban populations in twelve countries*. The Hague: Mouton.

Valentine, G. (2004). *Public space and the culture of childhood*. Ashgate: Burlington.

Yeung, W., Sandberg, J., Davis-Kean, P., & Hofferth, S. (2001). Children's time with fathers in intact families. *Journal of Marriage and the Family, 63,* 136–154.

STREET YOUTH'S LIFE-COURSE TRANSITIONS

Cecilia Benoit, Mikael Jansson,
Helga Hallgrimsdotter and Eric Roth

INTRODUCTION

Social science and media depictions of youth living on our city streets typically focus on their "risk behaviours," especially illicit drug use and unprotected sex, the social environmental challenges they face, in particular higher likelihood of sexual and physical assault and homicide (Tyler, Hoyt, & Whitbeck, 2000; Auerswald & Eyre, 2002; Pedersen & Hegna, 2003; Brooks, Milburn, Rotheram, & Witkin, 2004; Ensign & Bell, 2004; Raleigh-DuRoff, 2004; Hyde, 2005; Witkin et al., 2005) and their delinquent/criminal behaviour (Hartnagel, 1998). This focus on the multiple "risks" that street youth face has been accompanied by the search for determinants of the risk factors for street involvement, such as parental substance abuse and child neglect. Female street youth have been depicted as particularly vulnerable, partly because once on the street, they come under the control of male recruiters who make the girls drug-dependent and force them into trading sexual favours for money or in-kind goods. According to Bagley and Young (1987, p. 23), "the girl who finally tries prostitution is one who is already degraded and demoralized, in a state of psychological bondage, with grossly diminished self-confidence." Adults

Childhood: Changing Contexts
Comparative Social Research, Volume 25, 325–353
Copyright © 2008 by Emerald Group Publishing Limited
All rights of reproduction in any form reserved
ISSN: 0195-6310/doi:10.1016/S0195-6310(07)00011-7

who exploit these female street youth are believed to take advantage of their feelings of disconnectedness and low self-esteem and isolation (Silbert & Pines, 1981, 1982a, 1982b) and addiction to substances (Green & Goldberg, 1993). Yet, many females who were victims of childhood physical and sexual abuse do not end up on the street, nor do all those who were abused and end up on the street (male as well as female) become involved in prostitution, and, finally, many males and females who become involved in prostitution have no history of early abuse (Hagan & McCarthy, 1997).

While this risk-focused literature has tended to homogenise the street youth population, more recent scholarship has begun to shed light on their *heterogeneity* (Auerswald & Eyre, 2002; Hyde, 2005). This latter strand of scholarship has investigated, among other things, how differences in the timing of leaving home, the length of time on the street, and the particulars of specific street locales shape experience on the street, and the short- and long-term outcomes of becoming street-involved.

Common throughout all of these studies, however, is the assumption that street youth's involvement in "risky behaviours" places them on an "abnormal" trajectory compared to the "normal" life course of youth. Such a one-dimensional focus has the potential to stigmatise youth and deprive them of a sense of self. Ironically, many of the same behaviours, including frequent changes "in terms of love partners, jobs and educational status ..." (Arnett, 2005, p. 241) as well as high rates of drug use (Nelson & Barry, 2005; Schulenberg, Merline, Johnston, O'malley & Bachman, 2005), are seen as markers of the post-adolescent stage of *emergent adulthood* – the time period between adolescence, or biological maturity, and adulthood when young people are trying to separate themselves from their parents and in a transitory period before developing stable adult roles (Arnett, 2005, p. 114). We hypothesise, first, that the life-course trajectories of street youth are better understood as being temporally different rather than "abnormal" when compared to those of their same-aged peers; second, that street youth experience variations in their life course due to their position in the social stratification system and, third, that it is their social location together with key life-course events that determine different pathways to adulthood. In other words, it is not the risk behaviours that place street youth on a non-normative life-course trajectory but rather the timing and the socio-economic conditions under which these youth transition into emergent adulthood and adulthood that make them unique.

VARIABILITY IN YOUNG PEOPLE'S LIFE-COURSE TRANSITIONS

During the last decades, the life-course approach to human development has become a central topic in the social sciences. Psychologists have identified a number of pivotal markers accompanying life stages arranged chronologically by age – childhood, adolescence and adulthood (Heinz & Marshall, 2003). Childhood – roughly the first 12 years of life – has been depicted as an untroubled period of learning and play. Adolescence or the "teenage years", the stage when young people are no longer children but not yet adults, has been described as one of emotional and social turmoil as young people develop their own identities while still living with their parents or guardians and attending school (Schwartz, Cote & Arnett, 2005). Due to major shifts in social institutions, the transition from adolescence to adulthood has recently become extended to include an additional life stage – emergent adulthood – defined above as the years between biological maturity and entrance into stable adult roles. Emergent adulthood, which covers roughly the years between 18 and 25, and for some researchers extends to as old as 30 years (Arnett, 2005), is seen as marked by transitory residency, change in education programmes/fields, periodic employment mobility with bouts of unemployment, some economic independence, frequent changes of intimate partners, few responsibilities for others/dependents and experimentation with drugs (Schulenberg et al., 2005; Nelson & Barry, 2005). This stage is also seen as a time for intense identity exploration, focus on self, as well as the sense of endless possibilities mitigated somewhat by feelings of instability and vaguely defined social roles. Jeffery Arnett (2006, p. 120) argues that this life stage is "exceptionally unstructured by institutions". Compared with early childhood and even adolescence when family and school have relatively high control over a young person's day-to-day life, emergent adults are seen as free from these controls and not yet bound by the markers of career, marriage and parenthood that distinguish adulthood.

Many scholars take exception to Arnett's approach, however, arguing that it is ahistorical, ethnocentric and classist; instead, these scholars argue that the markers of the life stages of childhood and adolescence are historically fluid and culturally constructed (Hendrick, 1997; Gittins, 1998; Scheper-Hughes & Sargent, 1998; Levander & Singley, 2003). Historian Philippe Ariès (1965) reminded us 40 years ago that the idea of childhood itself was then a novel concept that very young children of both the upper and lower classes had been treated like "little adults" until into the twentieth century. Hugh Cunningham (1995) examined the historical records on children since the 1500s and concluded that the dominant middle-class notion of childhood in Western society, marked by ideas of domesticity and dependence, is a relatively recent understanding of childhood accompanying industrial capitalism. For instance, in pre-industrial Europe, it was common for children from both the upper and lower classes to not reside with their parents but rather to be in "circulation" in one way or another (Sá, 2000). The former were often sent out to a "wet nurse" at an early age and then later sent to boarding schools to acquire formal schooling, while young children from poor rural families were sent to work in better-off households to earn their own keep (Panter-Brick & Smith, 2000).

Other scholars have shown that society and culture continue today to shape the plural experiences of childhood around the globe. While in the latter half of the twentiethth century, high-income countries could afford to extend childhood for young people from the middle classes to include a stage of adolescence, allowing them time to learn the skills they needed in a high-technology workplace, this is by no means the norm worldwide. Bledsoe (1990), for example, notes that among the Mende of Sierra Leone fostering out rural children to better-off families in towns is commonplace, both as a strategy to manage family size and also for upward mobility. Similarly, working-class youth in Britain and Canada continue to be involved in paid employment while attending high school, and many "lads" drop out altogether before completing high school and instead move to full-time employment (Willis, 1977; Tanner, 1993).

In a similar manner, the markers accompanying emergent adulthood for street youth may begin at a different time than same-age youth and the sequence of the markers may also vary, depending upon street youth's early life experiences and current access to key resources. Thus, while for Arnett emergent adulthood is seen as a widespread "unprecedented phenomenon" (Arnett, 2006, p. 119) – a normative experience of today's young people that cuts across genders and other social groupings – sociologists argue that the timing and sequencing of the markers signifying emergent adulthood are likely to vary significantly, depending upon historical patterns, economic change, "knifing-off experiences" (such as mandatory military service, war, etc.) and social inequalities within particular cohorts (Shanahan, 2000; Bynner, 2005).

We draw on data from a mixed-methods longitudinal study of street youth conducted in a medium-sized urban region of Canada and a parallel study of a random sample of youth from the same geographical area in order to contribute to the above debate. We examine similarities and differences between the two groups in terms of the timing of their entries into the life stages of adolescence and emergent adolescence. Our findings show that rather than rebellious youth living a "high-risk" lifestyle, the risks faced by street youth are better understood as being the result of taking on the responsibilities of adulthood too early, and in the absence of familial and social supports.

THE TWO STUDIES: MATERIALS AND METHODS

Materials for our study came from two related studies conducted between 2002 and 2006.

Risky Business

Our first study, *Risky Business? Experiences of Street-Involvement* (henceforth referred to as RB) focused on the impact of street life on the health and well-being of a purposive sample of female and male youth (Benoit, Jansson, & Anderson, 2007; Jansson & Benoit, 2006). The data presented here draw upon the first two interview waves from an ongoing longitudinal study began in 2002 of street youth in the Census Metropolitan Area (CMA) of Victoria, British Columbia, Canada's westernmost city. Victoria, the capital of the province, is a middle-size city of 310,000, located between the larger cities of Vancouver (population = 2 million) and Seattle (population = 3.5 million).

Street youth – female and male – are a social concern in all three West Coast cities. Because of the lack of a standard agreed-upon definition, street youth include not only youth who live mainly on the street, but also "couch-surfers" who share shelter with intimate partners or friends, youth who are in and out of government care (also known as "system youth"), and youth who frequent shelters for the homeless.

The actual number of street youth is thus difficult to estimate with any rigour. Moreover, very few metropolitan areas have attempted to collect these kinds of data. In Seattle in the mid-1990s, 500–1,000 street youth aged 12–24 years slept on the street or in temporary shelters, and these estimates rise to as many as 2,000 if youth living in other unstable situations are included (Ensign & Bell, 2004). One study estimated that in 1990 there were 3,000–5,000 street youth in Toronto (Smart, Adlaf, & Walsh, 1992). Another study estimated that 6,000 youth aged 15–24 years stayed in various outreach facilities for street youth in Toronto in 1999 (Kraus, Eberle, & Serge, 2001). A third study estimated that in 2004 the number of street youth in Toronto in any given night was in the range of 2,000 (O'Grady & Gaetz, 2004). In Halifax, 300 youth used a youth drop-in centre between April 1 and July 31 in 2000; in Ottawa over 500 youth sought help in emergency shelters in the year 2000 (Kraus et al., 2001). None of these studies give reliable estimates of street youth by gender, although most studies suggest that there are more males than females in this vulnerable population but that the percentage of females is growing (Kraus et al., 2001; CIHI, 2005). We found no estimates of street/homeless youth in Victoria specifically. However, we assume, consistent with the studies mentioned above, there are 250–300 street youth, aged between the ages of 14 and 24 years, at any given time in Victoria.

Due to the particular characteristics of street youth, an assortment of sampling techniques was employed to reach participants. Staff at four community partner organisations that provide service to street youth helped establish recruitment strategies. Their location in the inner city provided access to subgroups of marginalised youth who live part- or full-time on the street, thereby enhancing our sample's representativeness. We also recruited youth through contacts with the Ministry of Health Services of British Columbia and other frontline health and social services in the metropolitan area. In addition, we advertised the study at various locales where street youth are concentrated. Finally, we employed a method referred to in the academic literature as "respondent driven sampling" (Heckathorn, 1997). This technique is especially appropriate for recruiting hard-to-reach or hidden populations who are stigmatised by the wider society, when no sampling frames exist, and acknowledgement of belonging to the group is threatening. Approximately half of the street youth participants were recruited to the project via this latter method.

Participants served as "seeds" and were each given three recruitment coupons to hand over to other youth whom they believed might come forward for an interview. This is based on the rationale that reclusive youth are more likely to respond to the appeals of their similar-age peers who have already participated in the research project, than to requests from more privileged adults from either the university or community agencies (Ensign & Gittelsohn, 1998). A $20 honorarium was provided for the first interview and participants received a $25 honorarium after completing subsequent interviews. The "seeds" were also paid a nominal honorarium of $10 for each peer who came forward to participate. Identified youth were asked to call on a dedicated cell phone number and anonymously answer a series of questions that assessed their age (they had to be 18 years or younger at the time of the phone call) and levels of involvement with the parent or guardian, the school system, the formal labour market activity and the street economy (e.g., pan-handling, petty crime, selling drugs and prostitution). We used a relatively conservative measure of street involvement (loose or no attachment to family and school, living on the street part- or full-time in the past month and making part or all money for survival through street activities). We hoped to access those least connected to societal institutions, and most likely to be facing health challenges.

The resultant sample includes 138 youth ranging in age between 14 and 19 years at the time they were first interviewed. Just over half of these participants identified as female (54 per cent). Street youth were interviewed twice in the first month, and we have continued to interview them every few months, depending upon their availability and their willingness to continue participating in the study. A relatively large number of research assistants have worked on this project, including former street-involved youth who were in their mid-to-late-20s and willing to be trained in interviewing techniques. These individuals were identified by our community partners as promising researchers. Health and social service professionals and graduate students who showed an interest in working part-time on the study were also recruited as interviewers.

The research instrument included closed- and open-ended questions. The individual interviews were tape-recorded with the participant's permission and ranged from 45 minutes to 2 hours, with the length depending primarily on the willingness of the youth to give thorough answers to the open-ended questions and the relevance of particular questions to their lives. We gave the youth the option to answer more sensitive questions, including those relating to sexuality, on a self-administered, written questionnaire. We believe this mixed-methods approach that deliberately gathers both qualitative and quantitative data from a group of research participants (Creswell, 2003) is especially useful for shedding light on the situation of hidden populations such as street youth because it enables us to quantify and qualify key variables, giving us an opportunity to triangulate both types of data on topics of interest and to elaborate on the meaning and experiences subsumed within survey statistics.

Responses to closed-ended questions were entered and analysed using SPSS 12.0 software. Analysis of responses to the qualitative probes and questions consisted of a number of sequential steps: the open-ended questions analysed for the paper were transcribed verbatim in word processor format. The transcriptions were independently read by two of the authors (Cecilia Benoit and Helga Hallgrimsdotter) question by question, and each then identified the central themes in the answers. The two authors then arrived at a common list of themes by question, based on an analysis of the separate lists they arrived at independently. The transcriptions were then coded thematically by the first author and a few transcriptions were coded by the other author. These transcriptions were compared to check for coding consistency/reliability. The first author did an initial analysis of the thematic data, and the other authors made further revisions.

While our overall project and associated research instruments produce both complete qualitative and quantitative data sets, for this particular paper, we have limited our analysis to a few key markers that were theoretically and empirically linked to street youth's life-course transitions. We have used our qualitative data as an interpretive resource for expanding upon the quantitative results (Morgan, 1998). This model of analysis, where one source of data is prioritised and the other treated as supplementary is a common strategy for integrating data in mixed methods research, as it is difficult to coherently integrate a full qualitative and full quantitative analysis within one paper (Morse, 2003).

Healthy Youth Survey

The second study, *Healthy Youth Survey* (henceforth referred to HYS), is also longitudinal, involving a randomly selected sample of youth from the same geographical area. To attain the sample, in 2003 we randomly telephoned 9,500 households in the Victoria metropolitan area and asked if they had a youth aged 12–18 years living there. Of the households that did, 82 per cent of parents/guardians agreed for their youth to participate and, of those, 78 per cent of the youth (664) agreed to participate. After attaining the consent of both the guardian/parent(s) and youth, face-to-face close-ended interviews consisting of survey questions on a range of topics, including the assets and resources of youth, their families and their communities, as well as individual, family and community or cultural risks for injury, were conducted with the youth in their own homes. The interviews occurred during the spring term (March through June). The youth received an honorarium of a $25 gift certificate for completing the research instrument. In 2005, the same random sample of youth, now aged 14–20, were re-contacted to participate in a second interview. Five hundred and eighty youth agreed to be re-interviewed, producing an 88 per cent response rate for the second interview. The comparative data presented below are drawn from the 580 youth who were interviewed twice. Of this subsample, 47 per cent identified as male and 53 per cent female.

Overall, the two samples from which our analysis is drawn – of street youth and the random sample – were thus approximately the same chronological age. We first present our results on the social backgrounds of the two populations and then link these results to a number of key markers locating them at different points in the life course.

RESULTS

Social Backgrounds of the Two Populations

Following the work of Link and Phelan (1995), we hypothesise that a deep understanding of the life-course transitions of street youth requires close attention to their early social conditions. Thus, in contrast to the dominance of epidemiological discourses regarding "risk factors", we predict that street youth's socio-economic status (education, income and occupation) is a "fundamental determinant" of their pathways to adulthood. The concept of fundamental determinant means that it is not dependent upon its relationship to more proximal behaviours, such as use of addictive substances, but exists independently of them (Link & Phelan, 2002). Below we examine socio-economic status using parents' education and employment status (as we were unable to get accurate family income data from the youth) and household stability and support during early childhood. We present these descriptive findings by gender when possible and include excerpts from the narratives of the street youth to the open-ended question: "I would like to begin by asking you to reflect back on your childhood. What stands out? What were the highlights? Who do you remember most from your childhood?" (Due to shortage of space, we have not presented the findings by Aboriginal/non-Aboriginal status, which we plan to do in a separate paper).

Parental Education
Table 1 indicates that the educational achievement of the parents or guardians with whom our RB participants lived the longest was comparatively low, with over one-quarter of both the mothers or female guardians and fathers or male guardians not having finished high school and less than 25 per cent having completed a college diploma or university

Table 1. Parental Education.

	Risky Business		*Health Youth Survey*	
	Father/male guardian (in %)	Mother/female guardian (in %)	Father/male guardian (in %)	Mother/female guardian (in %)
Did not finish high school	28.7	25.9	8.6	3.7
Finished high school	28.7	20.7	19.6	20.6
Finished job-sponsored training/trade school	10.7	8.9	11.3	3.7
Some college or university	10.7	19.3	12.7	19.9
Finished college or university	21.3	25.2	47.8	52.1
Total	100.0	100.0	100.0	100.0

degree. In the HYS, over 95 per cent of female parents or guardians, and over 90 per cent of male parents or guardians, had finished high school, and 48 and 52 per cent had completed a college diploma or university degree, respectively.

Parents/Guardians' Employment
Direct comparisons of parent or guardian employment were difficult between the two samples because the HYS survey asked the youth participants about "current employment situation" of parents or guardians while the RB survey asked about the employment situation of the male and female parent or guardian "with whom you lived the longest (while at home)". The available data show that labour market attachment was tenuous for the parents or guardians of the RB youth. Only a little under half of the youth in the RB study reported that their male parent or guardian was never unemployed and a further 14 per cent said they had been unemployed only once. The comparative figures for the female guardian were 30 and 17 per cent, respectively. Referring to the current employment status of their parents or guardians of the HYS youth participants, 88 per cent reported that their father was currently employed, and 85 per cent report that their mother was also working outside the home. Bouts of unemployment were also relatively common while the RB participants were growing up.

In fact, 55 per cent of females and 33 per cent of males were "unemployed several times", "usually unemployed" or "always unemployed".

In brief, what these data on parents or guardians' educational attainment and labour force engagement tell us is that the street youth in our sample come from social conditions of relative disadvantage. One of our participants described her early living situation this way: "Mmm, sort of a difficult childhood because my mom was always working and my dad was in jail so I pretty much had to take care of myself at home." A male participant spoke about the crowded conditions at home which he still visits from time to time: "My older brother is sleeping in the living room, my little brother under the stairs in a storage closet ... [M]y mom's got a room, but other than that it's like pretty hectic, it's constant bickering. No, no privacy ...." Another male participant spoke about the money problems in his early life: "there was a lot of money issues ... [L]ike they were, my mom was on disability and my dad has like all these, I guess my dad's on disability too, broke his back when he was younger and, so there was money issues."

Childhood Family Stability and Parental Support
Household stability and supportive relationships with parents or guardians can help buffer the impact of adverse social conditions due to poverty (Hertzman & Wiens, 1996; Shanahan, 2000). We collected information on the living situation of youth in the two surveys by asking them to indicate which situation they lived in for a month or longer for each year of life. The list of living situations was extensive, ranging from "(1) both biological parents", "(2) mother only", "(3) father only" to "(26) other, please specify". Figs. 1 and 2 show the percentage of youth at each age who are still living in the family situation into which they were born. The representation is similar to a standard demographic population pyramid (Shryock, Siegel, & Associates, 1976). The RB female and male participants experienced considerable disruptions in their family in their early years. By their 13th birthday, less than one-quarter of these youth were living in the same living situation they experienced during the first year of their life. By their 13th birthday, 34 per cent had lived in two family situations and 40 per cent had lived in three or more family situations. Many of the RB youth lived in families in which their biological parents or guardians lived in separate households. Thirty-nine per cent of these youth had never lived with both biological parents for a month or longer. Two-thirds of the youth had lived with their mother only or with the mother and an unrelated adult for at least one month before their 13th birthday, while less than one-quarter had ever lived with their father only or with the father and an unrelated adult.

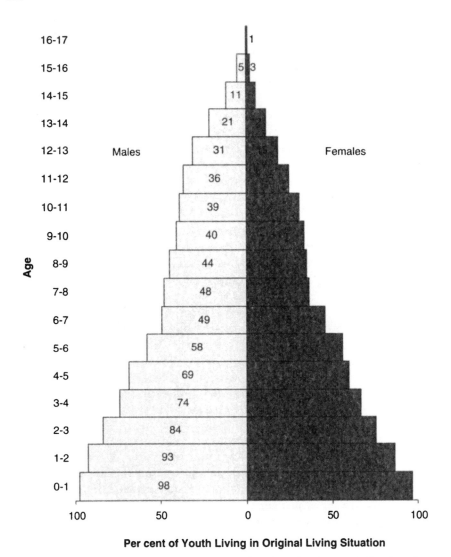

Per cent of Youth Living in Original Living Situation

Fig. 1. Per cent of Youth in First Living Situation, by Age and Gender, Street Youth.

Twenty-eight per cent of the youth had never lived with their biological father.

Male youth were more likely to have lived only in one living situation (27 per cent) than female youth (16 per cent) by their 13th birthday, but

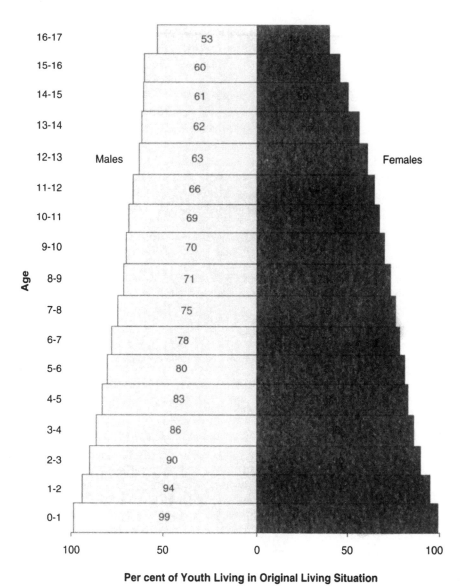

Per cent of Youth Living in Original Living Situation

Fig. 2. Per cent of Youth in First Living Situation, by Age and Gender, Random Sample.

female youth (64 per cent) were slightly more likely than male youth (56 per cent) to have spent at least one month living with both biological parents. Female youth were also slightly more likely than male youth to have lived with only one of their biological parents (alone or with an unrelated adult) for some time but were slightly less likely than males to have never lived with their biological father. In addition, 28 per cent of the RB participants had lived in a foster home at some point.

One of our female participants had this to say about her erratic living situation while growing up: "Ya, well, I was moving everywhere and I was getting shuffled from one place to the other and it was so hard to keep up." A male participant spoke about the lack of support in his early childhood and the caring burden he was expected to bear at an early age:

> Uh, my childhood was pretty rough, like I went through a lot and I think I went through ... [t]oo much for a child. I didn't really have a childhood 'cause I had to grow up too fast. I was already like, first time I was on the streets I was eleven and that was for like six months and then you know, moved back home and constantly getting kicked out and, and then I had to live with my sister ... and I had to take care of my nieces, my two little nieces, and it's like, I took on like, I don't know, it's like I was practically their parent, you know. I had to do everything for them, I had to cook, clean, you know, and do everything.

Another male participant described his childhood like this:

> Oh, I've been in so many foster homes where I've been beaten and, and just not fed really. It's like three times a day you're supposed to be fed and I only got fed like once and that shouldn't really be happening with children.

As Fig. 2 shows, the data available for the HYS youth tell a different story: about 60 per cent of them had only lived in one family situation by their 13th birthday. By that point, 20 per cent of these youth had lived in two, with the remainder having lived in three or more situations. Less than 1 per cent of the youth in the random sample said they had ever lived with foster parents. There were only small differences between female and male youth in the HYS. Within one or two percentage points, they were just as likely to have lived with both biological parents, their biological mother only, biological father only and never with their biological father.

We also investigated the quality of relationships our street youth sample had with the female and male parents or guardians with whom the youth lived for the longest time while growing up. When asked if their parents or guardians praised them for their achievements, just over one-third said that father or male guardian "usually" or "always" do. The figure for mothers or female guardians was higher, with over half usually or always offering praise.

On the other hand, about a quarter of the RB youth also said that their father or male guardian usually or always belittled them while they lived at home, and 20 per cent said their male parent ignored them. The corresponding figures for the mother or female guardian were 22 and 17 per cent.

Comparing male to female youth, it appears that while mother or female guardian was more likely to praise both female and male youth than was the male guardian, the difference in treatment was much more dramatic for male youth (63 and 36 per cent) than for female youth (48 and 41 per cent). The pattern of behaviour for belittling and ignoring was interesting because while 23 per cent of the female youth perceived that their father or male guardian belittled them "usually" or "always", the corresponding figure for mother was 28 per cent. This was the opposite pattern described by male youth (28 per cent about fathers and 14 per cent about mothers). While a substantially greater proportion of males than females declared that their guardians ignored them "usually" or "always" (just above 20 per cent of female youth versus just less than 15 per cent of male youth), a larger proportion of both genders said that this was the behaviour of their father rather than their mother.

One of our male participants spoke about his difficult relationship with his father:

> [M]y dad was always like angry at me. [W]hen I got home from school, he'd just be like yelling at me about like nothing, and then I would just like sit there and take it for a really long time and then when my mom got home I'd like be locked in my room and she would come and see what was wrong and then she'd go and talk to him. After that he wouldn't really talk to me, he'd just like make dinner and then go walk the dog and go to bed, and I'd just go to bed too. Then when I was like ten or eleven I started fighting back with him and like yelling at him for yelling at me.

One of the female participants said the reason why she much preferred living independently now was because:

> I came from everyone's always yelling and so stressed out and fighting and screaming and nothing's ever right, and it's not there, and it's just such a relief not to be there.

The HYS study included similar questions answered on a three-point scale about their mother and father currently. The data on these youth suggest a much more supportive environment. When asked if their male parent or guardian praised them, 80 per cent said it was "like him". When asked if their father belittles them, 84 per cent said "it was not like him", and when asked if he "ignores them" 89 per cent gave a similar negative response. The responses regarding mothers or female guardians to these three questions were even higher: 86, 91 and 94 per cent, respectively.

The differences between male and female youth were more consistent in the HYS. A greater number of youth responded that praising behaviour was associated with their mother than their father (83 and 78 per cent for male youth; 88 and 81 per cent for female youth). Both male and female youth were more likely to indicate that belittling and ignoring was not like their mother than they were to say the same about their fathers, although the differences were smaller for male youth (87 percent for male and 92 for female parent or guardian). In contrast, 81 per cent of female youth commenting on belittling said that this was not like their father, while 90 percent said this about their mother. The percentages for "ignores me" were 88 and 94 per cent for fathers and mothers, respectively.

These findings on the fundamental social factors separating the early lives of the street youth from same-aged peers in the random sample not only provide the context for understanding individually based risk behaviours, a dominant focus in the research literature, as noted above, but also provide evidence that street youth's life-course transitions occur in socio-economic and interpersonal contexts of relative disadvantage. Below we present data that suggest that these contexts of relative disadvantage alter the timing of life-course transitions. In particular, the street youth in our study appear to have moved beyond adolescence, and are, in many respects, experiencing at a different life-course stage – that of emergent adulthood.

Life-Course Markers of the Two Populations

Sociological markers of adolescence include co-residency with parents, full-time school attendance, financial dependence on parents or guardians, singlehood and few risk behaviours. Sociological markers of emergent adulthood include: transitory residency (own apartment, back with parents, living with friends, living with intimate partner, etc.), no longer in school, financial independence from parents, involvement in romantic relationships, and engagement in risk-taking behaviours such as use of addictive substances (George, 1993; Shanahan, 2000). We look at each of these markers in turn in order to examine differences and similarities in the life-course stages of the two groups of youth.

Residency Patterns
Fig. 3 shows the cumulative frequency distribution of first age at which the male and female participants in each study spent a whole year living without their biological parent, grandparent or other relative.

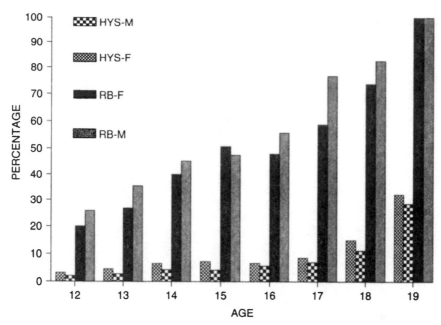

Fig. 3. Percentage of People Ever Having Lived a Whole Year Without Their Biological Parents, Grandparents or Other Relative. HYS-F, Healthy Youth Survey-Females; HYS-M, Healthy Youth Survey-Males; RB-F, Risky Business-Females; RB-M, Risky Business-Males.

Fig. 4 presents the data in a slightly different way by showing the cumulative frequency distribution of first age at which the male and female participants from both studies first "lived on their own" for at least 1 month, defined as with friends' families, boyfriend/girlfriend, with friends sharing an apartment/house/room, on the street, etc. The results from these two graphs show the dramatic differences in the residency patterns of these two groups of youth. By age 15, more than half of the RB participants had lived a whole year without their biological parent, grandparent or other relative whereas less than 8 per cent of the HYS youth had this experience by age 15. Looking at older HYS age cohorts (remembering that sample size declines as fewer and fewer observations are possible), it is clear that HYS youth with this experience are not anticipated to reach the magnitude of the RB youth until their early–mid- 20s.

Equally dramatic is the difference in the ages at which these youth first live on their own for a month or longer. Differences by the age of 15 are

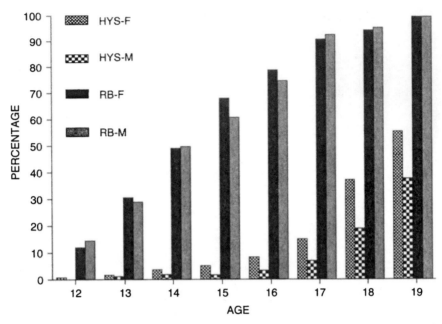

Fig. 4. Percentage of Participants Ever Having Lived a Month or Longer on Their Own; HYS-F, Healthy Youth Survey-Females; HYS-M, Healthy Youth Survey-Males; RB-F, Risky Business-Females; RBM, Risky Business-Males.

at least 10 times larger for RB youth than HYS youth. There are relatively few differences between male and female youth within these two samples, although female youth appear slightly more likely to both live on their own and live without a biological relative than their male peer. Gender differences in the RB sample are more complex, with males appearing to be more likely to live without a biological relative than their female peer at ages before 14. At age 14, female youth in this sample see a relatively dramatic increase, surpassing males until age 17.

School Attendance

The results for school attendance by gender for the two study populations show a similar pattern (Fig. 5) as found with early disengagement from the parental home presented above: by age 15, nearly two-thirds of the street youth are no longer attending the regular school system (including publicly funded "alternative schools" for youth experiencing problems in main-stream schools). This is in marked contrast to the HYS youth who are

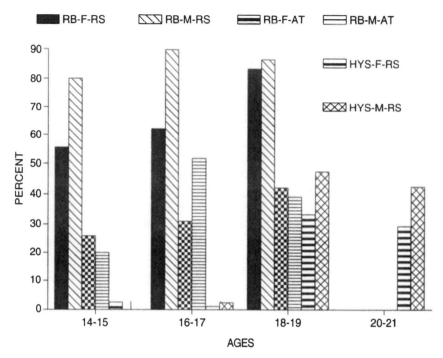

Fig. 5. Age-Specific Percentage of Participants Not Enrolled in School, Risky Business Females and Males Regular School (RB-F-RS, RB-M-RS), Risky Business Females and Males, Any Training (RB-F-AT, RB-M-AT), Healthy Youth Survey Females and Males Not Enrolled in Regular School (HYS-F-RS, HYS-M-RS).

almost universally enrolled in the regular school system until age 18 when there is a marked rise in non-enrolment following high school. However, a substantial number of RB participants were studying or receiving training in other ways, often via short vocational programmes, work preparedness programmes for youth or in voluntary self-directed learning programmes. Although male RB youth are more likely than their female peer to have withdrawn from the formal education system in the youngest age groups, there are few differences between males and females if other training is included. Among 16–17 year olds, however, more than half of all RB males are not in any training whereas almost 70 per cent of females are still accessing some kind of education or training programme.

What these data show is that HYS youth, whose parents overall are better educated and have higher-paying jobs, are more likely to remain in regular school than the RB youth. This is especially the case for males, which is also shown by the literature on education and social exclusion (Bourdieu & Passeron, 1977; Ready, 2001; OECD, 2006).

Financial Independence

Fig. 6 plots the percentage of HYS participants who worked during the current school year, compared to RB participants who worked in past 6 months. While the different periods considered in the two survey questions complicate direct comparisons, we make two observations. First, for both genders in the HYS labour participation generally increases with age. This is true in the final two age categories, where HYS participants, regardless of gender, have more labour-force participation than their same-aged counterparts in the RB study. Second, in contrast to the above, RB participants have higher labour participation levels in the earliest age interval. While the former finding indicates an earlier entry into emergent adulthood for the RB participants, the latter finding suggests that the RB youth do not become as

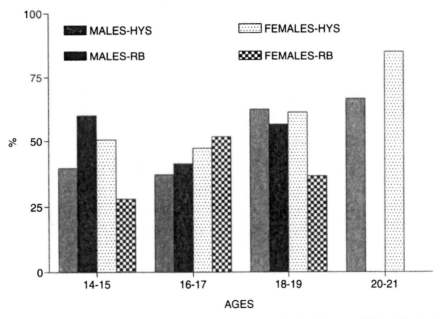

Fig. 6. Percentage of Healthy Youth Survey (HYS) Participants Who Worked During Current School Year Compared to Risky Business Respondents (RB) Who Worked in the Past 6 Months.

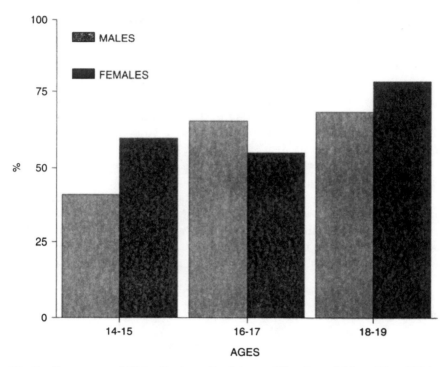

Fig. 7. Percentage of Risky Business Participants Who Earned More Than $70 in the Average Week from All Sources of Income.

well entrenched in the emergent adulthood life stage relative to the HYS youth.

However, the RB interview included a battery of questions on alternative sources of money such as panhandling, selling sex and selling drugs. The analysis of these data is presented in Fig. 7, showing the percentage of participants who earned more than $70 in the average week from all sources of income. These findings indicate a chronologically early approach to financial independence. This is particularly true for males, the majority of whom achieve this level of earning throughout the entire study period.

Intimate Partnerships
Another marker of emergent adulthood is the initiation of intimate relationships. In the HYS, this information came from the question about dating, with "dating" defined as "seeing someone or going out with

someone who is more than just a friend (could be a boyfriend or girlfriend)".
For the RB study, the corresponding question asked about being in a
"committed relationship". Fig. 8 depicts the age-specific results of these
questions for both samples. As previously found for labour force
participation (see Fig. 6), both male and female RB participants have
the highest levels in the earliest ages, with the HYS sample beginning at
low levels and then steadily increasing in the later age-groups. As with the
earlier data, our interpretation is that the RB youth are entering into
emergent adulthood before their same-aged HYS counterparts.

Other data on "ever pregnant/ever made someone pregnant" are
consistent with these findings: RB youth were more like to say "yes" to
this question during their teen years than counterparts in the HYS, and
females in both studies were more likely to answer positively. On the other
hand, there was little difference between the two groups with regard to the
use of protection when having sex: half of the street youth who engage in
vaginal sex said they "always" use a condom or barrier, and an additional

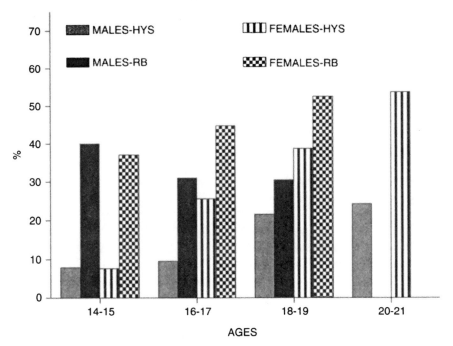

Fig. 8. Percentage of Healthy Youth Survey (HYS) Participants Currently Dating
in Comparison to Risky Business (RB) Respondents in a Committed Relationship.

21 per cent said they do so "most of the time". Fifty-nine per cent of the random sample of youth who said they were "sexually active" said they always use a condom when having sex.

Substance Use
The pattern observed above regarding residency, school attendance, economic independence and romantic relationships are also observed with substance use. While almost all the youth in the street youth sample have used marijuana in the last 6 months, use of this magnitude does not reach a comparable level in the random sample even by the age of 20–21 (Fig. 9). Interestingly, there are few differences in marijuana use between the genders in the younger ages but differences appear in the random sample among the older youth, with males declaring a slightly higher use. Analysis of the use of other drugs (hallucinogens and amphetamines) indicate that the female

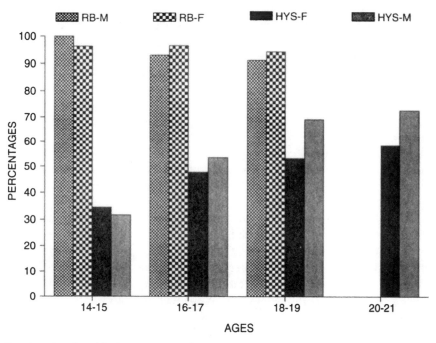

Fig. 9. Age-Specific Percentages of Survey Participants Who had Recently Used Marijuana; Risky Business Females and Males (RB-F, RB-M) Asked about Use in last 6 Months, Healthy Youth Survey Females and Males (HYS-F, HYS-M) Asked about Use in Past Year.

youth are heavier users of these drugs than male youth in the youngest ages with males being the heavier users in the older ages.

DISCUSSION

The results of this study call into question the assumption that street youth's involvement in "risky behaviours" during their teen years are what places them on abnormal and unhealthy pathways to adulthood. Our findings indicate, first, that one of the things at issue here are culturally constructed and class-sensitive notions of what are appropriate behaviours for specific chronological life stages. Whereas the youth in the random sample behave according to normative conventions associated with adolescence, the youth from the street-involved sample look more like their older counterparts – emerging adults – in many key respects. In particular, like young adults, street youth are living independently of their biological families, and are relatively deeply engaged in the economy (in their efforts to achieve some measure of economic independence). They are also likely to be in committed relationships that involve forming central emotional attachments outside their immediate family and to be experimenting with various drugs. Female street youth have, in most respects, become emergent adults before their male counterparts, indicating the importance of gender as a mediating variable between social conditions in early life and timing of life-course transitions.

As noted in the introduction, such normative notions of age-appropriate behaviour are contextually fluid. Currently normative life stages, such as childhood and adolescence, hold very specific cultural and historical provenances and are mediated by socio-structural backgrounds. Thus, what is considered acceptable for privileged youth is not viewed in the same light when applied to underprivileged youth. This disjuncture is very evident in the context of the lives of street youth; while drug use and frequent change of intimate partners are presented by some researchers as being part of a normal phase of identity building for emerging adults – indicating simply a desire to experiment with different identities and life experiences (Arnett, 2005; Schulenberg et al., 2005; Nelson & Barry, 2005) – for street youth, these are presented as "risks" for disease, addiction and morbidity.

This is not to suggest, however, that the differences between these two groups of youth are simply a matter of cultural construction and perception. The street youth captured in this sample come from backgrounds associated with disadvantage, and their early life experience is marked by poverty, instability and greater experiences of violence. In contrast, the middle-class youth who are "emerging into adulthood" in their very late teens and early 20s, and are the focus of the emerging adulthood literature, do so in the context of considerable social and family support.

In fact, the street youth in our sample, who seem to be experiencing early onset of this transitional phase, are unlike the more advantaged "emergent adults" in many ways. The transition between adolescence and adulthood for street youth is experienced in the context of a lack of social support and access to financial resources. They are thus "experimenting" with the markers and experiences of adulthood without a safety net. Even more important, however, is that the social conditions under which youth enter this transitional stage matter tremendously. In particular, the "fundamental determinants" (Link & Phelan, 1995) shaping street youth's gendered pathways to street involvement continue to make themselves felt as these youth transition into emerging adulthood: These include poverty, a chronic lack of shelter, unstable family relations, early severance of ties with educational institutions and a dependence on the informal economy.

We believe the advantage of examining street youth's activities through the lens of emerging adulthood is at least two-fold. First, it is a much less stigmatising perspective. Instead of understanding street youth through the vocabularies of risk, the emerging adulthood perspective suggests that the experiences of these youth be seen as part of a transitional phase, where experimentation with drugs, alcohol, sex, relationships and economic activity are expected parts of a process of identity building, and thus need to be evaluated along with social conditions before we can clearly conclude that it is primarily the experimentation that determine eventual outcomes. Second, viewing street youth through the lens of emergent adulthood has the potential to allow us to identify a useful site for social intervention. We believe, following Link & Phelan (2002), that the risk behaviours of street youth are "proximate" causes of their disadvantage and vulnerability, and thus interventions targeted at risk behaviours will be less effective in the long run than those that focus on the more structural causes. This means working towards providing the economic and social support that is necessary so that these vulnerable youth, like their more advantaged peers, can parlay the experiences of emerging adulthood into successful pathways to adulthood.

There are a number of limitations to the findings reported above. First of all, the street youth study is non-random and thus not necessarily representative of all street-involved youth in the region. Second, the random sample may underestimate the number of youth living in government care because of the inability of foster parents and many government workers to grant permission for youth to participate in the research. Also, data from both studies are youth's self-reports and we cannot assume they are unbiased. Parents' education and employment data are important proxy measures of family socio-economic status but do not provide a direct measure of family income, which is likely to be a key covariate. Finally, large parts of the data we presented for both studies are cross-sectional, and thus no firm causal conclusions can be drawn. Longitudinal analyses of the panel data are required to determine whether street youth's pathways to adulthood are normative or abnormal compared to youth in the general population.

CONCLUDING REMARKS

Until recently, street youth's life-course transitions have been treated as homogeneous and abnormal compared to youth in the general population. In this paper, we argue that this view is simplistic in the light of emerging evidence of the complex and multi-faceted transitions to adulthood being reported among young people in North America and Europe in late/post-modern societies (Shanahan, 2000). It may well be that other vulnerable groups of young people, like the street youth in our sample, are also facing reduced familial and social support, a shrunken period of adolescence and quick transition into adulthood and that this is especially likely to be the case for disadvantaged females. This is a topic that calls for further research so that we can place our preliminary findings on street youth in a comparative perspective.

The central theoretical contribution of this paper lies in applying the emerging adulthood perspective to the experiences of street youth. This perspective suggests that we understand street youth as much more than adolescents living a "high-risk" lifestyle. Instead, they are young people whose socio-economic and family backgrounds and the gender scripts of their society have pushed them prematurely out of childhood and adolescence and into a transition to adulthood. Furthermore, these "fundamental determinants" continue to shape how youth experience this transitional stage. In essence, thus, we argue that the long-term consequences faced by street youth are better understood as being the result of taking on the responsibilities of adulthood too early, and in the absence of familial and social supports.

REFERENCES

Ariès, P. (1965). *Centuries of childhood: A social history of family life*. New York: Vintage Books.

Arnett, J. (2005). The developmental context of substance abuse in emerging adulthood. *Journal of Drug Issues, 35*(2), 235–254.

Arnett, J. (2006). Emerging adulthood in Europe: A response to Bynner. *Journal of Youth Studies, 9*(1), 111–123.

Auerswald, C. L., & Eyre, S. L. (2002). Youth homelessness in San Francisco: A life cycle approach. *Social Science and Medicine, 54*, 1497–1512.

Bagley, C., & Young, L. (1987). Juvenile prostitution and child sexual abuse: A controlled study. *Canadian Journal of Community Mental Health, 6*, 5–25.

Benoit, C., Jansson, S. M., & Anderson, M. (2007). Understanding health disparities among female street youth. In: B. Leadbeater & N. Way (Eds), *Urban girls revisited: Building strengths* (pp. 321–337). New York: New York University Press.

Bledsoe, C. (1990). The politics of children: Fosterage and the social management of fertility among the Mende of Sierra Leone. In: W. P. Handwerker (Ed.), *Births and power: Social change and the politics of reproduction* (pp. 81–100). Boulder, CO: Westview Press.

Bourdieu, P., & Passeron, J. (1977). *Reproduction in education, society, and culture*. London: Sage.

Brooks, R., Milburn, N., Rotheram, M., & Witkin, A. (2004). The system-of-care for homeless youth: Perceptions of service providers. *Evaluation and Program Planning, 27*, 443–451.

Bynner, J. (2005). Rethinking the youth phase of life-course: The case for emerging adulthood? *Journal of Youth Studies, 8*(4), 367–384.

CIHI. (2005). *Improving the health of young Canadians*. Ottawa: Canadian Institute for Health Information.

Creswell, J. W. (2003). *Research design: Qualitative, quantitative and mixed methods approaches* (2nd ed.). Thousand Oaks, CA: Sage.

Cunningham, H. (1995). *Children and childhood in western society since 1500*. New York: Longman.

Ensign, J., & Bell, M. (2004). Illness experiences of homeless youth. *Qualitative Health Research, 14*, 1239–1254.

Ensign, J., & Gittelsohn, J. (1998). Health and access to care: Perspectives of homeless youth in Baltimore city, U.S.A. *Social Science and Medicine, 47*(12), 2087–2099.

George, L. (1993). Sociological perspectives on life transitions. *Annual Review of Sociology, 19*, 353–373.

Gittins, D. (1998). *The child in question*. London: Macmillan.

Green, S. T., & Goldberg, D. J. (1993). Female street worker prostitutes in Glasgow: A descriptive study of their lifestyle. *AIDS Care, 5*(3), 321–335.

Hagan, J., & McCarthy, B. (1997). *Mean streets: Youth crime and homelessness*. London: Cambridge University Press.

Hartnagel, T. (1998). Labour market problems and crime in the transition from school to work. *Canadian Review of Sociology and Anthropology, 35*(4), 435–459.

Heckathorn, D. (1997). Respondent driven sampling: A new approach to the study of hidden populations. *Social Problems, 44*, 174–199.

Heinz, W., & Marshall, V. W. (2003). *Social dynamics of the life course: Transitions, institutions, and interrelations*. New York, NY: Walter Gruyter, Inc.

Hendrick, H. (1997). *Children, childhood and English society, 1880–1990*. Cambridge, UK: Cambridge University Press.

Hertzman, C., & Wiens, M. (1996). Child development and long-term outcomes: A population health perspective and summary of successful interventions. *Social Science and Medicine*, *43*(7), 1083–1095.

Hyde, J. (2005). From home to street: Understanding young people's transitions into homelessness. *Journal of Adolescence*, *28*, 171–183.

Jansson, S., & Benoit, C. (2006). Respect or protect? Ethical challenges in conducting community-academic research with street-involved youth. In: B. Leadbeater, E. Banister, C. Benoit, M. Jansson, A. Marshall & T. Riecken (Eds), *Ethical issues in community-based research with children and youth* (pp. 175–189). Toronto, ON: University of Toronto Press.

Kraus, D., Eberle, M., & Serge, L. (2001). *Environmental scan on youth homelessness: Final report*. Ottawa: Canada Mortgage and Housing Corporation.

Levander, C., & Singley, C. (2003). *The American child: A cultural studies reader*. New Brunswick, NJ: Rutgers University Press.

Link, B., & Phelan, J. (1995). Social conditions as fundamental causes of disease. *Journal of Health and Social Behavior* (Special issue), 80–94.

Link, B., & Phelan, J. (2002). McKeown and the idea that social conditions are fundamental causes of disease. *American Journal of Public Health*, *92*(5), 730–732.

Morgan, D. L. (1998). Practical strategies for combining qualitative and quantitative methods: Applications to health research. *Qualitative Health Research*, *8*, 362–376.

Morse, J. (2003). Principles of mixed methods and multi-method research designs. In: A. Tashakkori & C. Teddle (Eds), *Handbook of mixed methods in social and behavioural research*. Thousand Oaks, CA: Sage.

Nelson, L., & Barry, C. (2005). Distinguishing features of emerging adulthood: The role of self-classification as an adult. *Journal of Adolescent Research*, *20*, 242–262.

OECD. (2006). *Education at a glance: OECD indicators – 2006 edition*. Paris: OECD.

O'Grady, B., & Gaetz, S. (2004). Homelessness, gender and subsistence: The case of Toronto street youth. *Journal of Youth Studies*, *7*, 397–416.

Panter-Brick, C., & Smith, M. (2000). *Abandoned children*. Cambridge, UK: Cambridge University Press.

Pedersen, W., & Hegna, K. (2003). Children and adolescents who sell sex: A community study. *Social Science and Medicine*, *56*, 135–147.

Raleigh-DuRoff, C. (2004). Factors that influence homeless adolescents to leave or stay living on the street. *Child and Adolescent Social Work Journal*, *21*, 561–572.

Ready, D. (2001). Finding or losing yourself? Working class relationships to education. *Journal of Education Policy*, *16*(4), 333–364.

Sá, I. (2000). Circulation of children in eighteen-century Portugal. In: C. Panter-Brick & M. Smith (Eds), *Abandoned children* (pp. 27–40). Cambridge, UK: Cambridge University Press.

Scheper-Hughes, N., & Sargent, C. (1998). *Small wars: The cultural politics of childhood*. Berkeley, CA: University of California Press.

Schulenberg, J. E., Merline, A. C., Johnston, L., O'malley, P., & Bachman, J. (2005). Trajectories of marijuana use during the transition to adulthood: The big picture based on national panel data. *Journal of Drug Issues*, *35*, 255–279.

Schwartz, S., Cote, J., & Arnett, J. (2005). Identity and agency in emergent adulthood: Two developmental routes in the individualization process. *Youth and Society, 37*, 201–229.

Shanahan, M. (2000). Pathways to adulthood in changing societies: Variability and mechanisms in life course perspective. *Annual Review of Sociology, 26*, 667–692.

Shryock, H. S., Siegel, J. S., & Associates. (1976). *The methods and materials of demography* (Condensed edition by E.G. Stockwell). New York: Academic Press.

Silbert, A., & Pines, M. (1981). Sexual child abuse as an antecedent to prostitution. *Child Abuse and Neglect, 5*, 407–411.

Silbert, A., & Pines, M. (1982a). Victimization of street prostitutes. *Victimology, 7*, 122–132.

Silbert, A., & Pines, M. (1982b). Entrance into prostitution. *Youth and Society, 13*, 417–500.

Smart, R. G., Adlaf, E. M., & Walsh, G. (1992). Adolescent drug sellers: Trends, characteristics and profiles. *British Journal of Addiction, 7*, 1561–1570.

Tanner, J. (1993). Resilient survivors: Work and unemployment among high school drop-outs. *British Journal of Education and Work, 6*(1), 23–43.

Tyler, K. A., Hoyt, D. R., & Whitbeck, L. (2000). The effects of early sexual abuse on later sexual victimization among female homeless runaway adolescents. *Journal of Interpersonal Violence, 15*, 235–250.

Willis, P. (1977). *Learning to labor: How working class kids get working class jobs.* New York, NY: Columbia University Press.

Witkin, A., Milburn, N. G., Norweeta, G., Rotheram-Borus, M., Batterham, P., May, S., & Brooks, R. (2005). Finding homeless youth: Patterns based on geographical area and number of homeless episodes. *Youth and Society, 37*, 62–84.

PART IV:
CHANGING DISCOURSES OF CHILDHOOD

CHILDREN, NEW SOCIAL RISKS AND POLICY CHANGE: A LEGO™ FUTURE?

Jane Jenson

INTRODUCTION

Recent intensification of the "politicisation of childhood" has been observed by analysts in numerous social science disciplines, and in a variety of public policy domains. Sociologists of childhood, for example, often attribute this greater politicisation both to shifts in the social construction of "social problems" and visions of children's agency (for example Mayall, 1994; Oakley, 1994, p. 17; Qvortrup, 1994; Livingstone, 2002, p. 13). Others observe this politicisation in changing patterns of defamilialisation and refamilialisation of social care and their implications for patterns of social solidarity (Leira & Saraceno, 2002 or Wincott, 2006, for example). Indeed, the politicisation of childhood – defined as the move from childhood being understood as primarily a family or parental responsibility to it being also a matter of public importance and concern – has emerged as a major theme in debates about "modernising" social policy paradigms (for example, Leira, 2002; Jenson, 2004; Esping-Andersen, Gallie, Hemerijck, & Myles, 2002).

The reasons suggested for the patterns of politicisation are varied. For one approach, operating at a macro-level of analysis, it is the inevitable result of late modernity and the embrace of the concepts of risk society and

Childhood: Changing Contexts
Comparative Social Research, Volume 25, 357–381
Copyright © 2008 by Emerald Group Publishing Limited
All rights of reproduction in any form reserved
ISSN: 0195-6310/doi:10.1016/S0195-6310(07)00012-9

individualisation (Prout, 2000 provides one overview), with some pointing particularly to the notions of "responsibility" underpinning governmentality practices in neo-liberalism (Rose, 2000, p. 1405 for example). Focussing on structured patterns of social relations, transformations in the work–family nexus as well as significant shifts in income distribution, a second approach identifies rising poverty and threats of social exclusion as the reason for a growing policy focus on children (Saraceno, 2001; Leira, 2002, Ch. 1). Numerous analyses also point to the strong linkage between the mounting popularity of the economic discourse of human capital and rise of child-centred policy perspectives both during and after neo-liberalism (for example, Myles & Quadagno, 2000; Saint-Martin, 2000; Lister, 2003; Dobrowolsky & Saint-Martin, 2005).

NEW SOCIAL RISKS AND PARADIGM CHANGE

This article shares the perspective of the second approach, focusing on the ways childhood has been politicised since the mid-1990s, in particular since what Porter and Craig (2004, p. 391) describe as the watershed year of 1997.[1] Over the past decade one dimension of the politicisation of childhood has involved devoting explicit public policy attention to children, to child poverty, to reconciling work and family responsibilities and to early childhood education and care (ECEC). In many countries, these policy foci increasingly arise as responses to what are termed the "new social risks." New social risks result from income and service gaps in post-industrial labour markets.[2] Compared to the labour market of the industrial era, there has been a loss of well-paid and traditionally male jobs in production and an increase in low-paid and often precarious service jobs sectors, with many families falling into the category of the "working poor." This is one social risk of inadequate income security. There has also been an increase in the female employment rate and virtually all adults are now expected to be actively engaged in employment. The male bread-winner model has been eclipsed (Lewis, 2001). Such changes in employment plus family transformations generate a higher risk of low-income and precariousness in several ways. For example, lone-parent families headed by women are significantly more likely to be in low-income. In addition, restructuring of labour markets and transformations of family and demography create challenges to traditional public as well as private assumptions about provision of social care. Inadequate access to social care for children is, then, also on the list of new social risks, when young families lack access to affordable and quality child care and yet all adults in the family must enter the labour force. In many ways, then, policy attention to new social risks has led to a politicisation of childhood.

Policy responses to the new social risks can be grouped under three inter-related categories: services for the elderly and disabled; services for families with children; active labour market policies. Comparison of spending levels in European countries between 1980 and 1999 reveals that across all welfare regime types, there has been an expenditure increase in all three categories. While the rates and amounts differ, there is no exception to the trend (Taylor-Gooby, 2004, Table 1.1, p. 16). Many protections against the "old social risks" – such as access to pensions; health care; primary, secondary and post-secondary education for example – addressed in the so-called golden age of the post-1945 welfare state have often been redesigned via privatisation or off-loading to the third sector. In contrast, the new social risks have received some infusion of public funds for services. According to Francis Castles (2005, p. 420), who compared the years from 1990 to 2001 across 21 OECD countries, the overall result is that "... although the pace of structural change has not been dramatic, it has been quite consistent, suggesting a developmental tendency of precisely the kind predicted by the 'new social risks' hypothesis." Across all regime "families," services have gained ground in the expenditure mix. With the exception of the Bismarkian continental cases, the shift was particularly pronounced in the last period for which he has data, 1998–2001 (Castles, 2005, p. 419). As Giuliano Bonoli (2005, p. 446) puts it:

> In a majority of OECD countries social programmes providing protection against new social risks are still at an embryonic stage, but virtually everywhere these issues are being discussed in public debates. There are big country variations in the extent to which NSR [new social risk] coverage has been developed, with the Nordic countries being at the forefront. However, even in those countries lagging behind in the adaptation of their social protection systems, essentially the conservative welfare states of continental and Southern Europe, some steps in this direction have been taken.

Levels of benefits, policy instruments and overarching goals have all changed. Families have been relieved of some responsibility for social care, for example, as public spending on and provision of ECEC has increased and moved in the direction of universality (OECD, 2001, 2006). New programmes have been instituted, relying on a variety of instruments to provide "payments for care" to the vulnerable elderly and disabled persons. Both mark a move away from post-1945 assumptions that families would take responsibility for the cost and provision of social care (Daly & Lewis, 2000; Jenson, 2004). Another example of change comes from the area of income security. Increasingly, reliance on wage supplements to the working poor makes the state and the market sectors jointly responsible for the *earnings* package. Again, the levels and instruments vary, but reliance on supplements to the earnings of the "working poor" reflects an understanding of market failure different from that underpinning policy design of the post-1945 decades.[3] Social knowledge and its statistical techniques are also being redesigned, as analyses focused on inequality and poverty at certain key junctures of the life course replace cross-sectional measures. Most broadly, notions of equality have been altered, focusing more on opportunities for the future than on the here-and-now and the development of all children (not only those "at-risk") has become the concern of states as well as families (Jenson, 2004). There has been, in other words, a shift in the policy paradigm.[4]

The proposition of this article is that such modifications in levels of benefits, policy instruments and overarching goals in response to what policy networks identify as new social risks have prompted creation of and adherence to a future-oriented policy paradigm, one that involves a significant level of politicisation of childhood. It is a policy paradigm that often evokes intergenerational solidarity and life-course risks and seeks instruments to limit them. The paradigm's instruments are multi-purpose, intended to support activation now and in the future. Thus, they respond to parents' need for support in reconciling work and family life, a mounting need as women's labour is mobilised in the post-industrial service economy. Beyond that however, ECEC services are intended to foster social inclusion by limiting the long-term and life-course effects of childhood poverty, while often evidencing less concern with the poverty of adults who are not parents of dependent children. Thirdly, a goal is to promote skills appropriate for the rapidly changing labour markets of the "knowledge economy," for future generations of workers as well as those in the labour force now, so that activation objectives can be achieved.

Convergence around ideas for a social architecture of prevention, investment and activation to reduce the effects of new social risks, prompt us to label it the *LEGO™ paradigm* (Jenson & Saint-Martin, 2006). As a paradigm, it shapes understandings of social risks, while providing policy prescriptions and suggesting instruments and even setting benefit levels. The consolidation of the LEGO™ paradigm for drawing and building a new social architecture to address the so-called "new social risks" is a significant factor in accounting for the politicisation of childhood. This politicisation is observed not only in the OECD world but also in the global South, promoted by international players such as the World Bank.[5]

At this point a caveat is in order. When we describe the LEGO™ paradigm, we are neither endorsing it nor claiming that it is being fully implemented (Jenson & Saint-Martin, 2006, p. 434). To say that a new paradigm is in place and that it focuses on new social risks does not mean that its discourse and instruments produce outcomes that correspond to its promises. The Keynesian macro-economic paradigm did not produce "full employment." The discourse of equality underpinning post-1945 welfare regimes did not produce "full equality," even in those countries most influenced by the principles of social democracy. Nonetheless, the Keynesian paradigm did give rise to policy analysis and interventions different from those of its predecessor liberalism and of monetarism, with its own outcomes and effects. When feminists identified post-1945 welfare regimes that were more "women friendly" than others, they could also document the differences in the norms and practices of social protection that distinguished them from those in which equality did not include a gender component. In other words, identifying the norms underpinning a paradigm is one type of analytic task. It is not the same as assessing outcomes, but it is a worthwhile task in itself for what it helps to understand policy communities' idea sets, diagnoses, prescriptions and interventions.

The next sections present the LEGO™ paradigm. In doing so, the article focuses on the notions of childhood and children that underpin it and identifies some of the ways in which expectations of childhood are altered when the paradigm's principles are adopted. The article concludes with a brief discussion of the politics of paradigm change.

THE LEGO™ PARADIGM

The name of this well-known toy is appropriated here in two ways. First, it is a metaphor, to describe convergence around some basic building blocks of a social architecture; three are identified. Second, its self-description actually allows us to capture the key features of the future-oriented, investment-centred activation strategy currently advocated as a blueprint for welfare state redesign in policy circles, one that involves a significant politicisation of childhood.

The company describes its *raison d'être* this way. It sees: "children as natural learners. These are precious qualities that should be nurtured and stimulated throughout life. ... 'Play' in the LEGO™ sense is learning. By helping children to learn, we build confident, curious and resourceful adults. For their future. And ours."[6] Moreover, while a toy, LEGO® is also appropriate for lifelong learning: "LEGO products are developed in such a way that there is something for all ages and stages of development. From kindergarten toddlers, schoolchildren and teenagers to young-at-heart adults. There's something for everyone."[7]

The corporate philosophy illustrates at least three key features of what we term the LEGO™ paradigm. First, it clearly focuses on *learning as the route to security* throughout the life course. Play is educational and useful because it fosters the capacity for continuous learning, flexibility and adaptability. Second, this philosophy has an *orientation to the future*. Children who play with LEGO now are already creating their future.[8] Finally, it suggests how activities in the present are ultimately *beneficial for society as whole*, and not only for the individuals themselves. Successful play in childhood enriches the community. This metaphor of constant learning, knowledge acquisition, involvement and engagement as well as the notion of open-ended results and variety is particularly appealing in the so-called knowledge-based world. Each of these three building blocks can be easily identified in current policy thinking and they all involve a politicisation of childhood. The next sections provide examples.

Learning as the Route to Security

In policy circles sensitive to the challenge of new social risks, security is defined as the capacity to confront challenges and adapt. Lifelong learning, for example, permits acquisition of new or updated skills; early childhood learning prepares this capacity. Rather than providing social protection, the goal of this new social architecture is to provide a trampoline that can constantly reinsert people into employment.[9] From this perspective, acquisition of human capital is proposed as a response to the changes associated with de-industrialisation, the growth of the service economy and, particularly, the emergence of a knowledge-based economy.

The LEGO™ paradigm's focus on learning extends the long-standing concern with formal education to other types and moments of learning. In the past, secondary and post-secondary education provided credentials for life. Now, technological change, labour force restructuring and corporate insistence on "flexibility" mean that there is a high risk that schooling and training undertaken in adolescence will become out-dated and new skills will have to be acquired. Moreover, for decades "full employment" was defined as only half the population. Now policies of activation seek to raise employment rates across the board; all women as well as men are expected to participate in the paid labour force. With such expectations, policy communities fear new patterns of exclusion will be entrenched, due to inadequate access to knowledge as well as the deterioration of skills because of withdrawal or exclusion from the labour force. The solution proposed is learning throughout the life course. Policy suggestions range from promoting a start in very early childhood to retaining the labour force's skills by encouraging the most experienced older workers to postpone retirement. Policies also include attention to groups "at risk" of inadequate skill acquisition or retention.

There is agreement that one critical building block is human capital acquisition, with learning being a key tool for adjusting to the new economy *and* for promoting social inclusion. One result has been increased focus on early childhood and pre-school children. While early childhood is obviously not seen as the only moment for learning, it is a privileged one.[10] For example, reflecting on a high-level conference entitled *Beyond 2000: The New Social Policy Agenda*, OECD documents called for (Pearson & Scherer, 1997, pp. 6–8): "A new approach to social protection [that] will have a stronger emphasis on interventions earlier in life and more preventive (and less remedial) measures. The goal would be to re-define equity and security in terms of barriers towards life-course flexibility ... ."

One important result has been growing attention to ECEC. Concerns about women's human capital are part of the analysis of new social risks. They are considered to be particularly at-risk of succumbing to exclusion from the knowledge-based economy, while there is also a sense that human capital is "wasted" when well-educated women withdraw from the labour force because social policy encourages familialist arrangements.[11] As a result, there has been a politicisation of child care around concerns about reconciling work and family (Leira, 2002, Ch. 2). The European Union, for example, has established the Barcelona targets for member states' provision of child care services.[12] Bismarkian welfare states have altered their appreciation of women's employment as well, and in consequence, child care services. Swiss and German family policies, for example, are moving away from the male breadwinner model and providing greater support for working mothers (Bonoli, 2005; Hausermann, 2005, for example).

Nonetheless, objectives for expanded ECEC go well beyond addressing parents' need to reconcile work and family responsibilities. Policy communities' definition of ECEC as part of *any* learning strategy is exploding, based on a growing body of scientific data, especially from longitudinal studies, of the long-term effects of early educational experiences. For example, the European Commission's Communication on Education and Training (European Commission, 2006b) asserts: "Pre-primary education has the highest returns in terms of the achievement and social adaptation of children. Member States should invest more in pre-primary education as an effective means to establish the basis for further learning, preventing school drop out, increasing equity of outcomes and overall skill levels."

The OECD has emerged as a flagship organisation in the transformation of "day care" into "early childhood education and care" (Mahon, 2007). It has undertaken an ambitious series of studies of ECEC, launched out of the 1996 Ministerial meeting on *Making Lifelong Learning a Reality for All*. The Organisation also reports that a clear pattern has emerged: "The trend in all countries is toward full coverage of the 3–6-year old age group, aiming to give all children at least 2 years of free publicly funded provision before beginning compulsory schooling" (OECD, 2001, p. 48 and *passim*). The international organisation supports this trend, in addition to recommending that parental leaves be long enough to provide care for and bonding with newborns but not so long as to allow mothers' own human capital to stagnate.

Countries such as the United Kingdom, that had been major laggards in the provision of even custodial day care, have undertaken to improve their ECEC services (Wincott, 2006). After its 1997 victory, for example, New Labour immediately announced a National Childcare Strategy and the creation of new spaces in nursery schools. In the run-up to the 2005 election, the Chancellor of the Exchequer Gordon Brown promoted his 10-year Strategy for Childcare as a key electoral plank, one that would supposedly give every child "the best possible start in life" (Dobrowolsky & Jenson, 2005, p. 219). This emphasis on early childhood in the LEGO™ paradigm takes a page from the book of some Nordic countries, where municipal governments are now required to provide a child care space to all pre-school child whether their parents are employed or not, in the name of achieving good developmental outcomes (OECD, 2006, Table 4.1, pp. 81–82).

Such an emphasis on universal provision means that policy goals for ECEC go well *beyond* the notion that child care is necessary so that mothers can seek employment, or to allow the reconciliation of work and family life. Pre-school education and early remedial interventions for developmental delays are deemed essential so that children will have the foundational skills to be life-long learners and avoid the long-term costs associated with precocious school failure (OECD, 2006, p. 12). This notion crosses regime types. For example, the Finnish government states that "growing and learning are understood to constitute a lifelong process. Upbringing at home and in ECEC forms the foundation for lifelong learning" (Finland, 2004, p. 8). In the liberal British welfare regime too, the government says: "childcare services need to be high quality, and need to reflect a child's different needs throughout its life" (HM Treasury et al., 2004, p. 17).

If new attention to quality in early childhood programmes reflects the politicisation of childhood inherent to the LEGO™ paradigm, there is still space, just as there was under the previous paradigm, for variation on three dimensions of instrument design: who cares, who pays and how child care is provided (Jenson, 1997, pp. 186–88). Such choices will have consequences for the specific implementation of the paradigm and the extent to which quality in ECEC is a goal. France, for example, has changed its answer to two of these questions in major ways over the last decades. In the past, most public expenditure for toddlers went to *crèches*. Now the state relieves parents of significant portions of the costs of care and there is little expectation that parents of infants and toddlers will do all the caring.[13] But, public spending has gone primarily to programmes that provide incentives to parents for hiring childminders, including those with no training. This policy choice is driven by the goal of supporting activation of the female labour force, both women with toddlers and women providing informal care for toddlers.[14] French governments have consciously and determinedly moved to reinforce the informal sector of child care, with major subsidies going to parents hiring babysitters and other informal carers for their infants and toddlers, despite the lower quality of such care and ample criticism from experts outside as well as inside France (Jenson & Sineau, 2001, Ch. 4; OECD, 2004).

The Nordic countries have gone in yet another direction in designing their instruments. These countries demonstrate less concern about increasing their already high female employment rates than do Bismarkian welfare regimes. Some have been, therefore, willing to use public funds to pay parents to provide child care for infants and toddlers as well as to subsidise private provision. In 1985, the Finnish carers' allowance was extended to parents providing their own child care until the child reaches age 3. Norway too offers parents a care allowance if they do not use public child care services. These choices are justified in terms of "quality child-rearing," supposedly allowing parents time to transmit their values to their children (Ellingsæter, 2003, p. 427; OECD, 1999, p. 26).

Although public funds still provide a significant share of the costs of child care, several central governments have also tried to off-load responsibility for provision to employers. The 2001 Dutch legislation on child care is based on an expectation that collective agreements will push employers into covering one-third of the costs. Income-tested subsidies to parents are available when employers fail to meet this expectation. This approach was part of a broader move to a supply-side approach that has raised fears about loss of quality control (OECD, 2006, p. 108).

As these examples show, shared appreciations of investments in human capital to protect against new social risks prompt a politicisation of childhood, albeit not always in the same way. In some cases there has been a focus on *children's pre-school education*, while in others the attention is more on the conditions for *activation of women* and therefore measures to support reconciliation of work and family life. In the latter case, babysitting and unregulated care may be considered sufficient. Most jurisdictions are refusing this stark choice, however, and they are being pushed to do so by experts in child development who stress the need for "holistic services" (for example, Moss, 2004, p. 9; also OECD, 2006).

Orientation to the Future

The emphasis in the LEGO™ paradigm on individuals and their human capital, both as ECEC and life-long learning, owes a good deal to practices initiated in some of the Nordic welfare regimes that pursued active labour market policies and universal ECEC in advance of them being promoted by the OECD, the EU and many national governments.[15] Thus, their contribution to the first dimension of the paradigm is significant. The focus on future life-chances described in this section, however, owes most to the emerging principles of liberal welfare regimes and international organisations such as the OECD and World Bank.

In the LEGO™ paradigm, social policy is future-oriented because of its investment theme. Investments imply a particular notion of time. They generate dividends in the future, whereas consumption (that accountants label an expense) is something that occurs in the present (Jenson & Saint-Martin, 2003, pp. 83–89). This position is reflected in a recent communiqué after a gathering of OECD social affairs ministers: "social policies must be pro-active, stressing investment in people's capabilities and the realisation of their potential, not merely insuring against misfortune," which is what the ministers considered post-1945 social protection did.[16] Notions of prevention quickly lead to a politicisation of childhood.

Many countries now choose to supplement the low incomes of the working poor and, especially those with children, the objective being to reduce the chance that children are subjected to a childhood of poverty.

Social knowledge about the relationship between childhood poverty and future life chances and circumstances are an important part of the policy discourse.[17] As UNICEF's experts at the Innocenti Centre put it, echoing a broad consensus in academic research (UNICEF, 2000, p. 3): "Whether measured by physical and mental development, health and survival rates, educational achievement or job prospects, incomes or life expectancies, those who spend their childhood in poverty of income and expectation are at a marked and measurable disadvantage."[18] New Labour in Britain re-iterates the analysis frequently: "Investment in children to ensure that they have opportunities and capabilities to contribute in positive ways throughout their lives is money well spent and it will reduce the costs of social failure" (HM Treasury et al., 2004, p. 2). Providing supplements to family income, in the form of cash transfers targeting children in poor households has become increasingly popular. The liberal welfare regimes have begun to use such cash benefits extensively (Mendelson, 2003), while Eastern European countries after 1989 shifted away from universal benefits to targeting (Barrientos & DeJong, 2006). The World Bank – no proponent of generous state expenditures – finds the investment frame a useful one for justifying new public spending, promising to invest in children and making a "business case" for such investments.[19] For its part, the European Union has begun targeting "children in poverty" with the notion being for many that there should be "children mainstreaming" (Heikkilä, et al., 2006, p. 21; Atkinson, Cantillon, Marlier, & Nolan, 2005).

Such future-oriented calculations imply a conception of equality different from the one that informed the post-war welfare state when social policy focused on redistribution and on fostering greater equality in the here-and-now (whether or not those goals were ever achieved). In contrast, the LEGO™ paradigm emphasises equality of life chances, a much more liberal philosophical stance.

Childhood is also often politicised when the acquisition of assets for the future becomes a policy goal. Many countries now promote the idea that children need to learn good saving habits and accumulate assets that will grow into the future.[20] Responsibility for making sure children both have assets and learn good middle-class saving habits is shared by governments and families, with governments setting up incentives for parents to save as well as providing assets directly to children. For example, along with other instruments for encouraging people to save, New Labour has instituted the *Child Trust Fund* which provides a "stake" to every newborn. In Mexico the conditional cash transfers (CCT) include asset accumulation mechanisms linked to bonuses for graduation (Luccisano, 2006).

The investment and savings theme in the LEGO™ paradigm has taken another form as well, encouraging individuals to take responsibility for their key life transitions, by saving money to exchange for time, including parenting time. For example, explicitly addressing the new social risks theme, the Netherlands recently introduced an individual life-cycle savings scheme. It is described this way by the Dutch Minister of Social Affairs (Geus, 2005):

> The money in the savings account can be used for various forms of unpaid leave, such as caring for children or ill parents, schooling, a sabbatical or, indeed, early retirement. This reduces the risk of unwanted withdrawals from the labour market, particularly by working mothers, and unnecessary absenteeism because of illness or disability.

The notion that time must be "saved" before it can be "spent" is quite different from the various sorts of leaves and career breaks developed to address "old" risks, such as childbirth or unemployment.[21] These were granted according to need rather than on the basis of good planning.

Benefits for Society as a Whole

The company promises that when children play with LEGO they are building not only "their future, but ours." For example, the 2002 Italian agreement to reform labour market and employment benefits was titled the "Pact for Italy," to indicate the extent of the general interest involved in, among other things, improving life-long learning and education.[22] There are several versions of the idea that combating new social risks enrich the collective good. One is a simple notion of prevention. For example, a report to the Government of Ontario, that has profoundly influenced Canadian policy discourse, puts the issues together this way (McCain & Mustard, 1999, p. 15):

> Over time, increased community-based initiatives and investment (public and private) in early child development and parenting will pay off through a population with better competence and coping abilities for the new global economy ... . This investment will be much more cost-effective than paying for remediation later in life, such as treatment programs and support services for problems that are rooted in poor early development.

But the larger idea is clearly expressed in a recent article entitled *Time to change. Towards an active social policy agenda* (Martin & Pearson, 2005):

> The evidence is there to show that active social policies can make a real difference to people's lives. And we must not forget that in doing so, active social policies not only

help the poorest and most disadvantaged in society. More and more productive workers mean healthier economies, and everyone gains from that. Active social policies can benefit us all.

There are two ideas embedded in this position: that work is the route to maximising individuals' well-being and that the well-being of society and social cohesion depend on such activity. These two ideas lie at the heart of strategies for confronting new social risks, and have resulted in the popularity of instruments to promote activation and benefit levels being set to "make work pay."[23] These ideas are linked to the politicisation of childhood in two ways: via the increase in mothers' employment and via concerns about preparing "all" children for active working lives.

Women entering the labour force have prompted a number of items to appear on the list of "new social risks"; we have already documented the consequences for ECEC services. Gone is any distinction (except for the small minority that might afford it) between those who should be active in the labour market, "bringing home the bacon" and those who should care for hearth and home, kith and kin (Lewis, 2001). But such public investment in services is described as having a societal dimension as well as an individual one. They are also meant to reap the long-term advantage for the whole society that subscribers to the LEGO™ paradigm believe will come from such spending. Britain's Chancellor of the Exchequer, Gordon Brown, is fond of repeating: "Our children are our future and the most important investment we can make as a nation is in developing the potential of all our country's children. Together we can ensure that no child is left behind" (quoted in Dobrowolsky & Jenson, 2005, p. 208). Also from a country that has relatively recently discovered the need for more investment in child care services, the Dutch Minister of Social Affairs, A.J. de Geus, put it this way: "… together we are working on the future of the European Union. A future which will benefit from good childcare!" (quoted in Jenson & Saint-Martin, 2006, p. 443).

POLICY CHANGE AND THE POLITICISATION OF CHILDHOOD

An intensified politicisation of childhood has occurred with the move towards the LEGO™ paradigm, a set of building blocks that include learning as the route to security, a future orientation, and the ways in which investing in children benefit the collective good. The next step in the analysis is to explore the ways in which this paradigm has taken hold, displacing earlier policy perspectives centred on the male breadwinner and his family as well as redistribution to achieve greater equality. Two types of explanations for the change must be considered. A first and most obvious is the pressure coming from fundamental transformations in the economy, the labour market and family and gender relations. Social changes in homes and at work have created the "new social risks" that generate a set of challenges for policy makers. A second explanation – the one developed here – while acknowledging the contribution of social change puts the emphasis on the development of new idea sets shared across policy communities as the impetus for paradigm change.

Sociology has a long tradition of analysing modernisation, and treating social changes as the drivers of policy design, especially transformations in family structures and practices, labour force restructuring and the age structure of society. When the welfare state first became an object of study, theories of industrialism were used to account for rising expenditure levels across the board and irrespective of party ideology (Myles & Quadagno, 2002, p. 36; Castles, 2005, pp. 412–413). This tradition was then widely criticised from a multitude of "politics matters" positions; the influential studies of welfare regimes, state institutions, or varied patterns of class and gender relations and power resource approaches all gained credence. There is now a tendency to return to macro-sociological explanations, however.[24] Focussing on globalisation, post-industrialism or a gender revolution some sociologists are again deploying structural arguments. Myles and Quadagno (2002, p. 45) describe one popular version of such analyses, the "service economy 'trilemma' in which postindustrialism means that countries must sacrifice full employment, fiscal balance, or equality. Policy makers can pursue two of these objectives but not all three simultaneously." This is a structural analysis par excellence. It leaves decision-makers to make choices only within the terms of the game set out by postindustrialism.[25] Indeed, Myles and Quadagno (2002, p. 46) ask: "Is postindustrialism the new iron cage for welfare states?"

This renewed enthusiasm for structural arguments can not provide an account of why there has been a politicisation of childhood, however.[26] Why have the challenges of post-industrialism generated a particular way of interpreting social risks and responding to them? If there is a "developmental tendency of precisely the kind predicted by the 'new social risks' hypothesis" (Castles, 2005, p. 420), it is still necessary to track the factors that have led to attention to the new social risks. As Hall (1993, p. 279, emphasis added) reminds us: "... policymakers customarily work within a framework of ideas and standards that specifies not only the goals of policy and the kinds of instruments that can be used to attain them, but also *the very nature* of the problems they are meant to be addressing." Beyond the definition of the problems, we must then trace their translation into strategies whose accent is on the future rather than the present, which display a willingness to promise spending more on "social investments" than on social protection as well as the other tropes of the LEGO™ paradigm. A focus on change in the labour market and even attention to family transformations can not provide full answers to queries about why there is a new paradigm. Social change does not, by itself, explain policy choices.

Political factors must be considered, including institutions and interests. As the concern of this article is with paradigm change, ideas must also figure among these factors (Jenson, 1989; Hall, 1993). Ideas allow coherence of interpretation, from diagnosis to intervention. They work at the front end of the policy process to provide an interpretation of the problem and they influence practice because they "constrain the normative range of legitimate solutions available to policy makers" (Campbell, 1998, p. 385). But ideas do not, by themselves, make change. There must also be an institutional shift in the "locus of authority over policy, achieved when the supporters of the alternative paradigm are able to secure positions of authority over policy-making" (Hall, 1993, pp. 280–81). In other words, there must be a change in policy communities, one that *may* follow from adjustments in the configuration of interests of political parties and eventually governments.[27] These newly empowered actors will bring their own interests to bear in making policy choices within key institutions. Therefore, to track the emergence of the LEGO™ paradigm we should look for the development, within policy communities, of coherence in interpretation of the challenges and the appearance in positions of authority of the promoters of the ideas.

We can see the emergence of a coherent position around the LEGO™ paradigm by the mid-1990s. It was anchored in a number of international institutions and national settings. At that time both international organisations and centre-left political parties began to turn away from the classical neo-liberal stances associated with Margaret Thatcher's British Conservatives, Ronald Reagan's Republicans in the United States and the Washington consensus for the global South. They sought an alternative (Porter & Craig, 2004, pp. 387–388, 391). Straightforward neo-liberalism had come to an ideational and a political impasse; the Thatcherite dictum that "there is no alternative" lost its political resonance, and this happened due to several reasons. The promised cutbacks in state activity and massive savings in state expenditures had failed to materialise (Huber & Stephens, 2001, p. 2).[28]

Social problems intensified. Poverty rates steadily mounted, especially among lone-parent and young families (Saraceno, 2000, pp. 165–166). Fears about social cohesion began to preoccupy policy-makers. Almost simultaneously, in a few years in the mid-1990s, institutions as widely diverse as the governments of France, the Netherlands, Britain and Canada, international organisations such as the OECD and the Council of Europe and the European Union made social cohesion a focus of their policy thinking (Jenson, 1998, pp. 4–5; Saraceno, 2001; Levitas, 2006, p. 124, 131). Instruments to foster social cohesion and ensure social inclusion joined their long-standing attention to employability and competitiveness, retained from the neo-liberal years.

It was long before the politicisation of childhood emerged within this idea set. By 1996 the high-level OECD conference of ministers and senior officials, *Beyond 2000: The New Social Policy Agenda* was calling for a modernised welfare state which would require:

> that social expenditures be focused on areas where returns are maximised in the form of social cohesion and active participation in society and in the labour market. As with all investment, this implies taking a long-term view of the costs and benefits ... . Such an approach implies greater investment in children and young adults, as well as the maintenance of human capital over the life course. (quoted in Dobrowolsky & Jenson, 2005, p. 205)[29]

Such thinking is part of "after neoliberalism," when the accent shifts from simplistic commitments to cutbacks to strategic "social investments," particularly investment in human capital, and when supply-side employability analyses give way to notions that activation requires some attention to the demand side of the labour market and the kinds of jobs it is creating.

These ideas circulated widely within international organisations. But beyond that, they were also taken up by numerous national governments (Deacon, 2001; Porter & Craig, 2004). The ideas made headway in influencing the design of policy when their promoters took over positions of authority in policy-making. They were particularly appealing to centre-left politicians and parties whose "modernised" programme depended on the promise to eliminate weaknesses in post-1945 systems of social protection that neo-liberals had identified and that had gained the latter popular support. Centre-left political actors relied on the themes of the LEGO™ paradigm, including about childhood, in order to transform their political identity, thereby serving their fundamental political interest in gaining and maintaining political power. They could take their distance from the traditional positions of their own party by claiming to reject any return to the "bad old days" of taxing and spending. They could claim to be "modern" by announcing what they had learned from the best of neo-liberalism. But they could also stress that new spending to fight child poverty and on social care meant they still retained their most basic traditional values and commitments to social justice. As Bonoli puts it, they could make a virtue of the vice of spending, allocating public funds to programmes that had not gained the patina of familiarity from the post-1945 decades (Bonoli, 2005, p. 442ff.).

In Britain, for example, the Labour Party had been striving since its disastrous defeats by the Thatcher and Major Conservatives to recast its identity, to become a "modern" party. "Modernisers" gained substantial ground during John Smith's brief tenure (1992–1994) at the head of the party. He set up the Commission on Social Justice (CSJ – sometimes termed the Borrie Commission) in 1992, symbolically choosing the 50th anniversary of the Beveridge Report. Many of the themes of the LEGO™ paradigm were present 2 years later in the Commission report, which was also a major site for the politicisation of childhood. For example, it declared: "the investment we make in babies and young children is wholly inadequate" (CSJ, 1994, p. 122), and asserted that "children are not a private pleasure or a personal burden; they are 100 percent of the nation's future" and that "the best indicator of the capacity of our economy tomorrow is the quality of our children today" (CSJ, 1994, p. 311). There were two action conclusions drawn: (1) "The first and most important task for government is to set in place the opportunities for children and adults to learn their personal best. By investing in skills, we raise people's capacity to add value to the economy, to take charge of their own lives, and to contribute to their families and communities" (CSJ, 1994, pp. 119–120); and (2) "the best way to help the one in three children growing up in poverty is to help their parents get jobs" (CSJ, 1994, p. 313). The CSJ was a source of many of the ideas and institutional innovations implemented by New Labour after 1997.

In 1997 the Liberal Party of Canada was struggling to regain some of its lost authority within the federation and chose to mount its struggle by relying on the themes of the LEGO™ paradigm. The 1997 Speech from the Throne (the government's statement of priorities) was one that clearly politicised childhood: "An optimistic country is one that chooses to invest in its children. Investments in the well-being of today's children improve the long-term health of our nation. A growing economy that creates jobs is the best guarantee for our children's future."[30] Such understandings led directly to policy action to redesign income security programmes, via the National Child Benefit and other measures (Jenson, 2004, pp. 182–183).

But it was not only the centre-left that had an interest in childhood being more politicised. In countries where the centre-right succeeded social democratic governments, they too could make use of the fact that childhood was politicised. Centre-right coalitions could finally achieve some of conservatives' long-standing goals of supporting parental care and privatising services, all in the name of re-equilibrating policy values.[31] They could appeal to the discourse of "quality child care" when supporting payments to promote parental care. However, the power of the activation themes in the LEGO™ paradigm, as well as the centrality of the notion of investing in human capital meant that the centre-right coalitions could not simply advocate a return to the past. Any incentives for parental care were confined to infants and toddlers. Non-parental care was not rarely rolled-back; indeed, in some cases it was extended (Ellingsæter, 2003, pp. 439–440). In part this was due to the power of the ideas, and in part to the fact that parties were frequently compelled to create coalitions and compromise around the ways to address new social risks (Ellingsæter, 2003; Bonoli, 2005; Hausermann, 2005). The consensus around a LEGO™ paradigm thereby took shape within state institutions under the aegis of these parties, seeking to broker a broad spectrum of interests and appeal to a wide variety of groups and categories of voters.

The European Union has come relatively late to the LEGO™ paradigm (Jenson, 2007). It has been more of a "policy taker" with respect to it, importing ideas and policy analyses from Member States and international organisations and then repackaging them as an interpretative frame for all member states. With respect to ECEC, for example, it has tended until recently to emphasise the reconciliation agenda more than the advantages of investment in pre-school programmes (Moss, 2004). In 2006, however, the Commission issued two communications in which a LEGO™ style of analysis was clearly present. One on education and training made the now familiar arguments about the payoffs of investing in ECEC (European Commission, 2006b, pp. 4–5) and the communication on the rights of the child advanced the notion of the long-term risks of child poverty (European Commission, 2006a). In both cases, the EU institutions were aligning their understandings of new social risks with the paradigm now predominant in many countries and international bodies.

CONCLUDING REMARKS

In the last decade the politicisation of childhood observed within a variety of disciplines and across many public policy domains has not been a chance event, nor is it sui generis. Rather, this article has documented the extent to which the politicisation of childhood is a key pillar of a new social policy paradigm taking shape in numerous countries and promoted within a wide range of international organisations as well as by the European Union. Recognition of and responses to new social risks by policy communities has prompted change of three types. Benefit levels have been adjusted to be sure. But beyond those the instruments of policy intervention and the very objectives of policy have been altered. Movement on the latter two, and especially the third, marks, according to Peter A. Hall's (1993) classic analysis, a paradigm shift. A coherent set of ideas has developed around the three dimensions of the LEGO™ paradigm, and these ideas have been carried into key political institutions by actors, especially parties in government, that have an interest in identifying themselves with "after neoliberal" policy stances or building a stable coalition with those who do.

The goal of this article was to document the coherence of the new norms, so as to render the extent of the change more visible. It is not, by any means, an analysis of the consequences of the politicisation of childhood. All this talk about children does not mean that because they are the object of policies children are thriving. Policies to fight "child poverty" leave many children and their parents with low and often inadequate income. Instruments to promote social inclusion result in many children and their families being little more than marginal insiders. Even talk about the importance of ECEC does not translate everywhere into adequate access to quality services for all the children who need them or all the parents who want them. Promises to provide assets to all children do not do much to undermine the income differences that support unequal class structures, ... and so on. While this article has described the paradigm shift, the next step is to assess its consequences.

NOTES

1. That year 1997 was one in which "... a range of critics assailed neo-liberalism's legitimacy, many from within the headline international financial institutions" (Porter & Craig, 2004, p. 391). It was the year of the Asian financial crisis and the year the World Development Report called for a more capable state as well as the year New Labour defeated the British Conservatives, that the OECD worried that structural adjustment policies were undermining social cohesion (OECD, 1997), that the Canadian government redesigned social assistance programmes via the National Child Benefit (Jenson, 2004), the Mexican government introduced its conditional cash transfers to support poor households with school-age children (Barrientos & DeJong, 2006), and so on.

2. For analyses using the concept of new social risks see, among others, Bonoli (2005), Taylor-Gooby (2004), Jenson (2004, 2007), and Armingeon and Bonoli (2006, Ch. 1).

3. Benefits paid as wage supplements may be "work-tested" (available to any worker whose earnings level falls below the line) or may be "child-tested" (available only to workers with low earnings and a dependent child). Britain's Working Tax Credit is an example of the first, and the Canada Child Tax Benefit is an example of the second.

4. In his classic article on policy paradigms, Peter A. Hall (1993, p. 278 and *passim*) defines a change in policy paradigm as a shift in overarching goals as well as techniques and precise settings. Change only on the latter two would lead, in his terms, to second or first-order policy change.

5. Reliance on many of the same policy instruments – income supplements; conditional cash transfers; child-testing of benefits – is not discussed here. For some discussion, see Barrientos and DeJong (2004, 2006).

6. From http://www.lego.com/build, consulted 26 July 2005.

7. From http://www.lego.com/eng/info/default.asp?page = lifelong, consulted 18 July 2006.

8. This may seem an unnecessary point, but debate over whether the politicisation of childhood should involve children "in the here and now" or "adults in becoming" is a lively one. See, for example, Lister (2003) and OECD (2001, p. 8).

9. Barrientos and DeJong (2004) describe a very similar politicisation of childhood involving many of the elements of the LEGO™ paradigm in the global South and focused on human capital. There, however, the shift is termed one towards "social protection" rather than social investment.

10. For examples of the LEGO™ paradigm's focus on learning by adults see Jenson and Saint-Martin (2006, pp. 435–37).

11. EU analyses have often focused on this risk. See, for example, *The Social Policy Agenda 2000–2005* (European Commission, 2000, pp. 14–15).

12. The EU targets are to provide childcare by 2010 to at least 90% of children between 3 years old and the mandatory school age and at least 33% of children under 3 years of age. Report of the Barcelona European Council, 15–16 March 2002, p. 12. Available on: http://europa.eu/european_council/conclusions/index_en.htm

13. The situation of infants and toddlers is most relevant here, because almost all pre-schoolers are in the educational system by age 3. However, but many of the subsidies provided are available for care of older children as well.

14. A recent overview of public support for child care costs shows France to have the most elaborate subsidy programmes directly targeted to informal care. Most other countries either do not fund it (providing subsidies only for formal care) or provide a general subsidy that may be used for some forms of informal care (Immervoll & Barber, 2005, pp. 59–62).

15. "This type of policy orientation, which also includes 'in-work' benefits or work subsidies, is sometimes seen as 'neo-liberal' and coercive, but actually has a long and honourable history as part of Swedish social democratic active labour market policy" (Ferrera & Rhodes, 2000, p. 5).

16. Final communiqué, Meeting of OECD Social Affairs Ministers, 1 April 2005. Available at: www.oecd.org/document/47/0,2340,en_21571361_34360727_34668207_1_1_1_1,00.html. Consulted 28 August 2005.

17. On the social investment and child poverty link in British social policy analysis see Dobrowolsky and Jenson (2005). For an overview of several international examples see Jenson (2004, p. 170).

18. The emphasis on investing in ECEC services so as to counter the detrimental effects of growing up in low-income is not new, of course. After 1945 publicly funded child care was meant to respond to "exceptional" cases – poor children at risk of inadequate parenting or children whose mothers had no "choice" but to seek employment (Jenson & Sineau, 2001, p. 246). However, as the OECD now notes (2006), ECEC is seen as a key preventive measure. See for example the recent Communication of the European Commission (2006b, pp. 4–5), where the investment benefits are graphed or the OECD's summary of its work on ECEC (2006), where the theme is constantly present.

19. See "Why Invest in Children and Youth?" On http://web.worldbank.org/WBSITE/EXTERNAL/TOPICS/EXTCY/0,contentMDK:20243901~menuPK:565261~pagePK:148956~piPK:216618~theSitePK:396445,00.html. Consulted on 31 July 2006.

20. For an overview of asset-building initiatives see OECD (2003, pp. 15–35).

21. For example, in the mid-1980s Belgium created a paid Voluntary Career Break to allow workers to meet family or other circumstances. They were not "saved for," and employers had to replace the worker on leave with another from the unemployment rolls (Jenson & Sineau, 2001, Ch. 3). In the case of maternity – and in contrast to "parenting time" – all countries in the EU 15 (except the UK) provide paid maternity leaves. This has been the case for several decades, since childbirth has always been treated as a health – and therefore "old" – risk. For details see www.childpolicyintl.org/maternity.html

22. Since the Pact was not signed by the largest union confederation, its relevance may be more symbolic than real.

23. *The International Reform Monitor, #9*, 2004: 8 reports that activation strategies have been adopted in virtually all the 15 countries it monitors. See http://www.reformmonitor.org

24. For one discussion see Castles (2005).

25. This notion of the trilemma is popular. See for example its use in Esping-Andersen et al. (2002, p. 187). Anne Wren (2001) argues that countries in each regime type might have made a different political choice, but all were basically constrained by being in the same "game."

26. They might, of course, help to understand the convergence around one dimension of it – public support for non-parental child care, as the service economy calls on women's work.

27. Obviously, not all changes in government lead to a change in paradigm. One of the very definitions of a stable paradigm is that its principles and practices are widely shared across the political spectrum (Jenson, 1989).

28. In the 1980s rates of growth in spending were 3.2% of GDP and it was only in the first half of the next decade that they began to decline (Castles, 2005, p. 416).

29. The report of this conference is found in OECD (1997).

30. Available in the Chrétien archives of the Privy Council Office, on: http://www.pco-bcp.gc.ca/default.asp?Language=E&Page=archivechretien&Sub=FactSheets&Doc=fact_sh19970923639_e.htm. Consulted 23 July 2006.

31. Ellingsæter (2003, p. 426ff.) describes how the victory of the centre-right in Norway in the mid-1990s brought such a move, in the name of "reinstating a balance" between non-parental and parental care as well as public and private provision.

REFERENCES

Armingeon, K., & Bonoli, G. (Eds). (2006). *The politics of post-industrial welfare society*. New York: Routledge.

Atkinson, T., Cantillon, B., Marlier, E., & Nolan, B. (2005). *Taking forward the EU social inclusion process*, Final Report to the Luxembourg Presidency. Available at: http://www.ceps.lu/eu2005_lu/report.cfm. Consulted 5 November 2006.

Barrientos, A., & DeJong, J. (2004). *Child poverty and cash transfers*. London: CHIP (Childhood Poverty Research and Policy Centre), Report #4.

Barrientos, A., & DeJong, J. (2006). Reducing child poverty with cash transfers: A sure thing? *Development Policy Review, 25*(50), 537–552.

Bonoli, G. (2005). The politics of the new social policies: Providing coverage against new social risks in mature welfare states. *Policy & Politics, 33*(3), 431–449.

Campbell, J. L. (1998). *Institutional change and globalization*. Princeton, NJ: Princeton University Press.

Castles, F. (2005). Social expenditures in the 1990s: Data and determinants. *Policy & Politics, 33*(3), 411–430.

CSJ (Commission on Social Justice). (1994). *Social justice: Strategies for national renewal. Report of the commission on social justice*. London: Vintage.

Daly, M., & Lewis, J. (2000). The concept of social care and the analysis of contemporary welfare states. *British Journal of Sociology, 51*, 281–298.

Deacon, B. (2001). International organizations, the EU and global social policy. In: R. Sykes, B. Palier & P. Prior (Eds), *Globalization and European welfare states. Challenges and change* (pp. 59–76). Houndsmill: Palgrave.

Dobrowolsky, A., & Jenson, J. (2005). Social investment perspectives and practices: A decade in British politics. In: M. Powell, L. Bauld & K. Clarke (Eds), *Social policy review #17* (pp. 203–230). Bristol, UK: The Policy Press.

Dobrowolsky, A., & Saint-Martin, D. (2005). Agency, actors and change in child focused future: 'Path dependency' problematised. *Journal of Commonwealth and Comparative Politics, 4*(1), 1–33.

Ellingsæter, A. L. (2003). The complexity of family policy reform. *European Societies, 5*(4), 419–443.

Esping-Andersen, G., Gallie, D., Hemerijck, A., & Myles, J. (2002). *Why we need a new welfare state*. Oxford: Oxford University Press.

European Commission. (2000). *Social policy agenda*. Communication from the Commission. COM (2000) 379 final.

European Commission. (2006a). *Towards an EU strategy on the rights of the child*. COM (2006) 367 final.

European Commission. (2006b). Efficiency and equity in European education and training systems. COM (2006) 481 final.

Ferrera, M., & Rhodes, M. (Eds). (2000). *Recasting European welfare states*. London: Frank Cass.

Finland. (2004). *Early childhood education and care in Finland* (ISSN: 1236–2123). Helsinki: Ministry of Social Affairs and Health.

Geus, A. J. de. (2005). Netherlands. Welfare to strengthen the economy. *OECD Observer, 248* (March).

Hall, P. A. (1993). Policy paradigms, social learning, and the state. The case of economic policymaking in Britain. *Comparative Politics, 25*(3), 275–296.

Hausermann, S. (2005). *Different paths of modernization in contemporary family policy. The political dynamics of reform in German and Swiss family policies since the mid-1970s.* Paper prepared for the ECPR Conference, Budapest, 8–10 September.

Heikkilä, M., Moisio, P., Riatakallio, V.-M., Bradshaw, J., Kuivalainen, S., Hellsten, K., & Kajanoja, J. (2006). *Poverty policies, structures and outcomes in the EU25.* Helsinki: Ministry of Social Affairs and Health.

HM Treasury, Department for Education and Skills, & Department for Work and Pensions. (2004). *Choice for parents, the best start for children: A ten year strategy for childcare.* Norwich: HM Treasury, December. Available on: www.hm-treasury.gov.uk. Consulted 15 March 2005.

Huber, E., & Stephens, J. D. (2001). *Development and crisis of the welfare state: Parties and policies in global markets.* Chicago: University of Chicago Press.

Immervoll, H., & Barber, D. (2005). *Can parents afford to work? Childcare costs, tax-benefit policies and work incentives.* OECD Social, Employment and Migration Working Papers, #31. Paris: OECD.

Jenson, J. (1989). Paradigms and political discourse: Protective legislation in France and the United States before 1914. *Canadian Journal of Political Science, 22*(2), 235–258.

Jenson, J. (1997). Who cares? Gender and welfare regimes. *Social Politics. International Studies in Gender, State and Society, 4*(2), 182–187.

Jenson, J. (1998). *Mapping social cohesion. The state of Canadian research.* Ottawa: CPRN, Study F|03. Available on http://www.cprn.org

Jenson, J. (2004). Changing the paradigm. Family responsibility or investing in children. *Canadian Journal of Sociology, 29*(2), 169–192.

Jenson, J. (2007). Social investment for new social risks: Consequences of the LEGO™ paradigm for children. In: J. Lewis (Ed.), *Children, changing families and welfare states* (pp. 27–50). Cheltenham: Edward Elgar.

Jenson, J., & Saint-Martin, D. (2003). New routes to social cohesion? Citizenship and the social investment state. *Canadian Journal of Sociology, 28*(1), 77–99.

Jenson, J., & Saint-Martin, D. (2006). Building blocks for a new social architecture: The LEGO™ paradigm of an active society. *Policy & Politics, 34*(3), 429–451.

Jenson, J., & Sineau, M. (2001). *Who cares? Women's work, childcare, and welfare state redesign.* Toronto: University of Toronto Press.

Leira, A. (2002). *Working parents and the welfare state: Family changes and policy reform in Scandinavia.* Cambridge: Cambridge University Press.

Leira, A., & Saraceno, C. (2002). Care: Actors, relationships and contexts. In: B. Hobson, J. Lewis & B. Siim (Eds), *Contested concepts in gender and social politics* (pp. 65–83). Aldershot: Edward Elgar.

Levitas, R. (2006). The concept and measurement of social exclusion. In: C. Pantazis, D. Gordon & R. Levitas (Eds), *Poverty and social exclusion in Britain.* Bristol, UK: The Policy Press.

Lewis, J. (2001). The decline of the male breadwinner model: Implications for work and care. *Social Politics. International Studies in Gender, State and Society, 8*, 152–169.

Lister, R. (2003). Investing in the citizen-workers of the future: Transformations in citizenship and the state under New Labour. *Social Policy and Administration, 37*(5), 427–443.

Livingstone, S. (2002). *Young people and new media. Childhood and the new media environment.* London: Sage.

Luccisano, L. (2006). The Mexican *oportunidades* program: Questioning the linking of security to conditional social investments for mothers and children. *Canadian Journal of Latin American and Caribbean Studies, 31*(62), 53–86.

Mahon, R. (2007). The OECD and the reconciliation agenda: Two blueprints. In: J. Lewis (Ed.), *Children, changing families and welfare states* (pp. 173–197). Cheltenham: Edward Elgar.

Martin, J., & Pearson, M. (2005). Time to change. Towards an active social policy agenda. *OECD Observer, 248* (March).

Mayall, B. (Ed.) (1994). *Children's childhoods: Observed and experienced.* London: The Falmer Press.

McCain, M. N., & Mustard, F. (1999). *Reversing the real brain drain: The early years study final report,* available at www.children.gov.on.ca. Consulted 1 August 2006.

Mendelson, M. (2003). *Child benefits levels in 2003 and beyond: Australia, Canada, the UK and the US.* Ottawa: Caledon Institute. Available at www.caledoninst.org

Moss, P. (2004). *Getting beyond childcare, quality .... and the Barcelona targets.* Speech prepared for the conference: Child care in a changing world, Groningen, the Netherlands, 21–23 October. Available at www.childcareinachangingworld.nl/results1.html. Consulted 29 July 2005.

Myles, J., & Quadagno, J. (2000). Envisioning a *third way*: The welfare state in the twenty-first century. *Contemporary Sociology, 29*(1), 156–167.

Myles, J., & Quadagno, J. (2002). Political theories of the welfare state. *Social Service Review* (March), 34–57.

Oakley, A. (1994). Women and children first and last. Parallels and differences between women's and children's studies. In: B. Mayall (Ed.), *Children's childhoods: Observed and experienced* (pp. 13–32). London: The Falmer Press.

OECD (Organisation for Economic Co-operation and Development). (1997). *Societal cohesion and the globalising economy. What does the future hold?* Paris: OECD.

OECD. (1999). *Early childhood education and care policy in Norway.* Country Note. Paris: OECD.

OECD. (2001). *Starting strong: Early childhood education and care.* Paris: OECD.

OECD. (2003). *Asset building the escape from poverty: An introduction to a new welfare policy debate* (DELSA/LEED/DC(2003)5). Paris: Directorate for Employment, Labour and Social Affairs.

OECD. (2004). *Early childhood education and care policy in France.* Country Note. Paris: OECD.

OECD. (2006). *Starting strong II.* Paris: OECD.

Pearson, M., & Scherer, P. (1997). Balancing security. *OECD Observer, 205*(April–May), 6–9.

Porter, D., & Craig, D. (2004). The third way and the third world: Poverty reduction and social inclusion in the rise of 'inclusive' liberalism. *Review of International Political Economy, 11*(2), 387–423.

Prout, A. (2000). Children's participation: Control and self-realisation in British late modernity. *Children and Society, 14*, 304–315.

Qvortrup, J. (1994). Childhood matters. An introduction. In: J. Qvortrup, M. Bardy, G. Sgritta & H. Wintersberger (Eds), *Childhood matters: Social theory, practice and politics*. Aldershot: Avebury.

Rose, N. (2000). Community, citizenship, and the third way. *American Behavioral Scientist, 43*(9, June–July), 1395–1411.

Saint-Martin, D. (2000). De l'ètat-providence à l'ètat d'investissement social? In: L. A. Pal (Ed.), *How Ottawa spends 2000-2001: Past imperfect, future tense* (pp. 33–58). Toronto: Oxford University Press.

Saraceno, C. (2000). Italian families under economic stress. *Labour, 14*(1), 161–184.

Saraceno, C. (2001). *Social exclusion: Cultural roots and diversities of a popular concept.* Presented at the conference on Social Exclusion and Children. Institute for Child and Family Policy, Columbia University, 3–4 May. Available on www.childpolicy.org, consulted 18 July 2006.

Taylor-Gooby, P. (Ed.) (2004). *New risks, new welfare.* Oxford: Oxford University Press.

UNICEF. (2000). *A league table of child poverty in rich nations*, Innocenti Report Card #1. NY: Innocenti Research Centre.

Wincott, D. (2006). Paradoxes of New Labour social policy: Toward universal child care in Europe's 'most liberal' welfare regime? *Social Politics: International Studies in Gender, State, and Society, 13*(2), 286–312.

Wren, A. (2001). The challenge of de-industrialisation: Divergent ideological responses to welfare state reform. In: B. Ebbinghaus & P. Manow (Eds), *Comparing welfare capitalism: Social policy and political economy in Europe* (pp. 239–269). Japan: Routledge.

INVESTING IN CHILDREN AND CHILDHOOD: A NEW WELFARE POLICY PARADIGM AND ITS IMPLICATIONS

Ruth Lister

INTRODUCTION

> Childhood often represents a central arena through which we construct our fantasies about the future and a battleground through which we struggle to express competing ideological agendas. (Timimi, 2006, p. 35)

> One critical part of the future is our children. The way we bring them up is an indication of how we feel about the future; and of course our attitudes to the young and ideas on how they should be educated reveal much about the present .... Without a strong sense of how we want the future to be, the government tends to revert to a default position, thinking mainly about how children will fit into the economy. (Davison, 2005, p. 7)

These quotations, taken from two British policy and political journals, are illustrative both of the contemporary politicisation of childhood and of the way children are frequently constructed in terms of the future they represent. After years of relative neglect, making Britain a 'contender for the title of worst place in Europe to be a child' (Micklewright & Stewart, 2000a, p. 23), children are now a primary focus of policy-making and of much political and media debate (Margo, Dixon, Pearce, & Reed, 2006). Prime Minister Gordon Brown has created a new government department of Children, Schools and

Childhood: Changing Contexts
Comparative Social Research, Volume 25, 383–408
ISSN: 0195-6310/doi:10.1016/S0195-6310(07)00013-0

Families. Dominant representations simultaneously frame children as investments in the future and as anti-social, unruly, disrespectful threats to social order in the present. Counter discourses represent children as citizens and rights-bearers who should be treated with respect by adults.

This is the political context for this article, which addresses the politicisation of childhood through the lens of what has been termed the new welfare policy paradigm of investing in children. The article starts by briefly describing its emergence and then argues that there are two broad models within this paradigm, which can be summed up in the ideas of a 'good childhood' and a 'profitable investment'.[1] The article will provide a critical analysis of the future-oriented 'profitable investment' model in which children figure as 'becomings' rather than 'beings' (to use the language of the new sociology of childhood) (Fawcett, Featherstone, & Goddard, 2004; Qvortrup, 2005).

Variants of the alternative 'good childhood' model, in which children are seen as 'beings', are being argued for by critics of the 'profitable investment' approach in the UK and, in a more normative section, the article will suggest what such a model might look like. It is one which fits well with the social democratic tradition of the Nordic welfare states. Of course, these are analytical models in which the differences are drawn more boldly than is the reality, and in practice an individual welfare state may draw on the elements of both. Nevertheless, governments who wish to adopt the investing in children welfare policy paradigm face a strategic choice as to whether to prioritise 'good childhood' or 'profitable investment' as the *primary* goal. Their decision will have implications for the nature of the policy regime that develops and for children themselves.

THE EMERGENCE OF THE NEW WELFARE POLICY PARADIGM

The new investing in children paradigm has been promoted by a number of international bodies, notably the OECD and the European Commission, over the past decade. In 1996, an OECD conference on the 'new social policy agenda' concluded with a call for a social investment approach, which prioritises investment in children and young adults. The 2000 EU Lisbon Summit saw investment in people as key to modernisation of the European social model. The Belgian Presidency of the European Union commissioned Gøsta Esping-Andersen and colleagues in 2001 to draw up a report on the new architecture of the European welfare states. The report, which has since been published in book form (and is discussed further below), articulates the general goal of 'a child-centred social investment strategy' as the foundation stone for this architecture (Esping-Andersen, 2002, p. 26). In an analysis of children's rights in the EU, the European Children's Network (EURONET) observes that:

> it is possible to discern the emergence at EU level of a social investment perspective over a social protection agenda – particularly in relation to demography, employment, education, and childcare – which has implications for children

and their place on the policy agenda (Ruxton, 2005, p. 19). From the standpoint of 'the good childhood' model, EURONET warns that, although such a perspective

> can have the effect of moving children and families higher up the policy agenda as improving their circumstances is seen to be an investment in society's future

it 'can simultaneously deflect attention from children's rights and well-being in the present' (*ibid.*). This is a theme developed further here.

MODEL 1: PROMOTING PROFITABLE INVESTMENT

The contours of the 'profitable investment' model are by now well known from the critical analysis of the 'social investment state', which represents one, rather dominant, approach to the new welfare policy paradigm of investing in children (see, for instance, Lister, 2003b, 2004, 2006a, 2006b; Dobrowolsky & Jenson, 2004, 2005). The exclusion of 'and childhood' is deliberate, for, as the quotation from EURONET underlines, the essence of this model is its future-orientation in which children represent an investment in the future so that the quality of childhood itself is largely overlooked. This section will briefly sketch the main outlines of the model, using Esping-Andersen's report to the Belgian Presidency and the experience of the UK as exemplars. The UK is the European welfare state in which the profitable investment model is most clearly embedded. Elsewhere, Canada stands out as the prime illustration of a shift towards a 'social investment state' under the previous Liberal administrations at the turn of the twenty-first century (Dobrowolsky & Jenson, 2004; Jenson, 2004).

Esping-Andersen's report represents one of the clearest articulations of the profitable investment model. Its instrumentalist philosophy is reflected in the dedication to the published version:

> For today's children who will provide for our welfare when we are old. It is for you – and hence for ourselves – that we desire the best possible welfare state. (Esping-Andersen, 2002)[2]

Here, children appear as the pension-providers of the future. More generally, Esping-Andersen argues that:

> if we aim for a productive and socially integrated future society, our policy priorities should centre on today's children and youths. Solid investment in children now will diminish welfare problems among future adults. (*ibid.*, p. 51)

Underlying this statement is a belief in the importance of investment in human capital, not just through education but more generally in children's welfare. This is necessary in order to avoid costly and less-effective remedial interventions in adulthood. Early childhood, in particular, emerges from the evidence as critical to future life chances. Thus, child-oriented family policy must be recast as 'social investment' (*ibid.*, p. 9). Such investment is necessary both to fight social exclusion and to promote economic competitiveness in Europe.

Child development and child poverty are identified as key targets for social investment, with the two very much interrelated:

> If childhood poverty translates into less education, inferior cognitive skills, more criminality, and inferior lives, the secondary effect is a mass of low-productivity workers, highly vulnerable to unemployment and low pay in the 'new economy'. They will yield less revenue to tax authorities and probably require more public aid during their active years. (*ibid.*, p. 55)

Therefore:

> minimizing child poverty now will yield an individual and social dividend in the future. And in the far-off future, it should diminish the risks of old age poverty. (*ibid.*, p. 55)

Key policy tools identified include universal, high-quality day care for children and support for working mothers (on the grounds that mothers' wages are critical to avoid child poverty).

Esping-Andersen's exposition has been very influential on New Labour thinking. He was invited to contribute to the third way Progressive Governance conference in London in July 2003. In his own contribution, Anthony Giddens (who coined the term 'social investment state') suggested that the approach he outlined, and in particular the priority it gave to preschool day care, 'forms a policy framework of relevance to a diversity of societies' (Giddens, 2003, p. 32).

New Labour's approach is less universalistic than that proposed by Esping-Andersen, who still identifies the Nordic social democratic model as 'comparatively well positioned to face the exigencies of post-industrial change' (Esping-Andersen, 2002, p. 14, 2005). Nevertheless, the priority that New Labour has given to tackling child poverty (with a commitment to its eradication by 2020) and to investment in early years programmes (including the flagship Sure Start scheme) could be interpreted as the adoption of his 'child-centred social investment strategy' in the context of a more liberal welfare state. As a key policy document on the child poverty strategy explains:

> since 1997, the Government has taken a much more active role in the provision of childcare and early years services, recognising that investment in the early years of a child's life can produce long-term, widespread benefits, especially for disadvantaged children. (HM Treasury, 2004a, p. 51)

Critique

In a country where attitudes towards children have been marked by their ambivalence, where child poverty levels soared in the late twentieth century and in which children's interests have typically been marginalised, the adoption of this child-centred social investment strategy represents a breakthrough. It has led to a significant increase in spending on both financial support and childcare/early-years services. Nevertheless, criticisms remain among both analysts and activists. While these criticisms are particular to New Labour's interpretation of the investing in children policy paradigm, they act as warnings of the limitations of the profitable investment model and as pointers towards what an alternative model focused on a good childhood might look like.

Only 'Becomings'?
The first concern is rooted in the distinction between seeing children as 'beings' in the present rather than just as potential adults or 'becomings'. According to Jens Qvortrup:

> colloquial expressions such as 'children are the future of our society', 'children are the next generation' and 'children are our most precious resource' tend to deprive them of an existence as human *beings* in favour of an image of them as human *becomings*, thus underlining the suggestion that children are not authentic contemporaries of adults. They are here, as it were, to be invested in .... It is children's fate to be waiting – patiently waiting to become an adult, to have their contributions recognized, to have a say in societal matters, to be part of the citizenry. (Qvortrup, 2005, p. 5, emphasis in original)

Such colloquial expressions are common currency in the profitable investment model: for example, the government explains that it is in 'the nation's social and economic interests' to ensure 'children get a good start in life' because 'children are the citizens, workers, parents and leaders of the future' (HM Treasury, 2004b, para 2.11). While it occasionally acknowledges that 'children deserve a secure, safe and happy childhood for its own sake', it quickly shifts into forward-looking gear, adding:

> and also because it provides the basis for them to make the most of their talents as they grow up, achieve their potential as adults and pass the benefits on to their own children. Support for children and young people is an investment in a skilled and productive workforce and a more cohesive society in the future. (HM Treasury, 2005, p. 41)

Thus, paradoxically, the iconisation of the child in the profitable investment model has involved the partial eclipse of *childhood* and the child *qua* child (Lister, 2003b; Prout, 2000). An alternative construction is provided by the Children's Forum who declared in their official statement to the UN General Assembly 'you call us the future, but we are also the present' (cited in Stasiulis, 2002, p. 508).

Childcare and education policies are more oriented towards employment priorities – current and future – than towards children's well-being in the here and now, despite the deployment of a discourse of well-being in official documents such as *Every Child Matters*, in which the Government articulated its broad strategy towards children. One casualty is the relatively low priority accorded to play (although this is beginning to change).[3] Thus, while one of the main 'outcomes' enshrined in the Children Act 2004 as a central element of well-being is 'enjoy and achieve', the specific aims attached to the outcome are geared towards achievement and the only mention of enjoyment relates to school, with no reference at all to play and leisure (Hudson, 2006). As the children's charity Barnardo's observes, this reflects a view of 'children as adults in waiting' whereas 'play and enjoyment are in their very essence about the quality of children and young people's lives' (Kelly, 2004, pp. 34–35).

For older children, the emphasis on achievement translates into an education system that has become dominated by frequent testing and by school league-tables with insufficient attention to the educational experience (although this is less true of the devolved administrations). The left-of-centre pressure group, Compass, warns that New Labour's:

> commitment to improving the life chances of children has been rooted in an approach to education that is controlling, instrumental and test-driven. Education is reduced to a means of preparing young people for the jobs market and improving national competitiveness. It is an approach to the learning process in which play, the imagination and creativity play little part. (Rutherford & Shah, 2006, p. 50)

This distortion of the educational experience has been the subject of increasing comment in the press. Teachers unions and the chief executive of the Qualifications and Curriculum Authority have all complained of the excessive load of assessment (*The Observer*, 26 March, 2006; *The Independent*, 1 and 3 May, 2006). A study by the education watchdog, Ofsted, found that reading for pleasure has been squeezed out of classrooms by the preoccupation with tests and targets (*The Independent*, 5 October, 2005). These concerns are reflected in research into measuring young people's well-being reported in a 'well-being manifesto' published by the New Economics Foundation. It warns that:

> our secondary education system is not supporting young people to naturally grow and flourish, which implies that they have lower well-being, both currently and across their lives, than they might have done if the education system

explicitly promoted 'individual and societal well-being both now and in the future' (Shah & Marks, 2004, p. 12).

The treatment by the education system of children as 'becomings' reflects an underlying adult instrumentality. In the words of Moss and Petrie:

> Purposes, functions, objectives and outcomes [of children's services] are usually defined by adults, and legitimated in relation to the needs of adults and the state of adulthood, that is, producing the required adult, in particular a competitive and flexible member of the workforce. (Moss and Petrie, 2005, p. 91)

In similar vein, Harry Hendrick observes that in New Labour's 'third way' children represent:

> a malleable form of human capital suitable for a variety of purposes: economic, educational, familial, generational and, not least representational, in the sense that with 'proper parenting' they may embody an ideal citizenship. In this respect, social policy embraces children in order to involve them in a kind of lifelong enterprise, usually and disproportionately on behalf of (adult) 'others'. (Hendrick, 2005, pp. 476–477)

Citizen-Workers of the Future?

A related concern is that it is primarily 'as citizen-workers of the future that children figure as the prime assets of the "social investment state"' (Lister, 2006a, p. 322). They rarely appear in official discourse as citizens of the present and, in particular, as citizens with rights. Key policy documents, most notably *Every Child Matters*, make no reference to the UN Convention on the Rights of the Child (UNCRC) to which the UK is signatory.[4] The parliamentary Joint Committee on Human Rights points to the failure to build 'a culture of respect' for children's human rights (cited in Williams, 2004, p. 421). An example is the tardy establishment

of a Children's Commissioner for England whose role was then defined
in law as 'promoting awareness of the views and interests of children
in England'. An amendment to the Children Act 2004 added that
the Commissioner 'must have regard' to the European Convention on the
Rights of the Child. Nevertheless, this has been widely criticised as too weak
in comparison with the remits of the Children's Commissioners of many
other European countries (including the UK's devolved administrations),
which are 'framed in terms of promoting and protecting children's rights' in
accordance with the UNCRC (Hudson, 2006, p. 232).

The UN Committee on the Rights of the Child also has been critical
of the Government's lukewarm attitude towards children's rights. In its
annual review of UK government action in response to the Committee's
2002 report, the Children's Rights Alliance for England concludes that
progress has been made on only 16 out of the Committee's 78
recommendations. The Alliance argues that 'there is a huge amount of
catching up to do, to avoid the international criticism of previous sessions'
(Children's Rights Alliance, 2005, p. 12). One of the recommendations,
which has been the object of considerable campaigning in the UK,
concerned parents' continued right to smack their children so long as it
constitutes 'reasonable chastisement' (rephrased 'punishment' following
the Children Act 2004). The Committee strongly criticised smacking as
constituting 'a serious violation of the dignity of the child' (CRC, 2002,
para. 35). The Children's Rights Alliance (2005) cites the European
Committee on Social Rights, which has declared the continued failure to
prohibit the corporal punishment of children within the family a breach of
Article 17 of the European Social Charter. The refusal to ban smacking in
part reflects a reluctance to acknowledge the rights of children against their
parents within the private sphere of the family in contrast with a greater
willingness to accede rights to looked after children who do not live with
their parents (Fawcett et al., 2004).[5]

Participatory rights are also uneven. On the one hand, it is increasingly
common for children's involvement to be sought in the development of
policies affecting them at both local and national level. On the other hand,
the quality of listening and responding has been questioned and

> many argue that, in spite of the rhetoric on participation, achieving the goal of meaningful
> participation of children in policy making remains as elusive as ever. (Spicer & Evans,
> 2006, p. 178; Neale, 2004a; Cairns, 2006)

In practice, what is called participation is more often than not a tick-box
exercise of consultation where the agenda is already set by adults, with

little or no accountability to the children (Tisdall & Bell, 2006). In a radio interview to mark his first day in post, England's first Children's Commissioner made clear that consultation does not represent genuine participation in decision-making, the case for which he made by arguing that 'children are now citizens'.[6]

Less Profitable Investments?

Another criticism, made for instance by Fawcett et al. (2004) and echoed at European level in the EURONET report, is that some groups of children are perceived to be less profitable investments than others. As EURONET warns, it can mean the prioritisation of 'the interests of children who are likely to become productive workers in the future over the interests of those who are less likely to do so (e.g. disabled children)' (Ruxton, 2005, pp. 19–20). This has certainly been the case in the UK. However, in response to criticism, the Government has now committed itself to improving support for families with disabled children and making disabled children a priority at both local and national level (Strategy Unit, 2005; HM Treasury/Department for Education and Skills, 2007).

Two groups of children who have been identified as particularly marginalised within the profitable investment model are: first, gypsy and traveller children, reflecting the second-class citizenship status of their parents and of gypsy and traveller communities generally (Cemlyn & Clark, 2005); and second the children of asylum seekers (Crawley & Lester, 2005; Fitzpatrick, 2005). A cross-party group of parliamentarians, with the support of the No Place for a Child Campaign, has published a paper criticising the detention of asylum seeking and other children for the purposes of immigration control. They argue that the UK Government 'is in contravention of a series of national and international legal guidelines and is failing to protect ... some of the UK's most vulnerable children' to the detriment of their 'health, education, and emotional needs' (Bercow, Dubs, & Harris, 2006, p. 2). Further strong criticism has come from the parliamentary Joint Committee on Human Rights (2007). A Welsh study of asylum-seeking children living in the community reveals 'how their rights are violated and routinely infringed by a state that seems to have forgotten that they are children' (Hewett, Smalley, Dunkerley, & Scourfield, 2005, p. 1). One interpretation is that the Government does not consider asylum-seeking children to be a good investment, in part because it does not see them as long-term residents and future citizens and does not wish them to see themselves as such (Lister, 2006a).

Antisocial Trouble-Makers?

A further cause for concern is that investment in children has been accompanied by increasingly authoritarian regulatory measures. These are designed to secure the investment in terms of promoting social cohesion and security and of turning children and young people into responsible adult citizens. As the then Prime Minister Tony Blair explained to MPs:

> One thing that we know is that the more we invest in young people at the earliest possible age, the better chance we have of making sure that they become responsible adults – hence the importance of programmes such as Sure Start. That is why it important that, as well as clamping down on antisocial behaviour, we should continue to invest in the education of our young people. (Blair, 2004, col. 1410)

Children (or more precisely children living in disadvantaged areas) are increasingly demonized as the perpetrators of antisocial behaviour and are described in the popular media as 'feral'. Nearly half of antisocial behaviour orders, the main weapon introduced to tackle antisocial behaviour, have been applied to children and young people.[7] The 'child of the ASBO' is required to be a responsible child. He (and it is more likely to be he than she) is, like the asset of the 'social investment state', a 'becoming adult', for early intervention in antisocial behaviour is justified in part as a means of preventing later problems in adulthood (Tisdall, 2006, p. 107).[8] This is in the context of an effective age of criminal responsibility in England and Wales of only 10-years old since 1998 – the lowest in the G8 countries other than the US and well below the EU norm (Allen, 2006). Children's and criminal justice organisations have condemned what they regard as the criminalisation of children (Allen, 2006; Squires, 2006). One consequence of such criminalisation, identified by Jessica Kulynych, is that the more the children are associated with disorder, the more likely is it that they are 'treated as problems to be addressed, not persons to address' (2001, p. 262).

Irresponsible Parents?

Finally, the responsibilisation of children is accompanied by that of parents. Parental responsibility is pivotal to policies on antisocial behaviour and social exclusion. The 'carrots' of supportive measures to support parents and enhance their parenting skills tend to be overshadowed by the 'sticks' of more coercive policies. Provisions include compulsory Parenting Orders designed to ensure that parents control their children's behaviour and punishment of parents whose children persistently truant.

Time and again, it is made clear that public policy will be deployed to encourage and, if necessary, enforce the responsibility of parents 'to bring up children as competent, responsible citizens' (Blair, 1998, p. 12). The gender-neutral language of 'parents' obscures the extent to which it is mothers who, in practice, bear the main burden of such policies (Scourfield & Drakeford, 2002; Lister, 2006a). The policies are 'both moralizing ("undeserving" children and "bad" parents) and individualized' (Tisdall, 2006, p. 113; Clarke, 2006). Individualisation means that insufficient attention is paid to the ways in which parental capacity is affected by the financial and material circumstances within which parenting takes place (Women's Budget Group, 2005).

MODEL 2: PROMOTING GOOD CHILDHOOD

It is no coincidence that the two countries typically used to illustrate the profitable investment paradigm of the 'social investment state' are the liberal welfare states of the UK and Canada (under the former liberal administration) in which social democratic, third way, governments forged an alternative to the neo-liberal governments that preceded them. The result is a distinctly hybrid form of welfare regime mixing liberal, neo-liberal and social democratic elements in what some scholars have dubbed 'post-neo-liberalism' (see, for instance, Roseneil & Williams, 2004). What distinguishes them as 'social investment states' is the particular configuration of social democratic and liberal/neo-liberal policy approaches and the dominance of the instrumentalist, future-oriented interpretation of social investment outlined above.

Yet, a strong commitment to social investment has long been the hallmark of social democratic regimes, and it is easier for such regimes to develop a different, more genuinely child-centred model of an investing in children policy paradigm. The Nordic model of childcare and education, with its more holistic, pedagogically informed approach, has developed a better balance between future-oriented investment on the one hand and a concern with the child *qua* child and with good childhood on the other.[9] Moreover, Helmut Wintersberger argues that it is

> much easier to combine the new rights of children enshrined in the UN Convention on the Rights of the Child with the architecture of the Nordic model. (Wintersberger, 2005, p. 216)

because citizenship rights are less tied to labour market position. He also suggests that 'a women-friendly welfare state is more likely to be child-friendly' even though women- and child-friendliness are not synonymous (*ibid.*).

The article turns now to sketch out what the main elements of a more genuinely child-friendly model might look like. It would be premised on recognition of children as 'beings' as well as 'becomings' and on an inversion of the instrumental subordination of the social to the economic. In other words, a *good childhood* would be valued in its own right as a central policy goal. Appreciation of this goal is reflected in the establishment in the UK of 'The Good Childhood' national inquiry by the charity the Children's Society, under the patronage of the Archbishop of Canterbury (http://www.goodchildhood.org.uk).[10] I propose here two key interrelated strands of what might make up a good childhood: well-being and citizenship.

Well-Being

Bradshaw, Hoelscher, and Richardson (2006) have developed an index of child well-being in the EU in response to the inadequacies of the EU's own official indicators. Their index attempts to operationalise the general principles enshrined in the UNCRC (see also Micklewright & Stewart, 2000b) and to combine the dimensions of well-becoming and well-being through eight clusters of indicators: material situation, housing, health, subjective well-being, education, children's relationships, civic participation and risk and safety. The centrality of children's material situation is emphasised. A childhood free of poverty provides the necessary platform upon which other elements of well-being rest.

In a summary league table based on the 21 countries for which adequate data were available, the Netherlands, Sweden and Denmark come top, followed by Finland and Spain, with the UK only 18th and ranked lowest among Western European members. The UK's lamentable record received considerable publicity when the subsequent UNICEF (2007) report on child well-being in rich countries, to which Bradshaw and his colleagues also contributed, was published. While Bradshaw et al. call for further research into possible explanations of the rankings, the UK's poor showing suggests that it has much to learn from other countries in promoting the well-being of its children. A number of organisations in the UK have started the work of formulating approaches that could help in this task.

One is the New Economics Foundation (NEF), which carried out an exploratory study into the well-being of over 1,000 children and young people aged 7–19. The research provided support for the NEF's view that well-being involves curiosity and personal development as well as life-satisfaction, and that this dimension appears to be linked to the ability to respond flexibly and creatively to life's challenges (Marks, Shah, & Westall, 2004). In their *Well-being Manifesto for a Flourishing Society* the NEF thus sums up well-being in the following terms:

> For people to lead truly flourishing lives they need to feel they are personally satisfied and developing, as well as functioning positively in regard to society. (Shah & Marks, 2004, p. 5)

The manifesto ends with the declaration that all policy-makers should ask:

> What would policy look like if it were seeking to promote well-being? This should be one of the defining questions of politics in developed countries. (*ibid.*, p. 17)

In similar vein, a report on the consumerisation of childhood by the National Consumer Council makes the case for a government annual 'children's well-being index'. This would combine the kind of 'objective indicators of the state of children' used in Bradshaw et al.'s index with 'subjective, survey-based data on how they experience the world' in key domains of their lives such as family, school, peer relationships, self-esteem, neighbourhood and consumer life (Mayo, 2005, p. 41).[11]

One key issue raised by the National Consumer Council report and elsewhere is that of children's mental health. Numerous newspaper reports have warned of a mental health crisis among children and young people in the context of political and public concern about the nation's mental health more generally. Typical was a front-page headline, which read 'Children on the edge. One in ten youngsters suffers mental problems as behavioural disorders double in 30 years' (*The Independent*, 21 June, 2006; see also Revans, 2005; Timimi, 2006). The recent media attention given to children's and young people's mental health problems may in part reflect a wider 'moral panic' about the state of childhood and what the Institute for Public Policy Research has identified as 'social paedophobia' (http://www.ippr.org.uk/pressreleases/?id = 2388) (Margo et al., 2006). Nevertheless, a report published by the British Medical Association indicates that the number of children with certain types of mental health problems has more than doubled in the past 30 years (*The Guardian*, 21 June, 2006). An earlier document from the Nuffield Foundation reported clear evidence of decline in the mental health of adolescents in the UK over the same period (Hagell, 2004). While this appeared to be part of a more general trend in industrialised societies in the late twentieth century, the Nuffield Foundation points to evidence that the situation may now be growing worse in the

UK, relative to other countries. It concludes that improving children's and young people's mental health requires 'commitment, input and investment from everyone involved in delivery of services to adolescents' (*ibid.*, p. 6).

It also requires a broader sensitivity to the effects of social and economic change. Some commentators believe that the rampant materialism of our consumer society fuelled by television advertising – much of which is directed to children and young people – is damaging their emotional well-being, particularly in the case of those on low incomes, contributing to worryingly high levels of depression and mental health problems. The Archbishop of Canterbury has argued that 'the right of children to justice involves challenging many of the habits of the advertising world in respect of children' (Williams, 2005, p. 38). There have been calls for stricter regulation of advertising directed at children and young people, with the economist Richard Layard, in his best-selling book *Happiness*, arguing for prohibition of all commercial advertising directed towards children, as in Sweden (Layard, 2005; Mayo, 2005; Margo et al., 2006; Rutherford & Shah, 2006; Williams, 2006).

Another source of pressure on children and young people, which is believed to contribute to their mental health problems, is the secondary education system. This, as mentioned earlier, is now dominated by a culture of testing and exams, which is seen as creating unnecessary levels of stress (Rowlands, 2006). Evidence in support of the damaging effect of the English schools' culture comes from the study of school children by the NEF. The NEF drew the conclusion that education needed to focus more on 'curiosity and personal development' and on 'living the good life' (Marks et al., 2004, p. 7). In short:

> we need to think about what components the curriculum requires to provide young people with the ability to live flourishing lives and to enjoy high levels of well-being. (*ibid.*)

Their work raises the underlying question of what education is for. Is it simply an instrumental mechanism for getting children through exams or is it also about the development of the whole child and the development of her 'capacities for a flourishing life' (Rutherford & Shah, 2006, p. 51)?[12] If the latter holds true, the process of the experience of the education system (which includes attention to how children relate to each other) is as important as the outcome.

The same question – what is it for? – can be asked of childcare. Monique Kremer (2006) identifies a number of 'ideals of care', differentiated according to the preferred locus of the childcare, the preferred providers and the primary objectives. These ideals help to make sense of the childcare policies pursued by different welfare states. According to the OECD:

> children's well-being and learning are core goals of early childhood services, but services for children under 3 have often been seen as an adjunct to labour market policies, with infants and toddlers assigned to services with weak developmental agendas ... . A challenge exists in many countries to focus more on the child, and to show greater understanding of the specific developmental tasks and learning strategies of young children. (OECD, 2006, p. 5)

The OECD also calls for 'respect for children's rights' and for their agency and states that

> Learning to be, learning to do, learning to learn and learning to live together should be considered as critical elements in the journey of each child toward human and social development. (*ibid.*, p. 7)

Peter Moss makes the case for going beyond

> 'childcare' to a discourse of holistic services for children, families and communities: holistic because they address the whole child, all families in the whole community (not just children with working parents) and serve many purposes and create many possibilities. (Moss, 2005)

He suggests that:

> Europe has strong traditions that can provide the basis for a holistic approach, for example: the theory and practice of pedagogy; the concept of education in its broadest sense; an understanding of early childhood services (and other institutions for children) as 'children's spaces'. (Moss, 2005, 2006)

A holistic approach, rooted in pedagogy, has, according to Lisa Harker, former chair of the Daycare Trust, 'regard for all aspects of children's well-being, including their social, emotional, health and educational development' (Harker, 2005, p. 22). It must also be sensitive to children with particular needs such as disabled children and minority ethnic children. Harker (2004) argues that the development of childcare provision in the UK needs 'better to reflect on the totality of a child's experience'. She holds up as a model the approach taken by the Italian city of Reggio Emilia which:

> is informed by an image of the child, not as an empty vessel into which the right ingredients must be poured, but as a being with extraordinary potential. Great emphasis is placed on encouraging curiosity and innovation, with both children and teachers engaged in a constant process of discovery. The child is not seen as a passive recipient of education or care, but as an active participant. (Harker, 2004)

In the comparative childcare literature, Denmark emerges as the main example of a welfare state that has adopted a social pedagogical philosophy of childcare, stretching back to the end of the nineteenth century (Borchorst, 2002). Childcare is regarded as a means of increasing children's well-being and the task of well-trained professionals who should be adequately remunerated (Kremer, 2006; Moss, 2006). The commitment to a universalist, pedagogically based childcare system has helped to legitimise public childcare and win public support, which has contributed to the system's resilience in the face of welfare-state restructuring (Borchorst, 2002; Michel, 2002; Kremer, 2006).

In some social pedagogical models, there is scope for children themselves to have a say in the provisions (Mahon, 2002; Moss, 2006). When asked by children's charities, children and young people identify having fun as important to their well-being (Kelly, 2004; Children's Society, 2006). For younger children, play and safe public places in which they can play are a high priority. Drawing on Danish experience, the charity Barnardo's has argued that 'good play experiences' should play a major part in plans for extended schools (Lundvigsen, 2006). According to Save the Children 'participation in play and leisure is critical to children's emotional well-being and self esteem' (Save the Children, 2005, p. 5). Regardless of the long-term benefits identified by child development experts, play has an intrinsic value for the experience of childhood (Hill & Tisdall, 1997). A UNICEF report observes that the right to play is enshrined in Article 31 of the UNCRC and that:

> there is a widespread view among child development experts that play is the very centre of children's spontaneous urge for development and should be understood as a core dimension of the quality of people's engagement with the world. (Lansdown, 2005, p. 19)

The full enjoyment of the right to play requires safe public spaces, which in the UK have become increasingly restricted to the particular frustration of children in disadvantaged neighbourhoods (Save the Children, 2005; Sutton, Smith, Dearden, & Middleton, 2007). In response, the Children's Play Council has piloted a toolkit for improving neighbourhood play spaces, which synthesises play and community development in a way which, when piloted, improved children's well-being and that of the wider community (Kapasi, 2006). Safe space to play represents one element in the development of a wider child-friendly public environment, as articulated by Kulynych:

> In general, we need to institutionalize opportunities for children to be "public" actors, and to be genuinely and safely in the public sphere. For example, in the area of urban planning, we need actual public spaces that are safe and appropriate for children, where children are welcome, and where children and adults can mix publicly together. We need

streets and transportation systems that are accessible to children. We need open and visible police presence in public spaces that does not assume that the presence of children signifies disorder. (Kulynych, 2001, p. 264)

Citizenship

Kulynych's plea for child-friendly public spaces is part of a 're-envisioning' of children's citizenship, which recognises children as 'political beings' with the right to occupy public space (Kulynych, 2001, pp. 262–263). This underlines the interrelationship between the two elements of a good childhood: well-being and citizenship, understood as both a status and a practice (Lister, 2003a). The link between children's well-being and citizenship is also made by Ben-Arieh and Boyer. They point out that, from the perspective of citizenship as a status, well-being depends in part on a firm platform of citizenship rights, particularly socio-economic rights (even if children enjoy some of these rights by proxy). Although children are, by and large, excluded from the citizenship rights enjoyed by adult citizens, they are recognised in international human rights conventions including those specifying distinctive children's rights. The European Commission has recently published an official Communication 'Towards an EU Strategy on the Rights of the Child', which *inter alia* promises a Commission Coordinator of the Rights of the Child. There is:

an urgent need for a comprehensive EU strategy to increase the scale and effectiveness of EU commitments to improve the situation of children globally and to demonstrate real political will at the highest possible level to ensure that the promotion and protection of children's rights get the place they merit on the EU's agenda. (European Commission, 2006, p. 2)

From the perspective of citizenship as a practice, Ben-Arieh and Boyer claim that:

being an active and involved child safeguards the child's well-being. In short, we want our children to participate not only in order to train them to become good citizens in the future but as means for securing their well-being as children in the present. (Ben-Arieh & Boyer, 2005, pp. 46–47)

They conclude that 'the issues of children's citizenship and children as citizens are of immense importance to children's well-being' (*ibid.*, p. 51). Citizenship as a practice is thus important to well-being in its 'eudaemonic' sense of the fulfillment of human potential and active engagement (Shah & Marks, 2004).

The nature of children's citizenship needs more thought than it has hitherto been given. It is not enough on the one hand to construct it in purely futuristic terms as in the profitable investment model, or on the other hand to simply assert, as some do in order to promote children's rights, that children are citizens, as if their citizenship were identical to that of adults. Understanding and strengthening children's citizenship can best be done by unpacking the key elements of citizenship – membership and participation; rights, responsibilities and equal status (developed further in Lister, 2007a, 2007b).

Underlying the question of children's relationship to citizenship is that of their evolving capacities – to participate and to exercise rights and responsibilities – and how these capacities are encouraged and recognised by adults. A UNICEF report is helpful here on the evolving capacities of the child. It concludes that:

> in societies throughout the world, more could be done to create environments in which children achieve their optimum capacities and greater respect is given to children's potential for participation in and responsibility for decision-making in their own lives. (Lansdown, 2005, p. xi)

This will, the report argues, require a cultural change:

> so that children are protected appropriately in accordance with their evolving capacities, and also respected as citizens, as people, and as rights bearers. (*ibid.*)

It makes the case for a review of the legal frameworks governing the acquisition of various citizenship rights because:

> the rigid application of laws prescribing ages at which certain rights come into play do not reflect the reality of decisions and levels of responsibility of which children are capable. (*ibid.*, p. 49)

The report assesses the advantages and disadvantages of the main models:

- fixed, prescribed age limits, as existing in most countries;
- individual assessment or a presumption of competence, with the onus on adults to demonstrate incapacity;
- fixed age limits but with the right of a child to demonstrate the necessary competence to acquire the right at an earlier age; and
- presumption of competence in all rights other than those at risk of being abused or neglected by adults for which fixed age limits would continue (*ibid.*, pp. 49–53).

It also cites a checklist used in New Zealand to help government departments and public bodies determine age limits in law and policy:

- Is a youth age limit really necessary?
- Choose the appropriate age, with reference to the UNCRC.

- Can it be justified?
- Consult young people.
- Be clear about the rationale for the limit in all public documents (*ibid.*, p. 53).

The report describes the efforts that have been made to assess children's competence, mainly with reference to medical consent. It would be useful to conduct a similar exercise in relation to the capacities necessary to exercise the rights and obligations of citizenship. At the same time, there needs to be greater recognition of the extent to which children are already exercising responsibilities of citizenship within particular cultural and socio-economic contexts – as workers, carers and participants in civic life (see, for instance, Stasiulis, 2002; Dearden & Becker, 2005; Miller, 2005; Zelizer, 2005).

It is with regard to this last aspect of citizenship that public policy can perhaps best encourage children's active participation as citizens on the one hand and public recognition of that participation on the other. Children's right to express an opinion and to have that opinion taken into account in any matter or procedure affecting the child is enshrined in Article 12 of the UNCRC. This participatory right is arguably of particular significance for children because they do not have the right to vote. Enabling children to participate both individually and collectively in decision-making and public debate through the development of appropriate mechanisms and procedures symbolises acceptance of children as members of the citizenship community. It also, the evidence suggests, strengthens their own 'sense of belonging' to that community and their sense of responsibility as well as helping to equip them with the skills and capacities necessary for effective citizenship (Cutler & Frost, 2001, p. 6; Guerra, 2005; Lansdown, 2005, 2006).

Writing about children's participatory initiatives in Latin America, Yves Cabannes suggests that 'the proven capacity of children to assume responsible roles can do as much as anything to promote respect for their particular perspective' (Cabannes, 2005, p. 208). In the context of the UK, Bren Neale has argued that the precondition of genuine participation is recognition of and respect for children. Indeed, she defines citizenship for children as 'an entitlement to recognition, respect and participation' and argues that 'these basic needs are as crucial to children's well-being as their needs for care and protection' (Neale, 2004b, p. 1). Children and young people themselves have identified respect from adults as an important element of their well-being (Children's Society, 2006; Lansdown, 2006).

Neale's position also suggests that children's claim to citizenship lies in both their equality with and difference from adults. They have been described as '"differently equal" members of society' (Moosa-Mitha, 2005, p. 386). Their continued need for protection is not incompatible with the right to participation and nor should the right to participation become an obligation, at the expense of the child's right to enjoy their childhood, as understood within specific cultural contexts (Stasiulis, 2002; Neale, 2004b). As the UNICEF report observes:

> one of the most fundamental challenges posed by the Convention on the Rights of the Child is the need to balance children's right to adequate and appropriate protection with their right to participate in and take responsibility for the exercise of those decisions and actions they are competent to take for themselves. (Lansdown, 2005, p. 32)

This point can be widened out to more collective forms of participation also.

CONCLUSION

This article has discussed the politicisation of childhood in the UK through the lens of the new welfare paradigm of investing in children. Children stand on the political stage primarily as both assets for the future and as unruly threats to social order rather than as recognised political actors or rights-bearing citizens. These different constructions of children reflect two alternative possible directions for the development of the investing in children paradigm. One, typified by the UK's 'social investment state', is the 'profitable investment' model. This does have real strategic value, particularly in countries such as the UK where children have been relatively neglected in social policy in the past. It is also helpful to a degree at EU level where it provides a rationale for the development of children's policy in the context of the continued subordination of social policy to economic and employment goals, although the publication of a communication on children's rights suggests the possible transcendence of the limitations of this model. However, the article has argued that there are dangers in pursuing a solely future-oriented instrumentalist approach. It has therefore proposed an alternative 'good childhood' model, which invests in *childhood* as well as individual children. Elements of this model can be found in the Nordic countries.

As stated earlier, 'profitable investment' and 'good childhood' are analytical (as well as normative) models, which, like welfare regimes, are ways of understanding dominant patterns in welfare states. It is usually possible to identify the elements of both models, in varying mixes, in actual welfare states. Moreover, an element of future orientation does not necessarily have to be instrumentalist and can therefore be combined with a good childhood model in a fruitful way.[13]

For example, the influential report of the Fabian Commission on Life Chances and Child Poverty focuses on the impact of child poverty on children's future life chances. Nevertheless, it explicitly rejects:

> narrowly instrumental approaches which concentrate exclusively on those outcomes in adulthood that relate to people's productivity as economic agents (Fabian Commission, 2006, p. 22)

and emphasises that:

> perhaps the most fundamental of all life chances is the chance to live a fulfilling and rewarding life, beginning in childhood. As such, children must be given the chance to enjoy a happy, flourishing childhood and to continue to thrive as they grow up. (*ibid.*, pp. 21–22)

In similar vein, the responses of British young people aged 14–16 to the question 'what are the most important things that make for a good life for young people?'

> indicated the importance of bearing in mind both the experiences of 'being' a child or young person and of 'becoming' an adult in thinking about the good childhood. (Children's Society, 2006, p. 6)

Whatever the exact mix of the two models, the central message of the analysis in this article is that, rather than investing in children simply as future citizens, a concern for a 'good childhood' needs also to prioritise all children's well-being and citizenship in the here and now.

NOTES

1. 'Good childhood – profitable investment?' was the title of the seminar held by ITLA, the foundation for funding Finnish Child Research, in Helsinki, March 2006, at which an earlier version of this paper was given. The article also draws on earlier work, notably Lister (2003b, 2004, 2006a, 2006b). It has benefited from comments from the referee and editors.

2. A similarly instrumentalist stance is adopted towards gender equality in a subsequent chapter on 'a new gender contract'.

3. Play is not ignored completely; indeed, the government has published a document on it (DCMS, 2006), but it has often been treated instrumentally in terms of 'the good' it will do to children (Gill, 2004). On the ground, local projects have, nevertheless, sometimes been able to carve spaces to promote play and the general enjoyment of childhood. And there are signs of growing recognition in government of the value of play for children's enjoyment and happiness (Lammy, 2007).

4. In contrast, relevant policy documents published by the Welsh Assembly Government are framed by a children's rights discourse. For instance, its child poverty strategy document is 'built on a core set of values in line with the UN Convention on the Rights of the Child' (Welsh Assembly Government, 2005, p. 9).

5. 'Looked after' is now the official term used for children in care.

6. The Radio 4 *Today* programme 1 July 2005.

7. Antisocial behaviour orders (ASBOs) are civil measures, which can be issued to anyone aged 10 years or over. 'They impose restrictions on the behaviour of individuals who have behaved in an antisocial way' (Blears, 2005, col. 53WS). Breach of an ASBO is a criminal offence, which can lead to a custodial sentence.

8. A 2006 *Action Plan on Social Exclusion* (http://www.cabinetoffice.gov.uk) promises a new focus on intervention in early childhood to prevent future social exclusion and criminal and antisocial behaviour.

9. However, there are concerns in Finland that policy has become less child-friendly over the past decade or so (Alanen, Sauli, & Strandell, 2004).

10. This follows an earlier, independent Commission on Families and the Wellbeing of Children, which raised some of the issues discussed here in its final report (National Family & Parenting Institute, 2005).

11. Save the Children has spearheaded an independent attempt at such an index, although not on an annual basis and has called for a regular UK-wide survey of children's well-being (Save the Children, 2005). The UNICEF (2007) child well-being report included three indicators of subjective well-being; the UK scored particularly poorly on the composite subjective well-being index.

12. Rutherford and Shah observe that elements of the approach they advocate have already been adopted in Wales.

13. The Republic of Ireland's National Children's Strategy, for example, combines a commitment to social investment in children with rights-based, participatory principles (at least on paper) (Pinkerton, 2006).

REFERENCES

Alanen, L., Sauli, S., & Strandell, H. (2004). Children and childhood in a welfare state: The case of Finland. In: A. Jensen, et al. (Eds), *Children's welfare in ageing Europe* (pp. 143–209). Trondheim: Norwegian Centre for Child Research.

Allen, R. (2006). *From punishment to problem solving. A new approach to children in trouble.* London: Centre for Crime and Justice Studies.

Ben-Arieh, A., & Boyer, Y. (2005). Citizenship and childhood. *Childhood, 12*(1), 33–53.

Bercow, J., Dubs, A., & Harris, E. (2006). *Alternatives to immigration detention of families and children.* London: No Place for a Child Campaign.

Blair, T. (1998). *The third way. New politics for the new century.* London: Fabian Society.

Blair, T. (2004). Oral answers. *House of Commons Hansard,* 11 February.

Blears, H. (2005). Written Ministerial Statements. *House of Commons Hansard,* 3 November, col. 53WS.

Borchorst, A. (2002). Danish child care policy – Continuity rather than radical change. In: S. Michel & R. Mahon (Eds), *Child care policy at the crossroads* (pp. 267–285). New York, NY: Routledge.

Bradshaw, J., Hoelscher, P., & Richardson, D. (2006). *An index of child well-being in the European Union*, Social Indicators Research. Available at: www.springerlink.metapress. com/home/main.mpx

Cabannes, Y. (2005). Children and young people build participatory democracy in Latin American cities. *Children, Youth and Environments*, *15*(2), 185–210. Retrieved 29 March 2006 from http://www.colorado.edu/journals/cye/

Cairns, L. (2006). Participation with purpose. In: E. K. M. Tisdall, J. M. Davis, M. Hill & A. Prout (Eds), *Children, young people and social inclusion* (pp. 217–234). Bristol: The Policy Press.

Cemlyn, S., & Clark, C. (2005). The social exclusion of gypsy and traveller children. In: G. Preston (Ed.), *At greatest risk. The children most likely to be poor* (pp. 150–165). London: Child Poverty Action Group.

Children's Rights Alliance. (2005). *State of children's rights in England*. London: Children's Rights Alliance for England.

Children's Society. (2006). *Good childhood? A question for our times*. London: The Children's Society.

Clarke, K. (2006). Childhood, parenting and early intervention: A critical examination of the sure start national programme. *Critical Social Policy*, *26*(4), 699–721.

Crawley, H., & Lester, T. (2005). *No place for a child. Children in UK immigration detention: Impacts, alternatives and safeguards*. London: Save the Children.

CRC (2002). *Concluding observations of the committee on the rights of the child: United Kingdom of Great Britain and Northern Ireland*. Geneva: Office of the High Commissioner for Human Rights. Available at: http://www.unhchr.ch

Cutler, D., & Frost, R. (2001). *Taking the initiative: Promoting young people's involvement in public decision-making in the UK*. London: Carnegie United Kingdom Trust.

Davison, S. (Ed.) (2005). Editorial: Opportunity knocks. *Soundings*, *31*, 7–9.

DCMS. (2006). *Time for play*. London: Department for Culture, Media and Sport.

Dearden, C., & Becker, S. (2005). Growing up caring: Young careers and vulnerability to social exclusion. In: M. Barry (Ed.), *Youth policy and social inclusion* (pp. 251–266). London: Routledge.

Dobrowolsky, A., & Jenson, J. (2004). Shifting representations of citizenship: Canadian politics of 'women' and 'children'. *Social Politics*, *11*(2), 154–180.

Esping-Andersen, G. (2002). A child-centred investment strategy. In: G. Esping-Andersen, D. Gallie, A. Hemerijck & J. Myles (Eds), *Why we need a new welfare state* (pp. 26–67). Oxford: Oxford University Press.

Esping-Andersen, G. (2005). Education and equal life-chances: Investing in children. In: O. Kangas & J. Palme (Eds), *Social policy and economic development in the Nordic countries* (pp. 147–163). Basingstoke: Palgrave.

European Commission. (2006). *Towards an EU strategy on the rights of the child*. Memo/06/266, Strasbourg: European Commission, 4 July.

Fabian Commission. (2006). *Narrowing the gap. Report of the Fabian Commission on Life Chances and Child Poverty*. London: Fabian Society.

Fawcett, B., Featherstone, B., & Goddard, J. (2004). *Contemporary child care policy and practice*. London: Palgrave.

Fitzpatrick, P. (2005). Asylum seeker families. In: G. Preston (Ed.), *At greatest risk. The children most likely to be poor* (pp. 92–108). London: Child Poverty Action Group.

Giddens, A. (2003). Introduction: The progressive agenda. In: M. Browne, P. Thompson & F. Sainsbury (Eds), *Progressive futures* (pp. 1–45). London: Policy Network.

Gill, T. (2004). Bred in captivity. *The Guardian*, 20 September.

Guerra, E. (2005). Citizenship knows no age: children's participation in the governance and municipal budget of Barra Mansa, Brazil. *Children, Youth and Environments*, *15*(2), 151–168. Retrieved 29 March 2006 from http://www.colorado.edu/journals/cye/

Hagell, A. (2004). *Time trends in adolescent well-being*. London: The Nuffield Foundation.

Harker, L. (2004). Lessons from Reggio Emilia. *The Guardian*, 11 November.

Harker, L. (2005). Europe knows best. *Community Care* (22 May), 19–25.

Hendrick, H. (2005). Conclusion. In: H. Hendrick (Ed.), *Child welfare and social policy. An essential reader* (pp. 475–479). Bristol: Policy Press.

Hewett, T., Smalley, N., Dunkerley, D., & Scourfield, J. (2005). *Uncertain futures. Children seeking asylum in Wales*. Cardiff: Save the Children Wales.

Hill, M., & Tisdall, K. (1997). *Children and society*. Harlow: Prentice Hall.

HM Treasury. (2004a). *Child poverty review*. London: HM Treasury.

HM Treasury. (2004b). *Choice for parents, the best start for children. A ten year strategy for child care*. London: HM Treasury.

HM Treasury. (2005). *Support for parents: The best start for children*. London: HM Treasury.

HM Treasury/Department for Education and Skills. (2007). *Aiming high for disabled children: Better support for families*. London: HM Treasury.

Hudson, B. (2006). User outcomes and children's services reform. *Social Policy and Society*, *5*(2), 227–236.

Jenson, J. (2004). Changing the paradigm. Family responsibility or investing in children. *Canadian Journal of Sociology*, *29*(2), 169–194.

Joint Committee on Human Rights. (2007). *The treatment of asylum seekers*. London: Stationery Office.

Kapasi, H. (2006). *Neighbourhood play and community action*. York: Joseph Rowntree Foundation.

Kelly, N. (2004). Child's play. *Community Care* (July 1–7), 34–35.

Kremer, M. (2006). The politics of ideals of care: Danish and Flemish child care policy compared. *Social Politics*, *13*(2), 261–285.

Kulynych, J. (2001). No playing in the public sphere: Democratic theory and the exclusion of children. *Social Theory and Practice*, *27*(2), 231–264.

Lammy, D. (2007). *Making space for children*. Available at: http://www.compassonline.org.uk

Lansdown, G. (2005). *The evolving capacities of the child*. Florence: UNICEF Innocenti Research Centre.

Lansdown, G. (2006). International developments in children's participation: Lessons and challenges. In: E. K. M. Tisdall, J. M. Davis, M. Hill & A. Prout (Eds), *Children, young people and social inclusion* (pp. 139–156). Bristol: The Policy Press.

Layard, R. (2005). *Happiness*. London: Penguin.

Lister, R. (2003a). *Citizenship: Feminist perspectives* (2nd ed.). Basingstoke: Palgrave.

Lister, R. (2003b). Investing in the citizen-workers of the future: Transformations in citizenship and the state under New Labour. *Social Policy and Administration*, *37*(5), 427–443.

Lister, R. (2004). The third way's social investment state. In: J. Lewis & R. Surender (Eds), *Welfare state change. Towards a third way?* (pp. 157–181). Oxford: Oxford University Press.

Lister, R. (2006a). Children (but not women) first: New labour, child welfare and gender. *Critical Social Policy, 26*(2), 315–335.

Lister, R. (2006b). An agenda for children: Investing in the future or promoting wellbeing in the present? In: J Lewis (Ed.), *Children, changing families and welfare states*. Cheltenham: Edward Elgar.

Lister, R. (2007a). Unpacking children's citizenship. In: S. Clutton, A. Invernizzi & J. Williams (Eds), *Children and citizenship* (pp. 9–19). London: Sage.

Lister, R. (2007b). Why citizenship: Where, when and how children? *Theoretical Inquiries in Law, 8*(2), 693–718.

Lundvigsen, A. (2006). *More school, less play? The role of play in the extended school in Denmark and England*. London: Barnardo's.

Mahon, R. (2002). Child care: Toward what kind of "social Europe"? *Social Politics, 9*(3), 343–379.

Margo, J., Dixon, M., Pearce, N., & Reed, H. (2006). *Freedom's orphans*. London: Institute for Public Policy Research.

Marks, N., Shah, H., & Westall, A. (2004). *The power and potential of well-being indicators*. London: New Economics Foundation.

Mayo, E. (2005). *Shopping generation*. London: National Consumers Council.

Micheal, S. (2002). Dilemmas in child care. In: S. Michel & R. Mahon (Eds), *Child care policy at the crossroads*. New York: Routledge.

Micklewright, J., & Stewart, K. (2000a). *The welfare of Europe's children*. Bristol: Policy Press.

Micklewright, J., & Stewart, K. (2000b). Child well-being and social cohesion. *New Economy, 7*(1), 18–23.

Miller, P. (2005). Useful and priceless children in contemporary welfare states. *Social Politics, 12*(1), 3–41.

Moosa-Mitha, M. (2005). A difference-centred alternative to theorization of children's citizenship rights. *Citizenship Studies, 9*(4), 369–388.

Moss, P. (2005). Getting beyond childcare ... and the Barcelona targets. Paper presented at the conference on challenges and opportunities faced by European welfare states. University of Oxford, January 7–8.

Moss, P. (2006). From children's services to children's spaces. In: E. K. M. Tisdall, J. M. Davis, M. Hill & A. Prout (Eds), *Children, young people and social inclusion* (pp. 179–198). Bristol: The Policy Press.

Moss, P., & Petrie, P. (2005). Children – Who do we think they are? In: H. Hendrick (Ed.), *Child welfare and social policy. An essential reader* (pp. 85–105). Bristol: Policy Press.

National Family & Parenting Institute. (2005). *Families and the state*. Bristol: The Policy Press.

Neale, B. (Ed.) (2004a). *Young children's citizenship*. York: Joseph Rowntree Foundation.

Neale, B. (2004b). Introduction: Young people's citizenship. In: B. Neale (Ed.), *Young children's citizenship*. York: Joseph Rowntree Foundation.

OECD. (2006). *Starting Strong II: Early childhood education and care, summary*. Paris: OECD.

Pinkerton, J. (2006). The Irish national children's strategy. In: E. K. M. Tisdall, J. M. Davis, M. Hill & A. Prout (Eds), *Children, young people and social inclusion*. Bristol: The Policy Press.

Prout, A. (2000). Children's participation: Control and self-realisation in British late modernity. *Children and Society, 14*, 304–315.

Qvortrup, J. (2005). Varieties of childhood. In: J. Qvortrup (Ed.), *Studies in modern childhood* (pp. 1–20). Basingstoke: Palgrave.

Revans, L. (2005). A stretched service. *0–19* (February).

Roseneil, S., & Williams, F. (2004). Introduction to the special issue. *Social Politics, 11*(2), 147–153.

Rowlands, J. (2006). *Childhood.* London: Compass. Available at: http://www.compassonline. org.uk

Rutherford, J., & Shah, H. (2006). *The good society.* London: Compass.

Ruxton, S. (2005). *What about us? Children's rights in the European Union. Next steps.* Brussels: European Children's Network.

Save the Children. (2005). *The well-being of children in the UK: Summary.* London: Save the Children.

Scourfield, J., & Drakeford, M. (2002). New Labour and the 'problem of men'. *Critical Social Policy, 22*(4), 619–640.

Shah, H., & Marks, N. (2004). *A well-being manifesto for a flourishing society.* London: New Economics Foundation.

Spicer, N., & Evans, R. (2006). Developing children and young people's participation in strategic processes: The experience of the Children's Fund initiative. *Social Policy and Society, 5*(2), 177–188.

Squires, P. (2006). New Labour and the politics of anti-social behaviour. *Critical Social Policy, 26*(1), 144–168.

Stasiulis, D. (2002). The active child citizen: Lessons from Canadian policy and the children's movement. *Citizenship Studies, 6*(4), 507–538.

Strategy Unit. (2005). *Improving the life chances of disabled people.* London: Cabinet Office.

Sutton, L., Smith, N., Dearden, C., & Middleton, S. (2007). *A child's eye view on social difference.* York: York Publishing Services.

Timimi, S. (2006). Children's mental health. *Public Policy Research, 13*(1), 35–42.

Tisdall, E. K. M. (2006). Antisocial behaviour legislation meets children's services. *Critical Social Policy, 26*(1), 101–120.

Tisdall, E. K. M., & Bell, R. (2006). Included in governance? Children's participation in 'public' decision making. In: E. K. M. Tisdall, J. M. Davis, M. Hill & A. Prout (Eds), *Children, young people and social inclusion* (pp. 103–119). Bristol: The Policy Press.

UNICEF. (2007). *An overview of child well-being in rich countries.* Florence: Innocenti Research Centre.

Welsh Assembly Government. (2005). *A fair future for our children.* Cardiff: WAG.

Williams, F. (2004). What matters is what works: Why every child matters to New Labour. Commentary on the DfES Green Paper. *Every Child Matters, Critical Social Policy, 24*(3), 406–427.

Williams, R. (2005). Who is bringing up our children? *Soundings, 31,* 35–42.

Williams, Z. (2006). *The commercialisation of childhood.* London: Compass.

Wintersberger, H. (2005). Work, welfare and generational order: Towards a political economy of childhood. In: J. Qvortrup (Ed.), *Studies in modern childhood* (pp. 201–220). Basingstoke: Palgrave.

Women's Budget Group. (2005). *Women's and children's poverty: Making the links.* London: Women's Budget Group.

Zelizer, V. A. (2005). The priceless child revisited. In: J. Qvortrup (Ed.), *Studies in modern childhood* (pp. 184–200). Basingstoke: Palgrave.

Printed in the United Kingdom
by Lightning Source UK Ltd.
135429UK00001B/85-90/P